Integrative Governance is a richly powerful, cross-disciplinary book. It captures the voice of Mary Parker Follett's work, the essence of German existential thought, and applications to governance. Moreover, the book cuts across disciplines including public administration, political science, economics, and sociology. In this sense, the book serves as a compass to navigate administrative theory in the 21st century through its accessibility and utility.

Arthur Sementelli, Florida Atlantic University, USA

Stout and Love have crafted a deeply intellectual, yet praxis focused text on integrative governance. It covers the expected topics, with a detailed philosophical account of governance being the value-added contribution. This text is a must for those responsible for constructing the genuine and nuanced integrative governance demanded by contemporary issues.

Robyn Keast, Southern Cross University, Australia

This book is an exemplar of how all books in public governance ought to make the philosophical foundations of the proposed argument explicit, to enable the most fruitful of dialogues in the field. My ontology is different than the authors' yet my admiration for such a thoroughly crafted work is paramount.

Edoardo Ongaro, The Open University, UK

Embracing an "attachment to existence" and defying the widespread skepticism and "sustained cynicism" of mainstream political science in the face of global crises, Margaret Stout and Jeannine Love have written a remarkable book. By articulating a relational, process-oriented and integrative approach to governance, they attempt to break the iron grip of rationalistic, dualistic, hierarchical, and economistic thinking on our understanding of state, citizen, nature and society, as well as our self-image as academic professionals. Drawing on the work of Mary Follett, Alfred Whitehead and their contemporary followers such as William Connolly, they systematically build a coherent and affirmative alternative that anchors the administrative, economic and democratic aspects of integrative governance in a process-based cosmology and epistemology. No one will walk away from this book without a wealth of new, inspirational insights.

Hendrik Wagenaar, King's College London,
UK and The University of Vienna, Austria

This book is an intense reflection and an extensive theoretical contribution to a unitary understanding and valuing of how to act in the complex processes of governance in our time.

It is not just a contestation of the resigned advocacy of traditional PA theories, nor an idle, cosmetic revamping of novelties advanced by Follett and other classical process theorists. Stout and Love offer testimony and committed persuasion for multiple ways of creative resistance to the seemingly uncontestable forces of growing global inequity, violence, and mistrust – the futility of which is a deception.

Ricardo Schmukler, University of Buenos Aires, Argentina

Margaret Stout and Jeannine Love have accomplished the extraordinary task of bringing the fullness of Mary Parker Follett's philosophy and scholarship to the field of public administration in their conceptualization of "integrative governance," an approach to governance (not government) deeply situated in Follett's principles of association and in radically democratic processes. Stout and Love adeptly show that now is the time to turn to integrative governance to aid in ameliorating the wicked and gnarly problems in this era of global, transnational governance. This book contains the seeds of transformational regime change, globally, transnationally, trans-disciplinarily, and trans-organizationally/trans-jurisdictionally. Read it.

Cheryl Simrell King, The Evergreen State College, USA

Integrative Governance

Dominant governance theories are drawn primarily from Euro-American sources, including emergent theories of network and collaborative governance. The authors contest this narrow view and seek a more globally inclusive and transdisciplinary perspective, arguing such an approach is more fruitful in addressing the wicked problems of sustainability – including social, economic, and environmental crises. This book thus offers and affirms an innovative governance approach that may hold more promise as a "universal" framework that is not colonizing in nature due to its grounding in relational process assumptions and practices. Using a comprehensive Governance Typology that encompasses ontological assumptions, psychosocial theory, epistemological concepts, belief systems, ethical concepts, political theory, economic theory, and administrative theory, the authors delve deeply into underlying philosophical commitments and carry them into practice through an approach they call Integrative Governance. The authors consider ways this approach to radical self-governance is already being implemented in the prefigurative politics of contemporary social movements, and they invite scholars and activists to: imagine governance in contexts of social, economic, and environmental interconnectedness; to use the ideal-type as an evaluative tool against which to measure practice; and to pursue paradigmatic change through collaborative praxis.

Margaret Stout is an Associate Professor of Public Administration at West Virginia University. Her research explores the role of public and nonprofit practitioners in achieving democratic social and economic justice with specific interests in administrative theory, public service leadership and ethics, and sustainable community development. Dr. Stout's first career was in human resource development, with a focus on work/life balance programming. Leading directly out of related experiences in state-wide and regional community and economic development initiatives, her second career was in community and youth development, serving as an executive director, project manager, and consultant to nonprofit and government agencies in Arizona. These experiences inform both her research and teaching through extensive and meaningful community engaged scholarship.

Jeannine M. Love is an Associate Professor of Public Administration at Roosevelt University in Chicago, Illinois. Her research analyzes rhetorics of individualism in political theory and practice, as well as social movements. Her work pays particular attention to issues of racial, economic, and food justice. Dr. Love's career in public administration began in 2000, when she began working as a child support caseworker in Columbus, Ohio. The practices she witnessed as a "street level bureaucrat," particularly the problematic marginalization of the country's poorest residents, continues to motivate her research and teaching.

Global Law and Sustainable Development

Series editor: Paolo Davide Farah

West Virginia University, USA and gLAWcal – Global Law Initiatives for Sustainable Development, UK

This series provides a new focus on the relationship between international law, economy, and trade, with special attention to what are commonly referred to as non-trade-related values and concerns. Through research and policy analysis the series sheds new light on a range of issues relating to good governance and human rights in the widest sense. It is held that the values supporting these issues are directly affected by the global expansion of world trade and need to be upheld in order to balance the excesses of globalization. Multidisciplinary in approach, the series integrates studies from scholars and researchers with a range of different backgrounds and interdisciplinary expertise from law, economics, political science, and sociology through to history, philosophy and natural science.

Available titles in this series:

The Reform of International Economic Governance
Edited by Antonio Segura Serrano

China's Influence on Non-Trade Concerns in International Economic Law
Edited by Paolo Davide Farah and Elena Cima

Integrative Governance: Generating Sustainable Responses to Global Crises
Margaret Stout and Jeannine M. Love

Forthcoming:

India's Foreign Economic Policy: Deciphering the Law, Economics and Politics
Julien Chaisse and Debashis Chaktraborty

For more information about this series, please visit: www.routledge.com/Global-Law-and-Sustainable-Development/book-series/ASHSER1419

Integrative Governance

Generating Sustainable Responses to Global Crises

Margaret Stout and Jeannine M. Love

Routledge
Taylor & Francis Group
LONDON AND NEW YORK

First published 2019
by Routledge

2 Park Square, Milton Park, Abingdon, Oxfordshire OX14 4RN
52 Vanderbilt Avenue, New York, NY 10017

Routledge is an imprint of the Taylor & Francis Group, an informa business

First issued in paperback 2019

British Library Cataloguing-in-Publication Data
A catalogue record for this book is available from the British Library

Library of Congress Cataloging-in-Publication Data
Names: Stout, Margaret, author. | Love, Jeannine M., author.
Title: Integrative governance : generating sustainable responses to global crises / Margaret Stout and Jeannine M. Love.
Description: Abingdon, Oxon ; New York, NY : Routledge, 2019. | Series: Global law and sustainable development | Includes bibliographical references and index.
Identifiers: LCCN 2018007738 | ISBN 9781138695733 (hbk) | ISBN 9781315526294 (ebk)
Subjects: LCSH: International cooperation—Philosophy. | Crisis management—International cooperation. | Sustainability—International cooperation.
Classification: LCC JZ1318 .S756 2019 | DDC 363.34/56—dc23
LC record available at https://lccn.loc.gov/2018007738

ISBN: 978-1-138-69573-3 (hbk)
ISBN: 978-0-367-47374-7 (pbk)

Typeset in Galliard
by Apex CoVantage, LLC

This book is dedicated to all those who have had and will have the courage and persistence to develop and pursue dispositions, relational styles, and modes of association based on the principles of Integrative Governance, whether it is in their homes, in their communities, in their workplaces, or in their governments.

Contents

Figures

Tables

Foreword

Paolo Davide Farah[1]

Integrative Governance: Generating Sustainable Responses to Global Crises by Margaret Stout and Jeannine M. Love represents an important contribution to the discussion about the best forms of global (and local) governance and alternatives to the existing ones.

It is a great pleasure for me to write this foreword, as both the authors have extensive experience as academics and practitioners.

Stout's research explores the role of public and non-profit practitioners in achieving social and economic justice with specific interests in administrative theory. She also has a strong interest in philosophical underpinnings, as shown in her previous books and the current one. She continues her passion for community development through action research and service learning projects as a faculty member. She employs a unique apprenticeship-style approach that was extensively recognized by her university through its Outstanding Public Service Award and Faculty Excellence in Civic Engagement Award, and the Community Development Society through its Outstanding Educator Award.

Before entering academia, Stout was president of WorkLife Strategies, Tempe, AZ which provided human resources management and strategic planning services in the area of work/life balance, with a specialty in dependent care needs assessment, program planning, and evaluation. She provided strategic planning and collaborative program design for regional economic development initiatives pertaining to quality of life and workforce development (Arizona Strategic Partnership for Economic Development). Later, she was founder and executive director of NewTown Community Development Corporation with a mission to create a sustainable urban village in the heart of the Phoenix metropolitan area. In this role, she completed community and economic development project development, implementation, management, evaluation, and reporting. She designed and facilitated community-based planning processes and authored two city-adopted neighborhood plans including all General Plan elements. She completed preliminary work for a Redevelopment District Plan and implementation plan for the Neighborhood Strategic Plans; successfully advocated for development decisions based on adopted Plans; provided leadership in the creation and adoption of mixed use zoning ordinances, transit-oriented design, light rail service, and free neighborhood shuttles connecting residents to regional transit; created and managed the multi-agency Tempe Child

1 Paolo Davide Farah, West Virginia University, John D. Rockefeller IV, School of Policy and Politics, Department of Public Administration and College of Law; West Virginia University, Energy Institute and Center for Innovation in Gas Research and Utilization (CIGRU); West Virginia University, Institute of Water Security and Science (IWSS). Founder, President, Director and Principal Investigator at gLAWcal – Global Law Initiatives for Sustainable Development. Senior Fellow at the IIEL – Institute of International Economic Law, Georgetown University Law Center. Editor-in-Chief for the gLAWcal Book Series "Global Law and Sustainable Development" and for the gLAWcal Book Series "Transnational Law and Governance" published by Routledge Publishing (New York/London).

Care Collaborative and its needs assessment process, service delivery plan, program design and implementation plan; developed a Family Child Care Network micro-enterprise program; developed a Comprehensive Housing Development Strategy with six distinct housing programs, including the implementation plan for a nationally unique Lease-to-Own program linked with Section 8 Family Self Sufficiency; and pioneered the formation of a Community Land Trust to ensure long-term housing affordability in a rapidly gentrifying community.

Love's research analyses the ways contradictory rhetorics of individualism impact policy in the U.S., with focus on implications for social, economic, and racial justice. She is interested in the ways these rhetorics are reflective of underlying political theory and grounded in political ontology, as well as exploring their implications for contemporary social movements in racial and economic justice as well as the potential for participatory democracy. These interests are likewise reflected in her two prior books collaboratively written with Stout, as well as the current volume.

Like Stout, Love is also a "pracademic." Prior to her academic career, she worked as a street-level bureaucrat in Columbus, Ohio. As a caseworker in child support enforcement, she managed over 700 cases as well as training other caseworkers and auditing their work. When the State of Ohio was found to be non-compliant with disbursement requirements under the Personal Responsibility and Work Opportunity Reconciliation Act, Love was part of a special task force created to audit all child support cases that had involved TANF benefits—a statewide project that refunded millions of dollars owed to current and former recipient caregivers. Throughout her time as a caseworker, she experienced first-hand the challenges of attempting to administer policies created in a top-down manner by elected representatives—policies that were often crafted from an upper-class perspective and had excessively punitive impact on lower income people, with racially disparate effects. She could see that the way policy was created and implemented was failing the people she was supposed to be "serving," and she had a sense that if we were going to improve public service, those who are directly impacted by policy need to have a voice in its creation—policy needs to be bottom-up. She wants to understand why our street-level bureaucracies were failing those they were meant to help, and to find better ways of serving the public. This led her to pursue graduate studies in Public Policy and Public Administration, as well as working in a variety of national policy think tanks focused on economic justice (Institute for Women's Policy Research, Center on Budget and Policy Priorities, and Urban Institute) during her graduate studies. These work experiences, along with her first-hand experiences navigating the Supplemental Security Income (SSI), Medicaid, and Supplemental Nutritional Assistance Program (SNAP) programs as a representative payee for her late partner, collectively influence her scholarly work.

As a faculty member of West Virginia University, John D. Rockefeller IV School of Policy and Politics and College of Law, member of the WVU Energy Institute, the WVU Center for Innovation in Gas Research and Utilization (CIGRU) and Institute of Water Security and Science (IWSS), USA and as Founder, President and Director of gLAWcal – Global Law Initiatives for Sustainable Development, through research, policy analysis and grassroots projects, I try to shed new light on issues such as good governance, human rights, right to water, rights to food, social, economic and cultural rights, labour rights, public health, social welfare, consumer interests, climate change, energy, environmental protection and sustainable development, product safety, food safety and security. All these values are directly affected by the global expansion of world trade and should be upheld to balance the excesses of globalization.

I share with Stout and Love this same pro-activism and vision of combining academic, highly scholarly work, and practice. Also for this very same reason, I believe that everyone who advocates for a similar perspective, should definitely read this book.

We live in peculiar times: on the one hand, many people enjoy an unprecedentedly high standard of living from a historical perspective. On the other hand, a considerable part of the population has a feeling that something went wrong, which is underscored by their feelings of discontent and uncertainty. Despite their potential to have positive impact on society, globalization and the rapid pace of technological development, including robotics and artificial intelligence, might shake up the lives of individuals as well as governance frameworks at global and national levels. The rules of play developed mainly in the 20th century can hardly keep pace with the developments of the 21st century. There is a longing for something new after the experiences with the -isms (fascism, socialism, capitalism etc.) of the 20th century.

It seems that Fukuyama's argument concerning the end of history with the ultimate win of liberal democracy requires serious rethinking and readjustment. As the example of China shows, authoritarian regimes making an effective use of the principles of market economy are able to enhance the standard of living of their populations, without any drawbacks, and gain more respect at international level without introducing substantial democratic reforms and compromising their authoritarian rule.[2] At the same time, it is also true that China had been gradually expanding its own systems of public participation and local governance with Chinese cultural characteristics. This narrative brought forward by China and other authoritarian countries against the risks of liberal democracies is more supported in the dynamics of political discourses, because as it happened between the two World Wars and all the events that led to the Second World War, liberal democracies are again showing the potential loopholes in their own systems. The risks that anti-democratic, xenophobic, and racist movements and political parties might develop and take the power through the democratic instruments should not be underestimated. They must be closely monitored and damage control must be made immediately to intervene when the core values of liberal democracies and their Constitutions are at stake.

For all these reasons, the adherents of liberal democracy can no longer see themselves as ultimate winners in arguments with their contenders; they need to justify their position and, eventually, acknowledge the need for adjustments in their views.

However, the real danger for liberal democracy might come from its core. The model of representative democracy seems to be less and less appealing, as many people feel unrepresented by those they have elected, a sentiment often truer in periods of economic recession and/or in areas of growing economic and human poverty. A reaction to these developments might be seen in the calls for more direct democracy. Unfortunately, as we live in the age of "alternative facts," even (at first sight) democratic instruments, such as referenda, might lead to destabilization and situations with an inherent conflict potential. The examples of the Brexit vote and the Catalan independence referendum demonstrate that the public might be vulnerable to misinformation and that elected representatives, blinded by their ambitions, might irresponsibly gamble with these democratic instruments. The similar risks of disinformation or even propaganda are also happening within regular election campaigns like in the recent presidential elections in the United States and in different European countries. These examples are often used by the proponents of representative democracy who argue that direct democracy undermines the democratic foundations of our societies and should not be used to decide about issues that are too complex. On the other hand, the calls for more direct democracy might also be seen as a sign that the model of representative democracy has shortcomings and needs certain rearrangements.

2 Paolo Davide Farah, Elena Cima (editors), *China's influence on non-trade concerns in international economic law*, Global Law and Sustainable Development Book Series, Routledge Publishing (New-York/ London), ISBN 978-1-4094-4848-8, September 2016, pp. 1–584.

Stout and Love see the solution for the governance dilemma in 21st century in a form of Integrative Governance. Resurrecting (among other influences) the timeless ideas of Mary Follett, the underlying solution for the issues of governance in the 21st century is seen in the re-appropriation of authentic collaboration and genuine relations. Linking the concept of Integrative Governance with the concept of radical democracy enables readers to see interpersonal as well as institutional relations in a holistic perspective, stripped of redundant layers of national, communal, or tribal identity. Such a *radically* human approach represents an underlying philosophical foundation for the functioning of participatory democracy that should be the polar star to follow. The consistent reasoning provided is urgently needed in this field, as many initiatives calling for participatory democracy seem to omit these fundamentals, without which failure is a constant recurrence.

It has to be said that strong liberalist principles do not create a fairer world on their own, but they risk facilitating a world ruled by unelected, authoritarian, and profit-driven (as opposed to human development oriented) organizations such as some (not all) multinationals. Private companies do what they are supposed to do to make a profit and otherwise benefit their shareholders. It is not formally and institutionally their role to self-regulate their actions if they are not requested to do so or if the rules of the game do not directly (laws and regulations) or indirectly (corporate social responsibility and accountability for the good public image of the company) impose to act accordingly.

As Stout and Love call out in their book and as I have also personally analysed,[3] food security might have a pivotal role in the paradigm shift from an import-export oriented model to the re-establishment of more locally oriented production. Achieving food sovereignty has become increasingly urgent considering the current economic crisis, the systemic problems created by the exacerbated import-export model, and a debit and credit system that is not sustainable and has brought our society down a dead-end street of defaults, unemployment, and social unrest, as seen in the examples of Argentina and Greece. This change would allow communities to re-appropriate control of local production including cultural components and choice of domestic production and consumption.

Similarly, a growing number of local communities are creating new and innovative ways for product commercialization like exchanges and trade with the use of alternative local currency as opposed to the use of cryptocurrencies or alternative currencies at a massive scale. The same can be said about other societies that are establishing methods or metrics to measure progress and growth beyond the GDP or similar common instruments.

One arena included in the original draft of this book is the potential for e-governance within these efforts. For instance, advancement in the field of technology and social media led Facebook's CEO, Mark Zuckerberg, to publish a bold statement on Facebook's potential to create a global community, which some observers read as a sort of political manifesto (or an elaborate marketing campaign). Be that as it may, such statements undoubtedly demonstrate that the new tech-aristocracy thinks about the future of governance in an age dominated by technology and artificial intelligence. It remains to be seen whether it is good or bad. We should also remind that in the U.S. the net neutrality is the pivotal concept. As Yuval Noah Harari notes, we cannot stop technological development, but we should be aware of its course and impact on our lives. A breakthrough in the field of artificial intelligence might

3 Paolo Davide Farah, "Trade and Progress: The Case of China," 30 *Columbia Journal of Asian Law*, 2016, pp. 97–107; Paolo Davide Farah, Elena Cima (editors), *China's Influence on non-trade concerns in international economic law*, Global Law and Sustainable Development Book Series, Routledge Publishing (New-York/London), ISBN 978-1-4094-4848-8, September 2016, pp. 1–584.

lead to the creation of a new 1% with more power and influence than ever before. The spectre of economic inequality painted by Thomas Piketty might then rise to a completely different level. Still, artificial intelligence might evolve into an all-knowing new God, creating new dimensions of wholeness and connections between people. It also remains to be seen whether experiments with cryptocurrencies, such as Bitcoin or Ethereum, are only the signs of a new economic "bubble" and attractive subjects of speculation or whether they have a real potential to set the basis for a new decentralized economic order based on blockchain technology.

Even algorithms might also become the new Satanic verses, burning democracy and free will into ashes, and action has to be taken. To prevent such scenarios from happening and to use technological developments to their fullest (positive) potential, solid (theoretical as well as practical) foundations of participatory democracy and governance are indispensable. In a positive scenario, they might serve as the basis for the *radically democratic* governance making the most of the progress characteristic for our times. In the worst-case scenario, they might represent a powerful counterforce to any efforts to silence the people's voice and serve as a tool of a new slavery.

Stout and Love lay important groundwork for the future of participatory democracy in the light of present challenges. The picture of Integrative Governance is painted on the grim background of the crisis of sustainability. The illusory certainties of the people in affluent Western countries are shaken up not only by progress in the field of technology and globalization, but also by (in many aspects) the deteriorating situation in the Global South. By applying a holistic approach, the book sheds an important light on the causalities between seemingly unrelated phenomena, such as the link between climate change, drought, and conflicts. The opinion that liberalism has enabled many countries to reduce poverty is correct, but at the same time and to a certain extent, what has to be examined is *at what costs*? In the long-term, has this wealth been achieved? The negative externalities of industrialization are enormous; the externalities of the excesses of globalization, free trade, and neo-liberal thoughts are even more dramatic, in terms of loss of quality of life, water and air pollution, climate change, environmental risks and natural disasters, health problems, and new diseases connected to industrialization without control and rules.

The recent wave of refugees (with more likely to come) that paralyzed Europe might be seen as a supplementary demonstration of a butterfly effect, when events in one part of the world put into motion unpredictable developments in distant countries. This might also be interpreted as an example of when the failure to act on the part of governments, the selfless work of the civil society and communities might intervene and to a certain extent compensate governmental failure. Several non-governmental organizations, which against all the odds, tried in any possible way to save many lives in the Mediterranean or grant shelter and care to those finally arrived in Europe are indeed good examples. Such welcome-initiatives demonstrate the potential of genuine collaborative practices, building bridges between people to overcome (or at least alleviate) the difficulties at the time of crisis.

Certain political movements might consider that negative discourses against globalization and internationalism are enough to deny what history and technological innovation and human desire have demonstrated for centuries. Interdependencies are a fact; the world is interconnected without a real possibility to controvert it. Any attempt to shut this down will have even more dramatic repercussion on a global level. This does not mean that globalization should not be more controlled or regulated; it is actually the opposite. Globalization must be regulated to balance an open society with a local concern and community governance that take care of the problems at local level. Stout and Love's perspective can help in this challenge.

As they note, cooperation between cities and the activities at the local level in the field of climate change adaptation and mitigation in the United States are examples of the potential collaborative governance holds. These activities nurture the hope that the short-sighted step of the United States' administration to pull the country out the Paris Agreement would not be the ultimate blow to global efforts to combat climate change. The international collaborations and partnerships among cities around the world, such as twinning and sister cities, help demonstrate that the needs and desires of their citizens might be similar, even in very different countries or contexts. Again, what has to be pivotal is respect and engagement beyond the diversities. The more we accept diversities, the more we can feel part of the same human community.

The economic crisis in Greece also gave birth to experiments with collaborative practices: for instance, in certain cases of companies that went bankrupt, workers took over the responsibility for the companies and chose to reinvent their management structure and business strategies. Hence, the new management of such companies might resemble cooperatives, strengthening not only the commitment to the company and its profit, but nurturing also the bonds between people. Paying attention to the bigger picture, their business strategies have often been reinvented to focus on environmentally sustainable products.

Naturally, every crisis is unpleasant and painful. However, it also shows us a mirror and offers a room for contemplation. And most importantly, it is in times of crisis that the need for genuine human collaboration is most urgently felt. Hence, the crisis provides us also with the unique opportunity to throw away our masks and become true *radicals*, i.e., to come back to our roots and resurrect our authentic selves.

As the authors correctly point out, not every form of collaboration is equally meaningful and effective. The lack of communication and coordination between international, national, and local levels might easily backfire in a form of mistrust, loss of credibility, and confrontational situations that might bring further conflicts and disorder. The often too technocratic top-down governance approaches, also characteristic to a certain extent for the field of international development, are increasingly criticized as too cumbersome and inadequately responding to local needs and cultural sensibilities. As a reaction to these critiques, alternative forms of cooperation begin to emerge and have to be examined and assessed. An example represents the South American concept of *buen vivir*, built *inter alia* upon the forms of cooperation characteristic for indigenous communities and considering the local conditions and cultural specifics. Similarly, as the multiple examples mentioned in *Integrative Governance*, ranging from quantum physics to indigenous beliefs, also the concept of *buen vivir* underscores the notion of wholeness and interrelatedness of human and natural worlds. At the same time, it represents an example of a bottom-up approach to governance as an alternative to the prevalent top-down approaches.

As I have mentioned in the foreword to Stout and Love's previous book, *A Radically Democratic Response to Global Governance: Dystopian Utopias*, social sciences and humanities are often two steps behind the developments in natural sciences and technology and react on these developments only when it is already too late. Similar to their previous book, *Integrative Governance: Generating Sustainable Responses to Global Crises*, to a large extent, erases this deficit and paints a vivid picture of a workable governance for the 21st century. The timeliness and practicality of the book is also emphasized by its transdisciplinarity and highly relevant case studies.

However, among all of these benefits of the book, one is especially noteworthy. Even though the starting point of the book rests in the realization that we find ourselves in the middle of multiple crises (falling under the scope of an overarching crisis of sustainability), which is naturally a rather depressing realization, the overall message of the book is *radically* positive: We have a unique opportunity to build a governance model based on meaningful participation. We have the know-how and the rest is in our hands. And that is extremely good news.

Professor Paolo Davide Farah
Editor-in-Chief for the gLAWcal Book Series
"Global Law and Sustainable Development" published
by Routledge Publishing (New York/London).

West Virginia University, USA and gLAWcal – Global Law
Initiatives for Sustainable Development, United Kingdom

Preface

This book is part of a larger project to conceptualize and advocate a radically democratic approach to governance in the global context – one that builds from philosophical argument but gets down to the particulars of practice (Stout and Love 2013, 2014a, 2015b, 2016, 2017). We offer a robust explication and affirmation of Integrative Governance, a radically democratic approach grounded in a rapidly growing body of work from a wide array of disciplines and worldviews that share an understanding of existence as a dynamic and relational, organic process. Many scholars argue that this alternative perspective has meaningful and positive implications for public policy and governance. However, these assertions and even prescriptions for alternative approaches typically lack a structure and framework that can anchor them into traditional understandings of the governance of groups, organizations, and societies in a manner that can *effect change in practice.* As public administration scholars and practitioners, we seek to fill that gap.

By *governance*, we mean all of the practices used to determine and produce collective action in any group context that affects the common good at any level of analysis: micro, meso, and macro. Drawing out the generic practices considered in "new public governance" (Osborne 2010), we include approaches to relational configurations, decision making, action, and evaluation. We find governance within and between all three societal sectors, however labeled (i.e., public, private, and nonprofit; government, market, and community; or political, economic, and civic). It is a concept that is both political and administrative (or managerial) and is intra-organizational, inter-organizational, intergovernmental, intersectoral, and transnational in the contemporary context.

By *global*, we imply that many common good issues transcend the boundaries of jurisdictions and nation-states, thereby demanding global governance of some type. However, a new approach is necessary, because, as Rosenau (1999) argues, global governance "suffers from a reliance on the artifacts of the very past beyond which it seeks to move" (287). Furthermore, in the absence of effective global governance, the forces of economic globalization have negatively affected every natural, societal, and political system. Herein, we explore the empirical evidence of these crises, as well as the theoretical failings of collaborative governance networks attempting to remedy the situation.

Thus, we come to this study of global governance from a *radically democratic* perspective. The term "radical" means going to the root or source (as opposed to going to extremes) (Davis 1990, Marx 1967). In reference to democracy, this means grounding theory and practice in the individual subject or world-citizen.[1] *Radical* politics shifts the subject from a unified People or particular group identity to each and every person. In radical politics rights are no longer tied to community identity, or state-based citizenship, but rather to one's humanity. *Radical* understandings of democracy move from liberalism's parties and elected representatives to direct, participatory democracy (Simons 2005). Thus, radical democracy is differentiated from conservative, liberal, and communitarian approaches to democracy (Tønder and Thomassen 2005b).

Finally, we argue that the *integrative* process is a more fruitful approach to governance than those typically found in practice – even those described as *collaborative governance networks*. The philosophical underpinnings of interconnection and the method of integration itself provide the nuanced differentiation needed to extricate the undermining tendencies of hierarchy and competition from collaboration. Its relational process ontology fundamentally alters governance ideas and practices in a way that may overcome the failures of global governance, while still achieving the primary aims of currently competing alternatives.

Part I sets the stage for Integrative Governance and why we believe it is necessary in the contemporary global context, one that is rife with global crises of sustainability and societal governance. Part II explains the meaning of integration and fleshes out the conceptual elements of Integrative Governance outlined in previous publications about our Governance Typology (Stout and Love 2013, 2014a, 2015b, 2016, 2017). Part III offers the reasoning behind our assertion that Integrative Governance is a better approach to generating sustainable responses to global crises and calls for its affirmation.

Note

1 We must note that the term "citizen" is problematic in radical political theory, given contested legal identities. We use the term in neither a nationalistic nor cosmopolitan manner that implies a unified identity. World-citizen simply means being a co-inhabitant of planet Earth.

Acknowledgements

The authors would like to acknowledge institutional support for research that enabled completion of this manuscript. Margaret Stout received support from the West Virginia University Senate Grants for Research and Scholarship 2012 (R-12-026), 2013 (R-13-049), and 2016 (R-16-003). Jeannine Love received support from Roosevelt University in the form of a Faculty Research Leave in fall semester 2012.

All figures in the book were crafted by Eve Faulkes, with the exception of Figures 2.1 and 12.1; we deeply appreciate her creative insight in illustrating complex concepts.

While all shortcomings are ours to own, we benefitted from early suggestions from the editors and peer reviewers of the book prospectus. Our colleagues Cheryl Simrell King, Robyn Keast, and Art Sementelli graciously provided feedback on the complete manuscript. We hope we have responded adequately, and believe their insights and suggestions have improved the manuscript, and we are deeply appreciative of their time.

We would like to collectively thank all of publishers of our previous work, all of which are appropriately cited and included in the reference list.

As an editorial note, any type of emphasis in quotes (i.e., bold or italic text) is in the original source, unless indicated by "emphasis added." In our own narrative, we use the gender neutral plural (they) rather than gender specific singular terms.

Part I

Situating Integrative Governance

Part I sets the stage for Integrative Governance and why we believe it is necessary. Chapter 1 provides an overview of the contemporary governance context and its social, economic, and environmental crises. We explain how the interconnected nature of these complex problems cannot be resolved by govern*ment* alone, and have therefore given rise to the concept of govern*ance*. Yet, historical governance approaches have failed to prevent or significantly mitigate these crises of sustainability and have even compromised the legitimacy of governance itself.

Chapter 2 presents an overview of contemporary governance theories that seek to resolve these shortcomings through network structures and collaborative practices, considering the manner in which governance theory is on an ongoing developmental path. We examine the ideal and why collaborative governance networks still fail to achieve the substantive and democratic benefits they promise.

Chapter 3 responds to these failures, considering the manner in which governance theory has been too insular to draw in the necessary ideas and practices to achieve its substantive and democratic goals. Empirically, it relies on insufficient objects of study to develop an understanding of collaborative networks. By anchoring itself to thin theoretical ground, governance theory is unable to respond to the world as it is now understood. It is philosophically misaligned with the ideal of collaboration and the reality of interdependence. Both intersectoral governance and sustainability create new objects of study that require a transdisciplinary approach – one that is *beyond* the grasp of any one discipline.

1 Complex global crises

> *OUR political life is stagnating, capital and labor are virtually at war, the nations of Europe are at one another's throats because we have not yet learned how to live together. The twentieth century must find a new principle of association. . . . Group organization is to be the new method in politics, the basis of our future industrial system, the foundation of international order. Group organization will create the new world we are now blindly feeling after, for creative force comes from the group, creative power is evolved through the activity of the group life.*
>
> – (Follett 1918, 3)

This chapter situates the need for Integrative Governance within the current context. "The world today confronts not one, but a series of interlocking crises – economic, political, social, and ecological" (Bookchin and Taylor 2015, loc. 81). Social crises arise in response to various forms of social strife and oppression, including forms of systemic discrimination and state-sanctioned violence. These tensions fuel both internal and international conflicts such as the civil war in Syria and NATO-led or sanctioned military actions in Afghanistan, Iraq, and Lebanon. They also manifest in civil unrest and a proliferating number of social movements, such as the Arab Spring, Democracy Now!, Occupy, and Black Lives Matter. Many of these social crises are driven, at least in part, by economic and environmental crises. Growing global inequality – both within and between societies – follows more than three decades of market deregulation, liberal global trade agreements, and government austerity measures (Elson 2017). Social and economic conditions are exacerbated by environmental crises, including extended droughts, super storms, flooding, and coastal loss (Gemenne 2015, Renner 2015). These interdependent crises generate a global *crisis of sustainability*.

While we discuss the escalating ideological crises associated with competing governance reform efforts elsewhere (Stout and Love 2016), here, we focus instead on the empirical conditions of the contemporary world and governance responses. Regardless of their ideological grounding and form, governments are meant to craft and enforce the rules by which society functions, including political, economic, and civil spheres. Governments must seek collaboration with others (e.g., other governments, nongovernmental organizations [NGOs], corporations, and citizens) to address issues beyond their narrowing scope and capacity or those that cross over national boundaries. Yet, even these institutional and intersectoral arrangements fail to mitigate the pressing social, economic, and environmental crises we confront. Violent conflict has not abated, economic catastrophe has not been avoided, and environmental disasters continue to become more frequent and extreme.

Globalization has replaced a state-based international system of governments with a decentralized, heterogeneous, intersectoral system of network governance (Keohane and Nye 2000). As a result, governing functions are increasingly likely to occur through associations of nation-states, associations of cities, partnerships of public and nonprofit agencies, and networks of affected citizens and stakeholders from across sectors. Nation-state sovereignty is impacted by expanding governance networks, thus creating a *crisis of government.* The meaning of governance is no longer grounded in a reified assumption that nation-states are "the foundation of politics" (Rosenau 1999, 287). Within this context, a new understanding of public agencies arises and national, institutional, and sectoral boundaries blur (Roll and Thomas 2014, Wachhaus 2014). We are now in an age of govern*ance* as opposed to state govern*ments* (Pierre and Peters 2000).

Although the terrain is well-traveled, to contextualize the need for this project, the following sections provide a brief account of today's empirical situation with a focus on three dimensions of sustainability: social, economic, and environmental. Each section describes the manner in which governance networks and social movements have arisen in attempt to address these respective crises, and then considers the forms of resistance these efforts elicit. This history details the transformation of nation-states into "network states . . . hailed as necessary to meet the challenges of increased complexity, interconnectedness, and globalization" (Bang and Esmark 2009, 14). Thus, what follows is simultaneously a historical overview of the formation of international and intersectoral governance institutions as well as the rise of the corollary crisis of government. From this vantage point, it becomes clear that the emergence of governance networks has resulted in a bifurcated populist reaction, one that may either return us to the protectionism of the past as nation-states reclaim the seats of power, or move us forward on a path toward radical democracy.

Due to their interconnectedness, disaggregating social, economic, and environmental crises is challenging. Likewise, due to the feedback loops among them, it is difficult to pick one as the start of a causal chain. For instance, one might point to economic policies that focus on growth, trade, and deregulation as underpinning both social crises and environmental crises. Alternatively, beginning the analysis with environmental crises allows for consideration of how climate change is a result of pro-growth economic policies that have also exacerbated social strife through environmental justice issues. Because we are particularly interested in understanding how all of these crises foment a crisis of government, we make social crises our point of departure.

Social crises

Social crises are evident in international military actions and civil unrest within nations. Social crises have myriad driving forces (e.g., histories of slavery, colonization, and genocide; competing worldviews; growing income disparities; corporate control of natural and economic resources; and dominating relationships between governments and the governed). Of the wide range of possible responses, mass protest, and violent conflict are the most visible (Kirton and Stefanova 2017). Here, we consider historical trends that have direct pertinence to the emergence of global governance and resistance to it, including relations among nations as well as relations between nation-states and their constituents.

International relations

International law was created due to a shared desire to establish global peace, or at minimum reduce the likelihood of unilateral acts of aggression. Its roots can be traced to the Peace of

Westphalia treaty of 1648 that ended the Thirty Years Wars among European nations, establishing an international system of sovereign state actors (Olsen and McCormick 2017) who engaged in diplomatic relations based on their own interests, ultimately backed by threat of force (Held 1992). In the aftermath of World War I, however, there was a move to foster international cooperation that would ensure a lasting peace among members; this was first envisioned as the ill-fated League of Nations (Office of the Historian 2017). In response to the enormous destruction of life and infrastructure in World War II (Favreau 2011), the goal of multinational cooperation was revisited and became viable with the creation of the United Nations (UN) in 1945 (Held 1992). Its founding charter stresses the goals of preventing war, protecting human rights, and bolstering international law by nations being "good neighbours" and uniting their strength (UN n.d.-b). The Charter was originally signed by 26 nations and has since expanded to 193 UN member states (UN n.d.-a).

Since then, UN-orchestrated treaties and organizations have steadily expanded international law to protect member states, individual rights, and natural resources. For instance, the Universal Declaration of Human Rights of 1948 outlined fundamental inalienable human rights of all persons during times of war or peace. Signatory nations pledged to protect and preserve the basic human rights of all persons within their borders in an attempt to curb some of the driving forces of social crises ranging from systemic oppression to genocide. The Declaration was supplemented by the Convention on the Prevention and Punishment of the Crime of Genocide of 1948, which authorizes punishment of member nations that engage in acts of genocide. Similarly, the Geneva Conventions, crafted in 1949, specify the requirements for providing medical assistance to the wounded during wartime and acceptable treatment of prisoners of war (ICRC n.d.). Other agreements aim to prevent conflict through the stewardship of resources, such as the 1962 Convention on the High Seas, which regulates activities within international waters.

The UN itself has also created several specialized agencies and committees. For instance, the Food and Agriculture Organization (1945) was created to address hunger worldwide through treaties, technical assistance, and policy recommendations (Ivanova 2014). The UN also continues its original focus on preventing and responding to conflict through its Security Council, which determines when and where UN Peacekeeping missions are necessary and can compel member states to assist. Its military counterpart is the North Atlantic Treaty Organization (NATO). Whereas the UN is a global deliberative body, NATO is a strategic alliance of Western nations who agree to combine military efforts in order to share the risks and benefits of collective defense (NATO 2017). NATO's founding treaty commits member states to the principles of the UN Charter and declares the shared values of consensus decision making, liberty, democracy, human rights, and rule of law (NATO 2017, June 2). Additionally, members agreed not to pursue unilateral military action.

Perhaps the most complicated example of international cooperation is the European Union (EU), which initially arose as the European Coal and Steel Community through the Paris Treaty of 1951in response to the enormous death toll and devastation of agriculture and infrastructure across Europe during World War II, as well as a centuries-long history of wars on the continent. As Olsen and McCormick (2017) note, the EU is an example of confederalism in which each state retains sovereignty for actions such as entering into international treaties; yet the EU has its own legislative system, a common currency and market, and EU citizens can cross member state borders at will.

Such international alliances are a global phenomenon. In 1945, several Arab states signed onto the Pact of the League of Arab States, forming the Arab League. Its goals were to coordinate political activities in the region, to improve financial matters of trade and customs, to address shared infrastructure, and to promote general welfare and public health in the region (LAS 1945). Responding to the Cold War and related conflicts in the region, a group of Southeast Asian states formed the Association of Southeast Asia (ASA) in 1961, which became the Association of Southeast Asian Nations (ASEAN) in 1967. The African Union was established in 1999 – out of the Organization of African Unity – to unite the nation-states on the African continent. Most recently, the Union of South American Nations (UNASUR) was created in 2008 (Flannery 2017).

While the vast majority of actors involved in these multilateral coalitions have been states, they work closely with NGOs to achieve shared aims, as noted in the UN's founding charter (Sidhu 2007). For example, the UN Security Council often works in tandem with Médecins Sans Frontières (Doctors Without Borders) to provide medical assistance in areas of military conflict during peacekeeping missions. The Geneva Conventions were developed at a conference convened by the Red Cross with 16 states and four charitable organizations (ICRC n.d.).

These multinational coalitions serve to solidify relations between various state actors and to provide mechanisms for allowing states to come to consensus and take action on a variety of issues from military intervention to common resource management to human rights. The perceived benefits of membership in these coalitions – and the risks of exclusion – have fueled the spread of new coalitions across geographic regions and the exponential growth in membership. They also mark the initial move away from solitary nation-states acting unilaterally for their own self-interest toward collaboration. Yet, global asymmetries of power remain intact in institutions such as the UN Security Council, whose decisions are made by majority rather than consensus, are binding rather than voluntary, and provides permanent positions and sole veto power to five of the ten members (Sidhu 2007). Similarly, power asymmetries and oppressive forces remain in play; many nation-states that have signed the Universal Declaration of Human Rights routinely fail to protect the rights of all persons within their borders.

Domestic governmental relations

Nation-states are also experiencing challenges from *within*. In nations with federal systems, the relationship between national and sub-governments is inherently agonistic. The ongoing negotiation and interpretation of constitutional policy making authority and implementation responsibility maintains a constant source of challenge to nation-state sovereignty. Dubnick and Meehan (2004) describe the dynamics of the last several decades as centrifugal, including both diffusion and dispersion of authority. This is evident in the late 1980s trends toward adoption of business practices and privatization of functions through both load shedding and contracting out to private organizations. As the authority and capacity of government bureaucracies are minimized through deregulation and budget cuts, agencies must enter public-private partnerships to tackle complex governance goals (O'Toole 1997b). These practices are often collected under banners of Reinventing Government (Osborne and Gaebler 1992) and the New Public Management (Barzelay 2001, Kaboolian 1998). The result of these trends is described as the "hollowing out of the state" (Milward and Provan 2000, Rhodes 1994).

However, with diminishing resources, devolution of authority has also meant significant budget cuts to grants in aid between levels of government. These austerity measures have left states and localities on their own to manage the social, economic, and environmental effects of globalization. In response, cities are creating their own networks to address common problems and share strategies with one another. Barber (2013) argues that cities are already more networked and globally interconnected through pragmatic collaboration than any grouping of sovereign nations. Formal associations go back at least to 1924 with the US Municipal League (now the National League of Cities), arising alongside the concept of the League of Nations. These municipal networks now include the City Protocol Network, the United Cities and Local Governments, the International Union of Local Authorities, Metropolis, the National League of Cities (US), CityNet, the European Union Secretariat of Cities, the US Conference of Mayors, and the Global Parliament of Mayors. Collectively, their agendas navigate myriad sources of interdependence: addressing global economic markets and crises, ensuring security in the face of global terrorism, responding to environmental degradation and catastrophes, leveraging global communications technology toward public participation, and increasing citizen engagement in governance. Recognizing the potential within these networks of localities, Barber (2013) argues for a sort of global parliament or World Assembly of Cities that "is already half-grown, waiting rather to be recognized, exploited, and formalized" (7).

The increasing devolution of responsibility to cities foments challenges to federal authority. For example, although the sanctuary city movement in the US began in 1979 in Los Angeles (H.B.C. 2016), this form of local resistance to national immigration policy has received renewed attention in response to actions by the Trump administration. Localities across the US and Canada have declared themselves "sanctuaries" for undocumented immigrants, placing restrictions on the extent to which local law enforcement voluntarily works with Immigration and Customs Enforcement (ICE) (Graber and Marquez 2016, Kopan 2017, Jan. 25). In March 2017, representatives of sanctuary cities across the US convened for the first time to share their determination and their strategies for facing these threats (Acevedo 2017, Mar. 27). Similarly, in response to slow federal action to curb human trafficking, NGOs, local businesses, and government agencies are forming regional networks of "slavery-free cities" (Allies Against Slavery 2015) or "slavery-free communities" (Slave-Free Community Project n.d.), taking steps to identify and support victims of human trafficking and ensure that all public and private supply chains are slavery-free.

Diffusion of authority is taken further through growing citizen demands for sovereignty, voice, and direct participation in self-governance, reflecting a trend in the narrative of democracy that has become increasingly participatory in character (Saward 2003). Indeed, the Worldwatch Institute's comprehensive review notes a common theme underlying the policy ideas and reforms analyzed: "the necessity of citizen empowerment and citizen responsibility" (Prugh and Renner 2014, 248). In effect, through such public participation efforts, communities have become the "'new' institutional site" of governance networks that are "mediating integration arrangements between increasingly disconnected citizen-state relations" (Brown and Keast 2003, 124). For instance, the participatory budgeting movement that began in Porto Alegre, Brazil, empowers citizens to determine how public funds will be spent; since 1989 it has spread to cities and local districts in Latin America, North America, Asia, Africa, and Europe (Participatory Budgeting Project 2017).

As further examined in Chapter 13, social movements often demand deeper democracy, greater policy influence, and a more citizen-centric society (Commonwealth Foundation 1999). For example, the Arab Spring of 2010 and 2011 began in Tunisia and spread to Egypt, Libya, and Syria as individuals occupied public spaces demanding democratic reforms (Haas and Lesch 2013). In the US, the Black Lives Matter movement emerged in 2012 and solidified in 2014 in response to killings of unarmed African Americans by police officers. This movement seeks to address state-sanctioned violence against black and brown individuals and to demand greater participation in crafting policies to affirm and protect their human rights (Garza 2014, Oct. 7) through mechanisms such as Campaign Zero (Campaign Zero n.d.).

While social movements are often specific to place or interest, new social movements share a trend toward solidarity (Day 2011). For example, the No Border Network (2004) challenges immigration and border policies as does the No One Is Illegal (n.d.) movement in Canada. Citizens stand in solidarity with undocumented residents demanding democratic rights for all. These calls for democratic inclusion within increasingly globalized networks of social movements create a new sense of world citizenship. Individuals are beginning to see themselves as interconnected within "a borderless world" (Chacón and Davis 2006, 292).

Hegemonic populism

These radically democratic sentiments are not shared by all. Some fear that "nation-states have been supplanted by network states" (Bang and Esmark 2009, 14) in which governments are increasingly unable to assert sovereignty through unilateral action (Scharpf 1993). Despite the disproportionate influence both the US and the UK carry within their alliances, their political leaders warn of dangerous erosion of national sovereignty and superpower status (Kettl 2000) as power shifts from national governments to international arrangements, agreements, and agencies (Cleveland 1993; Farazmand 1994). To reclaim the seat of power, politicians bypass sub-governments, appealing to citizens directly in new waves of nationalist protectionism. Strong illustrations of this trend are found in the US and UK, and it is becoming a growing trend within European states as well. Powerful rhetoric is used (e.g., us/them, good/evil, counter-terrorism/terrorism) to reinforce national identity and justify increasing state power to secure safety and democracy (Jackson 2005). This perspective is reflected in state, city, and citizen protectionism (e.g., "Build the wall!") that seeks to reinforce borders at the national level.

Frustration with this perceived loss of power can be seen in the appeal of President Trump's "America First" and "Make America Great Again" populism that disparages international alliances such as the UN and NATO. Similar nationalism is evident in the rhetoric surrounding the "Brexit" vote for the United Kingdom to leave the EU. The Leave campaign stressed border and immigration control, as well as throwing off the yoke of policies enacted by the EU parliament (Vote Leave n.d.). Unfortunately, this kind of populist rhetoric and international policy represent a "self-defeating approach," intensifying rather than alleviating the discontent it is purportedly meant to address (Chernus 2016, x). The initially welcoming responses to the Syrian refugee crisis in states like Denmark, Sweden, and Germany have been followed by a sharp uptick in far-right "Euro-sceptic" nationalist political activity by groups across Sweden, Denmark, Austria, Germany, and France (Allen et al. 2017).

Economic crises

Economic crises are seen in market crashes, recessions, increasing economic disparities across regions, and growing income gaps within nation-states. Economic disparities are often strongly correlated with race and ethnicity, and those who have faced histories of slavery and colonialism are often disproportionately impacted by economic crises (Darity and Nembhard 2000). The global economy is increasingly interconnected with a "complex interplay" of market forces and financial instruments that allow financial crises to spread at unprecedented rates (Kirton, Oldani, and Savona 2011). While the globalization of markets began with the rise of the nation-state in the sixteenth century (Held 1992), most accounts of contemporary market globalism begin with the formulation of the Bretton Woods System in 1944. Designed in the midst of World War II and in the aftermath of the Great Depression (Kirton, Oldani, and Savona 2011), this was the first attempt to regulate an international monetary system and create a "new world order" that would guide exchange rates, international lending, and international trade (Eichengreen 1993, xi).

Signatory nations sought to "liberalize international trade, encourage investment, and support the unemployed" (Eichengreen 1993, 627). Most notably, the agreement created financial institutions. The World Bank was envisioned as an institution for investing in reconstruction and development projects in war-ravaged Europe (Mason and Asher 1973, Vreeland 2007). The IMF was devised to oversee the pegged exchange rate (Eichengreen 1993). However, what would quickly become its sole task was to act as a credit lender providing emergency infusions of capital to stabilize economies of war-torn industrialized nations. The activities of both organizations quickly expanded beyond Europe to include, and then concentrate on, developing nations (Vreeland 2007). Both institutions have played pivotal roles in expanding the global market (Hardt and Negri 2000) through their loan conditions (Woods 2006).

To support these organizations' efforts, there has been a general proliferation of international governance organizations (IGOs) and nongovernmental organizations (NGOs). The Union of International Associations (2012/13) lists about 5,000 IGOs and 25,000 NGOs worldwide. Furthermore, private corporations have become increasingly involved in influencing free trade agreements to minimize barriers to production and trade in global markets (Nader 1993). The Organization for European Economic Cooperation (OEEC) was formed in 1948 as part of the ongoing efforts to stabilize global conflict and markets in the aftermath of World War II; it would become the Organization for Economic Cooperation and Development in 1961 (OECD 2017). The Group of Six (G6) was formed in 1975 in response to the 1973 oil crisis. It has a steadily expanding role (Hajnal 2007; Levy 2009), envisioned as a global "steering committee" (Cooper and Schrumm 2011, 229). The G6 expanded to the Group of Seven (G7) in 1976, and eventually the Group of Eight (G8) in 1997. This was expanded to the Group of Twenty (G20) in 1999, although the G8 retains a separate identity and significant power.

The combined efforts of IGOs and NGOs are supplemented by multinational and regional trade agreements. The General Agreement on Tariffs and Trade (GATT) first negotiated in Geneva in 1947 (Vreeland 2007) set the stage for the liberalization of international trade by reducing trade barriers such as quotas and tariffs (Zeiler 1999). The GATT was eventually supplanted by the World Trade Organization (WTO) in 1995, an organization created to further the GATT's aim of trade liberalization through monitoring and enforcing trade agreements and providing a forum for addressing trade disputes (Anderson 2000). By the time the WTO was formed, the GATT had increased from 23 nation-states to 128 members; it has since grown to 151 members, accounting for 96.4 percent of the world's trade (WTO 2017).

During this time, there has been a proliferation of regional trade agreements, such as the North American Free Trade Agreement (NAFTA), the Dominican Republic-Central America-United States Free Trade Agreement (CAFTA), the ASEAN Free Trade Agreement (AFTA), the Common Market for Eastern and Southern Africa (COMESA), the Economic and Monetary Community of Central Africa (CEMAC), the Economic Community of West African States (ECOWAS), the Economic Cooperation Organization (ECO), and the European Economic Agreement (EEA). Within these regional agreements, member countries can negotiate special terms of exchange; however, the WTO is responsible for oversight.

As the history of these intersectoral and international networks suggest, the current global economic system is ideologically grounded in free trade. As a result, the WEF (2010) argues that nation-states are no longer "the overwhelmingly dominant actors on the world stage" (8–10). This reallocation of economic policy power erodes nation-state sovereignty. IGOs, NGOs, and corporations are able "to exercise as much or even more authority" over national economic policy (Vreeland 2007, 1). Furthermore, because nation-states are the only democratically accountable parties within these governance networks, this dispersal of power raises deep democratic concerns (Wilde 2013). While decisions made by "quasi-regional or quasi-supranational organizations" promise greater control and flexibility for the parties, they often "diminish the range of decisions open to given national 'majorities' " (Held 1992, 21). With little democratic control by the citizens directly affected, IGOs, NGOs, and corporations are able to influence trade agreements that impose conditions that restructure entire national economies.

This danger is evident in loans given by the IMF and World Bank, and trade deals overseen by the WTO that are conditional upon the implementation of austerity measures such as mandatory cuts in public spending, privatization of public goods and services, deregulation, and reduction or elimination of trade barriers. Nations that request these loans are facing immediate crisis and have little bargaining (Vreeland 2007). Lenders seek "structural adjustments" to the economies of borrowers that generally favor wealthy nations and transnational corporations, often deepening existing wealth disparities, destabilizing the economies of developing nation-states, eroding public services, and allowing industrial nations to flood their markets with exports. These combined effects exacerbate debt and make developing nations less likely to be able to repay their loans (Immerwahr 2015).

These economic policies and trade agreements often reinforce global power imbalances that erode the sovereignty of developing nations while empowering multinational corporations and securing hegemony of the Global North (Hardt and Negri 2000; Stiglitz 2001). The GATT's most-favored nation clause is meant to prevent discriminatory trade practices; however, both the GATT and the WTO preserve the ability of more powerful nations to create and retain trade policies that are beneficial for themselves and transnational corporations, often to the detriment of poorer nations (Ritchie 1993; Zeiler 1999). Votes within the IMF and World Bank are determined by the size of a nation's economy (Vreeland 2007; Woods 2006). The G20 was created in response to these power asymmetries in an attempt to foster broader democratic inclusion in global governance (Bradford and Lim 2011; Cooper and Schrumm 2011).

Counterhegemonic movements

Even the superpowers are not immune to the negative effects of free market ideology. The hollowing of the state often results in deregulation and austerity measures that wreak havoc at the local level. Both unitary and federal governments are allocating fewer resources to cities due to policies that began with neoliberal reforms in the 1980s and accelerated during the Global Financial Crisis of 2008. For instance, in the United States programs are being cut and assets are being sold off to meet fiscal needs (Alperovitz 2013). Similarly, across Europe, cities have seen public funding slashed, privatization of infrastructure, and reductions in services (Schönig and Shipper 2016).

Once again, we see localities responding to these impacts through local action grounded in alternative networks. For instance the Transition Town movement in the US seeks to build community resilience to economic and environmental shocks through participatory processes within communities and idea sharing across networks of cities (Transition United States 2013). An increasing number of cities worldwide have created local currencies to incentivize buying locally and build community solidarity (Boik 2013, Feb. 5). Similarly, coordinated efforts between local governments and organizations, such as the Evergreen Cooperative's "Cleveland Model," strive to empower marginalized communities and build local wealth (Evergreen Cooperatives 2016). These approaches often combine the efforts of community land trusts (CLTs), community development corporations (CDCs), community development financial institutions (CDFIs), local nonprofit organizations, and worker cooperatives to strengthen and democratize local economic development efforts (Alperovitz 2013).

Within civil society, a number of social movements, often grouped within the category of anti-globalization or alter-globalization, have also grown out of response to the problems imposed by economic globalization. Many of these movements initially emerged in the Global South in response to economic hardships imposed by tree trade agreements or conditional loans from the IMF and World Bank. One of the best-known is the Zapatista resistance of 1994 in Chiapas, Mexico which emerged in response to the implementation of NAFTA and the devastating economic consequences for local farmers (Kopkind 2002); by the end of 1994, the movement had declared 38 autonomous indigenous municipalities (Hayden 2002). This led to the formation of the People's Action Network (Dixon 2014), a transnational network of grassroots social justice movements.

In 1999, this mantle was picked up at the "Battle of Seattle" – grassroots protests against the neoliberal policies of the WTO and the exploitative austerity measures imposed across the developing world by the World Bank and IMF (Cockburn and St. Clair 2000). Most recently, several social movements have arisen in response to the Global Financial Crisis and resultant economic policies. The Occupy movement began as Occupy Wall Street in 2011 in response to US policies such as the Troubled Asset Relief Program (TARP) that bailed out banks while leaving homeowners to face foreclosure and lose up to half their property values. Also in 2011, an occupation in Athens' Syntagma Square became the "Democracy Now!" movement (Tejerina and Perugorría 2013), a resistance against the austerity measures imposed on Greece by the IMF and the EU (Janssen 2010).

Most recently, the rise in American nationalist populism depicts US-led multilateral free trade agreements as detrimental to American manufacturing (Cassidy 2017). Thus, one of President Donald Trump's first executive orders was to quash the 12-nation Trans-Pacific Partnership (TPP) (Baker 2017, Jan. 23); and, his administration has insisted that the US will pull out of NAFTA if it is not renegotiated (Reuters 2018, Jan. 11).

Environmental crises

Arguably, environmental crises are the most prominent aspect of the crisis of sustainability. We live quite literally on the brink of destruction due to "serious compromise of the biosphere" (Prugh 2015, 134); without coordinated corrective efforts we face global natural calamities. Environmental crises are evident in the continuing trend of record-breaking global surface temperatures (2014, 2015, and 2016 were all record-breaking years). While the problem of climate change is the most obviously global in scope, impacts are felt locally in the water, soil, and forests necessary to sustain life: acidification and eutrophication of fresh and saltwater sources; rising sea levels; severe weather events from droughts to tsunamis; deforestation and soil degradation due to mass agricultural production and fossil fuel energy production and use; and, micro earthquakes linked to hydraulic fracturing for natural gas. As with economic crises, environmental crises are inextricably linked to social crises – both local environmental degradation and global climate change disproportionately impact developing nations and low-income communities of color both intra- and internationally (Bullard 2004).

While there is a long history of UN agreements pertaining to natural resources, the first concerted international effort to address climate change came with the UN Conference on the Human Environment (UNCHE 1972). The resulting declaration emphasizes stewardship of natural resources and minimization of environmental externalities, but also promotes the need for development and stresses nation-state sovereignty in determining environmental policy. This was followed by the 1992 UN Framework Convention on Climate Change (UNFCCC), which seeks to coordinate efforts to limit the rise in global temperatures (UNFCCC 2014); the first meeting in 1995 established the Berlin Mandate, which specified a process for reaching international agreement on protecting the climate system. Recognizing unequal contributions to climate change, developed nations were tasked with taking the lead in addressing global emissions while developing nations were given leeway to continue building their economies through industrialization (UNFCCC 1995).

These early measures set the stage for the adoption of the Kyoto Protocol in 1997 (amended in 2012 and extended to 2020), an agreement that legally binds signatory nations to targets for emissions reductions (UNFCCC 1997, 2014), that distinguish between Annex I nations, those with transitional economies, and developing nations. Failure to meet standards on time, along with the refusal of the US to ratify the agreement, led to renewed efforts to renegotiate an international climate agreement. This resulted in the Paris Agreement of 2016, in which individual nations established their own nationally determined contributions (NDCs) for reductions in anthropogenic climate change and set goals for assisting developing nations in meeting goals (UNFCCC 2017). Under the Obama Administration, the US joined 173 other nations and the European Union in signing the Paris Agreement, followed by official ratification.

Despite broad public concern regarding environmental crises, the nation-states that have contributed the most to the rise in global temperatures and yet face comparatively fewer effects of climate change refuse to engage or fulfill the requirements of environmental treaties. Industrial nations are loathe to give up their competitive advantage, and developing nations resent bearing the burden of climate change without reaping economic benefits. Additionally, it is critical to note that the impacts of climate change are not equally distributed. Developing nations, particularly small island nation-states, can be expected to face rising sea levels, drought, food insecurity, and increased poverty (IPCC 2014). Among developed nations, these impacts are most likely to hit urban areas the hardest, where poverty is often highly concentrated (IPCC 2014). Thus, the burden of global failure to address climate change swiftly and effectively will disproportionately fall upon low-income communities of color and nation-states within the Global South with histories of colonization and exploitation.

Rising municipalism

As with other international agreements, even the ambitious Paris Agreement faces strong criticism. Again sounding the alarm of nationalist populism, President Trump announced in

June 2017 that he was pulling the US out of the agreement, citing concerns about national sovereignty and economic growth (Shear 2017, June 1). On the other hand, environmentalists argue that even the goals set by signatory countries are too low to prevent exceeding a two-degree Celsius rise in global temperature (Irfan 2016, Nov. 3); to overcome these crises, there must be widespread "ecological literacy" (Orr 1992) and researchers must explore the root causes as well as ethical resolutions (Bookchin 2015b).

In the midst of these tensions, localities have been taking direct action. Over 90 percent of urban areas are located in coastal areas and over 70 percent of them are already feeling impacts of climate change (C40 2017). Thus, local governments have been seeking ways to address climate change. In the US, the National League of Cities' Sustainable Cities Institute provides a central clearing house for sharing information on sustainable policy and practices (SCI 2013); transnational alliances include the ICLEI (Local Governments for Sustainability), the Global Covenant of Mayors for Climate and Energy and the C40 Climate Leadership Group. Over 90 megacities within the C40 network made specific commitments to achieve the goals of the Paris Agreement – a recognition that local action is critical for success (C40 and Arup 2017). When the US pulled out of the agreement, mayors across the country immediately responded, and within a month mayors of 7,400 cities had pledged to continue to honor the commitments of the Paris Agreement (Boffey 2017).

There is also a long history of popular social movements in response to environmental crises; these efforts emerged alongside the Industrial Revolution with creation of the Commons Preservation Society in the UK in 1865 (Open Spaces Society n.d.). In 1962, the contemporary environmental movement was catalyzed with the publication of *Silent Spring* (Carson 2002) which documented the environmental impacts of chemical pesticides such as DDT (dichloro-diphenyl-trichloroethane) and sparked the creation of Earth Day in 1970 (Earth Day Network 2017). Subsequently, groups such as Greenpeace arose, formed by a network of activists organizing campaigns against nuclear armaments and for the protection of wildlife (Zelko 2013).

These efforts were reignited with the release of *An Inconvenient Truth* (Guggenheim 2006) in which Al Gore compiled incontrovertible scientific evidence of anthropogenic climate change. In 2014 climate negotiations by the Major Economies Forum in New York City provided the backdrop to the inaugural People's Climate March (Foderaro 2014, Sept. 21) which consisted of 2,646 synchronized climate protests in 162 countries (Peoples Climate March 2014). Some of the most impactful organizing is emanating from communities most harmed by environmental justice issues. For instance, Flint Rising Coalition, a coalition of community organizations, was created in response to the 2014 Flint water crisis – the coalition engages in "resident-to-resident" organizing and dialogue to identify community concerns and long-term goals (Flint Rising 2017). Similar grassroots mobilization is seen in organizations like the Little Village Environmental Justice Organization (LVEJO) and the Pilsen Environmental Rights and Reform Organization (PERRO) in Chicago. These organizations were created to combat the "disproportionate amount of pollution" (PERRO n.d.) their residents faced as low-income communities of color, and to "accomplish environmental justice" and "achieve the self-determination of immigrant, low-income, and working-class families" in these neighborhoods (LVEJO 2014). In 2016, members of the Standing Rock Sioux Indian Reservation rose up to protest the Dakota Access Pipeline planned to cross Lake Oahe and endanger their water sources. This initial protest sparked national response, resulting in resolutions of support from 300 tribes and First Nations as well as several cities, and the creation of Sacred Stone Camp – an occupation of nearly 4,000 "water protectors" (Standing Rock Tribe 2017).

A wicked situation

As can be seen in these brief explanations of social, economic, and environmental crises, they are mutually influencing, often coalescing to harm the most vulnerable simultaneously – those in poverty and people of color. Therefore, in the same way that societal sectors are artificial separations devised for analytical purposes, these three pillars of sustainability are inextricable from one another in a global system. The complex and deeply interdependent issues that comprise the crisis of sustainability are recognized as "wicked problems" in the policy and planning fields (Rittel and Webber 1973, 155). Unlike relatively tame and simplistic issues, wicked problems resist resolution because if only one aspect of the issue is addressed, the many others with which it is enmeshed will continue producing causal influences. In other words, each problem is potentially a symptom and a cause of others and addressing root causes is difficult. Furthermore, disagreements about both problem definition and resolution method abound in pluralist contexts – there are no "definitive and objective answers" (Rittel and Webber 1973, 155).

Because of their complexity and tendency to escape jurisdictional borders, wicked problems demand coordinated responses – a form of global governance, but not one that is unitary. There must be many democratic collaborative networks focused on particular complex problems (Hisschemöller and Hoppe 1995). Indeed, the outcome document of the Rio+20 summit, *The Future We Want*, describes the three dimensions of sustainable development as fluid and interconnected, opening up "opportunities for more integrative forms of governance" (Ivanova 2014, 142). Its New Sustainable Development Goals (SDGs) seek voluntary commitments from governments, corporations, NGOs, and citizens in the pursuit of long-term well-being for humans and the other species with whom we share the planet. As such, it is easy to understand claims that the complex problems can only be addressed through governance networks (Edelenbos and Klijn 2007, Kickert, Klijn, and Koppenjan 1997).

Whether the goal is peaceful coexistence, democratic voice, stable and thriving markets, or a sustainable and just natural environment, IGOs, NGOs, and social movements have arisen in response, collectively seeking to steer humanity toward a sustainable future. Intersectoral governance networks are deeply entrenched in social, economic, and environmental policy arenas globally, regionally, and locally. To a large degree, globalization has replaced an international system of nation-state governments with a decentralized, heterogeneous, intersectoral system of network governance (Keohane and Nye 2000). This array of institutions includes governments, private firms, and nongovernmental organizations that come together to focus on specific problems and opportunities, remaining structurally flexible in response to the changing contexts.

Similarly, social networks and movements arise and engage governance networks in their advocacy for a wide variety of issues. People want greater influence over the policies that might reverse our crisis of sustainability. Fortunately, there is a good fit between the wicked problem of sustainability and the demand for radical democracy. Given his understanding of wicked problems, Rittel (1972) offered a "second generation" systems approach to pragmatic problem solving and planning that heralded the collaborative and participatory governance practices that followed:

1 Bring together many different types of experts who view the problem and solutions differently;
2 Actively involve those who are experiencing the problem in planning;
3 Acknowledge the inherent subjectivity involved and the impact of moral and ethical commitments;

4. Employ a communicative process to develop shared understandings and find common ground among rationales;
5. Recognize that planning is politics;
6. Ensure that experts play a facilitative, educative role;
7. Approach the process with humility;
8. Maintain optimism;
9. Consider action strategies as adventures that may or may not work out; and
10. Keep open opportunities for argumentation.

Intractable, wicked problems require this type of egalitarian, participatory, deliberative democracy to enable open, inclusive learning processes to not only understand and resolve the problem, but to attain agreement on *how* to do so and to garner collaborative engagement in policy implementation (Hoppe 2011).

Considering the many IGOs at every level of government, the plethora of NGOs engaged in governance activities, and the myriad social movements seeking governance influence, at this point, it is hard to dismiss claims that we now live in a "network society" (Castells 2000). The combined result of these shifts toward intersectoral, intergovernmental, and global network activities largely supplant the study of govern*ment* with the study of network govern*ance* at all levels of society – local, regional, national, and international. We turn to this literature in Chapter 2 to uncover the ideals of collaborative network governance therein and the barriers that continue to hinder the kind of collaboration that might successfully address the wicked problems we face in an effective, egalitarian, democratic manner.

2 Governance network theories

As noted in Chapter 1, *governance* is a way to guide collective action toward the common good, while *government* is a formal legal-political entity. Governance *networks* are intersectoral groups of organizations, whether informal or formal, engaging in governance of a given geographic area or policy arena. Our review of the governance network literature from the early 1990s forward tells a developmental story that is still unfolding as we continue to learn more about the wicked social, economic, and environmental challenges we face. This trajectory has moved toward increasing calls for collaboration because, as Brown and Keast (2003) note, "When the goal is to resolve the more intractable social problems . . . or when systems change needs to occur, then collaboration may be needed" (124).

While critiques of governance can be found in myriad disciplines, and explorations of collaborative governance networks can be found in the corporate responsibility literature (Rasche 2010), the core literature on "governing without government" (Rhodes 1996) is located in the closely related disciplines of public administration, public policy, and political science. The latter discipline often focuses on changes to states, markets, and society (Bevir 2010, 2012; Jessop 2004; Kooiman 2003; Rhodes 1997b). Because we want to inform practice, we concentrate on the public administration and public policy literature on governance networks.

To develop a thorough understanding of the governance network literature, we reviewed numerous journal articles and books on the topic. Included, for example, are empirical large-n studies (Agranoff and McGuire 1998; Skelcher 2007), comparative case studies (Considine and Lewis 2003; Davies 2005; Feldman and Khademian 2002; Skelcher et al. 2007), qualitative analyses (Edelenbos and Klijn 2007; Hendriks 2008), and meta-analyses of previous studies (Ansell and Gash 2008; Emerson and Nabatchi 2015). The terminology used in this literature is inconsistent, including contradictory labels used interchangeably by various authors. These labels include: policy network, governance network, public management network, networked government, joined-up government, integrated governance, network governance, network management, participatory governance, new governance, collaborative network governance, collaborative governance, collaborative public management, interactive governance, and integrated governance. As pointed out by Parker (2007), not all network arrangements should be taken as evidence of governance. Similarly, there is a difference between the governance of networks themselves and the use of networks to govern. Furthermore, not all ways of working together within governance networks are collaborative (Keast 2016).

While carefully attending to substantive content as opposed to idiosyncratic labels, we organized what is known or proposed about governance networks – *collaborative* governance networks in particular. Through analytical synthesis, we identified ideas coherent with the definitions of networks, governance, and collaboration used in this literature, while identifying concepts that conflict with the stated logic and issues that cause failures to deliver promised benefits – in both utilitarian and democratic terms. The conclusions of these analyses are discussed in the following sections, offering extensive citation and quotation to capture the scholars' meaning, as opposed to our own thoughts on these topics.

A genealogy of the governance literature

Considering this literature chronologically, as illustrated in Figure 2.1, governance theory emerged in response to the global context in which independent nation-state control over public policy was weakening due to an expansion of international law and NGO involvement, independent action among cities and other regional governments, and participatory governance among citizens. Studies of public policy had long acknowledged that non-state actors were involved in the policy process (Pressman and Wildavsky 1979). Recognizing that these were not the "iron triangles" (Allison 1971) of mid-twentieth century national policy, Heclo (1978) reconceptualized these arrangements as policy issue networks – dynamic, cross-sector groups comprised of varying levels of government (local to international), corporations (often with multinational status), and NGOs attempting to influence public policy. Policy networks were also conceptualized as advocacy coalitions (Sabatier 1988). These non-state actors continually gained ground in steering public policy. Under the aegis of reinventing government and New Public Management, the state was hollowed operationally through the privatization of government functions through contracting and partnerships, along with the load shedding of resources and services (Agranoff and McGuire 1998; Milward and Provan 2000).

Therefore, the first issue of focus in the *governance* literature was the manner in which informal policy networks influenced national and international policy and how non-state actors had become increasingly influential (Agranoff and McGuire 1999; Klijn 1996; Rhodes 1997b). The new term for this phenomenon was "governance networks" – informal groups of state and non-state actors doing the work of governing. The term "network governance" also emerged, referring to the internal management of networks.[1] For the first decade or so, the majority of governance network studies focused on why they form (Alter and Hage 1993; Carlsson 2000; O'Toole 1997b, c; Rhodes 1997a) and whether they produce public value (Moore 1995).

As consensus grew that governance networks were here to stay, studies branched out into what characteristics they display (Agranoff and McGuire 1999; Salamon 2002) and how they operate (Brown and Keast 2003; Keast and Brown 2002; Keast et al. 2004). For example, scholars crafted typologies of networks (Agranoff 2003, 2006; Agranoff and McGuire 1998) to better understand the impacts of variations in structure, actors involved, and operating environments (Koppenjan 2007). Studies under the various labels of network governance (McGuire 2002), network management (Kickert and Koppenjan 1997), public management networks (Agranoff 2007; Agranoff and McGuire 2001), and collaborative governance (Koppenjan 2007) sought to understand the inner workings of networks. Studies aimed to identify the rules by which networks function and how they differ from hierarchical organizations (Considine and Lewis 2003; Klijn 2001), the challenges networks create for traditional management practices (Kickert, Klijn, and Koppenjan 1997; Agranoff and McGuire 2011; O'Toole 1997a), best practices for managing in networks (Agranoff

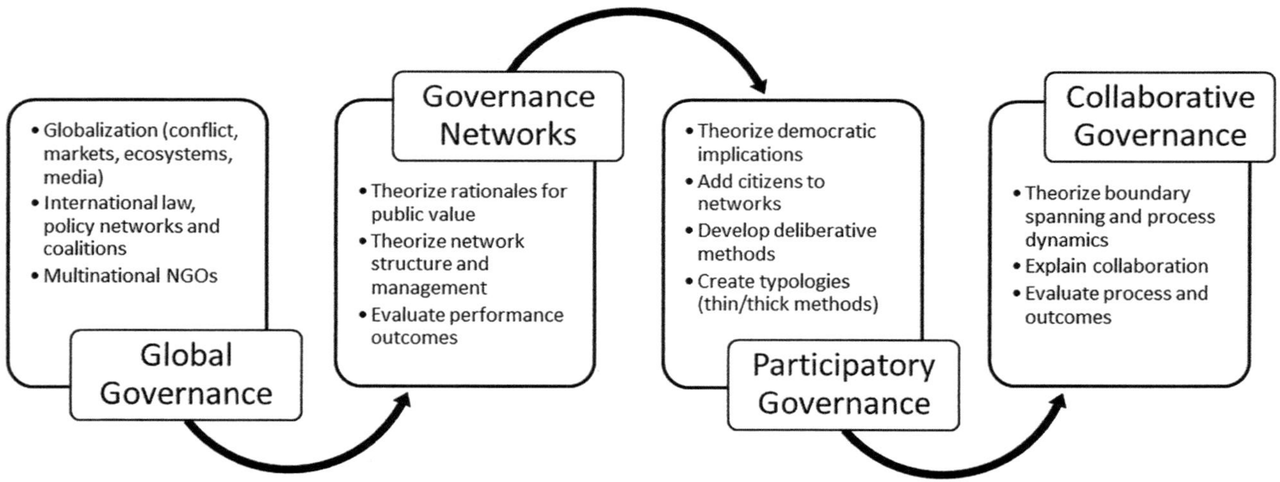

Figure 2.1 The developmental path of collaborative governance network theory

and McGuire 2001; McGuire 2002), and developing criteria for evaluation (Mandell and Keast 2007; Provan and Milward 2001).

More recently in the literature, democratic concerns emerged – both in terms of the degree to which internal operations reflect democratic principles and the external impact of governance networks. Studies of internal operations considered issues such as power asymmetries and rules of engagement (Agranoff 2005; Ansell and Gash 2008; Bingham, O'Leary, and Carlson 2008; Leach 2006; O'Toole and Meier 2004; Sørensen and Torfing 2011). Spurred by these concerns, ***collaborative*** governance (Emerson, Nabatchi, and Balogh 2012; Huxham 2000) and then collaborative governance ***networks*** (Silvia and McGuire 2010) came into use, identifying internal operational differences between network collaboration, government hierarchy, and market competition (Agranoff and McGuire 2001; Powell 1990; Salamon 2002) as well as differences between coordination, cooperation, and collaboration (Huxham and MacDonald 1992; Mandell and Keast 2007).

Studies of external impacts sought to determine whether governance networks were compatible with democracy (Sørensen 2002; Sørensen and Torfing 2003), often leading to distinctions between liberal representative versus deliberative democracy (Bogason and Musso 2006; Dryzek 2007; Hendriks 2008), majoritarian versus consensus decision making (Klijn and Skelcher 2007; Skelcher et al. 2007), and the possibility for networks to transform democracy altogether (Catlaw 2009; Hajer and Wagenaar 2003). Other studies focused on whether affected citizens, or at least their legitimate representatives, are included in the governance network (Bixler et al. 2016; Hendriks 2008). These studies made explicit arguments for greater public participation in governance networks, or ***participatory governance*** (Bingham, Nabatchi, and O'Leary 2005), which remains a topic of discussion in collaborative governance (O'Leary and Bingham 2009).

Because affected citizens are not always included in governance networks, two distinct types of collaborative governance networks are described in the literature (Stout, Bartels, and Love 2018): (1) those which focus primarily on achieving instrumental outcomes through ***organizational cooperation or coordination*** (Agranoff 2006, 2008; Agranoff and McGuire 1998; Ansell and Gash 2008; Bingham and O'Leary 2008; Fung 2006; Hartley, Sørensen, and Torfing 2013; Hertting and Vedung 2012; Kettl 2006; Koppenjan and Klijn 2004; Milward and Provan 1998; Provan and Kenis 2008; Sørensen and Torfing 2005b); and (2) those which focus on achieving both democratic and instrumental outcomes through organizational ***collaboration with citizens*** (Bingham 2009; Bingham, Nabatchi, and O'Leary 2005; Box 1998; Bryer 2009; Cooper, Bryer, and Meek 2006; Nabatchi 2010, 2012; Stout 2013). A recent work that claims to integrate this entire body of knowledge is the Collaborative Governance Regimes (CGR) framework (Emerson and Nabatchi 2015).

Defining collaborative governance networks

As a whole, the literature provides explanations of why governance networks form, their characteristics and dynamics, and their results. The discussion generally interweaves claims about their theoretical potential with explanations of what actually happens in practice and why collaborative governance networks fail to deliver promised benefits. Here, we have made an effort to disaggregate these discussions in order to craft an ideal-type definition of collaborative governance networks and to determine how to achieve greater success. Specifically, we consider collaborative governance networks' structural characteristics, function and purpose, and operational dynamics.

Structural characteristics

The term *network* refers to both structure and power dynamics (Koliba, Meek, and Zia 2011; Scharpf 1993). Salamon (2002) describes governance networks as an alternative to both hierarchical government control and market competition, while others suggest networks balance the two extremes of rigidity and open flexibility (Agranoff and McGuire 2001; Powell 1990).

Ideally, networks are groups that are open and accessible in terms of membership (Hendriks 2008; Koppenjan 2007), self-organizing (Carlsson 2000; O'Toole 1997b; Rhodes 1997a), and have a nonhierarchical (Agranoff and McGuire 1999, 2011; O'Toole 1997a; O'Toole and Meier 2004; Huxham 1996) or horizontal organizing style (Carlsson 2000; Klijn and Koppenjan 2016; O'Toole 1997b, c). While dynamic and "free-flowing" (Agranoff 2008, 329), they are also enduring institutional arrangements, as opposed to networking activities or ad hoc, temporary network relationships (Mandell 1999). Yet, the structure should be sufficiently flexible to accommodate changes both internal and external to the network (Huxham and Vangen 2000). Associations that do not bear these characteristics are another type of informal association, coalition, or formal partnership.

Function and purpose

Most generically, *governance* includes "the processes by which any complex activity or system is coordinated" (Seyle and King 2014, 20), as well as "the traditions and institutions by which [jurisdictional] authority . . . is exercised" (Kaufmann, Kraay, and Mastruzzi 2009).[2] In this sense, institutions are rules that structure societal action (Goodin 1996; North 1990), including enabling legal statutes, administrative rules and routines, social norms, and both formal and informal organizational structures (Imperial 2005). The focus shifts from government agencies to operational systems, functional roles, relationships, and actions. Combining this function with the structural characteristics outlined earlier, *governance networks* are voluntary, nonhierarchical, enduring relations between state and non-state actors (Rhodes 1997a), which can include governments, corporations, and nonprofits, from local to global levels of analysis.

Noting that theory is responding to a global context in which complex problems "cannot be solved or easily solved by single organizations" (O'Leary and Bingham 2009, 8), Kettl (2002) argues that governments are in search of "service coordination and integration with nongovernmental partners" (128). Therefore, governance networks make "decisions and actions within the private, public, and civic sectors" (Henton et al. 2005, 3) that produce significant public consequences (Nye and Donahue 2000). Toward that end, governance networks engage in the public policy process, which can include identifying a policy issue, advocating its position in formal agenda setting, formulating policy recommendations, making policy choices, developing resources, taking action, and evaluating outcomes (Sabatier 1999). Governance networks may focus on broad strategic planning and action, particular policy issues, specific projects, or simply information sharing (Huxham 2000).

It is widely accepted that seemingly intractable problems such as social and political conflict, poverty, and ecosystem degradation cannot be solved by independent organizations or nation-states alone (Alter and Hage 1993; O'Toole 1997c). Much of the governance network literature emphasizes the need to achieve greater public value in the face of these complex social, economic, and environmental challenges. Networks that span jurisdictional and sectoral boundaries are thought to be the only way to address such "wicked" problems (Agranoff and McGuire 1998; Huxham 1996). The coordination of activities produces shared learning and transfers of good practice between organizations (Huxham 2000) that creates new solutions and emergent knowledge (Agranoff 2005).

Rather than simply "tinkering" with administrative reform, Klingner (2004) argues that new approaches to governance offer the opportunity to re-engage with the ethics of political economy and the democratic role of governance (742). There are many criteria used to measure "good" governance, depending upon the values of the evaluator. For example, the World Bank's World Governance Indicators call for: voice and accountability, political stability and absence of violence/terrorism, government effectiveness, regulatory quality, rule of law, and control of corruption (Kaufmann, Kraay, and Mastruzzi 2009). The Worldwatch Institute calls for governance that: protects human rights, governs by consent, sustains natural resources, and coordinates specialization to increase efficiency and effectiveness (Seyle and King 2014). Governance networks offer strategies that are more inclusive, flexible, and adaptable (Alter and Hage 1993; O'Toole 1997c) in order to better achieve these utilitarian and democratic purposes.

The democratic rationale given for governance networks is to increase legitimacy (Donahue and Zeckhauser 2011). Leach (2006) notes that any collaborative initiative that has public implications should still meet traditional expectations of legitimacy: all applicable laws must be upheld, participants must be treated impartially, and activities must be transparent within and beyond the group. However, others argue for participatory governance because inclusiveness itself is of democratic value (Bogason and Musso 2006; Bryer 2010; Cooper, Bryer, and Meek 2006). Political theorists since Aristotle have extolled the opportunity to associate in the decisions by which one's community is governed as having inherent value for human beings and communities alike (Arendt 1998, 2005; Dewey 1934; Follett 1998; George 1929). Engaging affected citizens in participatory practices shares power among citizens in decision making through dialogue and deliberation, encourages citizen autonomy and independence, and provides a process for collectively pursuing the common good (Bingham 2009; O'Leary and Bingham 2009; Jun 2002). Traditionally marginalized groups and actors can achieve greater policy influence (Bixler et al. 2016; Klijn and Koppenjan 2000). Furthermore, the process of collaboration itself teaches the skills of self-governance (Follett 1998).

Governance networks that include affected citizens are described in definitions of "new governance" (Jun 2002), "interactive governance" (Edelenbos 2005), and "governance innovation" (Hartley 2006). These scholars draw upon the theory and practice of ***participatory governance*** (Bingham 2008; Bingham, Nabatchi, and O'Leary 2005; Nabatchi 2010, 2012; O'Leary and Bingham 2009). This literature focuses on government collaboration with citizens and civil society groups as opposed to other formal organizations (Stout 2010b; Vigoda 2002). It includes theories of ***citizen governance*** (Box 1998), ***deliberative democracy*** (Dryzek 1982, 1989, 1990, 1993, 2000; Fischer 2003; Forester 1999b; Fox and Miller 1995; Roberts 2004), ***communicative action*** (Habermas 1998c; Healey 1997, 2003; Innes and Booher 1999), ***substantive democracy*** (Box et al. 2001), ***participatory policy making and planning*** (deLeon 1997; Fischer and Forester 1993; Forester 1981, 1989, 1999b, 2009; Jenkins-Smith 1990), ***citizen participation*** (Arnstein 1969; deLeon 1992; Dryzek 1993; Fischer 1993; King, Feltey, and Susel 1998; Ventriss 1985; Walters, Aydelotte, and Miller 2000), and ***coproduction*** in implementation (King and Zanetti 2005; Sharp 1980; Whitaker 1980).

In regard to composition, Ansell and Gash (2008) argue that governance networks should be inclusive and transparent. The network must be supported by key actors both inside and outside the network and all operations must be visible to the public (Mandell and Keast 2007). Reflecting norms of participatory democracy, others argue all interests should be represented directly or by proxy, and all affected by the network's decisions and actions should be able to influence outcomes (Bryer 2010; Dryzek 2007; Hajer and Wagenaar 2003; Hendriks 2008; Leach 2006; Mandell and Keast 2007; Rhodes 1997a). To ensure influence is adequate, Agranoff and McGuire (2001) note traditional notions of accountability are replaced with notions of "responsibility, responsiveness, and the fostering of democratic ideals" (310). In some cases, these networks are even initiated by affected citizens themselves (Edelenbos and van Meerkerk 2016).

From this perspective, governance network actors are community members working together (Fung 2004) to create "meaningful public value" (Agranoff 2005, 41). While the purpose is utilitarian, it is in the democratically determined common interest. This reasoning inspired the creation of the Weil Program on Collaborative Governance at the John F. Kennedy School of Government at Harvard University (Henton et al. 2005). While originally conceptualized as the taxpayer's equivalent to shareholder value, public value is now understood as a measure of contribution to the common good by any actor (Meynhardt 2009; Meynhardt, Gomez, and Schweizer 2014). Its evaluation includes justice, fairness, and community building in addition to efficiency and effectiveness (Moore and Hartley 2008). Governance networks are therefore becoming a widely accepted approach to creating public value (Bryson, Crosby, and Bloomberg 2014).

Operational dynamics

Finally, we must define the meaning of *collaboration*, which includes who is in the network and how they work together. The literature offers normative explanations of the composition of collaborative governance networks, the manner in which power and authority is arranged, the resulting implications for leadership, the role of social capital in collaboration, and collaborative operational dynamics. Thus, developing a thorough definition of collaboration requires drawing from literatures pertaining to democratic micro-interactions and macro governance structures, which can inform one another to ensure that both *who* participates in the governance network (macro) and *how* they collaborate (micro) are congruent with democratic principles (Cohen 2008).

In regard to composition, given the open and inclusive characteristics of networks and the democratic purpose of governance noted above, only governance networks that include affected individuals fully meet the criteria of collaboration. By doing so, "Collaborative governance presents a promising holistic approach to civic engagement and public participation. It also provides an opportunity to embed governance systems and institutions with greater levels of transparency, accountability, and legitimacy" (Henton et al. 2005, 5).

The horizontal structure and inclusive membership of networks have implications for network operations. Thomson and Perry (2006) claim that collaboration has five dimensions: governance, administration, autonomy, mutuality, and norms. Restated, we argue that collaboration requires a particular approach to practice that demands norms of both autonomy and mutuality. Salamon (2002) describes "new governance" as a paradigmatic shift away from both hierarchy and competitive exchange toward cross-sector networks that operate through coordination and integration. Sørensen and Torfing (2007) describe governance networks as self-organizing, horizontal configurations of interdependent, autonomous actors contributing to a public purpose that are neither hierarchies nor markets. Networks display noncompetitive interactions among "independent but related entities" (Silvia 2011, 70) – they are in competition with shared challenges, not one another.

These norms are codified in both formal and informal operational rules which provide the social infrastructure and stability needed for networks to endure (Klijn 2001). Hajer and Wagenaar (2003) argue network members will work across differing institutional cultures to craft *new* rules for the network itself (9). To foster autonomy, no one is officially in charge of the network (Huxham 2000; Klijn 1996). Therefore, networks resist traditional forms of managerial steering (Rhodes 1997a) and all rules must be emergent and agreed upon by members (Mandell and Keast 2007). Similarly, mutuality means participants jointly make decisions about the rules that will govern their behavior and relationships and accept their enforcement (Gray 1989). Individual members can influence but not dictate decision making(Bingham, Sandfort, and O'Leary 2008). As a result, Agranoff and McGuire (2001) argue that it is impossible to determine which participants are principals and which are agents, and Feldman and Khademian (2002) replace principal-agent theory with relational reciprocity. Salamon (2002) emphasizes these as the cooperative operational tools of new governance.

In crafting these operational rules, it is imperative that networks remain inclusive, paying attention to both people and the processes used for interaction amongst organizational stakeholders and citizens (Bingham, Nabatchi, and O'Leary 2005). Because networks are not independent organizations or partnerships (Mandell and Keast 2007), collaboration requires replacing the approaches government previously used to establish mission and generate resources (Kettl 2006). Institutional design must accommodate both political and administrative functions, noting that collaboration "entails new roles in interaction" (Agranoff 2005, 41) that are described as "mutual engagement" (Agranoff 2008, 344) in which all members of the network are active participants (Bardach 2001; Huxham 2000) and leadership is emergent (Ansell and Gash 2008). In this new egalitarian context, managers lack authority to use carrots and sticks to motivate cooperation (O'Toole 1997a) – control is shared (Powell 1990) among co-equals (Feldman and Khademian 2002; Silvia and McGuire 2010) of "relevant and affected actors" (Sørensen and Torfing 2011, 853). Collaboration is therefore a synthesis that includes *self-organizing* coordination of labor and *reciprocal* cooperation that requires mutual change in order to determine and achieve common goals across organizational boundaries (Bingham, O'Leary, and Carlson 2008).

Various approaches can be used to "engage people constructively" in horizontal interactions (Emerson, Nabatchi, and Balogh 2012, 2). The modes of association identified in the literature include coordination, cooperation, and collaboration (Brown and Keast 2003; Huxham and MacDonald 1992; Mandell and Keast 2007); alternatively, these roughly align with managerialism, adversarialism, and collaborative governance (Ansell and Gash 2008). Coordination is a directed partnership that requires adjustment of activities in order to mesh with other network members, reflecting hierarchical, managerialist characteristics. Cooperation does not require adjusting individual goals or activities, but is rather a form of strategic partnership among network members, reflecting pluralist, market characteristics. Collaboration, however, requires adjustment to both goals and activities, producing shared aims and actions that simultaneously accommodates individual missions – the sought after win-win outcome (Huxham and MacDonald 1992; Mandell and Keast 2007).

Based on these egalitarian principles, "collaborative dynamics" (Emerson, Nabatchi, and Balogh 2012, 10) are defined as shared motivation, principled engagement, and capacity for joint action. All participants must be "able as collaborators" (Huxham 2000, 354), not just able to function within a cooperating partnership (Agranoff 2006; Agranoff and McGuire 2011). Collaboration is a process of mutually beneficial interactions, within situations of shared norms and rules, through which consensus, is reached by autonomous network actors engaged in formal and informal negotiation (Gray 1989; Thomson, Perry, and Miller 2009). As such, consensus building is generally understood to be a primary requirement for collaboration, and therefore proper network functioning (McGuire 2002).

In this context, traditional steering is replaced by a facilitative function in which leaders work to unite network actors (Klijn and Koppenjan 2000) in a variety of arrangements (Rhodes 1997a) through productive and purposeful interactions (McGuire 2006) to guide them toward a shared goal (Silvia 2011). The leadership role shifts from managing to enabling, which includes identifying network participants (*activating*), establishing operating rules (*framing*), generating commitment from various participants (*mobilizing*), and facilitating relationships to improve cooperation (*synthesizing*) (Agranoff and McGuire 2001; McGuire 2002; Silvia 2011). Similarly, Salamon (2002) defines the skills of new governance as activating participation, orchestrating collaboration, and modulating incentives to elicit cooperation. This leadership style is variously referred to as *collaborative* (Silvia 2011), *facilitative* (Ansell and Gash 2008; Bardach 2001; Bingham, Sandfort, and O'Leary 2008; McGuire 2006), or *integrative* (Silvia and McGuire 2010). Such leadership requires reflective practice (Argyris and Schön 1978; Huxham 2000) and high levels of interpersonal skill (Keast and Mandell 2013). For example, Silvia and McGuire (2010) note that integrative leaders also focus on building trust and maintaining social bonds to support effective collaboration.

To ensure the type of participatory influence and conflict resolution necessary to pursue and achieve consensus, real-time dialogue and deliberation are used to make decisions. This requires an "investment in process" (Agranoff 2008, 343), a commitment to the process (Ansell and Gash 2008), and faith in the collaborative approach (Leach, Pelkey, and Sabatier 2002). Participatory practices produce shared understandings through dialogue (Ansell and Gash 2008), a process which requires the willingness and ability to engage other perspectives (Huxham 2000). From that foundation, participatory deliberation leads toward consensus-oriented decisions (Agranoff 2006; Ansell and Gash 2008; Kickert and Koppenjan 1997) rather than "coalitional or power politics" (McCaffrey, Faerman, and Hart 1995, 612). This consensus building approach simultaneously builds commitment to the process outcomes (Ansell and Gash 2008) and to the group as a whole (Mandell and Keast 2007).

These deliberative processes must utilize "thick" forms of public participation (Nabatchi and Leighninger 2015) that involve, collaborate with, and empower community members (IAP2 2007). Members of the public are directly engaged in deliberation and given authority to decide for themselves what action will take place. Arnstein (1969) notes that even when using techniques associated with public participation, we must take care to assess the degree to which practices are inclusive, fair, and actually influence outcomes. Otherwise, genuine citizen power is at risk of devolving into manipulation, therapy, or mere placation, tokenism, and cooptation.

To ensure this type of process utilizes "true dialogue," is "genuinely deliberative consensus building," and fosters processes that are "transformative, or otherwise empowering" (Bingham, Nabatchi, and O'Leary 2005, 555), practitioners need skills in facilitation, collaboration, negotiation, and conflict management (Bingham, Nabatchi, and O'Leary 2005; Bingham, Sandfort, and O'Leary 2008). Bingham (2009) points to the methods articulated in dispute resolution and deliberative democracy as sources of guidance. While little instruction on the method is provided, the reflective process of goal analysis at the individual, organizational, and network level is recommended as a strategy to assist in achieving shared purpose (Vangen and Huxham 2012).

These negotiations may address rules of interaction, network purpose, decisions for action, among other concerns. Goals exist at multiple levels, vary in the extent to which they are made explicit, how strongly they are held, and the extent to which they require collaboration. This is likely to generate a combination of goal congruence and goal diversity in consensus building toward agreement and effective action. For example, Innes and Booher (2003) note that the norms of collaborative relationships, interactions, and practices generate second- and third-order consequences of improving deliberative capacity. Collaboration entails new ways of thinking and behaving (Waterhouse and Keast 2012) that recognize this complexity and, in doing so, produce "more effective problem solving, conflict management and governance" (Emerson 2009, 222). The results are proximal process and social outcomes such as improved joint decision making, shared meaning and understanding, and social capital (Rogers and Weber 2010). Thus, collaborative governance networks are venues to develop communicative capacity (Bartels 2015a).

Once shared purpose is determined, consensus-oriented practices are used for ongoing problem solving (Kickert and Koppenjan 1997). This includes joint planning and operationalization of resource allocation, roles, responsibilities, and task coordination to achieve shared goals (Chen 2008). This often requires "mutual adjustment" (Agranoff 2008, 344) in which collaborators "are simultaneously both craftsmen and raw materials in the developmental process" (Bardach 2001, 152). In these types of "knowledge-friendly cultures" (Agranoff 2008, 345), collaboration "aims to facilitate the exchange of ideas, mutual learning, and joint action through horizontal interaction between relevant and affected actors who have different kinds of resources and expertise" (Sørensen and Torfing 2011, 853). Innovation is possible when network members engage in critical reflection that produces mutually transformative learning that is jointly owned and supported. This requires an open-minded pragmatist approach to knowledge production and information synthesis (McGuire 2006) – a form of "interdisciplinary/interagency integration by exploration" (Agranoff 2008, 344), which includes continuous learning through evaluation (Mandell and Keast 2007).

These collaborative dynamics require high levels of trust (Agranoff and McGuire 2001; Huxham 2000; Huxham and MacDonald 1992; Mandell and Keast 2007; O'Toole 1997b), along with shared understandings and a commitment to the process and its outcomes (Ansell and Gash 2008). For this reason, social capital and community networks are praised for their capacity to generate and leverage trusting relationships and norms of mutuality and reciprocity to achieve collaborative integration (Brown and Keast 2003). Trust requires building interpersonal relationships and mutual understanding (Leach, Pelkey, and Sabatier 2002; Powell 1990) and is nurtured through the process of collaboration (Leach, Pelkey, and Sabatier 2002) wherein participants engage in open communication (Mandell and Keast 2007), including sharing information, resources, and leadership (Bardach 2001) to develop shared understanding and achieve mutual successes (Ansell and Gash 2008).

Gazley (2010) observes that assumptions of trust can be fostered through socialization as opposed to direct experience alone. In other words, the characteristics required for trusting relationships can be nurtured *prior* to the formation of new relationships. Without this shared culture, the social capacity to build relationships (Powell 1990) is needed to organize groups through which trust can develop (Agranoff 2008). This process requires significant investment of time and energy: "at least two years in many cases – and many cycles of direction setting, action and trust building" (Huxham 2000, 352). This process is most likely to be effective when relationships are "formed in the context of mutual respect and shared learning" (Stoker 2006, 41), and once trust develops it must be nurtured through "virtuous cycles of action" (O'Toole 1997b, 457) and assessed by considering how loosely or tightly actors are linked within the network (Mandell and Keast 2007).

Given this explanation of the ideal institutional design and dynamics for collaborative governance networks, while some traditional management skills are deemed useful in facilitating productive and purposeful interactions (McGuire 2006), new specialized skills are necessary for effective collaboration (Bingham, Sandfort, and O'Leary 2008; Kettl 2006; McGuire 2006; Kickert, Klijn, and Koppenjan 1997). Likewise, new indicators are needed to evaluate collaborative performance (Mandell and Keast 2007; Rogers and Weber 2010). Thus, attention must be given to building collaborative capacity (Kettl 2006), a group skill (Bardach 2001) required of all participants (Huxham 2000).

An ideal-type definition

Integrating the characteristics noted above, *collaborative governance networks* are open, self-organizing, nonhierarchical, multiscalar, intersectoral groups that engage affected citizens in determining and pursuing shared aims that produce the common good. They employ egalitarian practices of participatory democracy to ensure equitable and effective dialogue, deliberation, decision making, action, and evaluation.

The elusive collaborative advantage

The theoretical ideals of network structure, governance function and purpose, and collaborative operational dynamics are believed to have "collaborative advantage" over traditional governance approaches (Huxham 2000; Huxham and MacDonald 1992). Through collaboration, governance networks are able to meet "an objective which no individual organization could have met alone" (Huxham and MacDonald 1992, 50). Collaboration produces innovation because network members are empowered in participation and engage in critical reflection that produces mutual transformative learning that is jointly owned and supported (Sørensen and Torfing 2011).

While some scholars are dubious of this claim, even detractors largely agree that network structures can improve outcomes by removing rigid command and control governing structures as well as the excessive competition of markets. In this section, our analytical purpose is to critique the literature's content that *conflicts* with the logic of the ideal-type definition of collaborative governance networks. In some cases, the inconsistencies result from a critique of the normative ideals of networks and/or collaboration. In most cases, however, the literature depicts the manner in which actual governance networks differ from the ideal and explores why they fail to achieve collaborative advantage, raising questions about the purposes and operational dynamics of collaborative governance networks.

Instrumental failure

Governance networks emerged in response to both global crises of sustainability and a crisis of government. It would seem that a principal reason we fail to move the needle on crises of sustainability is that we have not yet figured out how best to link the *governed* who experience these crises with the *governors* who determine the response. Therefore, collaborative governance networks have both utilitarian and democratic purposes. Further, utilitarian purposes are interdependent with democratic means and ends.

In regard to sustainability, Brown (2002) observes that when collaborative governance networks attempt to integrate differences such as economic and ecological values, the conventional methods are "arbitral and corporatist approaches" (28) that negotiate compromises among parties within existing power asymmetries. This limits creativity as well as agreement across diverse interests. Unless governance actors believe that collective purpose determined with their own participation is the best way to achieve individual aims, there will be barriers to resolving the wicked problems we confront. In other words, our purpose in governance networks must be the pursuit of *common value*, which synthesizes both public and private value.

Huxham (2000) argues collaborative advantage depends in part upon the structural arrangement and membership composition of the group – in other words, the institutional design of the governance network. He argues we cannot revert to hierarchical strategies of single-minded, directive leadership, dominance by one organization or sector, or competition among policy actors. However, the literature is rife with rationales for forming governance networks that reflect these very tendencies. Unfortunately, although it is recognized that "interdependence is the key word in the network approach" (Klickert, Klijn, and Koppenjan 1997, 6), this is most often interpreted as mutual resource dependence and is explained in terms of self-interested motivations and quid pro quo "exchange relations, and/or common-interest based coalitions" (O'Toole 1997b, 117). From this perspective, networks form simply to produce individual benefits (Agranoff 2005). Even the term "collaborative advantage" is described as "achieving the objectives of each collaborating organization better than it could alone" (Huxham and MacDonald 1992, 50).

Much of the literature provides such individualist explanations for collaboration – networks emerge "from purposive, strategic design" (Skelcher 2007, 41) because organizations cannot achieve their goals without the resources of other actors (Klijn 2001; Klijn and Koppenjan 2000), or they seek to enhance efficiency, enable cost and risk sharing (Huxham 2000), and improve productivity and information gathering (Donahue and Zeckhauser 2011). Networks in this view are simply mechanisms for strategic exchanges of resources among mutually dependent actors (Klijn 1996; Klijn and Koppenjan 2000; Rhodes 1997b) with complementary interests (Powell 1990). Therefore, just like any other principal-agent relationship, network members may drain, rather than contribute to public value (Donahue and Zeckhauser 2011) and when they fail to cooperate, a deficit in incentives is blamed (Klickert, Klijn, and Koppenjan 1997). Provan and Milward (1991) call this a "resource-dependence" perspective, arguing it ignores normative explanations of network formation and coherence. We agree; these rationales mirror traditional intersectoral and international relations, rather than transforming them through mutualistic understandings of interdependence.

While the individual and community benefits of democratic participation are an important purpose of governance networks as presented, some argue that collaboration is not an end in itself (Imperial 2005; McGuire 2006) or that collaborative capacity is simply a personal benefit that accrues to participants, rather than members' agencies or the public (Agranoff 2008). Therefore, most of the focus is on whether or not collaborative governance networks improve democratic opportunity and influence. The resulting conventional methods to integrating different values among participants are therefore "arbitral and corporatist approaches" (Brown 2002, 28) that negotiate compromises among parties within existing power asymmetries. Therefore, rather than expanding social justice aims, many scholars note that when governance is extracted from traditional democratic institutions, those with greater ability to access governance networks can gain even more power and influence than they once had in formal government procedures (Lemos and Agrawal 2006; Shilling, London, and Liévanos 2009; Swyngedouw 2005; Skelcher, Mathru, and Smith 2005; Smith, Mathur, and Skelcher 2006).

To avoid creating this type of democratic deficit, many scholars seek to retain a guiding role for government agencies within collaborative governance – what some call the "meta-governor" role – to ensure both democratic collaborative process and responsibility for public outcomes (Koontz 2006, Mathur and Skelcher 2007, Sørensen and Torfing 2005a, 2009). Unfortunately, efforts to engage citizens under government's watchful stewardship merely seek coproduction of predetermined ends, appearing to have "domesticated urban movements and reconstituted them as service providers or quiescent partners in participation" (Bradley 2012, 216). Such so-called collaborative networks therefore do not adequately redress Arnstein's (1969) critique of "maximum feasible participation" in government programs. These processes are rarely delegated policy making authority (Cooper, Bryer, and Meek 2006; Fung 2004, 2006; Williamson and Fung 2004). Some even question whether public participation is becoming a new governance "tyranny" (Cooke and Kothari 2004). Although calls are made for "true equality in terms of knowledge, participation, power, and authority" (Bingham, Nabatchi, and O'Leary 2005, 555), we find that collaborators are either excluded or bring to the table power asymmetries grounded in their relative social, economic, and organizational status (Cohen 2008; Sabatier and Jenkins-Smith 1999; Huxham 2000; Huxham and Vangen 2000). These incursions in governance networks can reinforce "the privileging of strong and resourceful elites" rather than furthering democratic values (Sørensen and Torfing 2009, 234).

Incongruent operational dynamics

As can be seen, operational dynamics are implicated in instrumental success. As with all complex systems, "Networks near the edge of chaos – the compromise between order and surprise – appear best able to coordinate complex activities, and best able to evolve as well" (Kauffman 1995, 26). Even the most traditional public management scholars admit "self-organizing among actors of diverse interests can result in stable networked patterns that enhance social welfare" (O'Toole 1997a, 451). This potential requires egalitarian standing among participants, flexible deliberative processes, and mutual responsibility for generating and abiding by agreements (Mandell, Keast, and Chamberlain 2016). Attempts to control network dynamics through hierarchy or strategic competition hinder collaborative dynamics of creative emergence and cooperation.

These power relations are paramount to collaboration. An appropriate understanding of relational reciprocity diminishes fears of being controlled or defeated, enabling innovation in generating the common good. This egalitarian ideal can be difficult to achieve in governance networks that form with an intent to achieve individual interests. Unfortunately, even trusting relationships and norms of mutuality and generalized reciprocity are considered for their utilitarian value: a reduction in transaction costs, a sense of goodwill, increased loyalty to the network, and enhanced reputation of the collaborators (Agranoff 2008; Chen 2008). Therefore, trust develops if benefits are anticipated from network interactions (Edelenbos and Klijn 2007) and trust is hindered by assumptions of self-interest (McGuire 2002), strategic maneuvering for advantage (Scharpf 1997), and conflict over values and interests (Ansell and Gash 2008).

The assumption is that self-interest and conditions of uncertainty are disincentives to cooperation (Edelenbos and Klijn 2007; O'Toole 1997a) and network members will resist sharing information, resources, or risk (Agranoff 2006; Provan and Milward 2001). In a more laissez-faire approach, scholars use game theory to explain how network actors strategically adjust their own actions in anticipation of the actions of others to maximize their own interests (Klijn 1996, 2001; Klijn and Koppenjan 2000; O'Toole 1997a; Provan and Milward 2001). Repeated encounters will take care of overly "opportunistic behavior" (Edelenbos and Klijn 2007, 26). More hands-on recommendations encourage leaders to intervene in existing patterns of relations, restructure relationships, and build relationships to elicit cooperation and motivate action (Kickert and Koppenjan 1997). This is accomplished through the use of bargaining, persuasion, and incentives to strategically influence who participates in the network, what goals are identified, and how they are achieved (Feldman and Khademian 2002; McGuire 2006).

The meaning of nonhierarchical organization also appears to be widely misunderstood because this term refers to both formal (positional) and informal (competitive advantage) forms of hierarchy. In other words, nonhierarchy is not so much about what a network looks like in an organizational chart as it is about power dynamics – an interplay of form and action (Keast and Mandell 2013). While networks are described as emergent and self-organizing, in practice they are often "designed by government" (Davies 2005, 312), including framing of the network structure, rules, and roles (McGuire 2006). Scholars doubt that networks can form and function without command structures or the imposition of authority to manage uncertainty. Many networks maintain hierarchical characteristics (Agranoff 2006). Some scholars call for toning down "the conventional steering model" (Kickert, Klijn, and Koppenjan 1997, 11) with "a light touch" (Stoker 2006, 52), while others describe steering committees and formal organizations with staff (Huxham and Vangen 2000), directive roles for government agencies (McGuire 2002; Sørensen and Torfing 2009), or, in the most extreme examples, networks that are structured hierarchically under a lead agency as principal (Herranz Jr. 2008; Milward and Provan 1998; Moynihan 2005). Therefore, studies often highlight principal-agent (Coen and Thatcher 2008; Donahue and Zeckhauser 2011) or principal-agent-client (Provan and Milward 2001) relationships.

A meta-analysis of the "logic of governance" (Hill and Lynn 2005, 176) in 823 empirical studies found that despite claims that governance is increasingly horizontal, networked, and associational, it still tends toward hierarchy, regardless of whether the causal relationships studied are among governance actors, functions, or institutions.[3] In the end, governance typically involves governments in which authority and funding allocations remain hierarchical in structure and function. Even where positional authority is not in place, studies find that the member's own organizational "ethos" may not necessarily be suited to collaboration (Huxham and Vangen 2000). For example, there is often resistance to giving up authority (Agranoff 2006) due to concerns about maintaining sufficient control and accountability (O'Toole 1997a; O'Toole and Meier 2004), or stability and certainty (Davies 2005). As O'Toole (1997b) suggests, intra-organizational hierarchy is more influential on network members than inter-organizational lateral engagement. In anticipation of these concerns, Agranoff and McGuire (2011) explicitly reassure administrators that their organizational position remains intact, alongside the roles they perform in the network. When efforts are made to deemphasize hierarchical control and directives, recommendations advise leaders to instead draw upon market theories and strategies to foster cooperation (Considine and Lewis 2003).

These incursions of hierarchy and competition in governance networks mean that power dynamics are not egalitarian (Klijn 1996). Examining governance network power asymmetries is thus a key concern in the literature (Agranoff 2005; Ansell and Gash 2008; Bingham, O'Leary, and Carlson 2008; Leach 2006; O'Toole and Meier 2004; Sørensen and Torfing 2011). Disparities can result in networks that represent narrow interests (O'Toole 1997b; O'Toole and Meier 2004), that are "captured" by specific actors or groups (Bixler et al. 2016), and which reinforce the inequalities already present within society (O'Toole and Meier 2004).

There are a variety of reasons given for disparities of power within networks; however, control of strategic resources is often identified as the root cause (Agranoff 2004; Agranoff and McGuire 1998, 1999; Klijn 1996; Klijn and Koppenjan 2000; Rhodes 1997b). Those with limited control of resources are marginalized or excluded (Klijn and Koppenjan 2000; O'Toole and Meier 2004). Indeed, some argue that groups are only included if they control strategic resources and their cooperation is necessary to desired outcomes (Bixler et al. 2016; Hendriks 2008; Klijn and Koppenjan 2000). This can limit inclusion to key stakeholders (Stoker 2006) in order to maximize the impact of experts on decision making (Bixler et al. 2016). Others include all affected by the issue (Leach 2006; Sørensen and Torfing 2011), but argue to limit participation to representatives of those groups (Feldman and Khademian 2002; Hendriks 2008).

These dynamics directly conflict with the ideals of collaboration and follow from the failed purposes noted earlier. Neither the utilitarian goal of co-creating common value nor the democratic aim of engaging affected citizens are evident in the structures and power dynamics described. It is not surprising that the principal institutional design challenge appears to be the ability to overcome "conflicts and power issues" (Agranoff 2006, 61). There appears to be little knowledge of collaborative understandings of power and authority, which are relational, emergent, and generative (Rowlands 1997; VeneKlasen and Miller 2007). The literature follows zero-sum understandings of power: power over, power to (Klijn 1996), and power for or on behalf of others (Purdy 2012). In each instance, power is understood as a scarce resource to be distributed and wielded in an authoritarian or strategic manner, such as control over information and resources.

To be collaborative, we must co-create *power-with* one another, not simply share *power-over* (Follett 2003f). When power is understood as coactive and open-ended, diverse perspectives and ideas are welcomed. Power-with provides a sense of interdependent agency that enables a sufficient level of trust to share freely the information, knowledge, and resources that enable creative production of public value. This enables networks to "take advantage of emergent knowledge wherever it resides" (Agranoff 2005, 41). The literature argues that the benefit of inclusion is the creative synergy that is made possible by diversity (Hartley, Sørensen, and Torfing 2013) and the constructive role of conflict (Davies 2005; Koppenjan 2007; Agranoff and McGuire 2011). Yet even on this point, scholars worry that too much difference can prevent productive collaboration (Koppenjan 2007; Vangen and Huxham 2012).

These concerns reflect a lack of understanding of consensus-oriented dialogue and deliberation and reflect observations of domination or compromise, not integrative consensus. The literature is filled with arguments that consensus is unrealistic, and that it ignores power differentials and conflict, generating simplistic solutions to obtain agreement (Agranoff and McGuire 2011) and leads to the oppression of minority views (Koppenjan 2007) and groupthink (Edelenbos and Klijn 2007; Klijn and Koppenjan 2000). Furthermore, networks that fear competition (Vangen and Huxham 2012) or are too tightly coupled or close-minded are vulnerable to collapse or capture (Hajer and Wagenaar 2003).

For conflict resolution and trust-building practices, the literature draws from alternative dispute resolution, arbitration, mediation, and neutral assessment (Bingham, Sandfort, and O'Leary 2008; Edelenbos and Klijn 2007; Klijn 1996; Klijn and Koppenjan 2000). Strategies include bargaining, negotiation, and compromise (Huxham 2000; Imperial 2005; O'Toole 1997a).[4] One scholar even describes participatory, inclusive processes as "entrepreneurial strategies" (Page 2003). Rather than conflict *resolution*, conflict *management* tactics (Bingham, Sandfort, and O'Leary 2008) and even conflict *avoidance* (Huxham 2000) are recommended, which weakens trust and collaborative capacity among participants (Davies 2009). Some point out that the potential for conflict may sometimes lead managers to revert to tactics like regulation, mandated compliance, and centralized coordination (Davies 2005; Moynihan 2005). All of these tactics thwart participatory dialogue and deliberation (Hoppe 2011).

This is true even in explanations of collaborative governance networks that engage affected citizens. Public participation includes a variety of practices that vary in depth of input or feedback (Nabatchi and Leighninger 2015) and the actual degree of policy influence (Arnstein 1969). Participation within a representative democratic system can include "quasi-legislative processes" such as "deliberative democracy, e-democracy, public conversations, participatory budgeting, citizen juries, study circles, collaborative policy making, and other forms of deliberation and dialogue" and "quasi-judicial processes" of "alternative dispute resolution such as mediation, facilitation, early neutral assessment, and arbitration" (Bingham, Nabatchi, and O'Leary 2005, 547). Very few of these practices can be categorized as collaborative, because they are situated within systems of power that maintain dynamics of hierarchical authority and competitive advantage. As Dean (2017) notes, the truncated models of participation described by Sørensen and Torfing (2005a) and Bingham, Nabatchi, and O'Leary (2005) do little to achieve the ideal of participatory democracy.

Looking to what's presented as the most comprehensive, integrated theory, the Collaborative Governance Regime typology is organized according to *who forms the CGR* – self-initiated, independently convened, or externally directed (Emerson and Nabatchi 2015). While all three types could be evaluated as to whether they demonstrate collaborative operational dynamics, only self-initiated networks meet the ideal structural characteristics, and only those that include affected citizens meet the democratic purpose. In congruence with this differentiation, we find arguments in the literature that collaborative *methods* and collaboration *with citizens* are both necessary for creating public value, which includes both utilitarian and democratic outcomes (Bryson, Crosby, and Bloomberg 2014). Therefore, in assessing the instrumental value produced by network style organizing and collaborative governance (e.g., cost-efficiency, effectiveness, and degree of innovation), we must analyze the degree to which democratic values (e.g., participatory democracy) are enacted within the network and in interactions with its context (Sørensen and Torfing 2009).

In terms of collaborative dynamics, Huxham's (2000) oversimplification of collaborative governance as "all forms of and labels for, governance that involves people in working relationships with those in other organizations" (339) is problematic. We cannot simply lump together logically divergent dynamics of control-coordination-managerialism-hierarchy (externally directed), cooperation-competition-adversarialism-markets (independently convened), and collaboration (self-initiated) under the label "Collaborative Governance" and networks of varying compositions under "Regimes" (Emerson and Nabatchi 2015). To understand how best to achieve collaborative advantage – whether it is understood in utilitarian or democratic terms – the distinct characteristics of self-initiated networks operating through collaborative dynamics must be disaggregated from the other types.

In sum, egalitarian strategies seem to be nonsensical to most scholars in the governance network literature. Concepts like win-win outcomes, multiple leadership, and interdependent autonomy are described as "paradoxical" (Connelly, Zhang, and Faerman 2008). While scholars *describe* collaborative characteristics like power sharing, trust, shared meaning, understanding, empathy, conflict resolution, relationships, and creativity, they *explain* them with ideas drawn from their knowledge of hierarchy and competition. Even when collaboration is differentiated from hierarchical coordination and strategic cooperation, most explanations come from the mediation literature (Gray 1989; Wood and Gray 1991), social capital theory (Granovetter 1973; Putnam 1994, 2000), and collective action theory (Ostrom 1990). Theory remains grounded in assumptions of rational self-interest (Bevir 2010) – a logic that is fundamentally contrary to the egalitarian assumptions undergirding virtually every network and collaborative characteristic described.

To continue clarification of the meaning of collaborative governance networks, provide adequate rationales for their acceptance, and develop sufficient practical guidance, much work remains to be done. For example, as an alternative to the strategic negotiation and mediation perspective, we refer to the Progressive Era scholar, Mary Follett, who differentiates integrative collaboration from other "*modes of association*" (Follett 1919, 584), such as hierarchical domination and strategic competition. These distinctions make a difference to the quality of outcomes and the longevity of agreements. Based on her explanation, collaboration is a self-organizing, egalitarian, networked style of coordinating collective action amongst actors who are motivated to work cooperatively toward shared purposes determined through participatory processes that integrate perspectives. Therefore, coordination does not require authoritative direction and cooperation need not be strategic, if grounded in a different set of philosophical assumptions about human nature. Without a clear understanding of collaborative concepts like nonhierarchy, power-with, and integrative, consensus-oriented deliberative processes, governance networks will continue to struggle to achieve collaborative advantage. We unpack this argument further in Chapter 3, as we prepare to make our contribution to the gaps in theory and research in Parts II and III.

Notes

1 We note that Klijn and Skelcher (2007) align the term "network governance" with broader social arrangements and "governance network" with the activities of managing within networks – perhaps a reversal due to translation.
2 The phrase "in a country" is replaced with "jurisdictional' because authority can be exercised at international and subnational levels as well.
3 The studies included in the data set were published between 1990 and 2001 (inclusive) and used causal modeling of some sort, as opposed to historical analysis or descriptive case study, to understand multilevel or multi-organizational governance contexts, as opposed to single level, single organization studies. While the findings would be more compelling if the analysis was only of the 30-plus studies in the data set involving horizontal forms of governance – partnership arrangements, networking, coordination strategies, cooperative management, and services integration – even if it's a matter of proportional volume, hierarchy still overarches nonhierarchy in governance.
4 Anyone drawing from Fisher and Ury (1991) are using a misinterpretation of Follett's ideas (Stout and Love 2014b).

3 Advancing collaborative governance theory and practice

In Chapter 1, we argued that interconnected social, economic, and environmental crises of sustainability cannot be resolved by govern*ment* alone and have therefore given rise to the concept of govern*ance*, which includes intersectoral and intergovernmental networks that pursue the common good together. However, these governance networks have failed to prevent or significantly mitigate these issues and have even contributed to a rising crisis of government and democratic legitimacy. Huxham (2000) argues that in response to this complex global context we have no reasonable choice but to discover how best to collaborate in order to produce the common good. However, as argued in Chapter 2, if we wish to obtain the collaborative advantage imagined for resolving wicked problems while deepening democratic participation, we need a clearer understanding of the meaning and practices of *collaboration*.

Unfortunately, we have yet to find a clear paradigm-shifting explication of why and how we should govern collaboratively. We do not blame self-interested "human nature" or the impossibility of extricating hierarchy and competition from governance networks in the contemporary political economy for collaboration failures. Instead, we identify three reasons that governance networks fail to achieve collaborative advantage, each of which traces back to how they are studied and explicated: (1) insufficient objects of study; (2) insular perspectives; and (3) thin theoretical grounding and philosophical misalignment. These theoretical deficiencies, in and of themselves, present barriers to achieving collaborative advantage.

Insufficient objects of study

The governance networks studied are often those in which government plays a key role, whether they are formal public-private partnerships, informal networks of public and private agencies, policy advocacy groups, or instances of public participation. Most studies are conducted "where it is 'easiest' to create the data and models needed for quantitative empirical work" (Hill and Lynn 2005, 188). These networks tend to "reflect those who 'have access to the microphone' and whose voices are being heard, not those members of society who have no access or whose voices are silent" (Berry et al. 2004, 550). Therefore, they are populated by actors who have had little or no socialization, training, or experience in the art of collaboration. In fact, researchers note that administrators are poorly prepared, having been trained and socialized *against* behaviors like information sharing and seeking mutual benefit (Bartels 2016; Keast et al. 2004; Teisman and Klijn 2002). Therefore, without specific guidance and training in collaborative skills, we can expect performance failures (Huxham 2000).

Yet, these same problematic cases are used in theory building. Whether using historical analysis, case study, or formal hypothesis testing paired with sophisticated quantitative analysis, the goal is to "develop a body of empirical knowledge concerning what works and why" (Hill and Lynn 2005, 175). Theories drawn from individual empirical studies or meta-analyses cannot move far from incrementalism (Lindblom 2004) because they are drawing from the same pool of practices, few of which meet the characteristics of collaborative governance networks. These studies may teach bureaucrats some things about entrepreneurial strategy, but it will not assist them in collaboration. Networks cannot achieve collaborative advantage by combining authoritarian measures to quell uncertainty with strategic negotiation based on self-interest. We do not deny that these tactics are common within the current political economy, nor do we deny their negative effects on attempts to collaborate. However, we do argue that this empirical evidence alone will never provide insights on how to overcome these barriers.

Therefore, the objects of study need to be widened to include governance networks instigated in community contexts with diverse members, as opposed to like-minded coalitions. It may be that more associational forms of governance "reside in the less well illuminated areas beyond the transparent glare of data and methods used in these studies" (Hill and Lynn 2005, 188). One can find studies of collaborative governance networks that operate largely beyond government and then invite government to join in (see for example, Bartels 2015b, 2018; Elías 2010; Elías and Alkadry 2011; Stout 2010b; Verhoeven and Tonkens 2018). Such studies are much more informative in regard to collaborative dynamics. In fact, some of the most explicit and useful studies reviewed herein come from the environmental policy literature that explore governance networks that include affected individuals (Leach 2006; Leach and Pelkey 2001; Leach, Pelkey, and Sabatier 2002) and the recent "modest" approach taken by governance networks participating in "energetic society" groups in the Netherlands (van der Steen et al. 2015).

Insular perspectives

The collaborative governance network literature has captured well the struggles of intersectoral actors attempting to respond to the global crisis of sustainability as well as the problem of legitimacy in governance. The literature also clearly recognizes that hierarchy and competition both undermine the ability to collaborate effectively. However, most contributions build on the governance network literature itself, self-referencing within a fairly limited pool of empirical studies. This somewhat insular group of scholars is not seeing collaborative governance networks as ***a problem of political economy*** (Klingner 2004) that demands consideration of both normative (deductive) and empirical (inductive) theory.

Collaboration is a mode of association that is not native to traditional governance; it requires new attitudes, new skills, and new pedagogies, including new ways of evaluating whether network members are engaging in genuinely *collaborative* dynamics, as opposed to other modes of working together. While collaborative governance network scholars may *list* these characteristics and call for their evaluation, they do not draw broadly enough from other disciplines that can inform the meaning of collaboration. For example, alongside facilitation, dialogue and deliberation, conflict resolution, and joint problem solving, the literature lists practices that are associated with competition and hierarchy, such as bargaining, negotiation, mediation, and conflict management. We suggest this is because these are the only tactics fully explained in the literature with which these scholars are familiar.

We argue that remaining insular to the collaborative governance literature is a primary barrier to theoretical progress and recommendations for practice. Suggesting that public management is learning something new from studies of policy networks or social network analysis (Berry et al. 2004) is grossly insufficient. We must go much deeper into ethics, economic theory, political theory, and administrative theory in other sectors. To fully understand collaborative concepts, scholars need to reach beyond disciplinary boundaries to sources such as organizational behavior, micro-sociological theory, and social psychology (van Stokkom 2005). Guidance can also be obtained from fields of practice that use relationship-building, facilitation, dialogue and deliberation, conflict resolution, and joint problem solving, such as community development, social work, and restorative justice.

Thin theoretical grounding and philosophical misalignment

Explorations of collaboration generally end with description that "remains relatively superficial" (Keast and Mandell 2013). Little explanation and instruction in collaborative dynamics is provided and recommendations for practice are vague at best (Page 2010). We suggest the likely reason is a lack of familiarity with the theories that actually inform collaboration. Where description extends into explanatory discussion, it is generally informed by theories designed for either hierarchical or competitive contexts.

Edelenbos (2005) identifies the three main approaches to understanding institutions: political (macro-level systems), sociological (group level interactions), and economic (micro-level interactions). While some sources claim philosophical or theoretical grounding in deliberative democracy, the governance literature is deeply rooted in various rational actor assumptions at all three levels of analysis (Bevir 2010). This means the widely accepted theoretical foundations are firmly rooted in "rational choice institutionalism" (48), which combines both economic and sociological rationality – rational choice theory, institutionalism, systems theory, and regulation theory. These deductive assumptions are then used to explain network behavior. The resulting theories are deeply embedded in normative assumptions that are contrary to the nonhierarchical and noncompetitive logics put forth in descriptions of collaborative governance.

Similar rational actor assumptions are embedded in the forms of social capital theory (Putnam 1994, 2000) used to analyze networks; like game theory, components of trust and generalized reciprocity are attitudes developed through ongoing interaction and transactions with positive outcomes. Trust is generally depicted as an outcome of experience and familiarity and is therefore difficult to achieve in new relationships, particularly if a history of conflict is present (McGuire 2002, 2006). Similarly, norms of mutuality must be developed through experience (Ostrom 1990) and iterative processes of "mutual engagement and mutual adjustment" (Agranoff 2008, 344) in small overlapping aims (Huxham 2000). This occurs through ongoing interactions over an extended period time (Huxham 2000; McGuire 2002), preferably through face-to-face interactions (Ansell and Gash 2008).

Unfortunately, the literature's avoidance of normative theories that do not align with rational actor and power-over approaches to institutional analysis limits the ability to develop guidance for overcoming these barriers to collaborative advantage. These predispositions are a major hurdle to overcome when attempting to collaborate. We suggest that to achieve collaborative advantage, the assumptions must be reversed: We are socialized to distrust and anticipate self-interested behavior. These intransigent assumptions greatly underestimate the motivating force of a felt sense of interdependence and genuine desire to pursue common purpose. We argue that these are the more powerful motivators of effective collaboration.

This is where achieving collaborative advantage must begin. If more robustly informed by normative theory, collaborative governance network theory could produce a paradigm shift.

While an alternative framework has not yet "coalesced into a body of theory to rival the collective choice and principal-agent perspectives that predominate" (Page 2010, 247), there are ample resources from which to develop one. Unfortunately, collaborative governance network scholars do not go deeply enough into the philosophical rationales for collaboration to do so, often simply dismissing alternatives to mainstream theories as utopian or Pollyanna. For example, Agranoff and McGuire (2011) assert that the emphasis on consensus in collaboration depicts a "collaborative interactive nirvana" (266), while Imperial (2005) claims, "collaboration is not a magical cure for all governance problems" (311). This stance denies the capacity of philosophy and normative theory in the social sciences to effect change in practice. We cannot focus separately on normative standards (Arnstein 1969) or institutional design features (Fung 2003) – we must marry the two in order to make well-reasoned recommendations for improvements to practice. This allows us to avoid the pitfalls of empirically grounded theoretical frameworks that fail to identify "discreet, mutually exclusive" approaches (Dean 2017, 219).

Political and administrative theory and practice – the principal elements of governance – are framed by assumptions that can be traced back to a variety of philosophical commitments. As Foucault (1977) argues, micro- and macromodalities (the everyday and the structural) are mutually interdependent. In short, governance is always a matter of praxis and we need a way to break down this social phenomenon into its conceptual elements to get at underlying philosophical commitments. Specifically, ontological assumptions about existence prefigure our language and understanding of self, others, and the world around us. These understandings underpin psychosocial theories about individuals and groups and shape epistemological concepts about how we know and build knowledge; these ideas come together in belief systems, whether based on natural or metaphysical grounds. Philosophical commitments then shape ethical concepts about right and good, which in turn inform political, economic, and administrative theories about institutions, rules, and practices. Our experiences reinforce the originating beliefs.

We argue that collaborative governance network failures can be attributed to hierarchical and competitive dynamics linked to foundational theories – what we have previously called pathologies of collectivism and individualism (Stout and Love 2016). To emphasize, collaboration is not a compromise or middle ground between hierarchical consolidation and coordination on one side, and cooperation and competition on the other (Keast 2016).[1] As long as collaboration is conceptualized in this way, it will remain trapped on a continuum that only produces domination by or compromise with more or less hierarchical and competitive alternatives.

Because nothing in the collaborative governance network literature is defining collaboration or integration as a wholly different approach, the promised paradigm shift has yet to be sufficiently explicated, let alone achieved. Without this transformation, practices that seek collaborative advantage fail because they ultimately slip back into alignment with hierarchy or competition, as demonstrated in the many case studies and meta-analyses presented in the literature. Indeed, governance network scholars argue that the ostensible "paradigmatic" shift away from hierarchical government toward horizontal governance "is less fundamental than it is tactical: new tools or administrative technologies are being added that facilitate public governance within a hierarchical system" (Hill and Lynn 2005, 189). To achieve an actual paradigm shift, we need to identify a *fundamentally different* collaborative alternative to the consolidation-competition continuum.

Rosenau (1999) argues that the paradigms that flow from a governance ontology that assumes its foundational entities are nations and states cannot meet the needs of global governance. He insists a new ontology is necessary to fit new "purposes, processes, structures and loci" of governance in the global context (289). The combination of ontological and paradigmatic assumptions shapes our ability to see and make sense of key actors and their behavior. Indeed, as Rosenau (1999) notes, "ontologies are so deep-seated and so rooted as the bases of analytical habits, that they do not readily yield to evidence of obsolescence" (291). Nonetheless, this is precisely what we must bring to light. If our understanding of governance networks is grounded in rational actor assumptions, then we will anticipate competitive, self-interested behavior that can only be quashed through various types of incentives or control. Unsurprisingly, we fail to achieve collaborative results.

We argue that this is because network members are not actually *collaborating*. Rather, they are investing resources in trying to *coordinate* others who resist for various reasons or trying to *cooperate* with others in adversarial relationships. These efforts result in unsatisfactory ***domination*** or ***compromise*** and insufficient cost benefit. We tie this phenomenon back to the theoretical and philosophical drivers at play in governance network institutional design. These assumptions are mismatched to collaboration and must change in order to achieve collaborative advantage.

In essence, we cannot hold up aims of self-organizing control and self-motivated cooperation and then work toward it by manipulating incentives or managing behavior. The logics contradict one another. As illustrated in Figure 3.1, if we implement change at the tactical level while keeping a mismatched philosophy, eventually practices will revert to congruence with our most fundamental assumptions. The founder of the Holacracy management approach, calls this an "organizational pattern language" (Robertson 2014), apparently drawing from architecture and its premise that form follows function (see Alexander et al. 1977). As he notes, "How can we evolve some aspect of how we organize, when the innovations we try to use clash with the older paradigm still at play?" (Robertson 2015, 10).

If we merely try to change practices to achieve different results, the attempts are likely to fail. Recommended practices are likely to be executed incompletely or poorly because "governance systems reflect [a society's] worldview, values, and aspirations, transforming a governance system requires transforming the society, and *vice versa*" (Cullinan 2014, 74). If we do not attend to the driving commitments behind prescriptions for practice, we will continue to produce "muddled thinking" as well as "tensions that result from often unacknowledged definitional conflicts in real world participatory initiatives" (Dean 2017, 215). Bartels (2016) finds this to be true in local governance case studies; any time public administrators encounter citizens in collaborative efforts, they must overcome routinized organizational practices that contradict the logic and characteristics of citizen-driven participation.

To actually *change* governance practices in order to achieve better utilitarian and democratic outcomes, we need to work our way through all of the existing conceptual assumptions to the philosophical commitments in which they are anchored. While such beliefs and assumptions are very deep-seated, they are not immutable (North 1990; Sabatier 1988; Sabatier and Jenkins-Smith 1988). Governance theory need not remain tied to the rational actor lens. It is possible to devise political, sociological, and economic understandings of governance systems and interaction using other "organized patterns of socially constructed norms and roles" (Goodin 1996, 52). However, we cannot meet the call for transformation by merely presenting the alternative philosophy of a paradigm shift without digging into the details of practice.

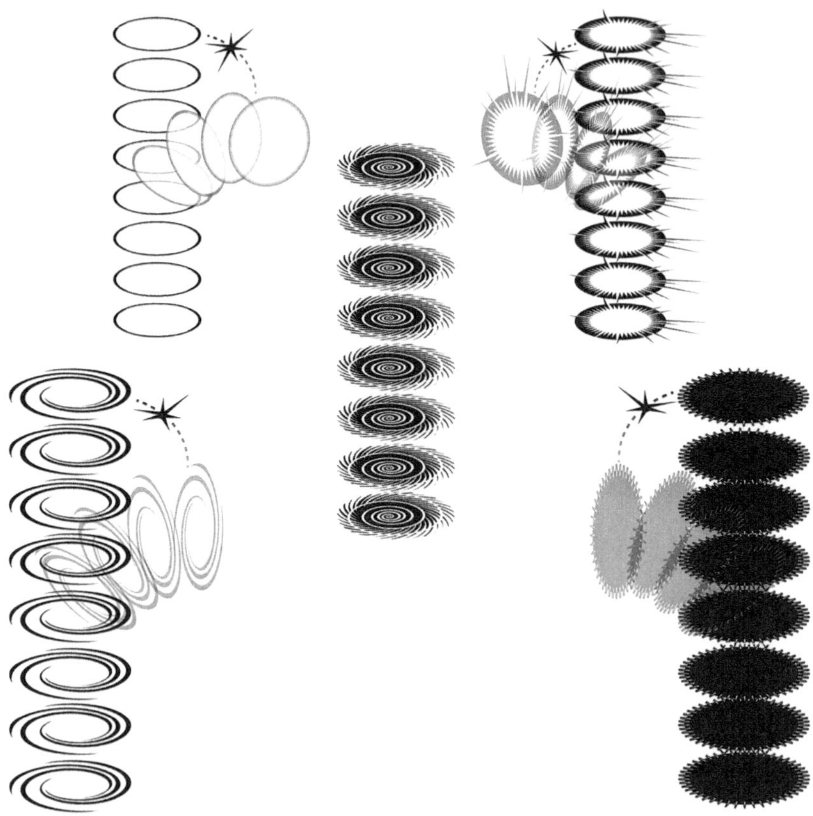

Figure 3.1 Philosophical misalignment in governance approaches

A transdisciplinary solution

Like Bevir (2010), we seek a more interpretive and critical understanding of governance networks to help us escape the trap of rationalism. That means we need to go to the philosophical source of those assumptions. This argument is in keeping with political scientist Dwight Waldo's (1984) claim that all political theory is based on a metaphysic, political theorist Steven White's (2000) argument that ontology prefigures political theory, and public administration theorist Thomas Catlaw's (2007b) assertion that political ontology prefigures administrative practice.

It has been claimed that "public administration exists to realize the governance of society" (Raadschelders 1999, 288). We appreciate that the field has always been one that studies the art and science of governance, drawing together sociology, political philosophy, organizational theory, psychology, ethics, economics, and others. Its "big questions" address both bureaucracy and democracy, considering ideas, emotions, philosophies, ideologies, myths, practices, procedures, institutions, technologies, and more (Waldo 1980). Corresponding research addresses the internal operations of public and nonprofit organizations as well as the relationship between institutions of governance and the polity (Box 2004; Frederickson 1971). From there, some public administration theorists seek to critique our role in the political economy (Kouzmin et al. 2009; Stout 2010a; Thorne and Kouzmin 2006). However, we contend the majority of scholars studying collaborative governance networks draw very narrowly from even these possibilities, let alone a broader disciplinary net.

Considering the global context described in Chapter 1, we propose that governance studies ask, "How can we most effectively and justly govern in a globally interconnected social, economic, and environmental system?" To answer this question, we first need to understand what *interconnection* means materially and socially. Then we need to understand interconnected knowledge and knowledge production. Then we can begin to consider the notion of how a system of belief (scientific or spiritual) grounded in physical, social, and intellectual interconnection informs an understanding of justice. From that basis, we can then consider effective ways to organize and administer political and economic systems and practices.

In other words, *governance in response to global crises of sustainability* is precisely the type of wicked problem that demands many disciplinary perspectives and should draw from both inductive and deductive theories. Governance cannot be the domain of a single discipline or purely empirical evidence. Governance is not only a generic social practice to be studied as an object of sociology. Nor is it simply an ideology to be explained by political theory. Nor is it solely a question of institutions to be studied by political science or organizational structures to be studied by management. Finally, governance is not simply a matter of actions and transactions that can be explained by economics.

Governance in a global context rife with wicked problems demands a holistic approach to both study and practice; it is at once *between* disciplines, *across* disciplines, and *beyond* each individual discipline's grasp. We can no longer separate micro and macro levels of action, global versus local phenomena, or specific cultural domains. We cannot divide this labor among independent disciplines. Our ways of understanding the world must be equal to its complexity. To govern our interconnected condition and achieve sustainability, we must dislodge disciplinary canons and make space for creative alternatives. As political scientist Benjamin Barber (2013) argues, even art and culture can help explain and promote the idea of the public, the idea of democracy, and the idea of interdependence. We argue that a *trans*disciplinary approach is necessary.

Transdisciplinarity is a post-normal-science response to conditions of dynamic intricacy in an era that is "increasingly Heraclitean" (Montuori and Donnelly 2016, 744). It "consists in creating a new object that belongs to no one" (Barthes 1972, 1).[2] However, through a process of convergence – what Gadamer (2013) would call horizon fusion – a coherent, shared understanding of the phenomenon is possible. Transdisciplinary studies draw from complexity theory, which is a combination of general systems theory and chaos theory used to study complex adaptive systems characterized by self-organization, mutual causality, uncertainty, emergence, interconnectedness, and interdependence. It demands intense creative capacity to imagine the horizons unfolding before us.

The preamble to the charter adopted during First World Congress of Transdisciplinarity describes issues underlying the crisis of sustainability: the need to understand both spiritual and material aspects of life, the impossibility of a universal identity, the danger of pursuing technological efficiency alone, the negative consequences of one-sided quantitative knowledge, and the unprecedented levels of income disparity among groups and nations (Nicolescu 2002). In response, the Charter points to the contemporary moment and its opportunity for transformational change in human beings and society, along with the role transdisciplinary study can play in such evolution.

Focusing on the social aspects of global systems, Clifford (1986) argues that cultural studies bring together many of the social sciences and humanities to understand "contexts of power, resistance, institutional constraint, and innovation" (2). These studies question the boundaries of civilizations, cultures, classes, races, and genders to "decode and recode . . . the grounds of collective order and diversity, inclusion and exclusion" (2). Thus, the "new object" of study is the relationship between the individual and the group – one that escapes the domain of any given discipline.

In sustainability studies, one of the first transdisciplinary sciences (Huutoniemi 2014), the new object of study is the nature of interconnectedness and interdependence within the global ecosystem. Even the US National Research Council (1999) notes that to achieve sustainability, integrative policy approaches are necessary; however, "*how* to achieve such integration in rigorous and useful research programs remains problematical" (283–284). In short, no one discipline can find solutions to the wicked problems contributing to the crisis of sustainability.

This understanding is evident in efforts to transform universities from collected siloes of disciplinary study to integrative programs targeting complex issues. As an example, Arizona State University (ASU) has been reinvented following a model its President, Michael Crow, calls "the New American University" (Crow and Dabars 2015). Among its design principles are goals to transform society and engage globally. Just as transdisciplinarity is inquiry-driven (Montuori 2005), ASU colleges, schools, and degree programs form around complex issues such as sustainability, social transformation, and public service and community solutions.

Integrative transdisciplinarity is a concept that emphasizes the relationship between parts, rather than a reductionist analysis of either the parts or the whole (Montuori and Donnelly 2016). In short, by understanding the relationships among parts and between the parts and the whole, the entire system and its parts are better understood. In this inquiry, we focus on the relationship between the individual and group with consideration of the global context. Specifically, the object of our inquiry is *governance in contexts of social, economic, and environmental interconnectedness*. We seek to understand the meaning of relationality and its implications for governance practice from a variety of disciplinary and cultural perspectives. Given the democratic imperative of such study, the inclusion of affected citizens in knowledge production is necessary. Joint fact-finding practices, including the use of both expert and non-expert knowledge for diverse perspectives on the problem, are at the core of a growing literature on post-normal science, extended peer review, and transdisciplinary research (Nowotny, Scott, and Gibbons 2001; Van Buuren and Edelenbos 2004).

In sum, to make developmental progress in collaborative governance networks, scholars need to expand their horizons to: (1) study governance networks that display genuinely *collaborative* characteristics and dynamics; (2) take a more *transdisciplinary* approach in such studies, including both philosophical and empirical inquiry; and (3) *explain in greater detail* the attitudes, knowledge, skills, and abilities required for effective collaboration. Without these adjustments, collaborative governance network theory fails to provide suitable guidance to practitioners.

Notes

1 We must note our very high regard for the outstanding work Robyn Keast and her colleagues have done and continue to do to understand the dynamics of collaboration. We simply disagree with this conceptualization.

2 While Barthes (1972) uses the term "interdisciplinary" in his essay on this approach to inquiry, what he described then is now defined as transdisciplinarity.

Part II

A transdisciplinary understanding of governance

The goal of Part II is to realign the aim of collaborative advantage with logically appropriate philosophical assumptions. Collaborative governance begins with an assumption of *interdependence*. However, to simply say, "we have to start at bedrock and *assume* that we are all already connected, just as we have assumed in the past that we were not" (Stivers 2008, 93–94) is insufficient explanation for a paradigmatic shift. Nor can interconnectedness be understood as something that has "happened" to us as "a natural, evolutionary human response" to the complexity of globalization (Bingham, Nabatchi, and O'Leary 2005, 555). Interdependence *has always been* the human condition within a globally interconnected system that includes social, economic, and environmental components. Our failure to understand this basic premise of existence has contributed to the wicked problems we confront.

Ontological interrelatedness represents a paradigmatic shift that requires robust explication and defense. The received ontological supposition of atomistic independence is undergirded by a fully detailed system of positive science in both its physical and social branches; it is defended by "the verdict of science" (Waldo 1984, 21). Associated assumptions of methodological individualism and attendant governance theories of hierarchical control and pluralist competition are grounded in a host of rationalist political, sociological, and economic theory. To casually replace the assumption of atomistic individualism with relational interconnection lacks the rigor required to do so convincingly.

If we are to supersede the Newtownian/Cartesian version of the universe and all it prefigures, a vigorous, transdisciplinary framework is needed. We must provide a conceptual map that logically links the integrative characteristics of collaborative governance networks to ontological assumptions, psychosocial theory, epistemological concepts, belief systems, ethical concepts, political theory, economic theory, and administrative theory. This enables us to trace the genetic code through ideas associated with governance. Methodologically, we employ transdisciplinarity to inform our understanding of both the global societal context and the structures and practices of governance. We identify integrative concepts in a diverse array of philosophical, scientific, and theoretical sources found in wide variety of disciplines, worldviews, and cultural belief systems, albeit those which have been marginalized by dominant perspectives.

Each chapter in Part II fleshes out the conceptual elements of Integrative Governance outlined in previous publications (Stout and Love 2013, 2014a, 2017, 2015b, 2016). We further unpack these concepts, drawing explanations from diverse literatures promulgating integrative characteristics. Our aim is to foster transdisciplinary cross-pollination by identifying shared concepts that can offer a foundation for broad-based discussion. Transdisciplinarity "does not strive for mastery of several disciplines but aims to open all disciplines to that which they share and to that which lies beyond them" (Nicolescu 2002, 149). This approach is similar to that of the American pragmatist, Mary Follett (2013c), who drew from many disciplines to identify correspondences, correlations, and "cross-fertilizations" (xvii) for the philosophical underpinnings to her "integrative process" and approach to governance of groups, organizations, and societies (Stout and Love 2015a). Through this diversity and open-endedness, we can develop an approach to governance that may be more widely adaptable and acceptable globally, as well as better fit to address the complex problems of sustainability.

Chapters 5–8 explore the philosophical elements of ontological assumptions, psychosocial theory, epistemological concepts, and belief systems. Chapter 9–12 explore the action elements of ethical concepts, political theory, economic theory, and administrative theory. The first four philosophical elements of the typology prefigure the latter four action elements of the typology. In this way the ideal-type depicts both what *is* (ontologically) and what *should be* (theoretically and ethically) – it describes what is believed to be the constitutive Good; both the source of good as well as good ends (Taylor 1989).

Some may criticize such attempts to create a "theory of everything." We argue that this is precisely what paradigmatic change requires. We must present a sufficiently robust explication of the world and humankind to scaffold the collaborative approach to governance we affirm. Using an *integral* approach means to integrate or bring together many aspects of the phenomenon under study (Wilber 2011). Indeed, "'An integral vision' . . . embraces science, art, and morals; that equally includes disciplines from physics to spirituality, biology to aesthetics, sociology to contemplative prayer" (Wilber 2011, loc. 249). However, transdisciplinarity does not aim to produce *totalizing* theories. Rather, its goal is to propose generative frameworks that can integrate new perspectives and raise different questions about phenomena that resist known approaches (Montuori and Donnelly 2016, 753).

For ease of comparison, we use the same Governance Typology presented in *A Radically Democratic Response to Global Governance: Dystopian Utopias* (Stout and Love 2016), explaining how the characteristics of each element are conceptual syntheses (as opposed to hybrids) of the various dialectical pairs generated by the four primary approaches to governance previously identified. Finally, we explore the integrative pathways that connect the primary approaches to the integrative alternative, indicating the feasibility of transformations in thinking and action.

4 The meaning of integration

The keystone of transdisciplinarity is the semantic and practical unification of the meanings that traverse and lie beyond different disciplines. It presupposes an open-minded rationality by re-examining the concepts of "definition" and "objectivity." An excess of formalism, rigidity of definitions and a claim to total objectivity, entailing the exclusion of the subject, can only have a life-negating effect.

– (Article 4 of the Charter of Transdisciplinarity, Nicolescu 2002, 149)

In Chapter 3, we argued that theoretical advancement requires transdisciplinary study of a wider range of collaborative governance networks to better understand the meaning of collaboration. *Integrative* governance provides the next logical step in the developmental path of collaborative governance network theory, because genuine collaboration is integrative.

However, we must dig more deeply into the meaning of this term than what has been provided in the governance literature thus far. Generally speaking, references to integrated or integrative governance are simply alternative labels for collaborative governance networks. The approaches named within integrated governance include networking, cooperation, coordination, collaboration, and partnership (Success Works 2002). Integrated governance is also used to refer to the assimilation of various internal control functions within an individual organization (PwC 2008). As a final example, integrated urban governance refers to policy unification across sectors (including public participation) and jurisdictions (horizontal) and between tiers of government (vertical), both in terms of decision making and implementation (Metropolis 2011).

References to integrated or integrative governance network theories and frameworks frequently refer to the amalgamation of several theories into a metatheory or framework (Emerson and Nabatchi 2015; Emerson, Nabatchi, and Balogh 2012; Millar and Abraham 2006; Sørensen and Torfing 2007). Integration is thus generally understood as *any way to combine things.* From this perspective, hierarchy and markets are understood as "the previous systems of integration" which must be replaced by "networked forms based on horizontal integration principles" as the "new mode for social connection" (Brown and Keast 2003, 107). This new mode emphasizes coordination, cooperation, or collaboration, but collaboration is not necessarily identified as essential to integration.

The design of governance arrangements, the nature of governance processes, and the forms of control used shift within this new mode. Dubnick and Meehan (2004) argue that integrative governance is a response to un-centering and de-centering trends in governance. As also noted by Cleveland (2000), de-centering (or decentralization) retains ultimate authority at the center, while un-centering generates multiple centers of authority. De-centering can still proactively require cooperation, while un-centering can only reactively incentivize cooperation. As an alternative, *emergent* integrative governance is often described in ways that build upon existing relationships, norms and rules, and governmentalities to ensure cooperation. The explication of the three types roughly corresponds to other definitions of coordination, cooperation, and collaboration. Unfortunately, such description replicates the pattern of explaining emergent integrative governance in rational actor terms of self-interested mutual adjustment and thus is not integrative in the manner in which we intend here.

However, a Canadian study addresses the need to adjust such dispositions, explaining that "joining up is a mind-set and a culture. It is not a system or a structure" (as quoted in Success Works 2002, 7). Similarly, city leaders argue that integrated governance means "a different administrative situation, a different way of thinking and a different way of setting about the problem" (Metropolis 2011, 3). Yet, while they discuss holistic and integrating administrative systems and decision maker mindsets, the driving concern is still one of achieving social policy efficiencies and economic development amidst global competition – even if also attending to the wicked problems of social, economic, and spatial inequity.

Page (2010) argues that integrative leadership is necessary for successful collaborative governance, wherein success is measured in terms of meaningful mutual influence during the process and improved policy outcomes. While he seeks a model that disables "guile," enables "sense-giving," and draws from aligned sources in interpretive policy analysis, community development, and conflict resolution, he does not quite make the transformational shift from established power dynamics and roles. Instead, he offers prescriptions for practice in a transitional setting in which dominating and strategic behaviors must be quelled by facilitative leaders. Therefore, a directive, as opposed to self-organizing, approach to framing the agenda, convening stakeholders, and structuring deliberation remains intact.

Rather than being a compromise or hybrid of hierarchical consolidation and coordination on one side, and cooperation and competition on the other, collaboration is a *dialectical synthesis* of the hierarchical need for order and unity and the competitive need for choice and autonomy. This means that collaboration achieves all of these objectives, but *through a completely different method*. To make sense of this claim, we first explain why meanings are important and how dialectical synthesis informs integrative meanings – including the meaning of integration itself.

Why meanings matter

The differentiation of hierarchical coordination and strategic cooperation from network collaboration is as close as the governance network literature comes to naming and defining integration as we do. From this understanding, only collaborative networks enable long-term and full integration of purposes, functions, risks, rewards, and the like (Brown and Keast 2003). We agree – but this requires a detailed clarification of the mutually exclusive characteristics of *integrative* collaboration, as opposed to hierarchical coordination and strategic cooperation. We must understand the philosophical assumptions and commitments that differentiate collaboration from coordination and cooperation as well as networks from hierarchical organizations and competitive markets.

The precise meanings of conceptual elements are critical to understanding the outcomes of collaboration, because ontological assumptions are encoded within language that serves to reinforce those assumptions through the shaping of consciousness, identity, belief, and knowledge (Derrida 1976; Gadamer 2013; Heidegger 1996; Lakoff 2003; Saussure 1960). As a tool of socialization, language is crucial in finding shared understanding and forming agreements. If we wish to have language that can help us comprehend relational interconnection and interdependency and the emerging governance innovations being used in response to wicked problems, we need rhetorical innovation – new concepts and new language (Hartley 2006). Mandell, Keast, and Chamberlain (2016) argue that collaboration requires new language because it makes a difference in how people conceptualize practice: "A transaction-based language is largely incompatible with the higher-level, interdependent relationships that exist within collaborative networks" (329). Thus, collaboration requires "reframing and renaming activities" (336).

As dialogue and deliberation scholars note, both the process and language used must be grounded in a fitting worldview (Parry 2004). We cannot approach a collaborative process using the language and techniques of hierarchical command and control or competitive strategy and negotiation. New ideas often require "the invention of new concepts as well as the redefinition of extant concepts using complex, technical and highly idiosyncratic terminology" (Jun 2011, 234). For example, Follett (1919, 1998, 2013c) rejects words that imply hierarchy and domination. To describe a different quality of relating, she creates new terms: *power-over* describes hierarchy and domination, while *power-with* describes nonhierarchical collaboration (Follett 2003f). Similarly, she rejects individualistic *authority*, replacing it with the non-positional *law of the situation* (Follett 2013a, 2013e).

As another example, in the management approach of Holacracy (see Chapter 11), roles and functions are phrased with verb-endings to indicate that they are continuing activities that are open to change (Robertson 2015). Problems or issues are "tensions" that hinder progress and solutions are "proposals" that are run through the integrative process of decision making. Roles are referenced rather than individual names to disaggregate person from position. People work *on* organizations, not *in* them or *for* them. Meetings are scheduled, but agendas are built during meetings, not beforehand. These micro-shifts in terminology carry the collaborative worldview into organizational operations, reaffirming the transformation recursively.

We also opt for carefully defining existing terms and crafting new terminology that attempts to accurately reflect integrative concepts. As becomes evident in the following chapters, the terminology of integrative concepts often requires some explanation. To describe a dynamic, interconnected universe in which all things are considered equal, we seek to develop terminology that is non-discrete (holistic or relational), non-binary (nonhierarchical), and gerundial (dynamic) in character (for detailed discussion, see Stout 2012).

Dialectical synthesis

For us, integration is a process through which a *synthesis* occurs, as classically understood. Dialectical logic has three developmental moments: thesis, antithesis, and synthesis (Adorno 1973; Popper 1940). This means that a *new* concept results from pre-existing and differing concepts confronting one another. It is not any of the original concepts, nor is it a simple hybrid; yet a synthesis retains important characteristics of each contributing concept. As Follett (1998, 2013c) explains, synthesis/integration represents an authentically *third position* that resolves the shortcomings of concepts in dialectical tension. Like Wang (2012), we argue that synthesis is the only way to resolve conflict and paradoxes while remaining open to further integration.

As an example, we cannot "leaven" a thesis with the antithesis, "for once we enter the framework of the former, we have already defined our terms in ways that contradict their very essence within the framework of the latter" (Sampson 1988, 21). Instead, we must offer a new concept that meets the core needs of both. In the example of individualism (thesis) and collectivism (antithesis), only relationalism (synthesis) holds both the part and the whole as distinct and of equal importance. Yet, these assumptions fundamentally transform all other concepts based on them.

Integrative Governance as a synthesis

The Governance Typology we are building from includes four primary approaches to governance that include both philosophical and practical conceptual elements. As shown in Table 4.1, the concepts composing the four primary ideal-types, Hierarchical, Atomistic, Holographic, and Fragmented Governance, are easily identified in practice, albeit never in perfect alignment because ideal-types are caricatures of logical concepts.

Putting these ideas into conversation with the collaborative governance networks literature, the four ideal-types loosely align with Robyn Keast's (2016) types of Consolidation (Holographic Governance), Coordination (Hierarchical Governance), Cooperation (Atomistic Governance), and Competition (Fragmented Governance).

As shown in Figure 4.1, the domain of each ideal-type is generated by a particular combination of two types of concepts. Hierarchical Governance is composed of collectivist and static concepts. Atomistic Governance is composed of individualist and static concepts. Holographic Governance is composed of collectivist and dynamic concepts. Fragmented Governance is composed of individualist and dynamic concepts.

The meanings of each conceptual element of the typology oppose one another in dialectical tension. As shown in Table 4.2, on the x-axis, the relational dialectic found in

Table 4.1 Primary governance approaches

Generic Elements	***Hierarchical Governance***	***Atomistic Governance***
Ontological Assumptions	static state, transcendent source, singular expression	static state, immanent source, plural expression
Language Characteristics	Discrete, Hierarchical	Discrete, Nonhierarchical
Psychosocial Theory	individuality	Individuality
Epistemological Concepts	Rationalism	Empiricism
Belief Systems	Monotheism	Naturalism
Ethical Concepts	Deontological Obligation	Consequentialism
Political Theory	Classical Conservative Liberalism	Modern Liberalism
Economic Theory	Welfare State	Market Exchange
Administrative Theory	Orthodox Administration	New Public Service
Generic Elements	***Holographic Governance***	***Fragmented Governance***
Ontological Assumptions	dynamic state, transcendent source, singular expression	dynamic state, immanent source, plural expression
Language Characteristics	Gerundial, Holistic	Gerundial, Discrete
Psychosocial Theory	Particular individuality	Singular Individuality
Epistemological Concepts	Idealism	Epistemological Anarchism
Belief Systems	Pantheism	Anti-Essentialism
Ethical Concepts	Moral Imperative	Moral Skepticism/Relativism
Political Theory	Socialism	Individualist Anarchism
Economic Theory	Collective Planning	Self-Sufficiency and Barter
Administrative Theory	New Public Administration	New Public Management

(Source: adapted from Stout and Love 2016)

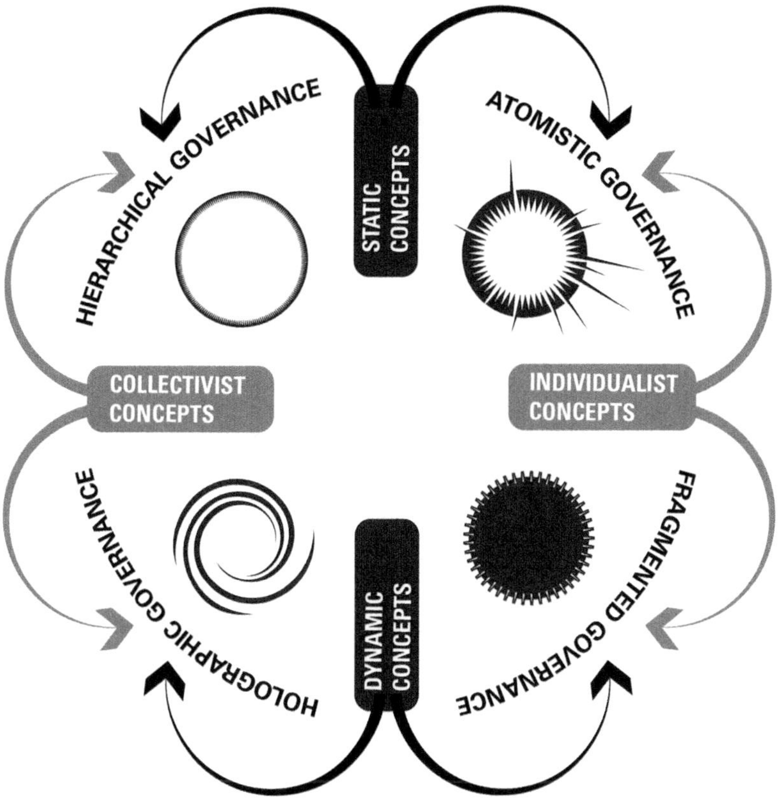

Figure 4.1 Conceptual composition of ideal-type governance approaches

Table 4.2 Political ontology dialectics

	Collectivist	*Individualist*
Static State	Ideal-Type 1 – *Hierarchical*	Ideal-Type 2 – *Atomistic*
Dynamic State	Ideal-Type 3 – *Holographic*	Ideal-Type 4 – *Fragmented*

(Source: adapted from Stout and Love 2016)

philosophical debates carries forward in collectivist versus individualist concepts. On the y-axis, the process dialectic of static versus dynamic state ontologies is found in divergent worldviews.

To continue the developmental path of governance theory, we develop a fifth ideal-type by identifying the synthesis of dialectically opposed conceptual pairs. Each chapter begins with an explanation of the dialectical syntheses at play in the element at hand. As shown in Figure 4.2, each element of the governance ideal-type has a relation-oriented dialectic in which collectivist and individualist concepts oppose one another and are synthesized by an Integrative relational concept. Each element also has a process-oriented dialectic in which static and dynamic concepts oppose one another and are synthesized by an Integrative

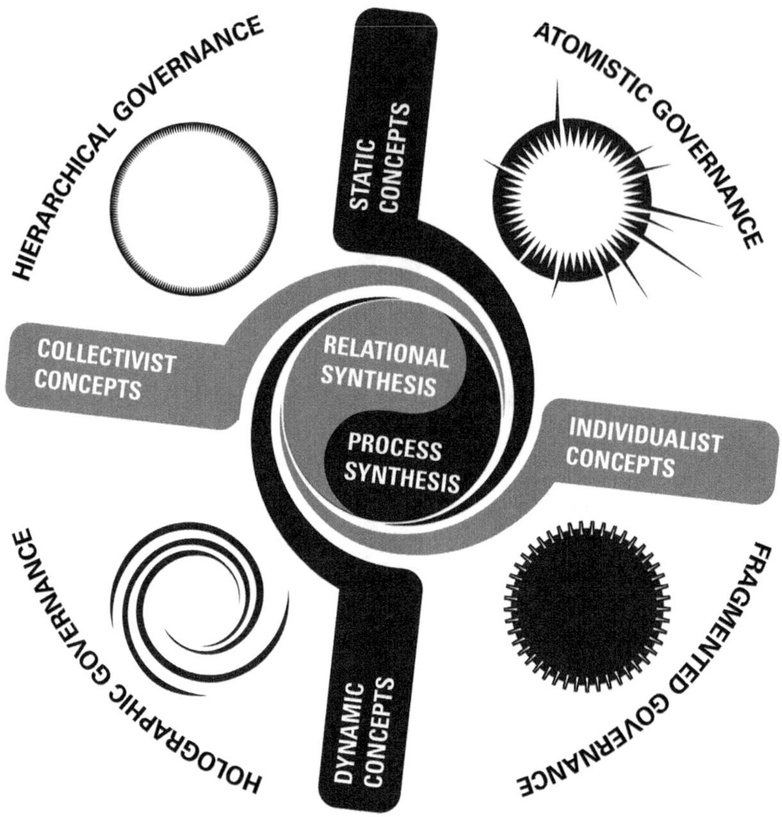

Figure 4.2 Integrative pathways for dialectical synthesis

process concept. In this way, *relational process ontology* weaves its way throughout the philosophical commitments and practices of Integrative Governance.

As a synthesis,[1] the new terrain of relational process ontology provides relational concepts (as opposed to either collectivist or individualist concepts) and a flexible, inclusive grounding for governance through process punctuated by moments of stability (as opposed to either static/dynamic concepts). Using this guiding logic, we construct the scaffolding of Integrative Governance. For each element, the concepts are arranged in a similar two-by-two matrix for dialectical synthesis. Once synthesis concepts are identified for each dialectic, we explore a wide variety of representative ideas that reflect those concepts, employing transdisciplinary inquiry to illuminate a plethora of examples. We must note that, while we come to these ideas from our own relational process perspectives, we are not embedded in all the disciplinary and cultural communities from which we draw and are therefore "outsiders" to some extent. We can only do our best to "reproduce as faithfully as possible" those perspectives (McCutcheon 2005, 17). Given the personal resonance of these ideas, however, we are optimistic that we do reasonable justice to these worldviews.

Through this process, the ideal-type of Integrative Governance emerges as shown in Table 4.3.

Table 4.3 Integrative Governance

Generic Elements	***Integrative Governance***
Ontological Assumptions	Relational Becoming
Psychosocial Theory	Ensembling individuality
Epistemological Concepts	Integral Knowing
Belief Systems	Co-Creationism
Ethical Concepts	Stewardship
Political Theory	Radical Democracy
Economic Theory	Coopetition
Administrative Theory	Facilitative Coordination

As noted, the resultant conceptual elements are identified using newly developed terminology. While these concepts are thoroughly unpacked in Chapters 5–12, we apologize in advance for the awkwardness of these terms! In the following chapters, we use *italics* to draw attention to the dialectical concepts employed in synthesis. The labels for each element's integrative synthesis meaning are shown in ***italicized, bold text***. To emphasize Integrative terms, we capitalize the label given to each element of the framework.

Note

1 In developing a synthesis approach we reject Burrell and Morgan's (2005) claim that "A synthesis [of ideal-types] is not possible, since in their pure forms they are contradictory" (25).

5 Ontological assumptions

Relational Becoming

The recognition of the existence of different levels of reality governed by different types of logic is inherent in the transdisciplinary attitude. Any attempt to reduce reality to a single level governed by a single form of logic does not lie within the scope of transdisciplinarity.

– (Article 2 of the Charter of Transdisciplinarity, Nicolescu 2002, 148)

We argue that to change the practices that generate the global crises we experience today, we must change our fundamental assumptions. From indigenous First Peoples[1] to the newest scientific discoveries, we find a shared understanding of existence that fosters social, economic, and environmental sustainability. This requires attentiveness to *political ontology* in order to bring together all aspects of life – human and other. For example, "new materialists" and posthumanists draw from the new physics and biology in particular, but also return to ontology for a radical reappraisal of materiality, revisiting "the most fundamental questions about the nature of matter and the place of embodied humans within a material world" (Coole and Frost 2010, 3). Following this approach, we consider the status of human and nonhuman alike, and all the biopolitical and bioethical issues that follow. These perspectives stress the generative character of existence and "turn to the Spinozist political ontology defended by Deleuze and Guattari" (Braidotti 2010, 212).

These perspectives also reengage political economy to critique the relationship between material life and geopolitical and socioeconomic structures, including posthumanist ethics (Braidotti 2013), political theory (Connolly 2011, 2013), post-anarchism (Rousselle and Evren 2011), and relational sociology (Donati 2014). These perspectives agree that we must explicitly reunite the political and the phenomenological with the ontological to resolve the crisis of sustainability we face. For example, Abram (1988) argues that Merleau-Ponty's eco-phenomenology "is destined to culminate in a renewed awareness of our responsibility to the Earth" (102).

The term "political ontology" has been used to describe complex assumptions about the nature of human being, identity, and social life and the reflexive relationship between ontology and political form (Catlaw 2007b, 317). Political ontology therefore prefigures approaches to governance; however, because it is taken as a given in most of the governance literature, one must look to a variety of other sources to identify and explain the assumptions in use, including philosophy, psychology, sociology, and theology. This brings us back to ontology proper – the most general branch of metaphysics concerned with the nature of being or existence, which generally stems from philosophy, religion, or physics. We argue that only relational assumptions demand the type of holistic attentiveness required to resolve the complex problems of sustainability. Furthermore, only a dynamic governance approach protects against hegemonic colonization in a global context. Thus, we turn to relational process ontology (Stout and Love 2015b) as a grounding for Integrative Governance.

As shown in Table 5.1, there are several dialectics at play in our Governance Typology. The horizontal relational axis consists of two dialectical pairs: transcendent versus immanent *source* of existence, and singular versus plural *ontological expression. Transcendent* ontologies assume that the source of existence is beyond that which exists, while *immanent* ontologies place the source within all actual things, beings, and places. *Singular expression* ontologies assume existence is whole (One) – it cannot be broken apart in some way, while *plural expression* ontologies assume existence is an aggregate of parts (Many). The vertical process axis shows the dialectic of *states* of existence: static versus dynamic. A *static state* ontology assumes that existence simply *is* (being), while a *dynamic state* ontology assumes that existence is continually changing (becoming). We label the four primary governance approaches holding various combinations of these opposing assumptions Hierarchical, Atomistic, Holographic, and Fragmented.

These opposing ontological assumptions can be traced back to the pre-Socratic Greek philosophers Parmenides and Heraclitus who offer differing conceptualizations of the nature of the One and the Many, transcendence and immanence, and being and becoming (Graham 2002, Heidegger 1992). The most recent formulation is ***abundance*** versus ***lack*** at the core of existence (Tønder and Thomassen 2005b), debating whether the nature of human being starts from embodied matter (ontological abundance) versus epistemological signification or social construction (ontological lack). While both positions tend to agree to the concept of an immanent void at the heart of existence, ontologies of abundance emphasize its nonmaterial potentiality while ontologies of lack see it as empty of both matter and worldly signification. The former focuses on the freedom to co-create while the latter focuses on freedom from domination in individual creativity.

However, a dialectical either/or is not necessary.[2] First, Heraclitus and Parmenides share the notion that the *source of existence* is within all things (immanent), although Parmenides asserts that it also exists as separate from those things (transcendent). Furthermore, the *ontological expression* of existence is singular (One), although Parmenides understands it to be a static unity (being) while Heraclitus considers it to be a unifying process (becoming). Finally, both agree that – at least in experience, if not also in essence – the singular source of existence (One) is expressed in plurality (Many). While Parmenides focuses on the fallacy of the multitudinous Way of Appearance, Heraclitus's admittance that the substance of the Many is the same presents a kind of monism. Thus, a synthesis of these similarities could reasonably be expressed as One-becoming-through-Many – a relational process perspective.

Turning back to the dialectics in our Governance Typology, to achieve a synthesis position, the relational binary dialectic of a *transcendent* versus *immanent source of existence* is resolved through ***embodiment***, which accommodates a nontheistic potential similar to transcendence because it accepts the nonmaterial as "real," but imagines an embodied creation

Table 5.1 Dialectical ontological assumptions

	Transcendent Source Singular Expression	***Immanent Source Plural Expression***
Static State	Hierarchical	Atomistic
Dynamic State	Holographic	Fragmented

(Source: Stout and Love 2016)

of the ontic more like immanence. There is no "beyond" that transcends the universe. Within all that exists, there is the capacity to co-create from non-temporal, nonmaterial potentiality. This radical form of immanence includes the material and nonmaterial within an open-ended whole. Thus, it can be understood as a "space *in between* immanence and transcendence" (Tønder 2005, 204).

The relational dialectic of a *singular* (One) versus *plural* (Many) *expression of existence* is resolved through ***relational assemblage***, in which unique entities co-compose an open-ended whole from a combination of potentiality, prior existence, and environmental influences. Each instance of becoming is happening in a relational assemblage that interconnects everything from quantum particles to the expanding universe as a whole. Stuart Hall (1998) describes this as an ontological point between the dialectic of "pure 'autonomy' or total encapsulation" (447).

Finally, the process dialectic of a *static* versus *dynamic state of existence* is resolved by ***creative emergence***, in which the process of becoming is punctuated with moments of full expression. This concept describes " 'a world in motion" where "everything is moving, even if some things are (temporarily) at rest" (Holm, Silentman, and Wallace 2003, 32).

Together, ***embodiment***, ***relational assemblage***, and ***creative emergence*** compose Relational Becoming. The notion of One-becoming-through-Many flips the assumption of One expressed through an illusionary Many on its head. Both the Many and the One are real, but the One can only be assembled by the Many through relational process. Becoming is a seamless emergent process of creative, relational assemblage from embodied potentiality to actuality. Thus, rather than referring to the One as discrete or all-encompassing and the Many as a set of distinct entities (one), we use the descriptor O/one to describe the co-creative power of singularities assembling the open-ended whole at micro, macro, and cosmological levels of analysis.

Ontologically, all entities at all levels of analysis – beings, things, and places – are relationally assembling entities. As shown in Figure 5.1, while the source of becoming is ***embodied*** at the center of the spiral, the porous boundaries and filaments suggest both relational interconnection and any whole as infinite and open-ended. The spiral formation is meant to indicate the dynamic process of ***creative emergence***. Below the surface of material appearances

Figure 5.1 Embodied source of Relational Becoming (O/one)

one finds "a world of change – matter coming together, dissolving, and coming together again" (Easwaran 2007, 24). This conception synthesizes ontologies of abundance and lack by assuming a foundational void – but one that is filled with creative potential that can be accessed. From this perspective, difference is "the constant play between presence and absence which simply renders impossible the attainment of either full presence (totality) or full absence (radical lack)" (Marchart 2005, 26). It is this dynamic quality that avoids the static reification found in ontological hybrids (Stout and Love 2016). ***Relational assemblage*** is the concept that synthesizes the problem of freedom. Rather than the complete autonomy idealized by notions of lack, becoming is a co-creative process that is mutually influenced by an entity's choices, previous existence, and relational interconnections.

While these ideas are clearly evident in Heraclitean philosophy, Alfred North Whitehead (1967), the founder of process philosophy, draws from Lucretius and Epicurean atomism. His "philosophy of organism" (Whitehead 1979, 7) describes actual occasions or entities in the process of becoming in a way that bridges timeless potentiality with time-bound actuality. Such a harmony depicts flux "in unbounded space" where "things [form] from the coming together" of streams of experience (Hernes 2008, 26). This understanding offers "a new creative synthesis" (Christ 2003, 224) that affirms a dynamic balance among classical dualisms like spirit/matter, One/Many, and self/other.

Aspects of both process and relational thinking are carried forward *in part* by German idealists, existentialists, phenomenologists, and pragmatists – including those who reject those labels. While not fully aligned with process philosophy, Spinoza's (2002) understanding of a holistic substance of being and experience reflects important aspects of the relational perspective, as does Heidegger's (1996) philosophy of being-with, and Buber's (1986) relational philosophy of I and Thou. The notion of being as a process of becoming can be found in Hegel's (1977) philosophy of dialectical becoming, Bergson's (1920, 2001, 2007) concept of *élan vital* in creative evolution, Husserl's (1982) concept of the lifeworld, James's (1909) psychology of experience, and Whitehead's (1979) philosophy of organism.[3] Both relational and process assumptions are drawn together in Nietzsche's (1968, 1969, 1977) life-affirming vital process of will as a synthesis of relational forces in eternal return, as well as Follett's (1919, 2013c) integrative creative process.

In more contemporary philosophy, there are some "affirmative" postmodern philosophers who, while idiosyncratically diverse, share a "philosophical and ontological intellectual practice that is nondogmatic, tentative, and nonideological" (Rosenau 1992, 16). They refuse absolutes, universals, foundationalism, and essentialism that infer either a static whole or transcendent source of being. However, many affirm a relational process of co-creation. Such views have also been described as "constructive postmodern" understandings (Griffin 2007; Griffin, Beardslee, and Holland 1989).

Specifically, ontologies of relational plurality and becoming can be found in Foucault's (1978, 1985, 1986) process ontology (see Rose 2007); Merleau-Ponty's (2012) unique phenomenology of the lived-body and eco-phenomenology; Derrida's conceptualization of *différance* as a process through which repetition and singularity occur relationally in each event of becoming; Deleuze's folding, unfolding, and refolding plurality of becoming (Deleuze 1991, 1994, 2001; Deleuze and Guattari 1983, 1987); Badiou's (2005) becoming anew in the event; Bennett's (2001) Epicurean-inspired enchanted materialism and other new materialisms (Coole and Frost 2010); a neo-Spinozist "radical immanence" (Braidotti 2013, 115); and Hardt and Negri's notion of immanent multiplicity and its inherent potential that combines collectivity and plurality (Newman 2011). Griffin (2001) calls this perspective "reenchantment without supernaturalism." Contemporary process philosophers place such thinkers in conversation with Whitehead (Cobb Jr. 2002; Faber, Krips, and Pettus 2010; Griffin 2007), as do some philosophers of science (Latour 1993; Stengers 2011). These assumptions also fit the rejection of essentialism in post-anarchism (Franks 2011).

Largely concurring with these philosophical explorations are a host of complexity sciences in physics, chemistry, biology, and neuroscience (Connolly 2011) as well as oceanography, geology, and climatology (Connolly 2013). Examples include Bohm's (1980) understanding of the quantum universe as an enfolded, unfolding, self-organizing order (also see Capra 1999; Zukav 1980); Ilya Prigogine's (1981) complexity theory in chemistry; the evolutionary biology of Maturana and Varela (1987), Stuart Kauffman (1993, 1995, 2010), Stephen Gould (1992), Brian Goodwin (2001), Steven Johnson (2001), and Lynn Margulis (1999); the deep ecology of Michael Bell (2006) and Fritjof Capra (1983); and the neuroscience of Antonio Damasio (2010), Giacomo Rizzolatti (2006) and V. S. Ramachandran (2012). The common understanding among these complexity sciences is that *systems* – whether they are physical, biological, social, or economic – are complex, dynamic, nonlinear, and relational. Change in one area of the system causes change throughout the system, regardless of the distance.

Building similar linkages from science to Hindu, Buddhist, and Taoist thought, quantum physicists Fritjof Capra and David Bohm argue that "the concepts of modern physics often show surprising parallels to the ideas expressed in the religious philosophies of the Far East" (Capra 1999, 17–18). Capra (1999) also notes similarities to both Heraclitus and the Native American spirituality described in Castaneda's (1971, 1973) ethnographies of the Yaqui sorcerer Don Juan. Bohm similarly notes the fundamental parallels between quantum physics and various Native American beliefs (Peat 2002). Others have observed "striking similarities and parallels" among the metaphysics of Hinduism and Native American thought (Ryan 2004, 28). In sum, "this view . . . can be found to some degree in all mystically oriented philosophies" (Capra 1999, 19).

Indeed, relational process ideas can be found in the worldviews and spiritual belief systems of many indigenous peoples around the world (Gyekye 1995, 1997; Stewart-Harawira 2005b; Waters 2004a; Wiredu 1996) and neo-pagan (York 2003) or "mystery traditions" (Adler 1986, 441). As one comparative religions study finds, "universal relationality and interconnectedness in process terms are exemplified through various Indigenous concepts, language structures, cultural and religious practices, and epistemology" (Daniels 2012, ii).[4] These cultures and worldviews share a "deep ontological alterity from Western notions of individualism" (Waters 2004a, xxv).

Within Western subcultures, contemporary process theology (Cobb Jr. 1965; Cobb Jr. and Griffin 1976; Keller 2003; Mesle 1993; Suchocki 1985) and feminist thealogies of the Goddess also reflect a relational process perspective (Christ 2003). The latter perspectives "have a much more radical understanding of the limitations of elite white male traditions of thought" (Christ 2003, 159). Indeed, feminism can be understood as "an ontological, spiritual revolution" (Daly 1973, 6). Therefore, mainstream Western philosophy requires "a comprehensive overhaul" (Zanetti 2004, 141).

While there are many nuanced differences among these varied sources, the common denominators are an assumption that being/becoming is relational and/or dynamic. These perspectives understand "the world as a network of interrelated events or momentary energy-events" (Wang 2012, 129). They refuse to bifurcate the holistic understanding of matter/nature and mind/consciousness/energy/spirit (Latour 2011). The substantive correspondences across these varied sources demonstrate the potential vigor relational process ontology could have in forming a shared system of thought and belief. Woven together, they stand to offer a robust alternative metaphysic to that of modernity (Latour 1993). It may be that this alternative "can be made plausible to more people and accepted by others as a worthy competitor for attention, if we draw upon multiple resources to express it" (Connolly 2011, 9).

Drawing on many such sources, we unpack the three integrated characteristics of Relational Becoming – ***embodiment***, ***relational assemblage***, and ***creative emergence***. However, we note that they are difficult to disaggregate for purposes of explication because they are mutually implicated.

Embodiment

Mainstream Western culture places physical (*immanent*) and metaphysical (*transcendent*) *sources of existence* in dialectical tension – the ground of being must be either one or the other. *Transcendent source* ontologies place the metaphysical in hierarchical priority over the physical, and extreme mysticism goes so far as to insist that the physical realm is merely a manifestation of the transcendent and distinction is an illusion. *Immanent source* ontologies deny the metaphysical altogether, in effect placing the physical in hierarchical priority over the illusion of the metaphysical. Skeptical postmodern thought denies all explanations of essential foundations, particularly those beyond human perception. In Relational Becoming, "There is more to reality than actuality" (Connolly 2011, 43). The dialectic of *transcendent* and *immanent sources of existence* is synthesized through the ***embodiment*** of potentiality – an "'ontology from within'" (Abram 1988, 112). As Wang (2012) explains, "transcendence and immanence generally occur together" (191). All material things hold within them the nonmaterial potential for ongoing becoming through time – hence the term ***embodiment***. Therefore, materialization must be conceived "outside of the dualism of the material and the ideal" (Coole and Frost 2010, 37).

Rather than dividing the physical and metaphysical, or denying one or the other, the material (actuality) and nonmaterial (potentiality) form an integral whole. ***Embodiment*** assumes "the spiritual and material dimensions of life form a dynamic unity" (Pulitano 2003, 26), whether the nonmaterial is interpreted as spirit, energy, consciousness (Christ 2003), or divinity (Adler 1986). The metaphysical and the physical are a relational whole of potentiality and its actualization. The source of becoming "is not transcendent in the sense of being totally outside nature . . . [it] is a naturally creative process" (Wang 2012, 179). Yet, these understandings redefine *immanence* as multidimensional in both spatial and temporal terms – actuality is measurable while potentiality stands ready to become.

Thus, ***embodiment*** provides a "sense of the numinosity of the natural" (Raphael 2000, 33). Numinosity seems to be the combination of the words numen (a spiritual force or influence that is often identified with a natural place, phenomenon, or object) and numinous, meaning supernatural and mysterious; filled with a sense of the presence of divinity (sacred); and appealing to the higher emotions or the aesthetic sense (spiritual). As such, it provides a bridge between vital or enchanted materialism and most other ontologies that focus on the metaphysical as opposed to the physical aspect of life, as will be discussed in Chapter 8. As Follett (2013c) explains, "the individual can create without 'transcending.' He expresses, brings into manifestation, powers which are the powers of the universe and thereby those forces which he is himself helping to create, *those which exist in and by and through him*" (116, emphasis added).

Embodiment is also conceptualized as a *fold* in existence. Merleau-Ponty replaces binary oppositions of material and nonmaterial with the notion of *fold* to indicate the multidimensional ontological attributes of the lifeworld (Coole 2010). In other words, there is no division of physical and metaphysical qualities, merely enfolded and unfolding aspects of embodied existence (Bohm 1980). Merleau-Ponty claims that Husserl caught a glimpse of this post-dualist ontology in his third existential dimension that unfolds between perceived dualisms – in other words, a synthesis. Deleuze (1992) further notes that the ontological fold is like Heidegger's concept of opening but he instead draws from process philosophers Heraclitus and Whitehead to develop the notion of the universe as a multiplicity of ontological folds that are like origami. Neither folds nor openings are empty – they are porous and dynamic, continuously folding and unfolding assemblages of existence.

However, *locating* the *source of existence* does not fully explain its characteristics. Heraclitus argues that the substance of each state of existence (potential and actual) is the same – there is an essence of potentiality that expresses itself in many becomings – "from all things one and from one all things" (Graham 2008, section 3.2, paragraph 4). This notion of "substance" is not dissimilar to the paradoxical quantum understanding of physical objects being both stationary and moving, or the dual nature of light as being both particle and wave; it is all energy, but its manifestation depends on how it is observed (Capra 1999). With all "things" ultimately being comprised of energy in motion, the dimensional differences lose differentiating boundaries and hierarchical ordering – everything is on a continuum of existence, drawing from the same source.

If potentiality and manifestation are simply different expressions of the same thing, where do potentials come from in the first place? This question brings up the classical ontological quandary of whether creation stems from nothing or from something. Western thinkers struggle with the concept of creative potentiality because the received ontological principle argued by Parmenides is that *nothing can come from nothing*. Rejecting *creatio ex nihilo*, even Whitehead claims that everything must be actual, placing one half of the source of becoming in God (Mesle 2008).[5] God nonmaterially actualizes "eternal objects," which are "the pure potentials of the universe," while the material world is comprised of "actual entities" which "differ from each other in their realization of potentials" (Whitehead 1979, 149). However, this necessarily places constraints on creativity – all that is possible already is. We argue that it is more logically coherent to consider potentiality as the other half of the dual ultimate: the unlimited capacity to co-create (Wang 2012) (see ***creative emergence*** later).

In creation from nothing, existence is actualized through the expression of infinite possibilities: "Potentiality becomes reality; and yet retains its message of alternatives which the actual entity has avoided" (Whitehead 1979, 149). A relevant discussion of creation from nothing can be found in contemporary philosophy. For example, using Badiou's set theory interpretation of ontology, Prozorov (2014a) argues there is an infinite proliferation of infinite quantities that cannot be subsumed under a totality. The set itself is an excess of the original elements, yet carries no quantitative value. There is a world beyond being where everything exists as *unreal* but potentially real. Beings are literally "woven out of the void" (Badiou 2005, 57). This void of actuality produces an infinite plurality of possible substantive worlds, with no possibility of any one's positive attributes to become universal.[6] Following this metaphor, the ground of becoming is *qualitatively* different but not *quantitatively* different, because while potentiality does not yet exist (quantitative addition), it contains possibilities that are beyond what actually exists at any given moment (qualitatively more).

While potentiality may lack substantive definition when unrealized, it is rich with possible attributes. Therefore, ontologies of abundance are more fitting to relational process. In some Native American traditions, for example, the non-temporal, non-spatial void is understood as the womb of all creative potential that is embodied in every part of a continually evolving, emergent universal whole (Mirror 2012). This is similarly explained by quantum physics: "we have the unlimited as the ground of everything" (Bohm 2004, 106). "Unlimited" here refers to both space and creative subtlety – the emergent implicate order can be anywhere and anything (Bohm 1980). The whole of existence is also infinite because potentiality is not bound by time and space (Stewart-Harawira 2005b).

Actual entities, therefore, "differ from each other in their realization of potentials" (Whitehead 1979, 149), but all conform to the same metaphysical principles of becoming and all share some degree of experience, from the quantum to universal level (Mesle 2008). Thus, at the ontological level there are no "firm distinctions between organic and inorganic or animate and inanimate" and "no definitive break between sentient and nonsentient entities" (Coole and Frost 2010, 10). This perspective can be described as a "radical immanence or immanent realism" (Connolly 2011, 76). However, what is expressed (or not) in the process of becoming is affected by all other entities also in the process of becoming. Thus, we turn to ***relational assemblage***, the second characteristic of Relational Becoming.

Relational assemblage

Relational assemblage is an ontological assumption that synthesizes a *singular* and *plural expression* of existence, in which the One is co-created by the Many in an emergent process. Looking to align chaos theory with a humanist ethos, the monist/particularist dialectic can be resolved by a complementary holism (Albert et al. 1986) that accommodates relational potentiality (Adams 2011). This understanding prioritizes neither the collective nor the individual, allowing the boundaries to soften, as indicated above in Figure 5.1. With the creative source of becoming (One) embodied within all entities (Many), all things are related by virtue of this common potentiality, and yet are differentiated and unique in their expression of it. Niebuhr (1970) describes this relationship as the One expressed through the Many, calling the phenomenon a "radical monotheism" in which a universal force imbues all and yet is manifested in each uniquely: "I am one within myself as I encounter the One in all that acts upon me" (122).

While the source of becoming "is not governing in the sense of being manipulative or overpowering" (Wang 2012, 179), it is not without constraints. Through ***embodiment***, the relation between the *source of existence* (One) and the entity (one) is transformed into mutual influence among all entities (O/one) in the process of becoming: "We create ourselves out of our relationships with" all other entities (Mesle 1993, loc. 826). Therefore "creation is always co-creation" (Christ 2003, 100) – it is relational. As Follett (2013c) explains, the process of co-creation is one of "reciprocal influence" in the "evolving situation" (57). There is an ongoing circular response "to a relating" (73). Similarly, Bohm (1980) explains that the implicate order is a complex pattern of relational movement, not a permanent arrangement of objects that change only within themselves. Like Follett (1998), Buddhists call this process "interpenetration"; it is an "essentially dynamic interrelation which takes place not only spatially but also temporally" (Capra 1999, 293). The dynamism of interconnection leads to emergent systems that are complex interrelations in which "no single event happens in isolation, no simple straight-forward cause and effect can be predicted" (Buchanan 2002, 18). Within this tangled world, systems are self-organizing with "millions of interactions occur[ring] simultaneously – when everyone changes the state of everyone else" (Strogatz 2003, 34). In other words, there is a "mutual reciprocity" (Cajete 2004, 55). In short, as the Indian philosopher Krishnamurty said, " 'To be' is to be related" (as quoted in Bohm 2004, 47).

Whitehead (1979) goes into great detail regarding relationality and assemblage in terms of time, shared ontological ground, and mutual influence in his explanation of the process of becoming, or "concrescence." In this process, there are three types of "prehension"[7] that co-determine what is actualized: (1) past experiences as an actual entity; (2) infinite potentiality; and (3) the interconnection with other actual entities. Across time, patterns form among these prehensions, but they are not predetermined. In the first type, "the new occasion [entity] draws the past occasion [entity] into itself" (Cobb Jr. 2008, 31), thereby enabling the actual entity to express continuity. Through creativity, novel potentialities "obtain ingression" (Sherburne 1966, 235), thereby enabling actual entities to change. Finally, contrasting actual entities "enter into each others' constitutions" (Whitehead 1979, 149), also enabling change. Thus, process philosophy asserts, "Connectedness is the essence of all things" (Morris 1991, 71). An actual entity "is not first something in itself, which only secondarily enters into relations with others. The relations are primary" (Cobb Jr. and Griffin 1976, 19). Indeed, "all actual entities in the world must be accounted for in some way, *by* and *in* every actual entity in the world. Every actual entity forms part of the constitution of every other actual entity in the world, however intense or trivial its relevance" (Daniels 2012, 115).

With this understanding of relationality at the individual level of analysis in hand, we must also consider how the principle moves out in wider levels of analysis. As Follett (1919) notes, when the focus moves from the parts to the integrated whole, the manner in which the parts are related becomes the phenomenon of interest. Connolly (2011) refers to this quality as "connectionism" (12). As feminist panentheism suggests, everything from the subatomic to the divine is interconnected and "the web of life is no mere metaphor" (Christ 2003, 70). Follett (2013c) describes this product as "a function of the interweaving between the activity of organism and the activity of environment" (79). First, there is the relating *within* the parts. Then there are relatings *among* the parts. Finally, there are relatings with the environment to accommodate the total situation engaged in the process of becoming. Thus, in what she calls a "whole a-making" (Follett 2013c, 102), "organism and environment do not 'express' but make wholes" (125) – a "dynamical construct arising over time" (Goldstein 1999, 52). Therefore, ***relational assemblage*** is an organic *growth* among holons or "holarchy" (Koestler 1967), as opposed to a superimposed "dominator" hierarchy forcing parts into a whole (Wilber 2011).

Whitehead provides a microcosmic explanation of ***relational assemblage*** that can be analogously applied at any level of analysis. Building on the concrescence of an actual entity, he describes a variety of compilations, making clear the relational character from the most basic to the most complex: "Though there are gradations of importance, and diversities of function, yet in the principles which actuality exemplifies all are on the same level" (Whitehead 1979, 18). Actual entities join together in what he calls "societies" at ever increasing levels of complexity – molecules, cells, trees, dogs, human beings, social groups, and so forth, all the way out to God. In fact, we do not perceive the microcosmic actual entities, but rather societies of actual entities at the macrocosmic level. We can perceive societies because they endure through temporal prehensions that are sufficiently similar to perceive them as discrete material beings or things. Yet, there is always the potential for major disruption in the process of concrescence, in which case what was perceived ceases to exist. Theoretically, this could mean instant materialization or dematerialization of entities (Griffin 1997). More common is the recursive process of Relational Becoming through which change in a society of actual entities is barely perceivable, such as maturation or aging.

The concept of society is used to emphasize the non-mechanistic, non-atomistic nature of organic becoming. A society is a group of actual entities connected in specific ways. Mainly, they share certain "defining characteristics" (Whitehead 1979, 34) in ways that enable the society to "hang together" (Mesle 2008, 106). A "nexus" is a grouping of societies that can either be non-social (chaotic) in nature or social in nature; "social nexus" is a structured society that has an enduring character through time that is described as a "personal order" (Whitehead 1979, 34). A complex "structured society" (100) is composed of multiple structured societies, generally described as subordinate to "dominant societies" (332).

The conceptualization of gradations of importance and complexity invites comparative value judgments that become particularly problematic when applied at the level of human society – what or who determines the hierarchy? Other relational perspectives avoid this paradox by avoiding hierarchical ordering from the start. For example, all differentiated functions are equally important in complex systems. Advances in biology have come to understand this relationality through studies of forms of life as comparatively simple as colonies of single-celled bacteria and as complex as human societies (Ben-Jacob, Shapira, and Tauber 2011). As Abram (1988) explains, Merleau-Ponty (1968) describes existence as "communal 'flesh'" (111). Natural systems exist in "nested relatedness" (Bird-David 1999, 77) from the "macroecosphere" to "biomes to microbial associations" (MacAllister 2011, 100). From this perspective, "everything in the natural world has relationships with every other thing and the total set of relationships makes up the natural world as we experience it" (Deloria Jr. 1999, 34). "We inhabit a world of becoming composed of heterogeneous force-fields . . . in and beyond the human estate" (Connolly 2011, 5). This "inherent connectedness to all life" (Tripathy 2006, 317) "urges us to think about all human projects in relation to the whole web of life, human and nonhuman" (Christ 2003, 180). Even the supposedly inanimate matter in our world is part of the creative process (Deleuze and Guattari 1987; Rico 2011).

Therefore, to eliminate the hierarchical notion of "gradations of importance" (Whitehead 1979, 18), we employ the Deleuzian understanding of rhizome (Deleuze 1994; Deleuze and Guattari 1987). While drawing from concrescence, rhizomatic assemblage – which is used both as a verb and a noun – is nonhierarchical in nature (Deleuze and Guattari 1987). "There are only multiplicities of multiplicities forming a single *assemblage*, operating in the same *assemblage*" (34). Bennett (2001) defines assemblage as complex "heterogeneous elements bound loosely together" (Connolly 2011, 27). Thus, ***relational assemblage*** produces both One and one of Many (O/one), all in a state of mutual influence. As Deleuze explains, "through movement the whole is divided up into objects, and objects are re-united in the whole, and indeed between the two 'the whole' changes" (as quoted in Badiou 2000, 39). Bohm describes this process as "dialogical" (as quoted by Nichol 2004, xv). Therefore, we must take care not to "produce the deception of a quantitative multiplicity which does not entail any qualitative shifts" (Braidotti 2013, 101–102).

In quantum physics, assemblage is explained quite clearly in the principle of influence at a distance as a natural occurrence (Griffin 2007). To some degree all things in the universe are co-creating a complex relational web of becoming. Donati (2014) describes this as an "inter-verse" (159) as opposed to a monistic universe or pluriverse composed of distinct and disaggregated parts. Bell's theorem of nonlocal causality "demonstrates that the universe is fundamentally interconnected, interdependent, and inseparable" (Capra 1999, 313). As has been demonstrated by experimentation, the very methods we use to observe and understand the world "play a role in producing the very phenomena they set out to describe" (Barad 2007, 207). As a result, our processes of understanding the world, the "apparatuses" we use, "iteratively reconfigure spacetimematter as part of the ongoing dynamism of becoming" (142).

In addition to the rhizome metaphor, relational assemblage is often conceived as interlocking networks of becoming or webs of many relationships, as in the Nuu-chah-nulth notion of "tsawalk" (Atleo 2005, 118). "The Indigenous understanding that all things interpenetrate and are relationally interdependent embraces a manifold of complexity, resembling a world of multifariously associated connections and intimate fusions" (Waters 2004a, xxv). Follett (1998) similarly describes ontological relation as "an infinite number of filaments" that "cross and recross and connect all my various allegiances" (312).

Relational assemblage suggests that the whole is not separate from its parts, nor is it simply an aggregate of its parts – it is an agential, related other constructed by the differentiated parts in synergistic relation. Such a composition

> cannot be reduced to the sum of the powers and qualities of the elements that have been combined with each other, nor can they be explained on the basis of these powers and qualities because the latter belong to a new relational structure.
>
> (Donati 2014, 59)

Therefore, the whole is its own differentiation from all of the parts and their multifarious groupings – "the many become one, and are increased by one" (Whitehead 1979, 21). Follett (2013c) describes this phenomenon as the "plus value" or "plusvalents" of creative experience – a law of "organic progression" (73).

In this sense, set theory (Badiou 2005, 2009) accurately describes the whole assemblage as a unique quantity, but rather than being empty of positive attributes, it holds the synergistic qualities generated by the relational parts that compose it. Nevertheless, it is not dominating in any sense because the self-organizing parts co-create ever-changing groups. The entire universe is becoming as its parts come into being and cease to exist. Furthermore, that which is "negatively prehended" (Daniels 2012, 115) or remains potential, rather than actualized, works on that which has become through what Nietzsche called " 'the powers of the false' " (Connolly 2011, 4) – the ongoing invitation to express new potentialities. Thus, ***relational assemblage*** is both a process and an expressed whole with infinite potentiality – "a unity to the plane of nature" that is not teleological or predetermined (Deleuze and Guattari 1987, 254).

Creative emergence

As explained in ***embodiment***, the source of existence is described as the ground of *becoming* (Christ 2003) rather than the ground of *being* (Tillich 1973) – existence is processual, rather than fixed. However, ***creative emergence*** synthesizes the process dialectic of *static* and *dynamic states of existence* by acknowledging that the process of becoming actual from a nontemporal, nonmaterial state is punctuated by moments of harmony or stability that can be perceived materially. Further, through ***relational assemblage***, "all-that-is" is engaged in this "co-creative project" (Beeman and Blenkinsop 2008, 104). As quantum physics explains, " 'matter' does not refer to an inherent, fixed property of abstract, independently existing objects; rather, '*matter' refers to phenomena in their ongoing materialization*" (Barad 2007, 151). Therefore, "emergence is an 'act of composition (syn-thesis)' . . . an act of coming into existence" (Donati 2014, 59).

Heraclitus describes the opposing processes of material formation and dissolution as the creative conflict through which all things become (Graham 2008). A similar proposition is made in physicist Niels Bohr's (1996) notion of quantum complementary wholes such as waves and particles (Graham 2002). Heraclitus argues that you can never step into the same river twice, but he acknowledges that you can step into an actual river. He claims that the only universal principle is change and all that exists is in a constant state of becoming and dissolving, creating a particular (dis)harmony or (im)balance in actuality at any given point in time. Vital materialism brings this idea back into conversation: "It is in these choreographies of becoming that we find cosmic forces assembling and disintegrating to forge more or less enduring patterns that may provisionally exhibit internally coherent, efficacious organization" (Coole and Frost 2010, 10).

Creative potential "expresses itself through the chaotic and generative void of positivity" (Braidotti 2013, 136) – we could say that "chaos is nature's creativity" (Briggs and Peat 1999, 19). Whitehead (1979) explains that moments of stability are reached in actual occasions (events), which happen in actual entities (materially concrete parts) and more complex societies of actual entities (observable things and beings). But actual occasions are "the final real things of which the world is made up . . . drops of experience, complex and interdependent" (Whitehead 1979, 18). These events "arise, become, and reach completion. When the becoming is completed they are then in the past; the present is constituted by a new set of occasions [entities] coming into being" (Cobb Jr. and Griffin 1976, 19). In other words, becoming is an ongoing flow of experience interspersed with moments of stability (Mesle 2008). Every event "is a creative act of synthesizing the world into a new unity" (Wang 2012, 131).

Japanese philosophy (Nishida 1992) expresses this as "the eternally unfolding present" (Cook and Wagenaar 2012, 5). As understood in Chinese Taoism, the *Tao* is "the way, or process, of the universe, the order of nature" (Capra 1999, 104). The symbol, *T'ai-chi T'u* or the *Diagram of the Supreme Ultimate*, places generic partners in relationship (see Figure 5.2). The shapes represent two embracing fishes, each with an eye the color of its partner (Wang 2012). Like the dissolving/becoming described by Heraclitus, the combined concepts of *yin* and *yang* contain all twofold expressions of becoming, such as receptive/active, dark/light, matter/energy, body/spirit, yielding/firm, female/male, intuition/reason, and so forth. The relational character or porosity of the two qualities within the whole is symbolized by the opposing color contained within each, indicating that each quality exists within the other – each fish is paradoxically both itself and the other. Each quality emerges from the other, making the whole of potential expression available to each. It is this both/and dynamic synthesis that differentiates it from the static holism of either/or dialectics.

This symbol also illustrates ontological dynamism by envisioning *yin* and *yang* in a state of rotational symmetry, representing the ceaseless motion of cyclic patterns of coming and going. When they are in a moment of balance, they appear as shown in the diagram. However, constant movement is indicated by the curved boundary between the embracing fishes. The two halves are engaged in a constant process of transformation in which "harmony" is sought (Wang 2012, 4). One can imagine the fishes rotating in position or their colors transforming and exchanging places through expansion and contraction of the "eye" within each: "The *yang* having reached its climax retreats in favour of the *yin*; the *yin* having reached its climax retreats in favour of the *yang*" (Needham 1956, 35). These moments of balance define the Taoist doctrine of the golden mean (Capra 1999), which recognizes

Figure 5.2 T'ai-chi T'u symbol (*yin/yang*)

that "harmony does not signify the imposition of uniformity, but rather the emergence of concord out of the allowance of discord" (Wang 2012, 4).

In the Diné (Navajo) worldview, this innate complementary process is described in the phrase, "*Sa'ah Naaghai, Bikeh Hozhoon*" (Maryboy 2004, 12). This is a phrase with no direct translation in English. The first half of the phrase refers to masculine energies while the second refers to feminine energies. The two qualities are dynamically complementary in the creating process of ***nanit'a***, or "balancing the flux" (12). Other indigenous spiritual traditions see "creation as a process of continuous action or coming into being" (Stewart-Harawira 2005a, 155). Waters (2004c) describes this as "interstitial being" (153) – the space where non-being and being come together, or the state of coming into being. Traditions of Goddess thealogy and paganism also hold that *change is*: "the whole universe is alive and changing, continually co-creating new possibilities of life" (Christ 2003, 45). Therefore, these worldviews tend to focus "on processes rather than goals" (Adler 1986, 38).

Deleuze and Guattari (1987) describe ***creative emergence*** as a dynamic of nonlinear movement and rest in which any given force field oscillates between periods of relative stasis and periods of imbalance and change followed by a new period of stabilization (Connolly 2010). Similarly, Bohm (1980) replaces the holistic term *hologram*[8] with the term *holomovement* to explain the dynamic nature of becoming in both parts and the whole. Quantum mechanics and experimentation verifies this view, showing that at both cosmological and layered subatomic levels, the universe is in constant relative motion: "The particles of the subatomic world are not only active in the sense of moving around very fast; they themselves are processes!" (Capra 1999, 203). These ideas have been translated into many other physical sciences through complexity theory (see for example, Prigogine 1981).

Process philosophy agrees that "the universe is a vast web or field of microevents" (Mesle 2008, 95). Furthermore, these events "are not parts of a process in the sense of steps in a process. There is one simultaneous process" (Follett 2003h, 198). Even in the early twentieth century, pragmatists recognized that "every advance in physics, physiology and psychology shows us life as process" (Follett 2013c, 118) – "a creating process" (119). To reflect this, "'Emerging' is the word which is being used more and more every day by scientists to denote the novelty wherever it appears in evolution" (Follett 2003h, 198). Instances of being come together in an emergent way (Johnson 2001), generating both ourselves and the world we live in through an ongoing process of co-creation.

Time is therefore an important element of ontology. Indeed, James, Bergson, Nietzsche, North, and Deleuze "all advance different versions of time as becoming" (Connolly 2011, 7). Assumptions of a static state are related to linear, regulated time, while assumptions of a dynamic state are related to nonlinear, complex time. The latter is a quantum physics view of time in relation to space, which is malleable. However, most understandings of temporality assume that it flows in one direction – from past to future through the ongoing portal of the present (Griffin 2007). The perception of time, however, is linked to the complexity of experience of each thing or being, with that perceived by humans being only one time register (Griffin 2008).

However, there are also non-temporal dimensions such as the realm of potentiality or the non-temporal, non-spatial state that existed before the Big Bang (Drees 1990). In this sense, creating happens in a mode of existence that is non-temporal and nonmaterial, while physical experience belongs to linear time. Braidotti (2013) differentiates these registers as *Chronos* (linear time) versus *Aion* (becoming time) (see 164). Thus, "we participate in at least two registers of temporal experience, action-oriented perception, and the slower experience of the past folding into the present and both flowing toward the future" (Connolly 2011, 4). Becoming is a process of emerging from one time register to another, from one spatial dimension to another, both of which are part of an integrated whole. Drawing on Nietzsche's (1968, 1969) philosophy of becoming, Connolly (2011) argues that fecund moments of eternal return happen in the non-temporal register: "The 'moment' is a protracted present in which, on occasion, movement back and forth between previously stabilized elements foments significant disequilibrium. This is a time ripe for 'accidents'" (111) – which is understood as creative becoming and change in regular, punctual time.

With the source of existence embodied in all that becomes, the process of becoming is neither directed by an external divinity or natural order of some sort, nor is it at the effect of pure chaos or completely autonomous. While mutually influenced in ***relational assemblage***, all entities possess "sui generis qualities and powers" (Donati 2014, 59). This agential "creativity is the ultimate behind all forms . . . and conditioned by its creatures" (Whitehead 1979, 20). In other ontologies, our choice might be "confined between an enchanted world created by design and a dry lifeless world jumbled together by chance" (Howe 2006). In process ontology, "creative freedom is understood to be inherent" (Christ 2003, 99). Bennett (2001) calls this agency "enchanted materialism" – a way of "conceiving matter as possessing its own modes of self-transformation, self-organization, and directedness" (Coole and Frost 2010, 10). Creation is a sacred expression of becoming in an open-ended multiplicity (York 2000).

Within this self-creating process, Prigogine's complexity theory and Whitehead's philosophy of organism both allow for differential degrees of agency in creation that Connolly (2011) notes is nonhierarchically distributed; there are different degrees of complexity that build on one another and different fields of becoming that interact with one another to constitute the world. Drawing from evolutionary biologist, Stuart Kauffman (1995), the levels of agency are: (1) proto-agency that arises with life or complex assemblage; (2) cultural agency that operates before and below language; (3) human agency that arises with values, meaning, and action (consciousness); and (4) complex agency in which actors operate in relation. The most complex level creates "inter-agential concatenations that exceed the previous reach of either party" (Connolly 2011, 27). This synergy is created through "*emergent causality*" which "can trigger novel patterns of *self-organization* in a thing, species, system, or being" (44).

Ontology focuses on the first level of agency – the creative agency inherent in all entities. This "enlarged human grasp of the intelligence and differential degrees of agency in other plant and animal species" (Connolly 2011, 7) is becoming more widely recognized in Western philosophy and science. Thus, along with all other entities, in "the doctrine of 'becoming'" (Follett 1998, 99) "men are the co-creators" (103). "Our universe is still unfolding and human beings are active and creative participants. Creativity is both the universe's ordering principle and its process, part of the greater flow of creativity in nature" (Cajete 2004, 47).

Relational Becoming

In sum, Relational Becoming is comprised of ***embodiment***, ***relational assemblage***, and ***creative emergence***. Coming into existence is an ongoing, emergent process of creative, relational assemblage from embodied potentiality to actuality. Perhaps the best summary of relational process ontology is provided by Bohm (1980), who describes the unbroken wholeness of existence as an emergent "implicate order" of cosmic relations which *en*folds the potentiality of all that *un*folds materially in space and time through "holomovement." In this explanation, he fully encompasses all three aspects of Relational Becoming. Enfoldment refers to the holistic nature of the universe – there is no "outside" (***embodiment***). If everything is both energy and matter enfolding potentiality, then the source of existence is embodied. Implicate order refers to the notion of interconnections among what is unfolding; in other words the unfolding process is a ***relational assemblage*** that generates the order of the universe. Unfolding means that potentiality is not directed or limited – becoming is a self-organizing process that cannot be predicted and controlled (***creative emergence***).

Integrative pathways

An Integrative synthesis must generate pathways that are easily traversed by those holding other positions. In the case of ontology, Relational Becoming must provide concepts that sufficiently meet fundamental assumptions within the other ontologies, or at least create a dialogical basis for creating shared understandings. As illustrated in Figure 5.3, we imagine the shared characteristics shown in Table 5.2 as pathways into a dynamic synthesis that is always open to contestation and change.

Referring back to our discussion of dialectical synthesis in the chapter's introduction, we know that to accommodate both the *transcendent sources of existence* found in Hierarchical and Holographic ontologies and the *immanent sources of existence* found in Atomistic and Fragmented ontologies, Relational Becoming assumes that creative potential lies within all things and beings – ***embodiment***. ***Relational assemblage*** accommodates both unified, *singular expressions of existence* found in Hierarchical and Holographic ontologies and *plural expressions of existence* found in Atomistic and Fragmented ontologies – One-becoming-through-Many. To accommodate the basic assumptions of both *static states of existence* found in Hierarchical and Atomistic ontologies and *dynamic states of existence* found in Holographic and Fragmented ontologies, Relational Becoming conceives of ***creative emergence*** as a process of becoming that is punctuated by moments of full expression.

The primary concerns of each distinct ontological position must also be addressed to establish a starting point for dialogue with the Integrative perspective, as shown in Table 5.2.

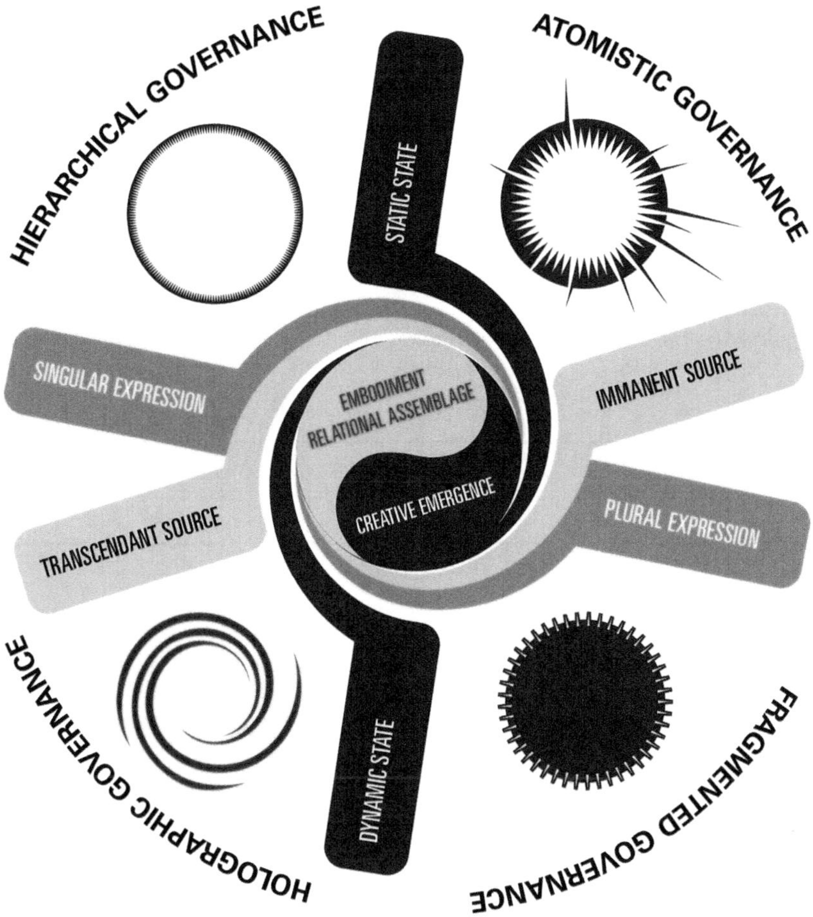

Figure 5.3 Integrative pathways for Relational Becoming

The Hierarchical position is primarily concerned with establishing stable ontological foundations that are ordered by something that is beyond the beings and things of the world. Relational Becoming conceptualizes an emergent order that enables a large degree of continuity through time in the ***relational assemblage*** of the past into each new moment of ***creative emergence***. The Atomistic position is primarily concerned with natural order produced through observable patterns of cause and effect. The natural immanence of ***embodiment*** provides a common scientific nomenclature with quantum physics, while the material results of ***creative emergence*** are observable in each event of ***relational assemblage***. The Holographic position is primarily concerned with an absolute relation within an immanent whole that is greater than the parts due to its transcendent source. ***Relational assemblage*** creates an open-ended whole, while the combination of ***creative emergence*** and ***embodiment*** generate synergy beyond simple aggregation. The Fragmented position denies anything transcendent and is primarily concerned with freedom from any externally imposed order, which the autopoietic process of ***creative emergence*** ensures, even if constrained by ***relational assemblage***.

Table 5.2 Integrating ontological concerns

Ideal-Type	*Characteristics*	*Primary Concerns*	*Synthesis Solution*
Hierarchical	*static state, transcendent source, singular expression*	Ontological stability ordered by something	***Creative emergence*** and ***relational assemblage*** produce an emergent, co-created order
Atomistic	*static state, immanent source, plural expression*	Ontological stability ordered by natural cause and effect	***Embodiment*** provides common ground with natural cause and effect that is observed in all instances of ***creative emergence*** into a ***relational assemblage***
Holographic	*dynamic state, transcendent source, singular expression*	Ontological relation within a synergistic whole	***Relational assemblage*** produces an open-ended whole that is synergistic due to ***creative emergence*** and ***embodiment***.
Fragmented	*dynamic state, immanent source, plural expression*	Freedom from ontological order	Autopoietic ***creative emergence*** ensures agency within ***relational assemblage***

Notes

1 These terms, along with others such as Native American and Aboriginal, are widely contested and no universally acceptable term is available. We use indigenous in our own writing, but maintain the terminology used by the various authors we are either paraphrasing or quoting, to ensure the specificity they desire.

2 The conflicts between Parmenides and Heraclitus may actually have resulted from inaccurate modern translations of remaining fragments of their writing (Heidegger 1992).

3 As important as process philosophy is to the understanding of relational process ontology, Whitehead was a product of a Victorian era and Western culture. For example, he uses static, binary concepts such as hierarchy and dominance. Thus, our attention to language helps to "criticize, improve, and, in some respects, transcend" Whiteheadian thinking (Mesle 2008, 2).

4 We must acknowledge the great value Daniels's study brought to expanding our review of Native American scholars – well beyond what we had reviewed in previous publications and conference papers.

5 In Whitehead's conception of dual ultimates or sources of existence, all potential already exists in God through eternal objects; an amendment of Platonic Forms that allows actual entities more agency (Mesle 2008, 98). The second ultimate is the creative process of becoming. That which is chosen defines the "qualities" and "relations" expressed in any given actual entity (Whitehead 1979, 191).

6 Prozorov (2014a) notes that this understanding of the void is similar to Lacan's (1956) Real, Deleuze's (1991) virtual, and Heidegger's (2012) event.

7 This term draws from the word "apprehend" in the sense of grasping (Mesle 2008).

8 In a hologram, the whole image can be constructed from any part of the recording medium. This metaphor is used in quantum physics to describe the principle of holism (Bohm 1980).

6 Psychosocial theory

Ensembling individuality

Any attempt to reduce the human being by formally defining what a human being is and subjecting the human being to reductive analyses within a framework of formal structures, no matter what they are, is incompatible with the transdisciplinary vision.

– (Article 1 of the Charter of Transdisciplinarity, Nicolescu 2002, 148)

Many social crises can be traced back to problems of identity that have become a focus of political debate and conflict. Donati (2013) argues that in the contemporary moment, social strife is "happening on the macro, meso, and micro levels" (33), attributing this phenomenon to the atomistic and hierarchical assumptions of modernity. The persistence of divisive identities both within and between nations foments social strife; however, we cannot promote a universal identity that demands colonizing homogeneity. Instead, we must "constitute a new mosaic of vigorous cultures that *enrich* the human condition and that foster its *advance* rather than fragment and decompose it into new 'nationalities' " (Bookchin 2015e, loc. 2267). Social systems must evolve through the " 'principle of relationality' " (Donati 2014, 9) as "the new glue of society" (43).

Psychosocial theories define understandings of human identity as well as the social bond. These concepts are necessary to flesh out understandings of political ontology, which describes assumptions about the nature of human experience, identity, and social life (Catlaw 2007b; Howe 2006). The ongoing proliferation of social crises around the world indicates that our very survival demands a transformation of psychosocial theory in order to discover "new ways of perceiving each other" (Carlsson and Ramphal 1995, 46), a perspective that is "universalistic in its view of humanity, cooperative in its view of human relationships on all levels of life, and egalitarian in its idea of social relations" (Bookchin 2015e, loc. 2267).

As shown in Table 6.1, the psychosocial character of individuality is made up of two dialectical pairs in our Governance Typology. On the horizontal relational axis, an *embedded social condition* means that pre-existing social institutions define identity and human relation through designated roles, with the difference being the strength of the social institutions framing identity. An *independent social condition* means that individuals have no *a priori* social bond; they are pre-social beings. The possibility of a social bond depends on whether or not there is a stable identity that can enter into social contracts.

On the vertical process axis, a *unitary identity* is contained within itself in a cohesive fashion (Descartes 1980), whether the subject is considered as part of a unified, singular whole or a group of singular subjects. From an ontological perspective of Being, the *unitary identity* also endures through time and experience. While the physical body may change

Table 6.1 Dialectical psychosocial theory

	Socially Embedded	*Socially Independent*
Unitary Identity	individuality	Individuality
Decentered Identity	Particular individuality	Singular Individuality

(Source: Stout and Love 2016)

over time (Mesle 2008) and characteristics may shift (Hales and Johnson 2003), there is a stable core identity that has a coherent, teleological narrative. A *decentered identity* is fluid and responsive to changes either internal or external to the subject (Deleuze and Guattari 1983) – the individual is a qualitatively different being at different times and in different contexts with multiple understandings of self at each given moment.

These characteristics prefigure the type of social relationship anticipated among individuals: individuality, Individuality, Particular individuality, or Singular Individuality.[1] The resulting matrix is very similar to the cultural and ideological system developed by Douglas (1996). The degree of agency in identity formation ("grid") combined with the social condition – the relationship between the group and the individual – ("group") forms four ideal-types: Hierarchy, Individualism, Egalitarian Enclave, and Fatalistic. These types pair respectively with ours.

The relational dialectic of *embedded* versus *independent social condition* is synthesized through ***relationality***. Human existence cannot be fully explained in simplistic physical terms, nor can it be limited simply to radically individual subjectivity. Human potential is located in an "intercorporeal depth" that is an "*intertwining* between self and world" (Coles 2005, 76, 78). It is this ontological understanding that informs new conceptions of both individuality and collective life (Patton 2005). Humans are born into social groups in geographic places. The individual is interconnected with others and the environment in a "nested relatedness" (Bird-David 1999, S78). Given Relational Becoming, the social bond is both innate and socially constructed; therefore, the social condition is neither complete unity nor pure autonomy. Within this context, ***emergent multidimensionality*** synthesizes the continuity of an authentic *unitary identity* and the dynamic multiplicity of a relationally reflexive *decentered identity*. Individual identities have porous boundaries that allow interrelation in formation (Bohm 2004). Furthermore, physical, intellectual, emotional, spiritual, and sexual aspects of each unique individual are complexly interconnected and reflexive. The "true individual" is therefore a "manifold being" (Follett 1998, 291); "a society of selves with a *center of gravity*, which acts to bind the multiple waves, states, streams, and realms into something of a unified organization" (Wilber 2011, loc. 1033). Braidotti (2013) refers to this as "nomadic subjectivity" and likens it to "the social branch of complexity theory" (86).

Taken together, ***relationality*** and ***emergent multidimensionality*** produce Ensembling individuality, as depicted in Figure 6.1. This process enables *identity* to emerge in reflexive responsiveness to both internal and external change, indicated by the unique spirals which are both porous and interconnected. Follett (1998) provides a vivid metaphor for this activity, imagining herself "surrounded by fringes, that . . . overlap and that by means of these I join with others" (60). She refers to this complex, relational understanding of humans as the "new individualism" (Follett 1998, 73). There have been other attempts to name and understand this form of individuality, including the "socially situated self" (Dudley 1996,

Figure 6.1 Ensembling individuality

84), the "self in relation" (Miller 1984), the "person-in-community" (Cobb Jr. 2007, 567), "cultural individuality" (Dimock 1937, 418), "ensembled individualism" (Sampson 1988, 16), and "the individual-in-herself in-her-difference in society" (Farmer 2005, 187). Each definition seeks to explain the necessary relationship between the individual and society. "Such a self would be autonomous yet social, individuated yet defined by nonconflicting interests, rational but embodied in numerous different social relations, expressive of individuality yet public in orientation" (Warren 1992, 13). Through interconnection we do not lose our uniqueness; our individual perspectives are what make interconnection not only possible but meaningful (Levine 2011). As Cobb (1981) explains, "each person is a unique locus of intrinsic value and a unique contributor to society" (19).

This reinterpretation of both individual and group psychology "gives us a new approach to the social sciences" (Follett 2013c, 79). Following this train of thought, Adams (2011) suggests a neo-Heideggerian phenomenology that reflects a "sociology of possibilities" (Vahabzadeh 2002, 343). Critical social theorists are now "analyzing current events and development in a way that is congruent with the pluralist, contingent rhythms of materialization" (Coole and Frost 2010, 25) – what we describe as Relational Becoming – in an effort to find a non-colonizing universal identity that can support social equity and sustainability. Keating (2013) refers to such identities as "open-ended, and polyvocal, transcultural universals" (118) which are contextually specific, flexible, and open to change.

Relational Becoming also broadens the social situation to include the nonhuman world (Bennett 2001; Braidotti 2013; Coole and Frost 2010). When *identity* is "based on the immanence of relations" (Braidotti 2013, 82) it must also include nonhuman creatures, things, and physical place. This requires "recompositions of both subjectivity and community" (Braidotti 2013, 83) that provide a non-binary understanding of being-with that positions humans in nature. In accordance with deep ecology, this perspective is neither anthropocentric nor biocentric (Adams 2011). Hardt and Negri (2005) describe this relational process as "becoming common" (103), noting this shift has positive implications for environmental as well as social sustainability.

These understandings are posthumanist because the nature-culture continuum becomes a categorical distinction rather than a dualistic opposition (Braidotti 2013). To dissolve such dualisms, Latour (1999) uses the term "actant" to describe all things and beings that are able to perform actions, produce effects, and alter situations. This is "a more phenomenological approach to embodiment" (Coole and Frost 2010, 19), one placing humans in a web of vital materializations that no longer privileges them. In this way, Ensembling individuality integrates the phenomenological and the ontological – the posthuman "subject is materialist and vitalist, embodied and embedded" (Braidotti 2013, 188).

Relationality

Ensembling individuality produces a synthesis between *embedded* and *independent social condition* through the quality of ***relationality*** – a concept that acknowledges we exist within interconnected webs in which all entities (humans, nonhumans, physical objects, and places) co-determine one another. Starting from a consideration of social embeddedness, this perspective asserts that humans "have always been associated together in living, and association in conjoint behavior has affected their relations to one another as individuals" (Dewey 1957, 97). This idea follows Durkheim's (1964) notion of organic solidarity, which develops in contexts where subsistence demands interdependence. In other words, humans are social entities, "persons-in-societies, not persons-by-themselves" (Walzer 1984, 326). Because it is not possible for individuals to be separated from social groups, "man's specific humanity and his sociality are inextricably intertwined. Homo sapiens is always, and in the same measure, homo socius" (Berger and Luckmann 1966, 51). Social embeddedness cannot be denied.

Yet, individuality also cannot be denied in our differentiated experiences of Relational Becoming (Christ 2003); thus, this *social condition* is not homogenizing. Just as new patterns and textures in cloth comes from the differences in the strands and how they are woven together, differences in the human and social world are essential. Mead (1967) argues the self emerges from the interactions and acts of communication with other individuals; there is no pre-existing self that exists at birth but only that which arises from interaction within the social sphere. Individuals are "capable of creating a 'self' through their intimate engagement with all others in their system" (Wheatley 2006, 20). Similarly, Dewey (1999) sees the first instance of individuality emerging spontaneously but unshaped; it "is not something complete in itself . . . it develops into shape and form only through interaction with actual conditions" (81). Whitehead (1979) similarly explains that change comes from taking in new qualities from eternal objects as well as other actual entities in the process of becoming.

Thus, "separatedness and relatedness are mutually necessary postulates" (Laing 2001, 25) – we are interdependent.

To illustrate this interdependent *social condition*, Follett (2013c) draws from "the *Gestalt* theory" and its "concept of wholes" (79). She begins with the concept of "figure and ground" in which she sees "a rough analogy to individual and situation" (109–110); these two wholes are mutually defining with each "determined, not only by its constituents, but by their relation to one another" (Follett 2003h, 185–186). We cannot "divorce person and situation" (Follett 2003c, 60). In fact, individuality can *only* be perceived in the context of others: "My individuality is difference springing into view as relating itself with other differences" (Follett 1998, 63) – "there is only self-in-and-through-others" (8). Thus, *identity* exists within "an ensemble of social relations" (Lykes 1985, 364) – a "social individuality" (Lykes 1985, 362) that is "identifiable only within a (constantly moving) context" (Alcoff 1994, 117).

This interrelation between individual and context represents what Follett (2003h) refers to as "the situation" – a "complex emergent whole, [that] is formed by the interacting, the relating, of the constituent factors" (198). She describes this process as "the circular reflex" which exists "on infra-personal, personal and social levels" (Follett 2013c, 59) – a process of "infinite interactions by which both individual and society are forever a-making" (Follett 1998, 61), wherein both intrapersonal and interpersonal processes have agential and reflexive characteristics. The individual and the community are "engaged in a contemporaneous formation" (Eze 2008, 386). All facets of the individual are in circular response with the environment, including other beings, things, and places. This means that "the individual is not adjusted to society; there is a creating relation between them. . . . We are making our environment anew all the time, but that new environment is at the same time recreating us" (Follett 2013c, 128). We are "active-social" subjects (Harmon 1981, 40).

Thus, ***relationality*** is both ontological becoming (***relational assemblage***) and psychosocial becoming. Buber (1986) expresses a combination of the two in his philosophy, describing relation as inherent to human existence: "In the beginning is relation – a category of being, readiness, grasping form, mould for the soul; it is the *a priori* of relation, *the inborn Thou*" (38–39). He calls this the *I-Thou* (subject-subject) relationship as opposed to the *I-It* (subject-object) relationship, explaining "when *Thou* is spoken, the speaker has no *thing*; he has indeed nothing" (20). Instead, "the primary word *I-Thou* establishes the world of relation" (21) in which the individual "takes his stand in relation" (20). There is "a feeling of all in each and of each in all" (Aurobindo 1957, 989).

Also providing a linkage between these levels of relatedness, Heidegger (1996) describes the "the everydayness of being-with-one-another" (121). At the social level, we experience being-with-one-another as the "*they-self*," a "pre-ontological interpretation" of self that is created by one's immediate relatings, or entanglement – it "articulates the referential context of significance" (121). He contrasts this with his notion of being-with, meant to reflect an "authentic" or ontological condition of relationality that we can never fully access experientially. However, Heidegger assumes that we are ontological monads in social relation. As Husserl notes, "if we start from individuals (i.e., monads), how can we explain the formation and existence of community?" – a problem Husserl never successfully answered (Duranti 2010, 10).

Therefore, many phenomenologists simply focus on ***relationality*** as an experiential, as opposed to ontological characteristic. All beings "are inevitably composed of other particularities through their felt relations with other actualities" (Wang 2012, 104). As explained by Duranti (2010), Husserl conceived of intersubjectivity as the basic condition of human existence, ranging from a minimal awareness of others to active coordination perceptually, conceptually, and practically. Specifically, co-presence in space and time enables us to imagine ourselves as embodied beings in one another's places. This sense of sharing the world in common makes forms of social interaction such as language possible. In the act of being aware of oneself as an experiencing subject in the world with other subjects, we understand ourselves as related. This recognition of the "we-relationship" (Schutz 1967, 164) begins in an implicit manner – one that is pre-rational. Therefore, even without concern for how we came to be, we experience our fact of relatedness as we recognize our common beingness.

Braidotti (2013) points to Simone de Beauvoir's being-woman-in-the-world as the starting point for a humanist feminism that introduces the embodied and embedded subject. Daly (1973) sees this relation, or "cosmic covenant" (177–178), as the ultimate goal of the women's movement – to create in all humans an androgynous expression of *I-Thou* (see Buber 1986).[2] Similarly, Christ's (2003) feminist interpretation of process philosophy explains that "the self is relational, social, embodied, and embedded in the world" (3). Thus, "taking relation as ontologically basic simply means that we recognize human encounter and affective response as a basic fact of human existence" (Noddings 2003, 4).

This relatedness also extends beyond beings and things to particular ***places*** for many indigenous peoples (Waters 2004c, b). In remaining hunter-gatherer societies, underlying belief systems often imbue all things, beings, and places with life and consciousness; therefore, these peoples see "their world as an integrated entity" (Bird-David 1992, 30). In other words, there is interdependence among the human and nonhuman world (Beeman and Blenkinsop 2008) – the "inter-*relation* human/animal" is "constitutive of the identity of *each*" (Braidotti 2013, 79). For instance, the Nayaka recognize humans as living in relation with animals, objects, and places. Further, "*As and when* and *because* they engage in and maintain relationships with other beings, they constitute them as a kind of person" (Bird-David 1999, S73). Thus, "Rather than viewing ourselves as being ***in*** relationship with other people or things, we *are* the relationships that we hold and are part of" (Wilson 2009, 80).

These perspectives are reflected in advances in biology which demonstrate that "the immediate surroundings should be understood not only as context but as an integratable part of organismic identity. The organism-environment complex co-evolves" (Ben-Jacob, Shapira, and Tauber 2011, 62). Integration within such systems can be so deep that symbiotic relationships between organisms "may generate morphological and metabolic change in either or both of the partners, and eventually even genetic dependencies" (MacAllister 2011, 96). Drawing from complexity theory, Briggs and Peat (1999) explain that "each of us as an individual is inter-connected to the systems of nature, society, and thought that surround and flow through us . . . within this same chaos is born all the physical and psychological order that we know" (4).

Thus, contemporary sciences – both social and physical – increasingly "rest on an enlarged sense of inter-connection between self and others, including the non-human or 'earth' others" (Braidotti 2013, 47–48). Connolly (2011) therefore refers to the social condition as the "human estate" (5) – a particular world of concern as opposed to the other force-fields of becoming with which we are related. This perspective has been called a "*zoe*-egalitarianism" (71) in reference to life or existence writ large. In effect, human ***relationality*** exists within an interconnected web that includes the whole of the Earth's ecosystem (Margulis, Asikainen, and Krumbein 2011). Humans are not in a place of dominance achieved through hierarchical position or competition – neither over or against our fellow humans *nor* over the nonhuman flora, fauna, and matter that makes up the rest of our world.

This perspective assumes that the self, "rooted as it is in relation, identifies *joy* as a basic human affect" (Noddings 2003, 6). We feel "joy in relatedness – whether in relation to persons, other living things, or ideas" (Noddings 2003, 132). Joy occurs during moments of happiness as well as in long-term reflection on the bittersweet whole, with all of its inevitable pain and sadness (Braidotti 2010; Christ 2003): "Beauty involves both harmony and contrast" (Mesle 1993, loc. 1322). Indeed, the Navajo call this relational approach to life the Beauty Way. Joy is not hedonistic or narcissistic pleasure – it is happiness with and for others in our acknowledgment of ***relationality***.

Emergent multidimensionality

Emergent multidimensionality is an understanding of self that synthesizes *unitary* and *decentered identity*. The mind-body dualism is dissolved and the self is composed of constantly changing and interlocking material and nonmaterial elements that interact with the environment. The human is not bifurcated between body and mind or spirit; such Cartesian dualisms make "the most obvious events of our embodied existence impossible" (Mesle 2008, loc. 474). Even Descartes (1980) himself admits there is a "mingling of the mind and body" (95). The interrelation of these aspects of self is reflected in several bodies of thought: phenomenological intersubjectivity assumes a natural unity of consciousness and body (Husserl 1982); process philosophy affirms "the body-mind continuum" (Christ 2003, 24); and many indigenous traditions understand human existence as an interconnected mind, body, and spirit (Henry and Pene 2001). In more contemporary philosophy, new materialism explores how the material, including human bodies, may be more similar to nonmaterial aspects of experience, including the human mind (Coole and Frost 2010).

Across these diverse sources, there is a shared refusal to bifurcate in any way the holistic understanding of matter/nature and mind/consciousness/energy/spirit (Latour 2011). "Subjectivity is multidimensional" (Haraway 1988, 586), because the human subject "is ontologically polyvocal," with physical, emotional, intellectual, spiritual, and sexual aspects of embodiment (Braidotti 2013, 93). As Follett (1998) explains, "since man is a complex of experiences there are many selves in each one" (20). However, identity is not merely an aggregation of traits because "no single characteristic of a man has much meaning until it is understood in its relation to his other characteristics" (Follett 2013c, 96). Personality is an "integrative unity, of a functional whole" (Follett 2003h, 185).

Desire plays a critical role in identity formation. However, an integrative perspective is decidedly not Freudian; desire is understood as a creative drive to change and develop, "as plenitude and over-flowing, not as lack" (Braidotti 2013, 136–137). Follett (2013c) explains that desire is also not a subject-object relationship with others and the environment. Just as "the self is always in flux weaving itself out of its relations" (Follett 1919, 577), individual desires are constantly being created anew in the relational situation: "personality is produced through the integrating of 'wishes,' that is, courses of action which the organism sets itself to carry out" (Follett 1919, 576). We are "internally influenced by the other such that one's own experience is partially constituted by the other," impacting our "moment-by-moment identity" (Oord 2005, 926). The multifarious desires within the individual are integrated in the process of psychological development, while the multitudinous desires of individuals are integrated in the relational group process of social development. Each desire is therefore always "an integrating desire which is continuously interweaving with the separate desires" of each member of the group (Follett 2013c, 112).Through this process both individual and group identities are generated.

These assumptions are reflected in transpersonal psychology, which incorporates the nonmaterial characteristics of human experience and identity (Ryan 2008). This school of thought highlights "experiences in which the sense of identity or self extends beyond (trans) the individual or personal to encompass wider aspects of humankind, life, psyche or cosmos" (Walsh and Vaughan 1993, 199). Early references to the term "transpersonal" were made by William James, who used it to refer to intersubjective perceptions (Ryan 2008); however, his understanding of consciousness (discussed in Chapter 7) clearly extends beyond physiological mind into the realm of the spiritual in his studies of religious experience (James 1997) and the philosophical underpinnings of his "transpersonal worldview" (Ryan 2008, 22).

Indeed, many prominent scholars of the late nineteenth century acknowledged the "spiritual dimension of the psyche" (Ryan 2008, 22) beyond the mind-body duality. These studies of "extraordinary subjective experience" (Sutich 1969, iv) have since included Jung's (1969) concept of the collective unconscious, Maslow's (1968) investigations of peak experiences and self-actualization through a "constant, never ending, fluxuating, and complex" (Maslow 1987, 7), "holistic-dynamic" process (15), and Grof's (1975) explorations of nonordinary consciousness. While perhaps not mainstream, and at times misinterpreted – as in the case of Maslow (see Duncan 2008) – these concepts have been quite widely adopted in the field of psychology.

More recently, Wilber (2011) developed a schema to explain psychosocial patterns that builds on the work of humanistic psychologist, Clare Graves (1970). Graves theorized that human development is the product of an open and dynamic bio-psycho-social system that evolves in relation to experiences within particular cultures (Lee 2002). Through empirical study, he identified a continuum of emergent, developmental waves that can be seen in both individuals and society. Beck and Cowan (1995) further developed this model, categorizing the first six stages as "first-tier" thinking, while the latter three are characterized as "second-tier" thinking. Each developmental wave decreases narcissism and ethnocentrism while increasing the capacity to take deeper and broader perspectives of human experience into consideration.

In contemporary social theory, ***emergent multidimensionality*** is sometimes referred to as intersectionality – the recognition that each individual has many dynamic components of self that are always interpenetrating and changing reflexively in the situation (Crenshaw 1989; Collins 1990). Without integration this can lead to "double consciousness" where one's various identities are placed into competition with one another for primacy (Du Bois 2003, 9). ***Emergent multidimensionality*** recognizes that the intersection – the place where these identities overlap within individual experience – is greater than the aggregated sum of those identities. "In attempting to work out a synthesis, the self has added a third element which is greater than the sum of its severed parts. That third element is a new consciousness – a "mestiza consciousness" (Anzaldúa 1987) – which dissolves the dualities of identity that create double consciousness (Saldívar-Hull 2000), while honoring the multiple dimensions of self.

This requires a "multilayered texture" of identity and experience such as that deeply rooted in feminist of color theorizing (Combahee River Collective 1995, 235). Black feminist theorizing, in particular, arose to resist the damaging homogenization in both the feminist and black power movements; the former erased the racialization of experience while the latter erased gender (Hull, Scott, and Smith 1982). Developing a notion of "multiple consciousness" (King 1995), feminists of color resist the homogenizing " 'monist' approach to liberation ideologies" (King 1995, 299) that require individuals to "pluck out some one aspect" of oneself "and present this as the meaningful whole" (Lorde 1995, 289) – an approach that erases differences within oppressed groups and thereby reinforces oppression (Hull, Scott, and Smith 1982). Instead, these theorists seek to draw out these multiple layers of self in resistance to the "*mythical norm*" inherent in hegemonic identities (Lorde 1995).

This complex understanding of individuality is therefore "without compromise to the *whole* of [individuals'] own identities" (Moraga 2015, xxi). To illustrate that identity formation need not be homogenizing, Cohen's (1997) explanation of queerness "stands in direct contrast to the normalizing tendencies of hegemonic sexuality" (438). Declaring oneself queer is a resistance to societal demands toward categorization, classification, or assimilation. In short, rather than demanding a subject position for a *particular* group identity or an erasure of dominating social identities, queering creates an opening for radical, relational identity. This type of individuality is neither socially isolated, nor "rooted in ideas of static, stable sexual identities and behavior" (438) that define group identity. In this non-hegemonic claim,

> queer people, acknowledging their contested identity, do the daily work of making these spaces whole, of crafting their own paths through and around institutions that exist to exclude them, and in so doing create ways of living in the world that open up the possibilities for others.
>
> (Lampmann 2016)

In this way, the queering of spaces (ideological and physical) is a broad demand for solidarity among all identities in the quest for autonomy and human flourishing within social systems. This " 'post-structuralist' approach" generates "a certain discursive space in which subjectivity can be reconfigured" by finding the "openings, interstices, indeterminancies, *aporias* and cracks within structures" (Newman 2011, 62). To generate these spaces, Anzaldúa (2004) calls for "a consciousness of the Borderlands" (729), one that exists at the thresholds between identities and experiences. Such openings provide the ongoing opportunity for constructive conflict and developmental harmonization in ever-increasing complexity, generating "an infinite multiplicity" (Deleuze and Guattari 1987, 254). As hooks (1990) argues, it is in these spaces of "radical openness" that we find "a central location for the production of a counter-hegemonic discourse that is not just found in words but in habits of being and the way one lives" (149). Considering these ideas, *identity* is "structured by multi-directional relationality" in "web-like, scattered and poly-centered" forms (Braidotti 2013, 164).

This radical and relational understanding of identity is post-Marxist because it no longer imagines the possibility of a substantive universal identity (Tønder and Thomassen 2005a). While allowing freedom in identity formation, radical perspectives promote agonistic respect and critical responsiveness to all differences, particularly those resisting social encoding. This perspective refutes the notion that identity is constitutive; society cannot exclude becoming, it can only place it in tension with expected subject positions, which is a social and political issue as opposed to an ontological one (Widder 2005). Therefore, the "we" orientation of ***relationality*** recognizes an undefined commonality that demands we keep open the definition of "us" (Tønder 2005). This prevents the binary of inclusion/exclusion that is inevitable when community is defined in particularist group terms. Instead, community identity is based simply on an inclusion that always maintains an open space, or unnamed part, that invites new members, new ideas, and new subjectivities into the community (Laclau 1996): "We, who are also parts of the moving present, create ourselves as we create an unknown future" (Dewey 1999, 83).

Through ***emergent multidimensionality***, the multifarious aspects of a particular person are in circular response creating *identity* in a unifying process. Understanding this complex process can ensure that "each and every individual is treated in her fullest human dimensions (psycho, socio, bio, spiritual, and other dimensions)" (Farmer 2005, xiv). However, because these dimensions are dynamic and in relation, each human is "a composite of the roles in which you participate, even though you overflow that composite" (Connolly 2013, 182). As in ***embodiment*** and ***creative emergence***, "one must still have chaos in oneself to give birth to a dancing star" (Nietzsche 1969, 17). Thus, echoing the process view of identity articulated by Emma Goldman (Bertalan 2011), poststructuralist anarchism depicts human identity as performative rather than essentialist (May 1994). From this dynamic, multidimensional perspective, a human is understood less as a life form that "progresses linearly through time" – in other words, less unitary – "and more as a dynamic network of linked points on a tangle-prone web" (Rico 2011, 259). Thus, human beings might be more aptly called human *becomings*.[3]

Ensembling individuality

Ensembling individuality combines ***relationality*** and ***emergent multidimensionality*** to understand personhood as emergent and multidimensional (physical, intellectual, emotional, spiritual, and sexual) and dynamic within a relational *social condition* that includes other human beings and all of creation. *Identity* is complex, including an integration of various aspects of self, others, and the physical environment. This changes one's developmental task to "'finding my place in the whole'" while recognizing that "my place is a matter of infinite relation, and of infinitely changing relation" (Follett 1998, 65). As Braidotti (2013) notes, "the posthuman condition urges us to think critically and creatively about who and what we are actually in the process of becoming" (86). Each person is a "self-generated mosaic" (Adams 2011, 132) that has no limits in its potential creativity (Bookchin 1994b).

Acknowledging both ***relationality*** and ***emergent multidimensionality***, the individual exists through "collaboration with all the powers of the universe. Man lives on several planes and his development depends on the uniting of them" (Follett 2013c, 145–146). It is this integration that produces "the 'balanced' individual" (123). In positive psychology the pursuit of authentic fulfillment acknowledges the very real and difficult problems people face, yet seeks to develop strength in all aspects of identity formation and expression – within the self and within relationships (Seligman and Csikszentmihalyi 2000) – calling on individuals to use their "signature strengths every day to produce authentic happiness and abundant gratification" (Seligman 2002, 13). Supporting this intrapersonal and interpersonal developmental process is precisely the project of the humanist school of psychology, which emphasizes the inherent motivation for growth and personal fulfillment – the pursuit of self-actualization (Maslow 1968; Rogers 1961) and Jung's (1970) individuation.

Implications for the social bond

Ensembling individuality and its assumptions of ***relationality*** and ***emergent multidimensionality*** have profound implications for the understanding of society that deserve specific attention. Both ontological and phenomenological understandings of ***relationality*** have been drawn together in relational sociology, which combines process philosophy with classical sociology from scholars who privilege relations over substance, including Marx, Weber,

Durkheim, Mead, Simmel, Dewey, Bourdieu, and Luhmann (Emirbayer 1997). Extensive expositions have been made by Donati (2011) and Crossley (2011), and the foundational assumption is that *society is constructed through relation*. Thus, as Donati (2014) argues, "it is necessary to elaborate a new theory of difference (as for personal and social identity), permitting us to understand it and manage it in a relational way" (148).

As an ontological condition, ***relational assemblage*** is a "bond" that interconnects all things that exist. It is a "co-presence" of human and non-human others in which our many intersections form "the relational bond that connects us" (Braidotti 2013, 169). Evans (1998) argues this inherent connectedness is expressed in the assumptions of advanced science – quantum theory, chaos theory, complexity theory, and contemporary ecological sciences. From this perspective, interconnectedness "binds all together within one continuous web of creation" (Stewart-Harawira 2005a, 155). It is a natural life force that is expressed through human thought, deed, and relationship (Dewey 1934; Follett 1998) that enables a "sense of commonality" (Stivers 2008, 100) or "impersonal fellowship" (Bohm 2004, 37). Thus, it is a form of resonance that does not imply a sense of warmth, affective tie, or inherent agreement (Catlaw 2007d).

From this ontological grounding, ***relationality*** moves from physiological circular response to psychosocial "circular behavior" (Follett 2013c, 99) that is intentional. Social agreements must be made consciously and actively by actual people (Arendt 1977). This is the fundamental "*reason* for dialogue" (Bohm 2004, 37). Through a social form of morphogenesis (Archer 1995; Donati 2014), active participation reinforces the social bond: "We belong to our community just in so far as we are helping to make that community then loyalty follows, then love follows" (Follett 1998, 59). This "social process is a process of coöperating experience" (Follett 2013c, 30) that "cannot be imposed by an outside body. It is essentially, basically, by its very nature, a process of auto-controlled activity" (Follett 2013g, 82). The tendency is toward cooperation because of the felt sense of interdependence (Duranti 2010) as well as the desire for belonging (Maslow 1943). With the assumption of ***relationality*** "authentic trust and openness can emerge in a group context, without its members having shared extensive personal history" (Nichol 2004, xviii–xix), yet allow for a "love evolved from some actual group relation" (Follett 1998, 193).

According to social construction theory, social practices produce social systems and institutions which, in turn, reproduce social practices that both constrain and enable action (Giddens 1984). Thus, the social bond is enacted in all social domains – in a "multitude of intertwining spheres" (Donati 2014, 35). This suggests that social institutions have the capacity to impact the expression of the social bond. Even if there is something that innately binds us together, it can be either hindered (generating fear) or fostered (generating trust) (Donati 2013). Individualist conceptions of the relationship between the individual and the group view the social bond as a problem to be solved (McSwite 2006). These perspectives seek autonomy (independence) from a subservient (dependent) condition (Gilligan 1995). Yet, the sense of difference of self from others, is "*the* problem of human living" (Bernstein 1991, 75). These atomistic views require social contracts that enforce trust and reciprocity, which, in turn, generate the social "lubricant" for effective interactions and the social "glue" of group identity (Putnam 2000). Such transactional conceptions of social capital reduce the social bond to its instrumental value (Putnam et al. 1983).

Relationality transforms dominating and transactional conceptions of the social bond; it is neither forged by a transcendent source (individuality), resultant from voluntary cause and effect (Individuality), established by being a part of the transcendent whole (Particular individuality), or impossible without coercion (Singular Individuality). Instead, ***relationality*** enables us to "realize the true force of the social bonds which knit men together, and which are the true foundation of a normal social life" (Goldman 2007, 49). The social bond is "an emerging, *sui generis* reality" (Donati 2014, 28). Adorno (1998) describes this social state as "differentiation without domination" (247). This relational condition offers a synthesis that is not based on societal norms, rules, or expectations, but rather a sense of difference without threat (Carr and Zanetti 1999). Each subject exists "within the web of the opportunities and constraints afforded by society" (Farmer 2005, 40), yet they also retain the power to influence these networks through their social relationships. Individuals exhibit intentional social action as opposed to reactive social behavior (Weber 1994a, b, c). Through this subject-subject interweaving of selves, the individual "is never yet embedded in the meshes but is forever free for every new possibility of a forever unfolding life" (Follett 1998, 295).

This praxis draws on ***emergent multidimensionality*** to offer insight into how we might actively renegotiate both ***identity*** and institutional context (Newman 2011), transforming both individuals and society (Keating 2013). For example Bookchin (2015e) notes that nationalism is a form of tribalism writ large; it is just another form of particularity or identity politics, but it is backed by the power of the state. All such particular identities generate barriers to finding human community across difference. In contrast, "to view the world today through a feminist of color lens shatters all barriers of state-imposed nationality" (Moraga 2015, xvi). However, it is equally important that both singularities and particularities challenge universal identity so that it remains open to new integrations, becoming ever more complex, inclusive, and adaptive – allowing for "variations in relation to other variations" (Follett 2013c, 70). Thus, the social bond exists between emergent multidimensional beings. In this context, social construction is a confrontation of difference that generates ever new integrations where "heterogeneity, not homogeneity" is sought (Follett 1998, 40) – the individual maintains a unique and authentic, yet dynamic, sense of self in relation.

Follett (1998) argues that the desire to engage in this co-creation is the fundamental purpose of social life: "an irresistible force compelling every member" (83). An individual's "sustenance is relation and he seeks forever new relations" (Follett 1919, 582), because "community is that intermingling which evokes creative power" (577). Similarly, for Whitehead the purpose of life is the "creative advance of the world" (Mesle 2008, 98). Relational experience is the "self-enjoyment of being one among many, and of being one arising out of the composition of many" (Whitehead 1979, 145). This generative power urges us on, "from the amoeba and its food to man and man, as the release of energy, the evocation or calling forth of new powers one from the other" (Follett 2013c, 303).

Similarly, the novelty generated through the interrelation between unique individuals "generally increases the enjoyment of experience; for the variety of possibilities that are actualized in an experience adds richness to the experience, and the element of novelty lends zest and intensity of enjoyment" (Cobb Jr. and Griffin 1976, 28). However, societies of entities also seek harmony among differences. Whitehead (1979) uses music to illustrate: Two voices singing different but complementary notes offer to the listener a simple enjoyment without much intensity. As the diversity of voices increases to a three- or four-part harmony, the diversity and complexity increase enjoyment and intensity. Indeed, "the criterion for progress is, therefore, richness of experience" (Griffin 2007, 45).

It follows that to generate the most creative experience, we must be sure that social groups enable "the whole field of desire to be viewed" (Follett 2003b, 39). The greater the number of desires brought into integrative process, the higher the level of synthesis that can be achieved. This reflexive understanding of the social bond becomes critically important as the underpinning for action-oriented theories: ethics, political theory, economic theory, and administrative theory.

Integrative pathways

An Integrative synthesis must generate pathways that are easily traversed by those holding other positions. Ensembling individuality must provide concepts that sufficiently meet fundamental principles within the other perspectives, or at least create a foundation for dialogue and the development of shared understandings. As illustrated in Figure 6.2, we imagine the shared characteristics shown in Table 6.2 as pathways into a dynamic synthesis that is always open to contestation and change.

Going back to our discussion of dialectical synthesis in the chapter's introduction we know that an Integrative understanding of the social condition must enable both a *socially embedded* sense of connection and a *socially independent* sense of autonomy. Ensembling individuality understands the social condition to be relational, but in a nonhierarchical and

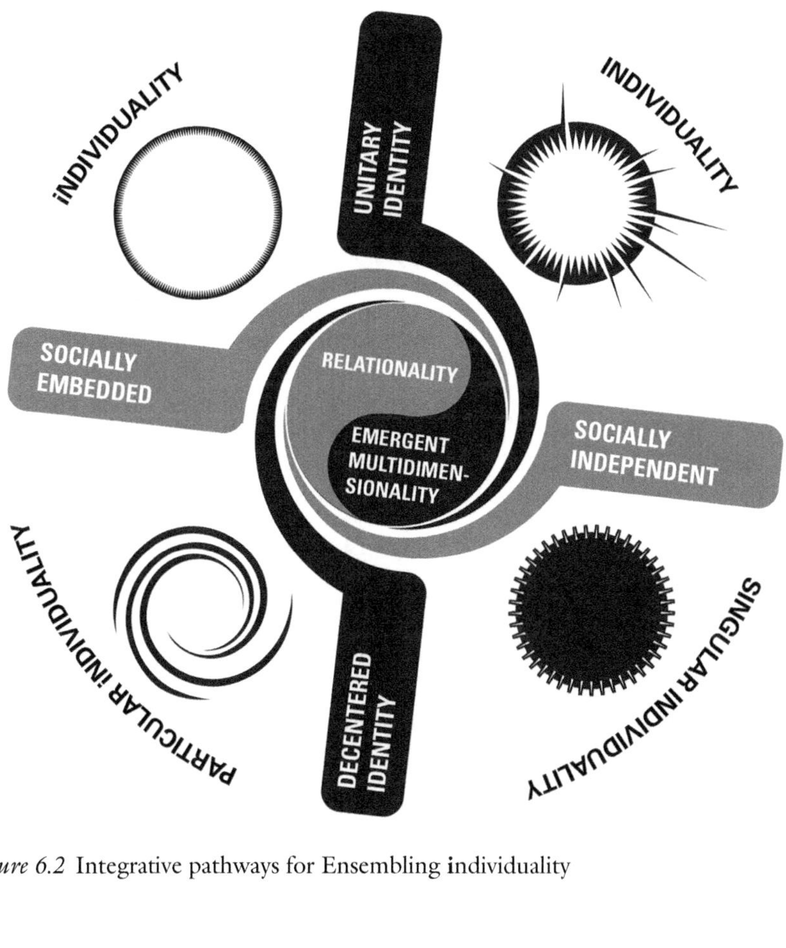

Figure 6.2 Integrative pathways for Ensembling individuality

agential fashion, thus preserving autonomy within ***relationality***. To meet the basic assumptions of both *unitary* and *decentered* understandings of *identity*, Integrative individuality must enable both continuity and change. Ensembling individuality establishes a process of identity formation that integrates various aspects of the self along with relational influences from other beings, things, and places. While it is fluid, ***emergent multidimensionality*** ensures that there is an authentic self that is not simply subject to the vagaries of social construction that accommodates a sense of continuity.

However, the primary concerns of each distinct position need to be addressed in order establish a starting point for dialogue with the Integrative perspective, as shown in Table 6.2.

The notion of individuality is primarily concerned with establishing an acceptable identity within society and carrying out that role successfully. Ensembling individuality conceptualizes an emergent identity that is responsive to the group through ***relationality*** and maintains continuity of characteristics of ***emergent multidimensionality***. The notion of Individuality is primarily concerned with autonomy in both identity and social relations, while accepting the minimal constraints of a social contract. ***Emergent multidimensionality*** ensures that there is agency in development of individual; however, this freedom is responsive to ***relationality***. Particular individuality is primarily concerned with clarity in social identity and relations, even as they change in response to society. ***Emergent multidimensionality*** and ***relationality*** combined ensure change is reflexive with the group. Singular Individuality is primarily concerned with freedom from social construction in identity formation. While no understanding of society can provide complete negative liberty, ***relationality*** ensures a large degree of agency for all identities, with consideration of their full complexity through ***emergent multidimensionality***.

Table 6.2 Integrating psychosocial concerns

Ideal-Type	*Characteristics*	*Primary Concerns*	*Synthesis Solution*
individuality	*unitary identity, socially embedded*	Group connection and stability of identity	***Relationality*** in identity formation; continuity in characteristics of ***emergent multidimensionality***
Individuality	*unitary identity, socially independent*	Autonomy in identity and social relations within a social contract	Agency within ***emergent multidimensionality*** is responsive to ***relationality***
Particular individuality	*decentered identity, socially embedded*	Clarity of identity within a changing group	***Multidimensionality*** allows for both continuity and change; ***relationality*** guides both
Singular Individuality	*decentered identity, socially independent*	Fluidity and autonomy in identity formation	***Multidimensionality*** allows for complex and fluid identity; ***relationality*** retains agency

Notes

1 The big/little distinction designates the assumption that the "big" (capitalized) concept is a social construction rather than an ontological fact, while the "little" (lowercase) concept is more ontologically accurate. We make these claims based on the impossibility of a human existing outside of the social group (Stout and Love 2016).
2 While we appreciate the move toward a more inclusive and nonhierarchical sense of identity, we acknowledge critique of Daly's work as overlooking the importance of difference within such a universal.
3 Thanks to Cheryl Simrell King for this clever self-descriptor.

7 Epistemological concepts
Integral Knowing

The transdisciplinary vision is resolutely open insofar as it goes beyond the field of the exact sciences and demands their dialogue and their reconciliation with the humanities and the social sciences as well as with art, literature, poetry and spiritual experience.

Authentic education cannot value abstraction over other forms of knowledge. It must teach contextual, concrete and global approaches. Transdisciplinary education revalues the role of intuition, imagination, sensibility and the body in the transmission of knowledge.
– (Articles 5 and 11 of the Charter of Transdisciplinarity, Nicolescu 2002, 150)

What knowledge is considered and how knowledge is constructed must change in order to resolve the social, economic, and environmental crises we confront today – they cannot be resolved using the knowledge base that enabled them to happen in the first place. Whitehead (1979) insists that consciousness "is the crown of experience, only occasionally attained" (267); however, this perpetuates hierarchical categorization based on complexity or sentience. We argue that the continuum of experience cannot be conceived hierarchically – doing so enables destruction of the physical planet in the same way that hierarchical differentiation between animate and inanimate entities, humans and animals, as well as between categories of humans, enables their abuse as commodities. Relational Becoming and Ensembling individuality demand *new ways of knowing* that are relational and nonhierarchical.

Indeed, some argue that global citizens must "see with new eyes and understand with new minds before they can truly turn to new ways of living" (Carlsson and Ramphal 1995, 47). Our interconnectedness calls for "a reconfiguration of consciousness, one that produces a new and different sense of subjectivity" (McSwite 1997, 14). Although we "tend to think of the subjective as pertaining to the self, and the objective to the world" where "the subjective is a matter of value, while the world is a matter of fact," these can no longer be held separate (Eagleton 2003, 137); we must join value and fact in the pursuit of sustainability. Such epistemological integration is a "pragmatist and feminist relational (e)pistemology" in which knowledge derives from an awareness of "how interconnected we all are, not just to each other personally, but also to our social environments, our cultures, past, present, and future, as well as our surrounding natural environment, and the forces of the universe as a whole" (Thayer-Bacon 2010, 2–3).

Epistemologies have long been a principal focus in governance scholarship because, as social theorists Michel Foucault and Bent Flyvbjerg argue, "power defines what constitutes knowledge and rationality; indeed, power ultimately defines 'what counts as reality'" (Brooks

2002, 91). Distinctive patterns of political decision making are based on "embedded assumptions and social constructions of reality" (Schneider and Ingram 1997, x). The bifurcation of philosophy and science enables the splitting of the *why* of phenomena from the *how*. Instead, we must use methods that enable us to consider both simultaneously (Stengers 2011). Whitehead (1967) argues that the metaphysical adventure of hope and the scientific adventure of experimentation must come together so that we can attend to that which is important for the situation at hand. These claims suggest that traditional approaches to knowing and understanding are not working; rationalism, empiricism, idealism, and constructivism (or epistemic anarchism) are not producing the knowledge needed to live sustainably.

Epistemological concepts describe how truth claims are justified and how knowledge is structured. As shown in Table 7.1, on the horizontal relational axis, *internal justification* means truth is validated by formal, intellectual logic (rationalism) or *a priori* belief (idealism). *External justification* requires verification *a posteriori* through systematic observation (empiricism) or through various "snapshots" of reality that are fixed through power dynamics (epistemic anarchism). On the vertical process axis, knowledge can be produced through either *foundational* or *coherentist structure*. A *foundational structure* offers a set of static truths upon which all knowledge is built in an axiomatic manner. *Coherentist structure* is produced by testing logical congruence amongst accepted truths.

Looking toward a synthesis, Ensembling individuality suggests we come to know the world within a ***relational*** social condition through an ***emergent multidimensional*** process of experience. We therefore experience the world through a dynamic process interweaving socially given concepts and individual perceptions. ***Embodied knowing*** resolves the relational dialectic between *internal* and *external justification* by using both types of information accessed in a variety of ways. The process dialectic between static *foundational structure* and dynamic *coherentist structure* is resolved through ***situated knowing***, which synthesizes subjectivity and objectivity through intersubjective agreement using the method of integration. Bringing the two ways of knowing together, consensus about what is "true" is established through a participatory process of knowledge production and mutual adjustment – "I know as I relate" (Bird-David 1999, S78).

Embodied knowing integrates concept (internal) with percept (external) by expanding accepted mechanisms of *justification* to include conscious, subconscious, and supraconscious ways of knowing. These approaches are found in a variety of disciplines and approaches to knowing, including panexperientialism (Tollefsen 2002; Wang 2012), tacit knowing (Polanyi 1974), intuition (Bergson 2007), holistic perception (Ferré 1998), and creative imagination (Braidotti 2013; Whitehead 1967). The importance of these alternative ways of knowing is recognized by a variety of spiritual traditions, psychotherapy, and even management theory – each of which has developed approaches for accessing ***embodied knowing***.

Situated knowing integrates subjectivity and objectivity in knowledge production. An excellent example is Haraway's (1988) "situated epistemology" and "situated knowledges,"

Table 7.1 Dialectical epistemological concepts

	Internal Justification	*External Justification*
Foundational Structure	Rationalism	Empiricism
Coherentist Structure	Idealism	Epistemic Anarchism

(Source: Stout and Love 2016)

which she argues move from the dichotomy of positivist universalism versus postmodern socially constructed relativism into the new terrain of "feminist objectivity" (583). Drawing from pragmatism, intersubjective agreement is grounded in what Susan Haack (2009) calls "foundherentism" – a *structure* of knowledge which dissolves the dualism between foundationalism and coherentism (117). Foundherentism allows for quasi-foundational truths that are determined through ***situated knowing***, and which are malleable, subject to ongoing intersubjective interrogation within epistemic communities, and open to contestation and re-evaluation. From a foundherentist perspective, "we need not give up the quest or hope of truth itself" – indeed we might combine "a pervasive fallibilism with a modest optimism about our epistemic condition" (Haack 2009, 284).

All humans are born into social groups, languages, and epistemic communities that mediate individual experience in various ways. Epistemic communities co-construct knowledge by drawing together ***embodied knowing*** and ***situated knowing*** in the process of forming intersubjective agreement. The experiential knowledge of ***embodied knowing*** provides input to the integrative process of ***situated knowing*** in which truth claims are affirmed through intersubjective agreement. These agreements are, in turn, justified through ***embodied knowing***. This cyclical, reflexive approach eliminates the "epistemological gap" (Ferré 1998) between the *internal* (mind) and the *external* (empirical world) because thought (hypothesis and analysis) and action (experience and observation) are intertwined in an ongoing process of knowledge production, justification, and structuration. Cook and Wagenaar (2012) refer to this as an "epistemology of practice" that addresses the "*eternally unfolding present*" (9).

Whereas traditional Western approaches to knowing split phenomena (objects as interpreted by human perception and understanding) from noumena (objects beyond reason as *things-in-themselves*) (Kant 1998), an Integrative approach follows the quantum physics assertion that "reality is composed not of things-in-themselves or things-behind-phenomena but of things-in-phenomena" (Barad 2007, 140). Similarly, psychologist Carl Jung explains that it is probable that "psyche and matter are two different aspects of one and the same thing" (as quoted in Shelburne 1988, 20), dissolving the mind-body dualism (Christ 2003; Gergen 2009; Haraway 1988; Mesle 2008). In other words, human perception is "embodied," not parsed out into "mind" beyond "matter" (Lakoff 2003). Phenomenology also considers the meaning of lived experience as a natural unity of consciousness and body (Husserl 1989; Merleau-Ponty 2012), conceptualized by Merleau-Ponty (1968) as "flesh" (111). In this sense, phenomenologists "adhere to a version of both 'realism' and 'idealism' at the same time" (Beyer 2013). Finally, for cognitive ecology, knowledge is "embodied, and richly multimodal" (Hutchins 2010, 712).

Despite the circular relationship in the *justification* and *structure* of knowledge, the following sections explore these ideas independently and then describe how they come together in what we call Integral Knowing, in reference to the inclusive intrapersonal and interpersonal epistemological processes that produce it.

Embodied knowing

Embodied knowing is a process that synthesizes *internal* and *external justification* of truth claims through a combination of experiential perceptions (e.g., panexperientialism, tacit knowing, intuition, holistic perception, creative imagination) and intellectual conceptualizations given by one's epistemic community. In this way, the testing of truth claims draws from both internal and external ways of knowing; "Justification is a matter of the *experiential anchoring* and *explanatory integration* of the subject's *evidence* with respect to a belief"

(Haack 2009, 192). At the intrapersonal level, each individual synthesizes understandings coming from all forms of experience – sensory perception, emotional response, the mind, the unconscious, and the spirit. Following from ontological ***embodiment*** and ***emergent multidimensionality***, we describe the information from these varied sources of experience as ***embodied knowing***.

Embodied knowing acknowledges that "experiential evidence, sensory and introspective, is the *only* ultimate evidence we have with respect to empirical beliefs" (Haack, 275), but widens the scope of *intra*personal experiences considered. For example, panexperientialism explains embodied experience as a form of knowing available to all beings, things, and places (Griffin 2007). Polanyi (1974) uses the term *tacit knowing* to explain the type of experiential or implicit understanding human beings have that is beyond formal, codified, explicit knowledge. Knowing in this way is felt rather than thought. Similarly, intuition, builds on tacit knowledge, allowing individuals to respond to new situations through insight gleaned from prior experience. Holistic perception draws together both physical and nonmaterial sources of information in a continuum consciousness, from sensory perception throughout various types of individual and transpersonal consciousness. These experiential forms of knowing enable creative imagination and reconceptualizations of previous knowledge.

At the *inter*personal level, ***embodied knowing*** acknowledges that psychosocial ***relationality*** mediates our subjective experience, particularly through mechanisms such as language and intellectual concepts given to us through our social groups and epistemic communities. This relational subjectivity mediates intrapersonal perception through phenomenological intersubjectivity.

Panexperientialism

Panexperientialism claims that all things (human and nonhuman, living and inert) experience (Griffin 2007).[1] Reconsidering ***creative emergence*** through an epistemological lens, "wherever there is a causal interaction, there is information, and wherever there is information, there is experience. One can find information in a rock – when it expands or contracts, for example – or even in the different states of an electron" (Chalmers 1996, 297). This suggests that from the quantum level up, all things and beings produce knowledge. Sentient consciousness, such as that of human being, is merely a more complex order of experience that exists along a continuum of experiencing (Griffin 2007). Recognizing this full multidimensional spectrum, ***embodied knowing*** extends beyond the physical senses and intellectual thought mediated by language to include "pre-sensory and pre-linguistic experiences" (Wang 2012, 125). It is an "undifferentiated, undivided, indeterminate 'suchness'" (Capra 1999, 29).

Wang (2012) argues that panexperientialism gives us "a capacity to respond experientially to other things, even if in an unconscious way" (106–107). Mesle (2008) explains that "There are not two kinds of substances – minds and bodies. There is one kind of reality – experience. But, experience has both physical and mental aspects" (39). Nonsentient objects do experience in an equally valuable manner – it is merely qualitatively different from other experiencing entities (Mesle 2008). Indeed, Whitehead (1979) notes "there is no absolute gap between 'living' and 'non-living' societies" (102) – all engage in the co-creative process of becoming.

Therefore, a better way to conceptualize differing experience is as a value-free qualitative differentiation of function, so that when concepts are applied to social action, dualistic and ranked meanings are not carried forward. Panexperientialism demands that all beings, things, and places be considered: "Situated knowledges require that the object of knowledge be pictured as an actor and agent" (Haraway 1988, 592), where "actants" are all things and beings that are able to perform actions, produce effects, and alter situations (Latour 1999, 303). As Tollefsen (2002) argues, "It is in experience that the world, as it were, communicates itself to us" (164).

Tacit knowing

Moving from raw experience into consciousness, knowing is sometimes referred to as a "gut feeling" or body knowledge – often referred to as instinct. Polanyi (1974) introduced the term tacit knowing to explain the type of personal understanding individuals have that is beyond formal, codified, explicit knowledge. Tacit knowing is visceral and experiential, sometimes understood as instinct or "gut feeling."

Tacit knowledge is often physically embodied, such as knowing how to balance on a bicycle or how to hammer a nail. Such actions are often learned through observation, imitation, and practice – in other words, through experience, as opposed to intellect. These skills once learned are enacted largely without thinking about them. Similarly, knowing is often *felt* rather than thought. Such human experience is "a situation lived and felt from the inside" (Connolly 2011, 97). In fact, people often are not aware of the knowledge they possess or how it may be useful to others. Polanyi (2009) argues that this implicit level of experience is where all knowledge begins, yet it is also difficult to transfer to another person because it is not always adequately represented by language.

Intuition

Intuition builds on instinct as a form of tacit knowing that comes from experience, it is a sense of knowing that has been attributed to creative aspects of the mind or the spirit, both of which are considered dimensions beyond intellect. Intuition arises from sensory perception joined with experience and the unconscious (Bergson 2007). Bergson (1913) argues that the conflict between realism (perception) and idealism (feeling) is resolved, "or rather dissolved by intuition" (75).

Flyvbjerg (2001) explains intuition as "the ability to draw directly on one's own experience – bodily, emotional, intellectual – and to recognize similarities between these experiences and new situations" (21). Intuitive perception includes a variety of subconscious and conscious inputs from the level of instinctual response to alternative states of consciousness. In other words, intuition is drawn from the whole of multidimensional experience without the filter of conceptual thinking. In this way, intuitive decision making "comes primarily from one's own body and is in this way at one with the performer" (18). Language can never describe this reality completely, and rational concepts are even more inadequate due to their simplifications.

Both psychology and philosophy claim that intuition comes from a source beyond the apprehension of ordinary consciousness. For example, Jung (1923) describes intuition as perception via the unconscious that can provide useful insights. As an example, "dreams have a psychic structure which is unlike that of other contents of consciousness" (Jung 2010, 23). William James (1997), among other psychologists of his time, describes at least two modes of consciousness; "Our normal waking consciousness, rational consciousness . . . is but one special type of consciousness, whilst all about it, parted from it by the filmiest of screens there lie potential forms of consciousness entirely different" (305). James conceives of this second mode of consciousness as "the spiritual dimension of the psyche" (Ryan 2008, 22). Each person has a spiritual self which is a felt (not thought) part of overall consciousness that leads a person to act in the physical world – what we might now refer to as the subconscious. James therefore considers various "kinds of mental activity in the stream of consciousness (including their embodiment and their dependence on habit)" (Smith 2013, § 4, para. 1).

Holistic perception

Holistic perception is a form of knowing that combines experience, tacit knowing, and intuition. This provides insights that rational consciousness does not access, thereby opening up doorways to creativity. Whitehead explains two basic modes of perception – "perception in the mode of causal efficacy and perception in the mode of presentational immediacy" (Mesle 2008, 57). Causal efficacy is carried-forward knowledge from other sources, which includes all past experience as well as knowledge gleaned through feeling and intuition. Presentational immediacy is associated with sense perception, which is mediated by causal efficacy through subjective experience. These perceptions meld to produce "perception in the mode of symbolic reference" (Griffin 2007, loc. 534).

Due to its inclusivity, we refer to this combination as holistic perception – the integration of all forms of embodied experience and consciousness, acknowledging that "there is participation *between* those distinctions . . . between thought and feeling" (Bohm 2004, 102). This approach to knowledge considers "not what we can know" in the purely cognitive sense, "but what we know" in the holistic sense (Stengers 2011, 9). Wilber (2011) categorizes this integral and holistic understanding as second-tier consciousness. Holistic perception enables the synthesis of subjectively and socially mediated conceptions with the perception of physical events. In other words, there is never a stark line between internal and external experience (Ferré 1998). As Whitehead (1967) explains, "All knowledge is derived from, and verified by, direct intuitive observation" (177). This might include sense perception, conceptual thought, memory, imagination, emotion, desire, and intuition. This means that experience includes conscious experience as well as semi-conscious and even unconscious mental processes, along with relevant background conditions implicitly invoked in our experience. This type of experience "involves the senses, and also something beyond. . . . It's perception of meaning . . . a more subtle perception" (Bohm 2004, 46). Thus, holistic perception includes sensory input, affect, and intuition – "not only scientific experiences but also religious experiences. It is a rich whole" (Wang 2012, 125).

These views of holistic perception are further developed by the field of transpersonal psychology in its consideration of the spiritual dimension of human life. Many studies attempt to understand the type of knowing that comes from non-ordinary awareness. For example, Maslow (1968) calls profound moments of understanding and happiness "peak experiences" (21). Similarly, states of "flow" are periods during which a person feels more whole and alive, yet without a sense of time (Csikszentmihalyi 1990). These experiences reflect the fullest realization of an individual's unique potential.

Holistic perception is often communicated in metaphorical terms in order to capture the whole meaning. For example, many Native American cultures use myths and stories, which, when told "in the language and cultural context . . . become powerful ways of knowing and living" (Maryboy 2004, 12). Taoists use paradox, Zen Buddhists use nonsensical riddles called *koans*, Zen masters use concise poetry like haiku, and Hindu gurus use myths. The value of this approach is recognized by psychoanalytical theory, particularly in the case of Jung's (1971) archetypes.

Creative imagination

Holistic perception provides insights that rational consciousness does not access, thereby opening up doorways to creativity. Whitehead (1967) insists that flights of imagination are essential to wise human participation in a world of becoming. This notion is reflected in posthumanist calls for "faith in the creative powers of the imagination" (Braidotti 2013, 191). Recognizing that creativity is necessary for the advancement of knowledge and progress of society, Connolly (2011) argues, "It is critical for thinkers to move back and forth between two registers of temporal experience: to dwell in fecund periods of withdrawal from action at some times and to intervene in ongoing practices at others" (15). These explanations of intentionally accessing holistic perception to develop new concepts from previously unconscious possibility leads to various practices developed for this purpose.

Accessing embodied knowing

Embodied knowing can be accessed through a variety of practices that seek to bring alternative states of consciousness into awareness. "One way in which they converge is in the act of self-reflection" (Eagleton 2003, 137). James (1890) describes this as tapping into "consciousness beyond the margin" (as quoted in Ryan 2008, 29). Through introspection and contemplation, one can access the subconscious for insight into deeper spiritual, moral, and intellectual questions. "The human spiritual dimension allow[s] individuals to be able to: respond to dreams and visions; accept them as representations of human potential; give these non-material realities symbolic expression" (Smith 2004, 118). Bergson (2001) describes this process as experiencing "duration" and Connolly (2011) argues that periodically dwelling in the non-temporal register of experience enables reflective awareness of the process of becoming. This is an experiential approach to knowing that is empirical but not empiricist (Bergson 1913; Ferré 1998), introspective but not idealist (Haack, 274).

Heidegger (1996) explains that curiosity leads one to ignore or flee from day-to-day being and become attuned with one's authentic sense of being – what he terms *Dasein* – which exists in a state of "being-in-the-world" (125). By entering the opening, clearing, or ontological mood, the grasp of linear time and physical perception is loosened from experience. There, one becomes aware of the "potentiality-of-being" (138) to the greatest degree possible, considering the limits of subjectivity. Prozorov (2014a) describes this process as "subtraction from the positive order of one's world" (75). Attunement thus uses a specific kind of seeing that is not purely empirically sensory ("perceiving with the bodily eyes"), but is something that "lets the being accessible to it be encountered in themselves without being concealed" (Heidegger 1996, 138). This leads to an understanding of "the primordial disclosedness of being-in-the-world" (138).

These realms of knowing can be accessed through a variety of practices found in both spiritual traditions and psychotherapy. Indigenous peoples often look to "dreams, visions, and intuitions" for "*revealed knowledge*" of the spiritual dimension (Castellano 2000, 24). Ceremonies such as the sweat lodge, sacred pipe, Native American Church peyote meeting, medicine wheel circle, and vision quest are used to access such intuitive knowing (Brown 2007; Bucko 1998; Hughes 2010; Maroukis 2012). These ceremonies often include fasting, sleep deprivation, and sensory deprivation to heighten awareness, along with drumming, singing, and dancing. These "ceremonies are primary means of instilling the attitude of expectant stillness that opens the door to full awareness" (Castellano 2000, 29).

Similarly, paganism considers the relationship between the material and the spiritual to be intentionally accessible (Adler 1986). Rituals are used by Neo-Pagans in order to access

Mystery knowledge – "teachings that cannot be grasped by the intellect alone, but only by the deep mind made accessible in trance" (Starhawk 1999, 183). To interpret dreams or experience, some consult with oracles such as Tarot cards, Druidic runes, astrological charts, palmistry, or the Taoist *I-Ching* (Book of Changes) in a process often called divination but which is better understood as a way to access intuitive knowing through archetypal wisdom. Thus, the interpretation of an oracle as a source of wise counsel is more apropos than prophecy. All such "divinatory techniques essentially work to focus awareness and engage the heightened intuition and perception" (Starhawk 1999, 183).

Eastern spiritual traditions often employ similar practices to access various forms of consciousness, including concentrated focus or mindfulness, breath work, mantras, body postures, and meditation. These practices seek to release everyday thoughts and sensations that crowd active consciousness in order to gain insight (Yogananda 1993). Mindfulness is "a state of consciousness that involves consciously attending to one's moment-to-moment experience" (Didonna 2009, 1–2). These states of consciousness are "achieved in a variety of meditative states" (Smith 2013, § 4, para. 1). In sketch, control of the body through breath and positioning cultivates mindfulness that is necessary "for the development of Insight" (Thera 2005, 69–70). Mantras invoke the use of specific words and sounds to induce resonance that attunes practitioners to alternative states of being. They are "a tool for connecting us with the spiritual wisdom and the energy of consciousness hidden in the universe as a whole" (Frawley 2010, 23) as well as "a powerful psychological tool for purifying and transforming consciousness" (Goa 2005, 10). As explained in Buddhism, mindfulness enables practitioners to reach "the exalted heights of the Factors of Enlightenment" (Thera 2005, 63).

Similar techniques are used in contemporary clinical psychology. Jungian psychoanalysis uses dream interpretation to bring knowledge from the unconscious into the therapeutic process (Jung 2010, 23). Hypnosis seeks to access this subconscious state more directly. Recognizing that alterations in states of consciousness are a part of everyday life, hypnotherapy induces a trance state to "sustain a state of attentive, receptive, intense focal concentration with diminished peripheral awareness" (Spiegel and Spiegel 2004, 19). Through this "dialectic between focal and peripheral awareness" (19), the unconscious can be brought into consciousness.

Similar practices are emerging in management and organization theory. Studies of entrepreneurial service businesses note that these "high-order dynamic capabilities" (Agarwal and Selen 2009, 431) are necessary for creative innovation. Therefore, these different types of knowledge must be cultivated (Eggers and Singh 2009). This approach is also developed in design thinking, a term used to describe integrative systems thinking, which involves distinct cognitive, attitudinal, and interpersonal aspects of creative, pragmatic knowing to explore *what might be*, as opposed to what is (inductive logic) or should be (deductive logic) (Dunne and Martin 2006).[2]

Contemporary thinkers urge us to pursue these practices in order to address our current predicament because "a collection of old precepts, habits, and standards of judgment are insufficient to an emerging situation" (Connolly 2011, 164). As Murdoch (1992) explains, "we must believe in our duty and ability to discover and make our own the truths which we first intuit or make out as shadows" (434–435). While intuitions "are neither especially in fashion in academic circles, nor highly valued scientifically" (Braidotti 2013, 191), the ability to intuit can and should be cultivated as it is essential to creative thinking. Connolly (2011) similarly argues that such "skills and sensitivities" are necessary as they allow us to continually respond to the "emerging situation" through the ongoing "formation of new maxims, judgments, concepts, and strategies" (164).

Relational subjectivity

Pragmatists argue we must utilize both theorizing and empirical observation to make sense of our world and actions (Dewey 1958). As Follett (2013c) notes, creative experience is "the place where conceptual and perceptual meet" (144). Experience as a whole includes "our perceptual experience, our personal experience, our social experience" (Follett 2013c, 113). All subjective perceptions of experience are therefore transformed by ***relationality*** – what one perceives is influenced by interconnections with other beings, objects, and places. In other words, "human knowing . . . is at bottom naturally relational" (Ferré 1998, 275); "our perception of the world is socially conditioned . . . we do not perceive in limbo" (Bogason 2001, 176).

While clearly a causality dilemma, because we are socially embedded, we come to know within epistemic communities. Husserl's (1982) notion of lifeworld explains the manner in which social forces such as language and culture structure how we perceive the world. These forces create a world-horizon that constrains what we expect from experience. In this way, "meaning is . . . an ongoing performance of the world in its differential dance of intelligibility and unintelligibility" (Barad 2007, 149). This perspective is carried forward in contemporary cognitive ecology with the recognition of cultural influences on thought (Hutchins 2010) – socially constructed concepts give us initial maps for navigating experience.

At the experiential level, Husserl (1982) describes intersubjectivity as the basic condition of humanity, a minimal awareness of others, and Heidegger's (1996) being-with understands subjectivity as relational – wherein recognition of relation begins in an implicit, pre-rational, manner. Co-presence in space and time enables us to recognize ourselves as different from one another and yet imagine ourselves in one another's places. In this sense, intersubjectivity has genetic and neurological foundations. For example, Jung (1969) conceptualizes the collective unconscious as an innate reservoir of knowledge in the structure of the brain that establishes predispositions toward basic human experiences. Contemporary brain research now refers to this as "genetic memory" that is encoded in species' evolving DNA, relating it to instinctual knowing (Llinas 2001, 190).

According to Gallese (2003), "The majority of the time our understanding of the situation is immediate, automatic and almost reflex-like" (520). Contemporary neuroscience attributes this pre-rational process to mirror neurons, which help us learn new skills by imitation. They also enable us to imagine trading places with another being, providing the neural basis for emotions such as empathy (Iacoboni 2008). We are "*therefore* able to join with one another, to see together without claiming to be another" (Haraway 1988, 586).

Neuroscience and neuropsychology explain that instantaneous, non-conscious activity in the limbic system broadcasts and receives emotions. This ability to "read" one another's emotional states happens nearly automatically when we are in face-to-face encounters; in this sense, "human beings are innate mind readers" (Johnson 2001, 196). In affective perception, verbal communication "is only a part of what is going on, in some cases only a small part, and one that can (and often does) distract us from the deeper meaning of our interpersonal encounters" (Stout 2007b, 80). Through nonverbal communication or body language, we "align our emotions with those of the people around us, and vice versa" (78). Therefore, the "effect of affect" (Catlaw 2007a) is important in ***embodied knowing***.

The concept of emotional intelligence (Goleman 1995) recognizes that both *inter*personal intelligence (the capacity to understand the intentions, motivations, and desires of other people) and *intra*personal intelligence (the capacity to understand oneself, including one's feelings, fears, motivations, and desires) (Gardner 1983) are necessary for fruitful interactions. For example, effective dialogue "requires *sensitivity* – a certain way of knowing . . . what's happening inside of you, what's happening in the group" (Bohm 2004, 45).

This type of conscious interpersonal awareness can also be traced to the notion of intersubjectivity (Duranti 2010). For sociologist Alfred Schutz, symbolic interactionism shows that

> knowledge of the social world is created intersubjectively through a mutual participation in each other's consciousness. By stipulating that there are sufficient commonalities in everyone's thought processes, it is possible for people to mutually share in each other's stream of consciousness.
>
> (Harmon 1981, 39)

This idea of transpersonal consciousness was first developed by William James (Ryan 2008). Through his empirical research "on 'extraordinary subjective experience,' 'supraconscious processes,' and subjective experience of the transcendental" (Ryan 2008, 24), James developed a theory of transpersonal consciousness – "a cosmic environment of *other consciousness*" (James, as quoted in Ryan 2008, 30). This relatedness enables us to generate "an earthwide network of connections . . . with deep filaments and tenacious tendrils into time, space, and consciousness" (Haraway 1988, 580, 588).

Situated knowing

Situated knowing draws together the forms of intrapersonal and interpersonal knowledge generated in ***embodied knowing*** and integrates them through an intentional, interactive process. ***Situated knowing*** therefore resolves the dialectic between static *foundational structure* and dynamic *coherentist structure* by synthesizing subjectivity and objectivity through intersubjective agreement. As understood in cognitive ecology, knowledge is "profoundly situated" and "social" (Hutchins 2010, 712). Knowing occurs within a context of ***relationality*** that includes environment, people, animals, plants, objects, and place. This is more than mere "contextualism" (Haack 2009) or "perspectival truth" (Miller and Fox 2001). Distributed cognition explains that understanding emerges from and is distributed across the system in which it is situated (Hutchins 2014). Knowers are inextricably embedded in and actively shaping their knowledge communities, often referred to as epistemic communities (Haas 1992) or communities of practice (Lave and Wenger 1991). Such epistemic pluralism reflects the many contexts in which meaning making occurs (Farmer 2010).

Situated knowing is produced within "complex networks of mutual influence" (Ferré 1998, 272). Sense-making occurs within a relational context and truth systems are amended through a process of intersubjective agreement. This requires us to redefine both subjectivity and objectivity as they are no longer distinct. Passion cannot be separated from reason, fact cannot be divorced from value, object cannot be distinct from subject. Indeed, even rationalists agree a pure distinction between fact and value is impossible; they are interdependent (Habermas 1998a). As Marx and Engels (1998) query, "Does it require deep intuition to comprehend that man's ideas, views on conceptions, in one word, man's consciousness, changes with every change in the conditions of his material existence, in his social relations, and in his social life?" (58).

As described earlier, relational subjectivity considers the manner in which external factors influence perception. For example, the collective unconscious, genetic memory, affect, intersubjectivity, symbolic interactionism, and transpersonal consciousness enable mutual understanding. In turn, relational subjectivity provides a grounding for relational objectivity – one that is an intentional composition of subjective perspectives. While relational objectivity does not deny the existence of an objective world, it rejects the notion that it can be perceived from a non-subjective position. Instead, relational objectivity is generated through intersubjective agreement. Each of these concepts is unpacked in the following subsections.

Relational objectivity

Objectivity is transformed by ***relationality.*** While there is a physical world of objective phenomena we hold in common, our understanding of it can only be intersubjective, influenced by interconnections with other beings, objects, and places. Each of us views this world from a different perspective (Arendt 1998). Rather than imagining a disembodied, all-seeing objective position assumed by positivist science, Eagleton (2003) explains that "objectivity does not mean judging from nowhere" because "only by standing at a certain angle to reality can it be illuminated for you" (135). This is sometimes described as a "horizon" or "the range of vision that includes everything that can be seen from a particular vantage point" (Gadamer 2013, 313). Knowers "reflect the particular locations in which they find themselves, thus leading to the idea that the unique experiences either of individuals or of the groups to which they belong are productive of 'situated' knowledges" (Ruccio and Amariglio 2003, 15). Thus, every person and group has their own particular vista that establishes the limits of their perception and understanding of the world. This is reflected in the concept of positionality, which recognizes that intersecting aspects of self (e.g., race, nationality, age, gender, sexual orientation, class, gender identity, etc.) influence "the information that becomes encoded as 'knowledge'" (Madge 1992, 295).

Merleau-Ponty's eco-phenomenology extends this notion of situated knowledge into the nonhuman world (Brown and Toadvine 2003). He claims objectivity is reciprocally constituted by countless organisms within a field of mutually impacting material relationships. Bird-David (1999) describes an indigenous "relational epistemology" that draws knowledge not only from human, but also environmental relation. For instance, the Nayaka report talking with the trees in the forests in which they live. This phrase "is shorthand for a two-way responsive relatedness with a tree – rather than 'speaking' one-way to it, as if it could listen and understand" (S77). Taking this further, studies in ecology have found that trees share information with one another, such as warnings of an aphid attack (Babikova et al. 2013). This communication occurs through mechanisms such as the mycelial network – a web of fungi that connects their root systems – and by the release of chemicals, or smell, into the air (Wolleben 2015).

Follett (2013c) also reminds us that facts themselves are determined by their situatedness, explaining that "the value of every fact depends on its position in the whole world-process, is bound up in its multitudinous relations" (12). Mannheim (1997) describes this as "relationism" in which "all the elements of meaning in a given situation have reference to one another and derive their significance from this reciprocal interrelationship" (76). Any change in context, or observation of new information, changes the meaning of other facts: "This means, among other things, that when a factor is added to or subtracted from a situation, you have not that situation minus or plus that factor, for all the rest will be changed" (Follett 2003h, 192).

One rationale for being as inclusive as possible in forming relational objectivity is that it leads us closer to an approximation of objective truth at any given time. Only by continually joining together many situated knowledges can we craft some semblance of objectivity. Knowledge of the natural world is "created from observations by many persons" (Castellano 2000, 23), representing "a convergence of perspectives from different vantage points, accumulated over time" (24). Indeed, objectivity "is possible only thanks to *more and wider experience*" (Ferré 1998, 275).

However, remembering that relational subjectivity mediates our perception, relational objectivity mitigates coercive power dynamics in social construction. Knowledge is structured by a system of conventions accepted by the epistemic community's participants. When co-created, the power of knowledge is not coercive or constraining. Therefore, we must formulate a way to reconcile perspectives in a manner that is inclusive and participative. This is where the intentional process of forming intersubjective agreement comes in.

Intersubjective agreement

Intersubjective agreement brings together relational subjectivity and relational objectivity through the method of integration. Phenomenology considers how conscious beings make meaning together through active coordination perceptually, conceptually, and practically (Husserl 1982). Similarly, in cognitive ecology "perception, action, and thought" are understood as "inextricably integrated" (Hutchins 2010, 712). In such praxis, "subjectivity and objectivity thus join in a dialectical unity producing knowledge in solidarity with action, and vice versa" (Freire 2011, 38).

In the pursuit of intersubjective agreement, truth claims emerge from an organic process that is self-organizing and cooperative as opposed to hierarchically or majority-imposed (Tollefsen 2002). In contrast to the contemporary norm, it "is not, first, scientific investigation, then some method of persuading the people to abandon their own experience and thought, and lastly an acclaiming populace. The social process is a process of cooperating experience" (Follett 2013c, 30). Remembering that inclusivity is important to relational objectivity, we must also reiterate the notion that knowledge is power. For this reason, knowledge production must be "power-sensitive" (Haraway 1988, 589), utilizing "engaged, accountable positioning" (590) that fundamentally transforms the logic of discovery.

This concern also has practical implications. For example, Schmidt (1993) notes that relying only on expert technical knowledge while ignoring experiential wisdom can lead to devastating outcomes. All "players" are needed for creative innovation (Eggers and Singh 2009). This broader epistemological "repertoire" is considered necessary to improve practice because it is often the case that those most intimately involved in a situation know more about what is important than the most formally trained outsider (Schreurs 2000). Thus, "phronetic research" blends together "a polyphony of voices, with no one voice, including that of the researcher, claiming final authority" (Flyvbjerg 2001, 139). Similarly, participatory action research engages all those affected by the inquiry in framing research questions, gathering and analyzing data, and drawing conclusions (Bartels 2012).

Because the purpose is to come to a situated and shared understanding of the truth, it is helpful for participants to adopt "an experimental attitude toward experience" (Follett 2003c, 50–51). In addition, "communicative capacity" (Bartels 2015a), or "the ability to dialogue . . . is crucial" (109). The ability to engage in "genuine discussion" (Follett 1998, 210) as opposed to debate is critical to intersubjective agreement because it "often takes ingenuity, a 'creative intelligence,' to find the integration" (163). This means that each participant "will entertain any hypothesis, she will consider any evidence" (James 1955, 61) in order to move "from a monological ('I know') to a dialogical position ('Let us explore')" (Gergen 2009, 220).

What Follett (2013c) calls "the method of integration" (178) is a particularly effective approach to foster the kind of dialogue and deliberation necessary to produce shared understanding and agreement. Its synergistic effect produces more creative, effective, and long lasting outcomes because nothing is lost through exclusion, domination, or compromise. Integration seeks "the interpenetration of the ideas of the parties concerned" (Follett 2003g, 212) through a dialogic "interpermeation" (Follett 1998, 209). Truths "are discovered by argument, evidence, experiment, investigation" (Eagleton 2003, 109).

The integrative method consists of four general phases that tend to be iterative in nature: (1) dialogic sharing, (2) disintegration of positions, (3) comparative revaluation, and (4) deliberative synthesis. *Sharing* invites all participants to contribute *a priori* perspectives to the process. Each individual within the epistemic community shares with others their understanding of the situation: How do they perceive the facts? What experiences contribute to a more complete perspective? Just as Follett (2013c) describes "experience meetings" (212), Arendt (1998) likens this process to individuals engaged in discussion around a table. The table maintains our separation as distinct subjects with unique perspectives while providing a common space for generating shared experience. Through dialogue, we develop our understanding(s) of the world and ourselves.[3] The group may also seek new information by engaging in "a cooperative gathering of facts" (Follett 2013c, 17) that may help fill gaps or illuminate a common perspective. Following from ***embodied knowing***, participatory learning processes include both qualitative and quantitative data and methods of collection, analysis, and exchange to enable transdisciplinarity and the use of both expert and non-expert knowledge.

Once all known facts and understandings have been articulated, *disintegration* can begin. In this step, fully formed conceptualizations are broken down into smaller, more nuanced ideas to facilitate analysis. The facts that have been gathered are examined to identify the perspectives and values they reflect. Through discursive practices "part of the world becomes determinately bounded and propertied in its emergent intelligibility to another part of the world" (Barad 2007, 149). This type of analysis "must be balanced with synthesis – placing the part that we have come to know by close analysis in the context of all its relations, which will continually impact on that which we thought we knew, and thereby transform it" (Castellano 2000, 30). Gadamer (2013) describes this process of synthesis as a fusion of horizons.

Revaluation "is the flower of comparison" (Follett 2003b, 38) that precipitates an organic change of opinion through dialogue about perceptions, experiences, and facts. Care is taken to consider the implications of apparent conflict and why it occurs. Experiences and perceptions that reflect apparently different interests are examined to discover underlying commonalities (Forester 1999a). In this step, participants are able to see the situation from other perspectives, enabling "constructive conflict" (Follett 2003b, 30), a deliberative comparison of difference that seeks creative synthesis. This is not mere compromise; instead, "through an interpenetrating of understanding, the quality of one's own thinking is changed" (Follett 2013c, 163), opening up the possibility of developing shared understandings.

The resulting commonalities lay the groundwork for deliberative reintegration. The *synthesis* outcome is the shared sense of truth that fits the experiences of all engaged in the situation, the substance of which is often different from anything that was originally shared. Any remaining differences or disagreements are deliberated in light of rationales given and commonalities identified. Once a communicative agreement (Habermas 1998c) is reached, these truth claims must remain open to interrogation and reconsideration as the situation changes or participants enter into or leave the conversation. In other words, the process of integration is continual and iterative. As Follett (1998) notes, "You cannot bottle up wisdom – it won't keep – but through our associated life it may be distilled afresh at every instant" (130).

In a global context, the process of integrating knowledges must continue across epistemic communities and communities of practice in order to develop mutual understanding and to gain acceptance of truth claims (Duranti 2010). Since each situation is merely an interlocking part of the total situation (Follett 2013c), iterative fusions of multiple horizons at many possible levels of analysis are necessary. Ongoing integration across these communities develops ever-greater understandings of truth, or truth-through-relationship (Knitter 2002). Through these interlocking networks, all forms of knowing interweave and inform one another, bringing the most localized knowledges together in a more nuanced mosaic of transdisciplinary, polyvocal, cross-cultural wisdom.

Integral Knowing

Integral Knowing combines ***embodied knowing*** and ***situated knowing***. These forms of knowing are at once perceptual and conceptual, explicit and implicit. This "creative experience" pursues a *synthesis* of "concept and percept" (Follett 2013c, 280). In this way, "the spiritual and material dimensions of life form a dynamic unity and can be translated into concrete action" (Pulitano 2003, 26). Each member of an epistemic community accesses their own ***embodied knowing*** while engaging in a process of intersubjective agreement with others, thereby co-creating ***situated knowing***. Truths generated in this process remain open to ongoing questioning, evaluation, and change – a key component to all aspects of the pragmatist approach to truth seeking (Dewey 1958; Follett 2013g). Therefore, no truth claim is made in a definitive, reified manner. Truths can become untrue when they no longer fit coherently or are no longer practically useful (James 1955). We can also be mistaken about our observations or interpretation; cooperative sense-making helps generate coherence, learning from errors, and adjusting accordingly.

However, this does not mean that knowledge production falls into a purely subjective or parochial relativism. Through ongoing integration across epistemic communities, intersubjective agreement accommodates reasonable approximations of objective knowledge at increasingly larger scopes. Truth is verifiable to the extent that thoughts and statements correspond with experience across communities. Indeed, the "only test of probable truth is what works best in the way of leading us, what fits every part of life best and combines with the collectivity of experience's demands, nothing being omitted" (James 1955, 61) – truths must "be accountable to experience" (Ferré 1998, 275). This idea of truth being what works for many people in many places is given a variety of names: reliable, comformal (Ferré 1998), and truth-indicative (Haack 2009).

In sum, Integral Knowing employs a "practice of objectivity that privileges contestation" (Haraway 1988, 585). Truth is not something "out there" to be discovered or verified, but is something that is co-created through the social process, involving the experience of all (Eagleton 2003). Integral Knowing is derived from "cooperative relationships between persons and other persons, and between persons and the world" (Tollefsen 2002, 159). Knowing is "dependent and relational. It must be infinite and open-ended" (Wang 2012, 120). Through intersubjective agreement, "we learn how to connect the conceptual and perceptual planes, how to let every fact contribute to those principles which by use again in the factual world becomes again transformed, and thus man grows – always through his activity" (Follett 2013c, 141). In this way, Integral Knowing produces "progressive experience" (54) that expands our understanding – as individuals and a society.

Integrative pathways

An Integrative synthesis must generate pathways that are easily traversed by those holding other positions. In the case of epistemology, Integral Knowing must sufficiently address fundamental concepts within the other epistemologies, or at least create a basis for dialogue and shared understandings. As illustrated in Figure 7.1, we imagine the shared characteristics shown in Table 7.2 as pathways into a dynamic synthesis that is always open to "contestation, deconstruction, passionate construction, webbed connections, and hope for transformation of systems of knowledge and ways of seeing" (Haraway 1988, 585).

Going back to our discussion of dialectical synthesis in the chapter's introduction, ***embodied knowing*** resolves the relational dialectic between *internal* and *external justification* by integrating perceptual and conceptual information and therefore drawing on a broader array

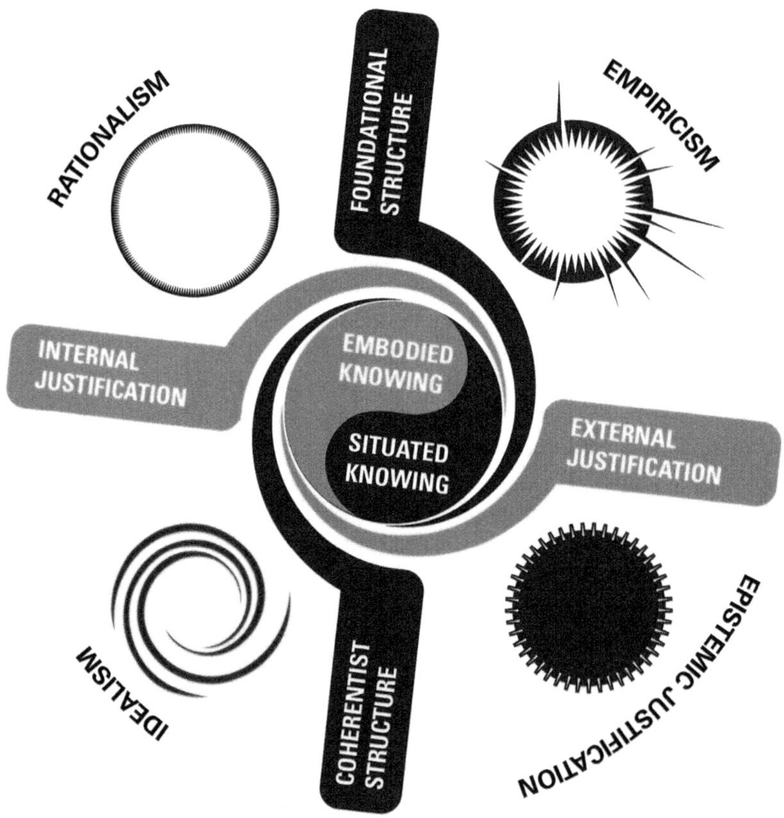

Figure 7.1 Integrative pathways for Integral Knowing

of sources of information in examining truth claims. ***Situated knowing*** resolves the process dialectic between *foundational* and *coherentist structure* by producing agreed-upon foundations from which to test logical congruence of new truths while the foundations themselves remain malleable. Consensus about what is "true" is established through a participative knowledge production process that can move from the most local to global scope. Within this process, both subjectivity and objectivity are redefined as relational in character. However, the primary concerns of each distinct ontological position must also be addressed in order to establish a starting point for dialogue with the Integrative perspective, as shown in Table 7.2.

Rationalism is primarily concerned with the use of reason to guide both knowledge production and the justification of truth claims through deductive logic from foundational truths. ***Embodied knowing*** includes cognitive information, while ***situated knowing*** provides a process for reasoning through intersubjective agreement resulting in temporary foundations for knowledge. Empiricism is primarily concerned with knowledge being produced and confirmed through physical observation. ***Embodied knowing*** includes sensory experience, while ***situated knowing*** provides the "reality check" of relational objectivity. Idealism is primarily concerned with ideas making sense within the cultural context and feeling right in terms of personal experience. ***Embodied knowing*** includes tacit and intuitive knowledge, while ***situated knowing*** enables coherence with accepted truths. Epistemic Anarchism is

Table 7.2 Integrating epistemological concerns

Ideal-Type	***Characteristics***	***Primary Concern***	***Synthesis Solution***
Rationalism	*foundational, internal justification*	Reason guides production and justification of knowledge logically consistent with foundational truths	***Embodied knowing*** includes cognitive sources of information; ***situated knowing*** provides moments of stability through intersubjective agreement
Empiricism	*foundational, external justification*	Objective physical observation of phenomena guides production and justification of knowledge provide epistemic foundations	***Embodied knowing*** includes sensory experience; ***situated knowing*** generates relational objectivity that is subject to intersubjective agreement
Idealism	*coherentist, internal justification*	Ideas are consistent with systems of belief and feel right	***Embodied knowing*** includes tacit knowledge and intuition; ***situated knowing*** enables a sense of coherence within the group
Epistemic Anarchism	*coherentist, external justification*	Ideas are consistent with personal experience	***Embodied knowing*** ensures consideration of subjectivity; ***situated knowing*** addresses power dynamics and inconsistencies

primarily concerned with the manner in which mediated perception is involved with knowledge production – inconsistencies between truth claims of others and subjective experience are rejected. ***Embodied knowing*** ensures consideration of subjectivity, while the process of integration in ***situated knowing*** ensures that power dynamics and inconsistencies are located and addressed.

Notes

1 The related idea of *panpsychism* holds that there is a universal mind, soul, or life force in which all entities participate and which informs perception beyond the purely physical or neural functions. This theory assumes only entities with *consciousness* are participants (Skrbina 2005).
2 Ideally, designers work with end-users to co-create solutions through divergent dialogue and convergent deliberation (Brown 2011). Thus, design thinking uses the integrative process.
3 These explanations of deliberation often draw upon Habermasian communicative rationality, which is misaligned with the assumptions of Relational Becoming. Communicative action (Habermas 1998a, c) is a highly rational approach to deliberation that relies on predetermined understandings of right and is heavily weighted toward argumentation and persuasion. It is not specifically designed for building consensus through mutual responsiveness and often results in compromise or *de facto*, if not overt domination (Kim and Kim 2008; Mansbridge et al. 2006; Bartels 2013).

8 Belief systems

Co-Creationism

Transdisciplinarity constitutes neither a new religion, nor a new philosophy, nor a new metaphysics, nor a science of sciences.

Transdisciplinarity leads to an open attitude towards myths and religions, and also towards those who respect them in a transdisciplinary spirit.

No single culture is privileged over any other culture. The transdisciplinary approach is inherently transcultural.

– (Articles 7, 9, and 10 of the Charter of Transdisciplinarity, Nicolescu 2002, 150)

As noted in the discussion of contemporary social crises, conflict over belief systems is often an identified source of civil and global conflict. Conflicts between belief systems often extend into the sphere of governance. Indeed, since the Enlightenment, there has been a battle over which belief system would hold primacy in governance: science or religion. Clearly, the current century's War on Terror is rhetorically grounded in a competition between monotheisms (Christianity and Judaism versus Islam). The desire to spread belief systems through conversion has also been a justification for colonization; in particular, this has reflected a hierarchical ordering that favors monotheisms (Christianity and Islam) over pantheistic and panentheistic belief systems. Similarly, cultural appropriation of belief systems and the practices of colonized and oppressed cultures – especially for profit – have also engendered deep conflicts among racial and ethnic groups.

We suggest that the intensity of these conflicts is in large part due to the pivot point belief systems hold between theory and practice. Dilthey (1988) explains that a belief system is "a state of affairs bound up not only with mythical thought, but with metaphysics, and with self-reflection" (158). Further, Connolly (2011) argues that faith disciplines perception; it establishes anticipation. Drawing on our Governance Typology, ontological assumptions shape our understanding of existence, psychosocial theory guides our understanding of human beings, and epistemological concepts determine how we come to understand experience. Belief systems build upon these philosophical assumptions, translating these understandings into a cohesive worldview that establishes the foundation for the behavioral purposes, structures, and practices that follow.

We therefore measure our experiences against the philosophical assumptions embedded in belief, always seeking to restore experience to the expectation when it is not met. How one responds to the increasingly problematic human predicament hinges on one's beliefs and whether we feel a sense of personal agency and responsibility to respond. Therefore, to change action we must understand the implications of seeing the universe, the world, and the people in it in a particular way. While we do not personally practice or appropriate any one of the traditions discussed herein, we assert that identifying common ground among belief systems that hold an understanding of relational process will enable us to "invite positive political connections across differences of creed and affinities of spirituality" (Connolly 2013, 126). This echoes Huxley's (1964) call: "What we now need is a multitude of participants to take part in the great discussion and to join in the search for the larger truth and the more fruitful patterns of belief which we confidently believe is waiting to be elicited" (226).

Connolly (2011) queries, "Does a growing minority sense, with varying degrees of articulateness, that we participate in a larger world of becoming with numerous sites of creative power? If so, it may be timely to augment that appreciation" (16). Huntington (1996) argues that a global civilization is slowly emerging that reflects a healthy universalism that is neither imperialist nor mere acceptance of international pluralism, but rather is a shared awareness, exploration, and expansion of commonalities. This type of dialogue is a common practice in religious pluralism. Theologian Paul Knitter (2002) describes four responses to religious difference: (1) replacement of one with another; (2) fulfillment of one through another; (3) acceptance of irreconcilable differences; and (4) dialogue to identify commonalities.

Adding a more pragmatic alternative, Wang (2012) argues that we need not relinquish systems of belief in order to attain harmonious complementarity. He illustrates by explaining the manner in which core Chinese principles of peaceful coexistence, mutual transformation, and openness to change have been expressed in Confucianism, Taoism, and Buddhism. He explains that these shared ideas have kept the three belief systems in harmony without the "imposition of uniformity, but rather the emergence of concord out of the allowance of discord" (4). This harmonism goes one step further than dialogue by assuming a relational notion of mutual transformation rather than mere coexistence or complementarity.

This argument suggests the need for dialectical synthesis. As shown in Table 8.1, belief systems hold in tension two primary dialectical pairs. On the horizontal relational axis, existence is believed to be made possible either by a metaphysical *theist creator* or a natural process of *materialist creation*. These creation stories generate widely held dichotomies of divine versus earthly, metaphysical versus physical, spiritual versus material, and sublime versus mundane. On the vertical process axis, the competing assumptions are whether the source of existence is *eternal* or *changing*.

To develop a synthesis belief system, the relational dialectic between a *theist creator* versus *materialist creation* would be resolved by including both nonmaterial and material aspects of creation. Following Relational Becoming, we use the term ***sacred immanence*** to add the normative character of belief to the nonmaterial creative potential embodied within all expressions of materiality (creators). Everything contains the generative void of potentiality for *creatio ex nihilo* in the co-creative process. From this foundation, the whole of creation could be conceived as God/Goddess.[1] However, God/Goddess is more likely to be

Table 8.1 Dialectical belief systems

	Theist Creator	*Materialist Creation*
Eternal	Monotheism	Naturalism
Changing	Pantheism	Anti-Essentialism

(Source: Stout and Love 2016)

envisioned as a synergistic product of co-creation that adds qualitative value to all contributing entities.

One philosophical approach to this problem uses mathematical set theory (Prozorov 2014a). If the One (or God/Goddess) is the ultimate set of sets, the set needs to be understood in relation to the items in the set (the Many) whether they are subsets or individual parts. Is the set (One) quantitatively different from the parts (Many) that comprise it? If so, is the set outside of the parts? Does the set exist *a priori* to the parts? Or is there simply a qualitative difference between the composing parts and the set they create in relation to one another? An Integrative explanation would argue that the set (One) is both quantitatively and qualitatively different from the included parts and sets of parts (Many), but it cannot exist without those parts, nor does it exist *a priori* to the parts.

The process dialectic of *eternal* versus *changing* understandings of creator/creation must also be resolved. Both the unchanging laws of God and Nature and the ever-changing character of the universe and the self must be accommodated in some fashion. Again following Relational Becoming, both stable and changing characteristics are included in the process of becoming, which is punctuated with moments of full expression – each moment or event in which the nonmaterial becomes material. We use the term ***co-creating*** to infer that creation is ongoing in every moment of linear time, while not forgetting the ***relationality*** of ***sacred immanence***.

Whereas philosophical schools of thought may be dissected and recombined, this approach is not appropriate for belief systems that must be taken *in toto*. Because no belief system we are aware of fully reflects the Integrative perspective, this chapter will review several traditions that hold principles that logically align with Relational Becoming, Ensembling individuality, and Integral Knowing. Consideration of each belief system as a whole offers a starting place for dialogue. However, taking religious pluralism to the furthest degree possible, mutual transformation Wang (2012) suggests the possibility of an eventual synthesis into a shared belief system. An Integrative belief system would seek to do just that, while maintaining acceptance of diversity among traditions of practice in the process. Through such religious pluralism, people of diverse faiths and creeds "learn about each other's values, share their stories, and foster understanding of their traditions . . . it can generate mutual respect for diversity and establish important areas of common ground as well" (Warren 2001, 263).

Following this pluralistic approach, we will keep belief systems intact in this chapter rather than parsing them into component principles. We begin with process theology, then consider the pertinent aspects of indigenous spirituality, neo-paganism, posthumanism, and new materialism. Drawing from a variety of sources, we offer a beginning sketch of what an Integrative system of belief might look like. We call this belief system Co-Creationism as a placeholder label.

Panentheism and process theology

Panentheism allows for metaphysics without theistic or "radical transcendence" (Connolly 2011, 74) and "affirms the sense of unity or connection affirmed by pantheists while retaining the sense of differentiation and individuality" (Christ 2003, 66). The German philosopher Karl Krause coined the term in 1828 in his search for a synthesis of monotheism and pantheism (Chisholm 1911). Panentheism means all is *in* God as opposed to all *is* God (pantheism): "Pan*en*theism suggest that God is both in the world, immanent, and also beyond the confines of mere matter, also transcendent" (Biernacki 2014, 2). In other words, “Panentheism seeks to avoid either isolating God from the world as traditional theism often does or identifying God with the world as pantheism does” (Culp 2013, 1).

A fair amount of discussion of panentheist thought takes place in the process theology literature, although panentheism is not exclusively Christian (Mesle 1993). For example, Griffin (2007) equates panentheism with ***naturalistic theism*** that can be found in feminist panentheist thought (see for example Christ 2003; Keller 2003) which seeks a synthesis in which divinity is ontologically immanent and plural as opposed to transcendent and unitary (Frankenberry 2011). Charles Hartshorne (1984) is a principal proponent of this naturalist line of thinking in process theology.

However, the notion that all unique expressions of being are in God and yet are not simply parts of God requires some detailed explanation of certain aspects of Whiteheadian process theology proper.[2] As explained in Chapter 5, without God, creativity is the ultimate principle that moves all things within the relational process of becoming – the process of concrescence. However, Whitehead’s acceptance of the philosophical assumption that nothing can come from nothing (*nihil fit ex nihilo*) leads him to argue that what is potentially actualized by any entity must already exist in an actual entity. Whitehead solves this conundrum by making God the full expression of all potentiality in an actual entity (Mesle 2008). He therefore develops a system of dual ultimates, or sources of becoming, asserting that God *embodies* creative potentiality and is equivalent to all other actual entities ontologically and quantitatively, but also different from others in a qualitative sense (Griffin 2004).[3] “God is not to be treated as an exception to all metaphysical principles, invoked to save their collapse. He is their chief exemplification” (Whitehead 1979, 343).

God’s dual nature reflects this dipolar source of existence. In his “primordial nature,” similar to the mental pole of all other actual entities, God expresses all creative potentiality. In his “consequent nature,” similar to the physical pole of all other actual entities, God is the synergistic sum of all actual entities. We will therefore consider Whiteheadian descriptions of God as either creative potential or God as the sum of everything, while highlighting aspects that do not align with the assumptions of Relational Becoming.

God as creative potential

Through God’s primordial nature, the non-temporal enduring objects of possibility are not only actualized, these possibilities are oriented toward a particular aim. God’s ordering of values is determined based on his experience of all other actual entities (Mesle 1993). Because God has the greatest degree of experiential complexity and because God is in direct relation with everything, ***relational knowing*** necessitates that his knowledge is the most complete among all of creation and therefore most fully considers the experiences of all: God is “the most moved mover” (Epperly 2014, loc. 580). With this superior knowledge, God seeks to influence the becoming of all other actual entities. We “experience God’s ‘lure’ toward some of those possibilities over others” (Mesle 1993, loc. 834). “The initial aim is the causal force of the past, combined with God’s presentation of the relevant possibilities *and* a ‘lure’ toward some rather than others” (Mesle 2008, 102).

Process theology believes that through ***relationality***, God encourages all other entities to actualize potentialities that will produce good, beauty, love, and truth, thereby generating the metaphor of God as “poet of the world” (Whitehead 1979, 464). Yet, following prescriptions for nonhierarchy, process theology recognizes that rather than being coercive, God’s power is merely persuasive. Based on the relation between God and other actual entities, process theologians embrace “a *limited* God who participates in a world of becoming without . . . governing it the way an omnipotent deity would" (Connolly 2011, 75). ***Relationality*** further means that all of creation influences God's valuation on an ongoing basis. "In a world of becoming, God and humanity are co-present" (107). Without the divine spark of creativity "the world could not become" (Mesle 1993, loc. 843), but without individual autonomy and choice it *would* not become because experience "does not exist until the creatures create it" (loc. 938).

Therefore, focus remains on the process through which we are creatively transformed by God toward the good during creative becoming (Wieman 1946). In other words, "We cannot do it to ourselves or make it happen. We are saved by grace alone through faith" (Cobb Jr. 1993, loc. 1897). God has perfect knowledge of what could be best at any given time and calls us toward it in the co-creative process. Process theology uses terms such as good, love, beauty, truth, health to express what can be more generically understood as that which is most appropriately responsive to the experience of every part of creation (Mesle 1993). While only God can know this, without unilateral power, absolute control, or predetermination, it is creation's responsibility to heed the call. This relational power and agency is the source of failures to achieve what is good: "God must continually take the decisions of the creatures and work with them – whatever they may be" (loc. 885). Thus, from a process theology perspective, "prayer should be an act whereby we center ourselves around and align ourselves with the sacred" (loc 1601), seeking to hear and heed God's call.

God as the sum of everything

Reflecting ***relational assemblage***, Whitehead (1979) argues that God's consequent nature is the prehension of all satisfied actual entities in the world – the quantitative sum of all that is in an eternal present: "The many become one and are increased by one" (Whitehead 1979, 21). There is nothing "beyond" God but unexpressed creative potential. However, as discussed earlier, Whiteheadian process theology places that unexpressed potential in God as well. Thus, God is co-created by everything that is becoming and is the fullest expression of being at any particular moment. In this sense, God is the universe's poem – one that is written by the co-creative becoming of all actual entities as they draw from pure potentiality, their past, and relation to others in the process of concrescence. However, based on God's status as an actual entity, there is a bidirectional relationship that establishes ongoing co-creation *of* God and *with* God. Some even suggest that God is mutually answerability to humankind (Christ 2003; Griffin 2004; Kearney 2001; Niebuhr 1963, 1970). In this sense, God is a synergistic outcome of all actual entities and God is contributing to that co-creation in each moment of becoming by embodying and ordering creative potential in the form of eternal objects.

Aligning process theism with Relational Becoming

The difficulty of aligning Relational Becoming with Whiteheadian process theology rests primarily in the generation of a subject called God. Such identification opens the door to notions of representation – claims to hear and speak for that subject. Moreover, that subject is differentiated from all other subjects – God is not physically embodied, while all other actual entities are. God has the greatest knowledge of experience and is therefore best situated to determine value and aim. God has already actualized all possible enduring objects that actual entities may choose to express. These characteristics are misaligned with an Integrative understanding of Relational Becoming because all forms of "greater than" or "more than," have a tendency to fall into the traps of dualism, hierarchy, and power imbalances. While Whiteheadian process theology holds that "by reason of the relativity of all things, there is a reaction of the world on God" (Whitehead 1979, 345), this mutual influence is not equal. Indeed, others recognize that Whitehead's explanation creates a nearly unresolvable paradox between determinism and freedom in becoming (Mesle 2008).

Another barrier to alignment with Relational Becoming is the fixation on the material basis of creation – that everything comes from something, which either means from God itself or from some eternal substance. If potentiality in the form of eternal objects is already actualized by God, then ***creative emergence*** is constrained to extant possibility as opposed to an unknown and unlimited potential. This truncates the agency and experience of all actual entities (including God). Connolly (2013) likewise suggests, "It may be that his [Whitehead's] doctrine of eternal objects . . . reduces the scope of possible creativity in the world" (163).

A nontheistic interpretation of process philosophy instead places unexpressed potential within all actual entities (Mesle 1993), thereby reflecting ***embodiment***. Indeed, at the most expansive level, process theology "urges us to think about all human projects in relation to the whole web of life, human and nonhuman" (Christ 2003, 180). Rather than relying upon God's lure toward particular values, both values and the desire to pursue them come through ***relational assemblage*** and ***creative emergence***. The more aware we are of relation, the more we comprehend and care about what is most widely experienced as loving, good, true, and beautiful – to create it for others also creates it for ourselves. This awareness guides the co-creative process of becoming – we lure one another. From this view, prayer would become a practice of increasing such awareness and intentionally seeking to understand how to contribute to these values.

This perspective would consider the synergistic whole as a qualitative factor in co-creative becoming (Mesle 1993). For this type of explanation, we turn to the American Progressive era process thinker, Mary Follett. As explained in Chapter 5, without benefit of the contemporary term *synergy*, Follett (2013c) explains the organic growth of creative experience within what she calls the "total situation" (55). In the process of becoming, "organism and environment do not 'express' but make wholes" (125). She also rejects the notion that the whole is "a quiet Beneficence" (101); "nor are subject and object 'products' of a vital force" (55). Instead, she insists, "that kind of religion which consists of contemplation of otherworldliness is the easy way, and we take to that when we have not enough vitality deliberately to direct our life and construct our world" (Follett 1998, 103).

Thus, the "plus value" or "plusvalents" (Follett 2013c, 73) is not God, but rather the synergistic value generated by groups of any type through the complex process of co-creative becoming that is simultaneously happening within parts, among parts, between parts and the whole, and among all of these and the collective products of their relatings. In other words, apparently distinct situations are interconnected to generate the synergistic total situation. This whole is both quantitatively and qualitatively more than the aggregate sum of the parts; this is the total situation, which only exists through those interacting beings and, in turn, adds value to them.

Translating into the language of Whitehead's actual entities, we might say the total situation is the synergistic outcome co-created by all actual entities at any given moment – the aggregate plus one. This is the parts plus the whole – and in every moment the total situation affects their becoming. The universe is composed by many situations: galaxies are made up of solar systems; solar systems are made up of stars, planets, and other celestial bodies; celestial bodies are made up of inorganic and/or organic things and beings; things and beings are made up of cells; and so forth. However, a process view understands that all of those situations and actual entities are mutually influencing the universe as the total situation – the parts are co-creating the universe and the universe is contributing to that co-creation.

If one must use the term, "God" would not be an actual entity but would rather be the synergistic value of all creation in the eternal present that can only act through other actual entities. Ontologically, the spark of creativity can be considered the innate will to power – the desire to experience within all things and the desire to share that experience with others for increased enjoyment. Potentiality can be considered that which remains latent within all actual entities at any particular moment. The synergistic sum created among beings can simply be understood as the value created by relational process that inheres to all of its parts. Through the relational process of becoming, all entities call to one another to pursue what is valued.

These descriptions align perfectly with Relational Becoming and could be the basis of a coherent belief system. Based on ***relational assemblage***, God could be considered the synergistic sum of the parts – the total situation – but not as an entity. Assuming the ontological principal of ***creative emergence***, God cannot be conceptualized as the embodiment, expression, or source of creative potential – potential must be unlimited and organized in the creative process of becoming. From this perspective, "creativity is the ultimate reality of the universe, presupposed by every instance of actuality" (Wang 2012, 150). In short, creative potentiality – the essence of becoming – is within and expressed by all things and beings through ***embodiment***. Therefore, it may be best to draw from those who are re-conceptualizing Whitehead without God (Ford 1977, Sherburne 1967), or non-theist process philosophers (Mesle 1993, 2008).

Indigenous spiritualities

The basic tenets shared by many indigenous traditions were described in Chapter 5 as integral to the conceptualization of Relational Becoming as a combination of ***embodiment***, ***relational assemblage***, and ***creative emergence***. This section builds on that foundation by considering the implications of these concepts for spiritual practices.

Maori scholar Makere Stewart-Harawira (2005a) outlines a set of principles she argues are common to many indigenous peoples, the most central of which is the "profound interconnectedness of all existence. This principle governs all relationships . . . between all human beings, between all other forms of life, and binds all together within one continuous web of creation" (155). Spiritual law guides "interconnections between the molecules of existence and the nature of the energy that binds them" (Stewart-Harawira 2005b, 39). Similarly, according to some traditions of Native American spirituality, energy transforms into materiality and back again, but never disappears (Waters 2004a). This is similar to the universal law of conservation of energy understood by physics; energy cannot be destroyed but can be transformed into other forms, including light, sound, movement, and material mass. The "Great Mystery" – as opposed to the anthropomorphized Great Spirit – is the sacred act of coming into being as energy or material that cannot be adequately explained in human terms (Means 1995, 241).

Assuming there is agency inherent in creative becoming, indigenous belief systems generally support the possibility of calling things into being as an intentional act of co-creation. "The human spiritual dimension allowed individuals to be able to . . . translate the potential into the actual" (Smith 2004, 118). In this way, "the spiritual and material dimensions of life . . . can be translated into concrete action" (Pulitano 2003, 26). This "allow[s] individuals to be able to: respond to dreams and visions; accept them as representations of human potential; give these non-material realities symbolic expression" (Smith 2004, 118). It is this direct connection between the physical and metaphysical that enables intentional co-creation.

To guide the aim or purpose of co-creation, indigenous spiritualities are often guided by an understanding of ***relational assemblage***. Every element of the natural world, both animate and outwardly inanimate (e.g., water, earth, air, and fire), has its own unique life force (Stewart-Harawira 2005a) that is interdependent (Beeman and Blenkinsop 2008). Therefore, the beingness in all things is honored in reciprocal relationship and underlies a deep sense of stewardship and respect for all of creation. A common theme in Native American cosmology asserts, "We are no better or worse than any of our relations, because the metaphysics of respect (interdependency) sustaining our fundamental relations with Mother Earth are relations of equality" (Verney 2004, 135). All things are related and "express 'a natural democracy,' in which humans are related and interdependent with plants, animals, stones, water, clouds, and everything else" (Cajete 2004, 46). Further, the use of the phrase "all my relations" extends the concept of ***relationality*** beyond the physical realm to include "the dwelling place of the sky and the soul of the Earth . . . and the multitude of energies that power the cosmos" (Briggs and Peat 1999, 146).

As noted in Chapter 6, this relational perspective combined with the assumption of Ensembling individuality leads to a particular understanding of self, community, and place. Many indigenous peoples experience an intimate connection to territory – the categorical label itself refers to a human relationship with that place, rather than as an independent object (Daniels 2012). "It is through our spiritual (metaphysical) connection with Mother Earth that we are able to teach our philosophy of communal living among all life in the universe" (Verney 2004, 135).

This relationship to the land is particularly strong in Australian aboriginal belief systems that understand human spiritual being and physical place to be fully interdependent (Brigg 2007). The term Country refers to both a particular place and the human sense of that place, while Dreaming refers to that which brings them both into existence and orders their relations. Similarly, in the Navajo tradition, both remembering and imagining place "inform each other in complex ways" (Basso 1996, 6). These interactive principles guide the Law or way of living together in place. Taken together, there is a "fusion of being and political existence in Country through Dreaming and Law" (Brigg 2007, 409). Ontologically speaking, if the proper Dreaming rituals are not completed, Country will cease to exist. As noted by Native American scholars, "This is reflective of one of the oldest ecological principles that have been incorporated as metaphysical, and practical rules for human conduct" (Cajete 2004, 55). Most recently, this relationship between spirituality and place have emerged in the concept of re-indigenization. This notion recognizes that all first peoples around the world once held to belief systems intimately tied to the land, and by integrating oneself spiritually with place, indigeneity can be recreated (Bust 2005; Cajete, Mohawk, and Rivera 2008; Nelson 2015).

Following from these beliefs, indigenous ceremonies, stories, and rituals tend to reflect relational process assumptions (Bastien 2004). These practices often use circular and spiral symbolism to represent endless change and movement (Pulitano 2003). For example, in Pueblo cultures, the spiral represents the transformational nature of ***embodiment*** and ***creative emergence*** – from energy/spirit to matter and back again (Jojola 2004). In New Zealand's *kaupapa Maori* (Henry and Pene 2001) the double spiral – resembling a DNA double helix – represents pre-existence and potentiality, time and space, spirit and matter, past and future. The space between the spirals represents the dialectical synthesis of such dualities (Stewart-Harawira 2005b). Through spiritual practices, these concepts are contemplated and enacted in order to intentionally bring good into being. As the anthropologist R. R. Marett (1914) wrote of pre-animistic religion: it "is not so much something thought out as danced out" (xxxi).

Neo-pagan traditions

As with indigenous spirituality, some tenets of paganism and neo-paganism were described in Chapter 5 as reflective of a combination of ***embodiment*** and ***creative emergence***. Here we also highlight the notion of ***relational assemblage*** and consider the implications of these concepts for morality and spiritual practices.

The term "pagan" comes from the Latin term *paganus* that Romans used to refer to conquered peoples who lived in the countryside.[4] The term is most commonly used to denote pre-Christian European belief systems such as druidic and hellenistic traditions; however, some argue that paganism is more appropriately applied to a wider range of ancient and indigenous traditions from across the globe (York 2003). Most broadly, paganism is a label given to ancient nature religions throughout the world, which would include early Hinduism, Taoism, and Shinto along with indigenous spiritualities as uninterrupted traditions of spiritual practice that pre-date contemporary monotheisms (Bonewits 2007). It should be noted, however, that this broader application of the term is not without controversy; the pagan label is one created by European Christians and applied broadly to denote any non-Christian religion and to justify colonization (York 2003). As such, applying the term in this way reproduces Christian Eurocentrism and erases important differences between belief traditions.

The term neo-paganism emerged in the 1960s and 1970s as a general label for a variety of religious movements dating back to the mid-nineteenth century. Its adherents seek to reclaim aspects of ancient wisdom and traditional rituals while combining them with contemporary ideals such as humanism and feminism, or by interlacing them with other religious traditions from around the world.[5] Radical Christian monotheism shares similarities by arguing that the principle of being itself is divine (Niebuhr 1970), or as pagans might say, sacred (Adler 1986). Whether considering the nonmaterial and material, biological and inorganic matter, or human and other creatures, co-creation is "a dynamic partnership or colloquium of potential equals" (York 2003, 162).

In his book *Contemporary Paganism*, Graham Harvey (2011) observes that most neo-pagans rarely indulge in theology, but rather offer a worldview to be appreciated. As Starhawk (1999) describes witchcraft, neo-paganism is "a religion of poetry, not theology" (8). A common denominator among these practices is "an essential this-worldliness" (York 2000, 7), providing emphasis on ***embodiment***. Divinity is understood as immanent, ever changing, and deep with all things and beings; nature and all aspects of human existence are considered sacred; a multiplicity of deities or sacred archetypes of all genders is accepted; and, a commitment is made to balance feminine and masculine characteristics and power in all acts (Ellwood and Partin 1987). References to Goddesses and Gods in these traditions are typically metaphorical representations of spiritual principles, not actual entities.

These beliefs are practiced through intentional ritual creation, often employing circle or spiral symbolism. Neo-pagans reflect the understanding of ***relational assemblage*** with rituals that connect their experiences to the larger cycle of life and root them in both time and place. This sense of ***relationality*** beyond the human is reflected in rituals that are oriented to nature – the four directions, the cycle of the seasons, the movement of the sun, the changing phases of the moon, the ebb and flow of the human life cycle and death – as well as timeless, archetypal understandings of the human experience. They are designed to strengthen the relationship with all of nature and reconnect the various dimensions of self – physical, mental, emotional, sexual, and spiritual.

Non-duality is reflected in that cycles of seasonal light celebrate fruition, fullness, and action while cycles of seasonal darkness honor the natural need for rest, emptiness, and reflection. Practices include meditation, breath work, prayer, invocations, singing, chanting, drumming, dancing, re-enactments of symbolic dramas, pouring of libations, making offerings to a fire, and feasting – often conducted in nature. Many neo-pagans have personal altars where they meditate, pray, and perform rituals to conduct spiritual work. "Deep spirituality involves the ***direct investigation of the experiential evidence disclosed in the higher stages of consciousness development***" (Wilber 2011, loc. 1386). Through such practices, neo-pagans seek a re-sacralization of their experiences, their lives, and the world. These acts of reenchantment are meant to attune participants to divinity and to cure the alienation of modernity and its attendant injustices, psychological damage, and environmental destruction.

Posthumanism and new materialism

For many non-theist believers, humanism has offered a reasonable foundation for a system of belief and its attendant moral and ethical guidelines. However, its retention of a hierarchical dualism between human beings and all other parts of creation precludes it from inclusion in an Integrative belief system. As has been noted of theist beliefs, "for all their flaws, traditional religions often foster a sense of interconnection . . . even with the whole of creation" (Christ 2003, 111). Traditional humanism and scientific materialism fail to do so; furthermore, both reject the nonmaterial aspects of existence required for an Integrative belief system. In contrast, contemporary adherents to posthumanism and new materialism give attention to both of these issues, as noted in their contributions to Relational Becoming.

Posthumanism and new materialism both move beyond anthropocentrism, thereby extending prescriptions for practice to include all of creation in a nonhierarchical manner. An early exploration of this interrelationship can be found in Gaia theory, a concept proposed by James Lovelock (1972) and further developed with Lynn Margulis (Lovelock and Margulis 1974). The Gaia hypothesis proposes that organisms interact with their inorganic surroundings on Earth to form a self-regulating, complex system that contributes to maintaining the conditions for life on the planet. Thus, organisms co-evolve with their environment and so biota and abiotic systems mutually affect one another.

The co-evolutionary aspects of the hypothesis have been demonstrated by subsequent scientific study, particularly through study of the symbiotic relationships between mitochondria and human DNA as well as complex relationships among soil bacteria, atmospheric conditions, and Earth's surface temperature (Lovelock 1995; Margulis 1999). Starting in 1985, regularly scheduled conferences have been held on the topic by academic and scientific societies, securing its place as a counter argument to Darwinian evolution (Joseph 1986). The co-evolutionary concept has even made its way into popular culture through Michael Pollan's (2001) argument that plants have evolved in relational response to human desires for sweetness, beauty, intoxication, and control.

This and other deep ecology hypotheses (Capra 1983; Næss 1973) emerged in the early 1970s when alternative spirituality traditions were taking hold in Western society. They were readily adopted by many neo-pagans – even the name Gaia refers to the Greek goddess personifying the Earth, the primal Earth Mother. However, scientists object to this common misinterpretation, stressing that Gaia is "not an organism," but "an emergent property of interaction among organisms" (Margulis 1999, 119). This clarification is sought by many who wish to remain purely scientific or philosophical in their explanation, not muddying the waters with spirituality and religion.

An early expression of this perspective can be found in evolutionary biologist Julian Huxley's (1964) notion of the mind-body continuum (rather than duality) and his argument that experiences which transcend the ordinary, those we consider divine or worthy of awe and adoration, are still part of nature, not beyond it. Therefore, he sought an understanding of divinity without God, and of our active role in evolution, redefining it as "not truly supernatural but *transnatural* – it grows out of ordinary nature but transcends it" (223). In this sense transcendence refers to a quality that is beyond mundane value or current understanding, but not beyond the natural world or our potential grasp of it. This is reflected in what Connolly (2011) refers to as "*mundane* transcendence" (74).

Others, on the other hand, are not afraid to more fully embrace religious or spiritual concepts in what Braidotti (2013) calls "a post-secular turn" (35). For example, Mies and Shiva (2014) call for "a new cosmology and a new anthropology which recognizes that life in nature (which includes human beings) is maintained by means of co-operation, and mutual care and love" (6). They describe this ecofeminist belief system as a wholly different form of universalism based on "life-sustaining networks and processes" (13), but explain that ecofeminism is simply a new term for an ancient wisdom. Similarly, while terms used like "vital" (Coole and Frost 2010) and "enchanted" (Bennett 2001) may differ in terms of their connotations, these perspectives acknowledge a special nonmaterial dimension of existence. As process naturalism explains, "sacredness is not a magical or mystical quality. . . . It isn't a thing or stuff. It is primarily a way of experiencing the world" (Mesle 1993, loc. 1792). It can be experienced in relation to any entity in any moment; "A world of becoming distributes affective and creative power widely rather than condensing the latter into a single divinity or concentrating both in the human estate" (Connolly 2011, 15).

Proponents of posthumanism and new materialism generally leap straight from ontological discussion to consideration of social action. However, such scholars also admit there is something akin to faith involved;

> This project requires more visionary power or prophetic energy. . . . Prophetic or visionary minds are the thinkers of the future. The future as an active object of desire propels us forth and motivates us to be active in the here and now of a continuous present.
>
> (Braidotti 2013, 191)

Similarly, it is argued that it takes the intuitive and prophetic vision of "a seer" to identify "how crucial shifts in the pace of events and the timing of responses are to the world" (Connolly 2011, 153). To take such actions, belief is necessary – one that does not rely on "either divine providence or ready susceptibility to human mastery" (79) as found in both theist and humanist belief systems. Drawing from complexity theory, Briggs and Peat (1999) urge "letting go, accepting limits, and celebrating magic and mystery" (7).

Others challenge us to follow Nietzsche in developing an expansive love of the world – *amor fati* – a love of fate (Braidotti 2013), or a sense of "existential gratitude" (Connolly 2011, 168). Such faith enables participation in intentional co-creation and lessens anxiety in the face of the human condition. With full recognition of the serious environmental, economic, and social issues the world faces and the dangers they pose to humanity, a belief system in which "existential vulnerability and gratitude are delicately interwoven" (Connolly 2013, 180) will lead us to care for the world rather than resent that predicament. It is decidedly not a naïve optimism or faith. However, such realism also need not lead down a nihilistic path. Instead, a belief based on a disposition toward "positive existential attachment" (Connolly 2010, 195) is generated by "feelings of abundance and joy that emerge whenever we sense the surplus of life over the structure of our identities" (196) – a non-theist, positive, existential spirituality.

Co-Creationism

While certainly not a doctrine or actual belief system, the hypothetical principles of an Integrative belief system can be drawn from naturalistic process theology, indigenous spirituality, neo-paganism, posthumanism, and new materialism.

The relational character of creation is expressed through a faith in and affirmation of everything in the universe as co-creators. Theologian Jerome Stone (2015) uses the term "immanent sacred" as a descriptor for such co-creators. Following Relational Becoming, the notion of ***sacred immanence*** adds normative value to ontological assumptions in the following tenets:

1 The not yet manifested void of creative potentiality is the embodied source of creation – it is the nonmaterial waiting to be made manifest by all existing things, beings, and places.
2 All things, beings, and places are considered entities in their own right as particular assemblages.
3 All things, beings, and places are sacred and divine as co-creators.
4 All characteristics perceived as dualities or differences are equally valued.

Adding the understanding of creation as a dynamic process, ***co-creating*** is a concept that encompasses the following tenets:

1 Creation is a relational, dynamic process within and among all things, beings, and places, all of which are interconnected and interdependent.
2 The universe in its entirety (or God/Goddess) is the ever-changing synergistic outcome of co-creation that adds qualitative value to all that is becoming.

Taken together, Co-Creationism is a belief in a sacred but immanent process in which all things, beings, and places draw from the embodied void of creative potentiality in a relational process of becoming. Sacred acts of faith are designed to increase understanding of these principles and to celebrate their implications for living well together. Faith is understood as an affirmation of existence, an abiding love of and responsibility for the world and our part in co-creating it. Rituals include a wide array of expressions, from the contemplative to the celebratory. "Every major wisdom tradition contains, at its core, a series of contemplative practices, and, at their best, these contemplative practices disclose the transrational and transpersonal waves of consciousness" (Wilber 2011, loc. 1463).

Those holding to these principles or expressing these sacred acts of faith would likely be loath to declare them as doctrine, dogma, or a declaration of faith, instead considering them as expressions of truths about existence as they understand it, with full recognition of their contestable and changing nature. Thus, our identification of these principles is simply an effort toward solidarity with acknowledgement and respect for distinctions across particular faith perspectives and practices. An Integrative belief system, like an integral belief system, "does not seek to impose its belief structures on others, but invites each and all to develop their own potentials, therein to discover their own deep spirituality" (Wilber 2011, loc. 1473). This approach seeks "a conviviality of differences through reflexivity to reach common ground" (Donati 2014, 147). It considers "whether it is possible to forge a new pluralist assemblage composed of minorities of various times who diverge on belief and creed while sharing positive affinities of spirituality across those differences" (Connolly 2011, 13). In this spirit, we embrace relational secularity (Donati 2014) and invite those holding to some or all of these principles to consider with us their implications for practice. For those who are not so aligned, we pause to consider how we might enter into productive dialogue.

Integrative pathways

An Integrative synthesis must generate pathways that are easily traversed by those holding other positions. This is what is required to pursue interfaith dialogue. In the case of belief systems, Co-Creationism must provide concepts that sufficiently meet fundamental principles within the other belief systems, or at least create a basis for dialogue toward shared understandings. As illustrated in Figure 8.1, we imagine the shared characteristics shown in Table 8.2 as pathways into a dynamic synthesis that is always open to contestation and change.

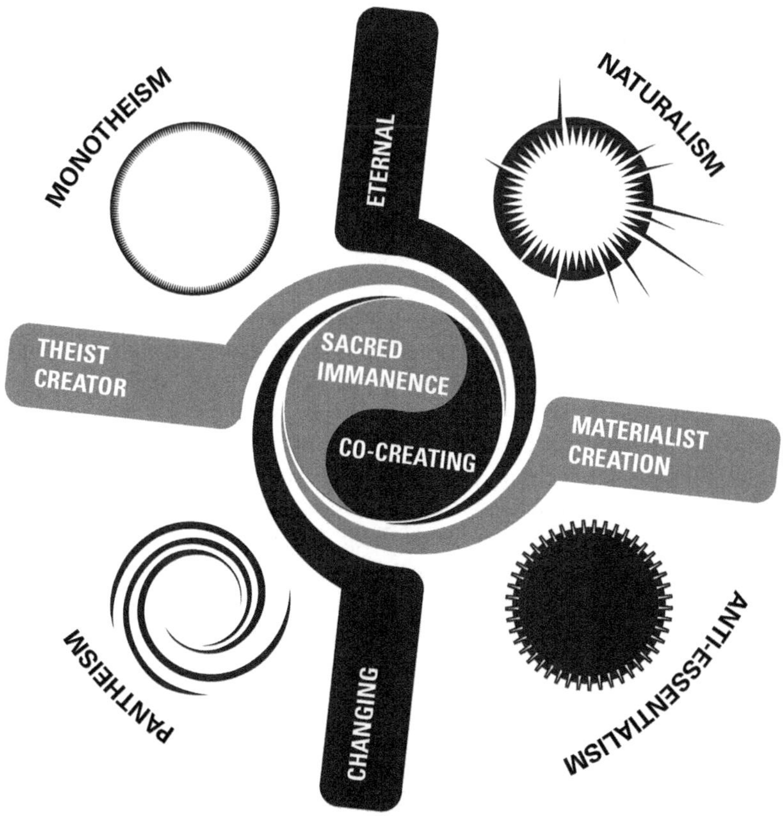

Figure 8.1 Integrative pathways for Co-Creationism

Table 8.2 Integrating belief system concerns

Ideal-Type	*Characteristics*	*Primary Concerns*	*Synthesis Solution*
Monotheism	*eternal theist creator*	A divine entity that orders creation	***Sacred immanence*** recognizes creation as sacred, while the synergistic effect of ***co-creating*** can be understood as divine
Naturalism	*eternal materialist creation*	A system of cause and effect that follows laws that can be observed and known without attribution to nonmaterial forces	***Sacred immanence*** is materialist, while ***co-creating*** includes mutually causal relationships
Pantheism	*changing theist creator*	A divine entity that enfolds and imbues all of creation	***Sacred immanence*** recognizes all things, beings, and places as sacred and engaged in ***co-creating***
Anti-Essentialism	*changing materialist creation*	No externally imposed systems of belief or stable universal identity	***Sacred immanence*** is materialist, while ***co-creating*** retains individual agency

Going back to our discussion of dialectic synthesis in the chapter's introduction, we know that a dialectical synthesis must accommodate both *theist* assumptions found in monotheism and pantheism alongside the *materialist* assumptions of naturalism and anti-essentialism. ***Sacred immanence*** holds that the nonmaterial and the material are joined in the process of ***co-creating***. Furthermore, as co-creators, all contributing entities are considered holy or blessed and deserving of deep appreciation due to their association with not-as-yet manifested potentiality and the awe-inspiring process of co-creation. Because the notion of God/Goddess resonates deeply within all theist belief systems, ***sacred immanence*** can also accommodate this conceptualization as either a representation of creative potential or the synergistic sum of everything. Yet, ***sacred immanence*** also acknowledges the unique and independent characteristics of each and every thing and being. This materialist and individualist understanding is safe ground for science, humanism, and anti-essentialism alike. To meet the basic assumptions of *eternal* belief systems (monotheism and naturalism) some sort of stability is required. In order to meet the basic assumptions of *changing* belief systems (pantheism and anti-essentialism), variation must be accommodated. ***Co-creating*** achieves both principles through its dynamic, relational process that draws from timeless potentiality to produce an evolving synergistic outcome. However, the primary concerns of each individual belief system must also be addressed in order establish a starting point for dialogue with the Integrative perspective, as shown in Table 8.2.

In understanding the source of existence as a timeless, unchanging, metaphysical being, Monotheism asserts a divine being that is separate from and hierarchically above the physical universe, establishing a fundamental dualism within the whole. The process of ***co-creating*** dissolves this dualism; however, ***sacred immanence*** maintains the characteristic of divinity allowing space for a concept of God/Goddess. Pantheism asserts an ever-changing, transcendent divinity that expresses itself through the parts of the whole, thus establishing non-duality. ***Sacred immanence*** enables nonhierarchical difference within the whole by acknowledging that all things, beings, and places are sacred, while acknowledging the unique parts that are ***co-creating*** the whole. Naturalism denies any form of noumena and asserts a material world made up of many individual phenomena set into causal motion through some sort of observable event (i.e., the Big Bang). Its belief systems include both atheistic science and secular humanism. ***Sacred immanence*** acknowledges the materialist nature of existence and allows for an understanding of its importance without need for a deity, while ***co-creating*** acknowledges mutually causal relationships. Anti-Essentialism refutes all belief systems as grand narratives that a radical plural must refuse, and is particularly suspicious of claims about truths beyond the physical and social world. ***Sacred immanence*** accommodates material phenomenon as a core feature of existence – the material is the chalice of co-creation and so it is honored and respected and does not require a reified grand narrative. Because ***co-creating*** acknowledges the agency of each individual entity, it retains a substantial amount of autonomy.

Notes

1 We remain concerned with this caveat, agreeing with Julian Huxley (1964) that these individuals, "like Dr. Tillich and many other modernist theologians, seems to me, and indeed to any humanist, to be trying to ride two horses at once, to keep his cake and eat it. He wants to be modern and meet the challenge of our new knowledge by stripping the image of God of virtually all its spatial, material, Freudian and anthropomorphic aspects. But he still persists in retaining the term *God*, in spite of all its implifications of supernatural power and personality; and it is these implifications, not the modernists' fine-spun arguments, which consciously and unconsciously affect the ordinary man and woman" (222).

2 Acknowledging the problem of phallogocentrism (Derrida 1981), for this discussion of process theology, we will simplify by using God as the term representing all theist (theo/thea) ideations of the divine entity (God/Goddess), using masculine pronouns.

3 As Connolly (2005) notes, this understanding of a limited God was also put forth by James (1909) in his explanation of a pluralistic universe.

4 This summary is paraphrased from the Neo-Paganism.com website (Neo-Paganism.com 2015) unless otherwise noted. This website provides a thorough and well-written overview of the commonalities held by a variety of traditions identified with paganism.

5 Earlier movements include Freemasonry, Rosicrucianism, Theosophy, Spiritualism, and Druidism, as well as Afro-Diasporatic faiths such as Voudoun and Santeria. More contemporary movements include Goddess spirituality, Witchcraft, Wicca, Druidism, ecofeminism, deep ecology, bioregionalism, the Mythopoetic Men's Movement, Neo-Shamanism, and the New Age Movement.

9 Ethical concepts

Stewardship

The transdisciplinary ethic rejects any attitude that refuses dialogue and discussion, regardless of whether the origin of this attitude is ideological, scientistic, religious, economic, political or philosophical. Shared knowledge should lead to a shared understanding based on an absolute respect for the collective and individual Otherness united by our common life on one and the same Earth.

– (Article 13 of the Charter of Transdisciplinarity, Nicolescu 2002, 151)

As we move from philosophical assumptions into practice, we extend the ontological, psychosocial, and epistemological commitments found in an Integrative belief system into praxis. Worldviews prefigure particular attitudes and norms of behavior in practice. Therefore, faulty ethics are often assumed to be the culprit in social, economic, environmental, and governance crises. Furthermore, attempting to resolve their "underlying factors . . . is an ethical endeavor" (Bookchin 2015b, 2923). As environmentalist and social activist Paul Hawken (2007) queries, "If there is a web of life, if human beings are part of a vast living system, what are the moral implications?" (72). It is clear that "positing radical interrelatedness has concrete ethical implications" (Keating 2013, 49).

Many argue that the ethical dimensions of the crisis of sustainability require that we take a more critical and reflexive stance toward the underlying drivers, attending to "practices of domination and the unequal parts of privilege and oppression" (Haraway 1988, 579). Braidotti (2013) suggests we are confronted with "a double ethical urgency" because morality as commonly configured no longer serves to guide action toward sustainability, and we need a new ethic immediately if we are to survive (112–113). This ethos must guide us to "live in such a manner that the fulness [*sic*] of life may come to all" (Follett 1998, 353), pursuing "the flourishing of nonhuman organisms and ecological systems" (Oord 2005, 928).

To achieve such sustainability, it has been argued that effective global governance "will require the articulation of a collaborative ethos" (Carlsson and Ramphal 1995, 5). This shared ethic should accomplish what international law is meant to provide: a public morality that is at once local and global, democratic in process, and voluntary in adoption (Held 1992). This would therefore reflect key aspects of Benhabib's (2006) pan-human cosmopolitanism as well as Braidotti's (2006) notion of global, nomadic citizenship.

Integrative Governance offers a new approach to formulating public ethics for political, economic, and administrative practices, while imbuing it with a fitting sense of morality. Specifically, an ethic of Stewardship can do so because it calls for care for both self and others. Although stewardship is a concept that "belongs to the most ancient strands of our Judeo-Christian heritage" (Hall 1990, 49) as well as Confucianism (Weiming 1996), it is responsive to "the explicit problems and needs of our own historical moment" (Hall 1990, 123) – namely, the crisis of sustainability that confronts us. Stewardship's sense of mutual care and relational mindfulness supports sustainability and good governance by considering the social, economic, and environmental implications of decisions and actions to all concerned. "Collectively, we are stewards of the earth" (Gray 2001) – sharing mutual rights, responsibilities, and answerability.

As shown in Table 9.1, a synthesis position must address the dialectics found in the four primary governance types. The horizontal relational axis shows the dialectic of prioritizing *Right* or *Good* as a *normative structure* for determining action. *Right* is generally defined by the group as a moral judgment regarding means, while *Good* is generally defined by the individual as beneficial or desirable ends. The vertical process axis shows the dialectic between *external criteria* and *internal motivation* as *sources of ethical guidance. External criteria* can either be guidelines for action provided by a source we feel obliged to follow, or found in the anticipated results of our chosen actions. *Internal motivation* is felt personally, but can be understood either as a societal norm or a personal preference.

An Integrative ethic must ensure that both group-imposed norms of *Right* and individual determinations of *Good* are considered as normative guidelines so that neither a predetermined universal right nor a pluralistic or relativistic good dominate an individual's choice making. Habermas (1998a) describes this synthesis position as lying between norms and facts. Both group and individual perspectives are brought together through the ethical concept of ***reverent interconnectivity*** – an axiological ethic (Brady 2003) of mutual care and relational mindfulness that goes beyond transactional understandings of mutuality. This ethic follows directly from the sense of ***sacred immanence*** found in Co-Creationism. Its moral code demands that we respect the inherent value of all entities as co-creators.

An Integrative ethic must also ensure that neither *external criteria* nor *internal motivation* are reified as absolute determining factors. Habermas (1998b) calls for discourse ethics that are only discoverable through deliberative communication with others.[1] When principles are co-determined through participative rather than exclusive practices, they are no longer coercive. Furthermore, active engagement in formulating those principles engenders the internal motivation to abide by them. Therefore, a synthesis of *external criteria* and *internal motivation* is found in a participative determining process that produces ***emergent principles.***

Considering ***reverent interconnectivity***, Stewardship privileges neither *Right* nor *Good.* As Gadamer (2013) argues, this approach to ethics "embraces both means and end" (332). We cannot "know the right means in advance," nor can there be any "anterior certainty concerning what the good life is directed toward as a whole" (331). Instead, principles emerge "as part of the stuff of the situation, as part of the warp and woof of our concrete life" (Follett 2013c, 142). It is "from all the intermingling" of *Right* and *Good* within the situation "that a new thought may be evolved" (142). Considering ***emergent principles***,

Table 9.1 Dialectical ethical concepts

	Normative Right	***Normative Good***
External Criteria	Deontological Obligation	Consequentialism
Internal Motivation	Moral Imperative	Moral Skepticism/Relativism

(Source: Stout and Love 2016)

Stewardship is neither an impersonal ethic of reasoned justice nor a personal ethic of emotional care – it is a synthesis (Haas and Deetz 2000). It is neither objective nor subjective – "it is both; we look at the matter quite differently" (Follett 1998, 278). We need not "choose between a moral atomism and general ethical laws" (Follett 2013c, 142).

Williams (1999) identifies three ethical models for determining right and achieving the common good. The covenant suggests a transcendent moral authority over individuals that determines what is right, similar to our Deontological Obligation and Moral Imperative ideal-types. The contractual approach defines the public good through a pluralist social contract, similar to our Consequentialism, and resisted by Moral Skepticism/Relativism. Finally, stewardship requires the individual and community to act in a way to protect future generations. We argue that Stewardship and its commitment to interconnectivity between the present and the future best fits an Integrative approach to ethics. It provides the external criteria of both social covenants and contracts, while generating the internal motivation that inspires such personal commitment.

By definition, a steward is "a person morally responsible for the careful use of money, time, talents, or other resources, especially with respect to the principles or needs of a community or group" (Neufeldt 1996, 1315). The term is used broadly across fields as diverse as theology, science and technology policy, environmentalism, organizational management, economics, financial planning, philanthropy, and public policy. While often emphasizing fiduciary trusteeship, the original meaning of stewardship is a spiritual responsibility for humanity, the earth, and a shared moral purpose (Hall 1990). Within an Integrative ethic, such responsibility is shared and mutually answerable; we are all stewards.

As a respectful, relational actor, the steward is neither a servant nor fully autonomous: "Stewardship is the exercise of comprehensive and dedicated responsibility for a valued practice, institution, resource, relationship or group" (Selznick 1998, 68). However, this relationship is not a transactional principal-agent arrangement: "The responsibilities of stewardship go beyond mutuality. They call for a deeper commitment to selected objects of moral concern" (Selznick 1998, 68). The steward's actions are "prompted by an urge, an impulse, a motive from within" (Morro 1932, 19). This behavior is not dictated by external or formal agreements – a steward's ethics are not bound by norm, rule, law, or code, but rather by a covenant of care.

The moral commitment evoked by an ethic of Stewardship is imbued with a sense of ***reverent interconnectivity*** that is grounded in the philosophical commitments to Relational Becoming, Ensembling individuality, Integral Knowing, and Co-Creationism. Whether infused with a sense of spirituality or religiosity, the ethic of Stewardship links this relational worldview with normative standards for action: "the essence of this . . . is as important for ethics as for physiology or psychology" (Follett 2013c, 88). If we deeply respect our interconnectivity we will seek to do what is relationally considered right and produce what is good for both ourselves and the group.

This morally-infused understanding of mutuality "is reflective of one of the oldest ecological principles that have been incorporated as metaphysical, and practical rules for human conduct" (Cajete 2004, 55). It is also present in process theology which argues that "feeling, sympathy, relationship, creativity, freedom, and enjoyment are the fundamental threads that unite all beings in the universe, including particles of atoms and the divinity" (Christ 2003, 3). We likewise see this understanding of community in posthumanism, postcolonialism, feminism, ecology, and environmentalism, all of which "rest on an enlarged sense of inter-connection between self and others, including the nonhuman or 'earth' others" (Braidotti 2013, 47–48). Thus, relational mindfulness evokes an ethic based on interconnection between the human and nonhuman environment – "an affirmative bond that locates the subject in the flow of relations with multiple others" (Braidotti 2013, 49).

Emergent principles are determined through a participative process through which all individuals co-determine what is right and good, thereby generating an authentic commitment grounded in experiential ownership. Mesle (1993) calls this a "committed relativism" (loc. 1312) that enables legitimate value judgments without resorting to claims of absolute right or wrong. This is essential because "seldom is any side right in that absolute sense" (Follett 2003e, 251). It requires open-mindedness and responsiveness to each situation in order to interpret the meanings situationally. Drawing forward ***situated knowing***, this approach to "moral knowledge" must likewise "respond to the demands of the situation of the moment" (Gadamer 2013, 331). Lloyd (1996) calls such a locally situated approach to universal ethics "a collaborative morality" (74), and Eze (2008) describes it as "realist perspectivism" (395). This is not unlike a critical ethical stance that is skeptical of dominant narratives, morally reflective, compassionate toward the generalized other, and interpersonally responsive (Zanetti 2004). As an example, some theories of communitarian democracy keep norms and values open to informed critique by the community (Kahne 1996).

Reverent interconnectivity

Reverent interconnectivity is an ethical stance that synthesizes *Right* and *Good*. It engenders a subject-subject relationship, as opposed to a transactional subject-object attitude found in instrumental explanations of mutualism, generating both mutual care and relational mindfulness in reciprocal relationship. Following from the philosophical commitments in Relational Becoming, Ensembling individuality, Integral Knowing, and Co-Creationism, ethics must be aligned with the "self-in-relation" (Miller 1984). This interconnectedness "governs relationships between all human beings, between all other forms of life" (Stewart-Harawira 2005a, 155). As Keating (2013, 162) explains,

> individuals who see themselves as integral parts of all that exists recognize their interdependence with others. This recognition fuels both the desire for social change and the assurance that individual actions – no matter how insignificant they may seem – can and do impact others.

Therefore, the assumption of ***relationality*** must carry forward into decision making and action. To the extent that there is a "constitutive good" (Taylor 1989), it is ***relationality*** itself; interconnection is both the source of goodness and expression of goodness. As Noddings (2003) argues, relation is "identified as the human condition that we, consciously or unconsciously, perceive as 'good'" (5). Therefore, "We want to be *moral* in order to remain in the caring relation" (5). Follett (1998) explains, "What is morality? The fulfillment of relation by man to man. . . . This ordering of relations is morality in its essence and completeness" (333).

This deeply respectful, "I-Thou" relationship (Buber 1986) undergirds what some feminists call an "ethic of care" (Gilligan 1982, 1995). Connolly (2011) describes the stance as a "generative ethic" (80) that cultivates a care for the world and motivates us to produce principles, responsibilities, and obligations pertinent to our mutual interdependence. From this perspective, "morality is not the refraining from doing certain things – it is a constructive force" (Follett 1998, 53). Following Nietzsche, some even describe this as an "ethics of joy" based on the potential depth of existential appreciation of the world (Bennett 2001,

131–159). Braidotti (2010) calls on Deleuze and Nietzsche to explain that the "ethical challenge" lies in "cultivating joyful modes of confronting the overwhelming intensity of *bios-zoe*. This implies approaching the world through affectivity and not cognition" (210). This type of mutual care is neither grounded in a sense of personal affection, nor a sense of resource dependence. Rather, it is the ethical implication of our multidimensional interdependency with the world. Therefore, ***reverent interconnectivity*** fosters more than transactional mutuality – this sensibility generates both mutual care and relational mindfulness in reciprocal relationship.

Mutual care

Recognition of ***reverent interconnectivity*** encourages us to care about all beings and places, motivating us to co-determine what is right for ourselves and our interdependent communities. At a basic level of dependence, "ecological stewardship . . . acknowledges that this is the only place we live, and it implies the need for ongoing care of the planetary ecosystem so as to maintain its capacity to support and nurture all of humanity indefinitely" (Prugh 2015, 136). In other words, for our own sustainability, "we had better have a care about the world in which we live" (Mesle 1993, loc. 826). However, ***reverent interconnectivity*** deepens this sense of care to one of "biophilia, love for humanity and nature" (Fromm 1997, 101) that produces a generalized "presumptive care for the diversity of life and the fecundity of the earth" (Connolly 2011, 79) – one that re-enchants the world and our love for it (Howe 2006).

Noddings (2003) takes "the caring relation as ethically basic" (3). Lyons (1983) found evidence that there are two distinct ways of describing the self in relation to others: connected or separate/objective.[2] These are linked to personal affective care and transactional interest. Alternatively, the ethic of care "revolves around the central insight, that self and other are interdependent" (Gilligan 1982, 74). Thus, the human condition is a "relation of natural caring" (Noddings 2003, 5) and the desire for mutual wellbeing extends beyond the transactional *quid pro quo* reasoning of social contract reciprocity. An ethic of care is defined from this relational perspective which argues "the activity of care enhances both others and self" (Gilligan 1982, 74). This contrast is also illustrated in distinction between a "feminine" ethic of care and a "feminist" ethic of care (Gilligan 1995); the former prioritizes relationships by subjugating self to others in a form of altruism or self-sacrifice, while the latter is rooted in an ontological condition of being-in-the-world together.

Mutual care, therefore, does not necessarily imply a feeling of warmth, personal tie, or inherent agreement but, rather, reflects the necessary implications of Relational Becoming. Kropotkin (1902) explains this type of mutuality "is a feeling infinitely wider than love or personal sympathy" (xiii). Similarly, Follett (2003a) explains mutual care "will keep us not only from a false individualism, but also from a false altruism" (82). The sense of care thus reflects a recognition that "Our interests are inextricably interwoven" (Follett 1998, 81). This results in a synthesis of individualist self-interest, collectivist service, and charitable beneficence, transforming all three through a sense of interdependence. Thus, mutual care imagines human beings as naturally engaging in free association that is prone toward reciprocity rather than demanded by a social contract (Carson 2006). As George (1929) observes, while such care need not be understood as altruism, "there is yet a force which overcomes and drives out selfishness" (463).

Whitehead (1979) describes this "emotional force" (15) as empathy, which begins with a non-cognitive awareness of the intrinsic value of others – "feeling the feeling *in* another and feeling conformally *with* another" (162). It is also a sense of mutual loyalty that is gradually built up through our empathetic ability to "think and feel together" (Follett 1998, 47). According to Husserl (1982), the intersubjective empathic experience occurs by moving from unconscious awareness of the other to imagining ourselves in the other's position. Empathy enables the individual to set aside personal perspectives in a "disinterestedness" that is "a kind of compassion or fellow-feeling" (Eagleton 2003, 133) that enables one "to feel the values and feelings of others – their hope, fears, joys, sorrows, loves, and suspicions – to create our own lives and values in response to them, and then to relate back to them in ways that show that we have taken them creatively into our own life first" (Mesle 1993, loc. 1376). Through empathy, we recognize ourselves in the joys and suffering of others and identify with them through compassion. Wang (2012) argues this empathetic imagining of the other is key to peaceful coexistence.

Humanists, both secular and theist, often refer to this type of empathy as love. In this use, love is not personalized affect but rather empathy put into action. This meaning is reflected in the concept of *agape*, which is broadly understood as a form of universal love or "the interdependence of sympathy" (Oord 2005, 926). As with other understandings of mutual care, this approach synthesizes self-love and other-regarding love: "These needs are coequal and synergistic: neither derives from the other, and the full actualization of one is dependent on the full actualization of the other" (Hart 1989, 102). Thus, love is depicted as actions aimed at promoting mutual wellbeing, taking "into account, to varying degrees, the life of the individual, local community, and global community" (Oord 2005, 928).

This innate "seed of care" (Connolly 2011, 79), however, must be nurtured and therefore depends upon "the actors and on the social networks to which they belong" (Donati 2014, 61). In other words, we must generate social systems that reinforce mutual care through an "affirmative ethics" which "is based on the praxis of constructing positivity" (Braidotti 2013, 129). As "trust, affect, care, and responsibility for one another" (Sitrin and Azzellini 2012, 98–99) are nurtured within the practice of community, individuals experience a "personal transformation" in which they "become 'more human'" (99). Kropotkin (1902) argues that mutualism emerges through this type of social evolution, "to always larger and larger agglomerations, so as to finally embrace one day the whole of mankind, without respect to its diverse creeds, languages, and races" (224).

Relational mindfulness

Reverent interconnectivity fosters "a responsible attitude toward our experience – a conscious and responsible attitude" (Follett 2003c, 50). Keating (2013) explains that once we have an understanding of "ourselves as radically interrelated, we react thoughtfully as we engage with others; we learn to pause and self-reflect" (49). This kind of call for active reflection upon the mutual impacts of our actions is reflected in the Golden Rule, or law of reciprocity, found in many religions and spiritual traditions. Adding an element of self-interest to further motivate reciprocity, the Hindu and Buddhist notion of ***karma*** suggests that one's actions have a cause and effect relationship on one's future experience (Bowker 1997). This notion is also found in the Wiccan Rede (Traditional n.d.) invoked in neo-pagan practices as a reminder to live an ethical lifestyle:

> Bide the Wiccan Rede ye must, in perfect love and perfect trust.
> Eight words the Wiccan Rede fulfill: An harm ye none, do as ye will.
> Ever mind the rule of three: What ye sends out comes back to thee.
> Follow this with mind and heart, and merry ye'll meet and merry part.

This focus on reciprocity draws forward Ensembling individuality. Each person is expected to be "aware of the needs of others as well as being aware of what the individual can do for the good of the group" (Cordova 2004, 178). As an example, the Lakota people describe right living as the "Good Red Road of balance and reciprocity that can only be found in relation" (Burkhart 2004, 15). We refer to this type of ethical agency as *relational mindfulness*, in which people – both on their own and within groups – continually seek to be attentive to the possible implications of their decisions and actions for all other entities that may be affected. This requires continuous reflection on, "To whom or what am I responsible and in what community of interaction am I?" (Niebuhr 1963, 68).

If the notion of community must reflect all that is within the sphere of mutual effect, how community is defined in any given instance may vary from the micro-local level to the macro-global level. Because everything is interconnected, "each point of existence has a certain ring of primary influences, but each of those primary influences has its own ring of influences which partially overlaps and partially extends beyond the circles of the others" (Suchocki 1985, para. 17). In other words, each person impacts the macro-system (MacAllister 2011). This so-called butterfly effect is quite profound, because "everything affects everything else in a relational world" (Suchocki 1985, para. 17) – "we actually make a difference in the whole of this awesome universe" (para. 18). This mindfulness of both the imagined and actual gives new meaning to the old adage of "think globally, act locally."

Starting with the relationally mindful person, the human condition is one of "person-in-community" (Cobb Jr. 2007). For this reason, Braidotti (2010) calls for "an ethical regrounding of social participation and community building" (204) and Furman (2004) calls for an ethic of community. Because morality is relational rather than covenanted or contractual, it could also be conceived as a community compact or statement of intent (Walker 1998). However, due to our global interconnections, "the responsible self is driven as it were by the movement of the social process to respond and be accountable in nothing less than a universal community" (Niebuhr 1963, 88).

This breadth of existing humanity is further extended to include nonhuman beings "an eco-philosophy of multiple belongings" (Braidotti 2013, 49) as well as future beings in "inter-generational accountability" (192). As Keating (2013) insists, we must consider "*all* others (both human and nonhuman others), no matter how different or distant they might be" (46). However, anthropomorphizing animals is flawed. While all other beings are co-creators and therefore subject to relational mindfulness, the ethical agency and responsibility attributed to each varies – nonhuman beings and places cannot be held to the same standards of mutual care and relational mindfulness.

In regard to places, many indigenous traditions interconnect human being with territory (Monture-Angus 1999) and exhibit a "profound and deeply rooted sense of place and relationship with the entirety of the natural world" (Suzuki and Knudtson 1992, 10) and sense of interconnection and respect for all of creation (Stewart-Harawira 2005a).[3] As one Native American scholar explains, "It is through our spiritual (metaphysical) connection with Mother Earth that we are able to teach our philosophy of communal living among all life in the universe" (Verney 2004, 135). Similarly, in some Australian aboriginal ontology, the interacting concepts of a physical place, the human sense of that place, and the sacred process through which they are brought into being guide the way of living together in place. There is a "fusion of being and political existence in Country through Dreaming and Law" (Brigg 2007, 409). Ethically, if human Law is not congruent with spiritual guidance (Dreaming), the place and all beings within it (Country) will be harmed, which includes the deciders and actors themselves.

In sum, ***reverent interconnectivity*** entails reflecting with care upon the generalized other most broadly conceived – a community of all beings and places affected by an action, both now and in the future. The ethical "we" must include the full continuum of human and nonhuman beings, places, and those yet to be born or created. Indeed, many Native American peoples close public statements and prayers with the phrase, "For all my relations" (Waters 2004a) in acknowledgement of this entire interconnected web of creation.

Emergent principles

Emergent principles are ethical concepts that synthesize *internal motivation* and *external criteria* through the method of integration. From the perspective of ***reverent interconnectivity***, each individual is responsible for being in moral conversation with both the generalized and actual other at all times (Benhabib 1992). As Follett (1998) argues "we do not follow right, we create right" (52). She claims this perspective generates "a system of ethics which has three conceptions in regard to right, conscience and duty" (52). Specifically, it is "a related conscience" (56) that is determined through a group process that she calls "the method of integration" (Follett 2013c, 178). The process is integrative and relational rather than procedural and transactional.

As introduced in Chapter 7, the integrative process entails activities of: (1) sharing, (2) disintegration, (3) revaluation, and (4) synthesis. In the case of ethics, rather than seeking intersubjective truth, the process seeks to determine right and good; "the ranging of multiplicity into that which is both means and ends" (Follett 2013c, 82). To be most effective in determining right action and good ends, integrating begins with a relational attitude Follett (1998) describes as "*the will to will the common will*" (49). As Braidotti (2010) explains, an adequate ethical question is "One that is capable of sustaining the subject in his or her quest for more interrelations with others, that is, more 'Life,' motion, change, and transformation" (215–216). This relational disposition engenders a cooperative style of relating in which we are willing to consider others in our decisions and actions.

To be most inclusive and to ensure the highest level of agreement in regard to outcomes, integration uses participative "*modes of association*" (147) that employ "genuine discussion" (Follett 1998, 210), as opposed to debate. However, the process of integration assumes difference and the potential for conflict exist within all social groups (Follett 1919, 1998, 2003b). Today, we would call integration a process of dialogue and deliberation toward consensus building (Susskind, McKearnan, and Thomas-Larme 1999; Yankelovich 1991) or a conflict resolution process (Forester 2009; Yankelovich 1999).

Sharing invites all participants to contribute their unique and often deeply held value commitments (Forester 2009). To accommodate both types of normative guidance – *external criteria* and *internal motivations* – integration must include desired ends based on perceived facts and socially-determined values. However, to find mutual understanding, participants must employ sincerity and honesty in communication, as well as a willingness to hear, suspend judgment, and respect value positions with which they may vehemently disagree (Bohm 2004). Young (1997) notes that "through listening across difference each position can come to understand something about the ways proposals and claims affect others differently situated" (69). Keating (2013) refers to this as "listening with raw openness," a process of "opening ourselves and really *hearing* what others say" (52). This is a demanding process requiring a willingness to trust others and the process initially, but it is self-reinforcing through ongoing dialogue (Freire 2011).

This type of dialogue requires "a place where there is no authority, no hierarchy, where there is no special purpose – sort of an empty space, where we can let anything be talked about" (Bohm 2004, 49). A skilled facilitator can help create a space that supports and makes easier the sharing of deeply held values and beliefs (Box 2004; Forester 1999b; Stivers 1994, 2000b). However, this also requires skill from participants as well, including "*sensitivity* – a certain way of knowing how to come in and how not to come in, of watching all the subtle cues and the senses and your response to them" (Bohm 2004, 45). This ability is often called "emotional intelligence" (Goleman 1995, 2011) or "communicative capacity" (Bartels 2015a).

Disintegration explores participants' conceptions of right and good, breaking them down to understand specific meanings, where they come from, and why they are held. This process illuminates common ground and shared beliefs as well as differences and value trade-offs among mutually exclusive conceptions. Keating (2013) describes this as finding "points of connection" (42) that create a "woven linkage – a synergistic, alchemical combination between sameness, similarities, and difference" that "position difference within a larger context, a more visionary framework" (42–43). As these differences confront one another, *revaluation* enables conflict resolution (Forester 2009) through "constructive conflict" (Follett 2003b, 30) and *transvaluation*, a process through which challenges to existing values creates new shared values (Starcross 2004). Through this deliberative process, *synthesis* is found in ***emergent principles*** shaped from both common ground and new insights.

Emergent principles must always be grounded in the situation at hand, but with consideration of the broadest and most inclusive total situation, considering ***reverent interconnectivity***. As Follett (2013c) explains, "We want to find the law *of* the situation *in* the situation and yet still be guided by law and not by personal or national whims or a narrow self-interest" (152). As such, "knowledge of the particular situation . . . is a necessary supplement to moral knowledge" (Gadamer 2013, 331). These types of situationally determined principles are neither relativistic nor universal; they consider individuals, particular groups, and the whole of society, from the local to the global. Therefore, the resulting conceptions of right and good are more just because no one is excluded from consideration and the integrative determining process does not allow for domination and compromise. These ***emergent principles*** represent "a unifying of interests benefiting and developing individuals, benefiting and developing society" (Follett 2013c, 48). This resolution of responsibility to others and self is beneficial not only for society, but for the individual as well (Harmon 1990).

While what is considered in the integrative process encompasses the broadest scale of society, Follett (1919) argues that social agreements of this nature can legitimately be made only through "actual group association – the *practice* of community" (584). This participation is necessary to synthesize *external criteria* with *internal motivation*. When people take part in determining right and good, "no mandate from without has power over us" because "it is no longer a prohibition but a self-expression" (Follett 1998, 53). A sense of commitment to acting upon what is determined is ensured not through the binding authority of law or contract, "but in the fact that it has been produced by the community" (Follett 1998, 130). Thus, loyalty to ***emergent principles*** is experientially founded and all share responsibility for demanding and giving obedience to what has been co-created.

In sum, the integrative process assumes that human beings are capable of determining right and good together, accommodating difference and disagreement while moving toward consensus. The answer to the ethical questions of how one should act (means) or what is good (ends), are discovered through dialogue and deliberation with consideration of all within the situation – those beings and places that will be impacted now or in the future.

This requires a commitment to an "us" broadly conceived because "the wider its circumference the truer will our judgments be" (Follett 1919, 580). The resulting public ethic is inherently mutualistic due to its basis in ***reverent interconnectivity*** – subject-subject relations that produce a sense of fellowship that transforms justice from a hierarchical structure of sympathy to an egalitarian foundation of empathetic understanding. All share responsibility for demanding and giving obedience to ***emergent principles*** through a sense of experientially founded loyalty. This determining process can be used to guide the means and ends chosen in all aspects of social life, including political and economic systems and the manner in which they are administered.

Stewardship

The ethic of Stewardship combines the sense of ***reverent interconnectivity*** and a commitment to ***emergent principles.*** The philosophical assumptions of interconnection in how we become, form our identities, and come to know the world create a reverence and care for all of creation. This care motivates a sense of mutual responsibility and answerability for our actions. Stewards are neither self-interested nor self-sacrificing, but are rather mutually caring and respectful of the sanctity of all human beings and all of creation. Therefore, Stewardship is often described as an important function given a high level of responsibility, but one that requires humility because it is committed to a shared moral purpose and beholden to the authority of the community.

Referring to the ideal-type model developed by H. Richard Niebuhr (1963), the dialectic formed between *man-the-citizen*, who is answerable to the social order, and *man-the-maker*, who determines the social order, is resolved in *man-the-answerer* who is agential, yet mutually obligated *with* others. There is no external source providing the substantive content of an ethic; there are no predetermined moral mandates. Nor are we free to autonomously determine and pursue the good we desire. We must maintain both an ongoing sense of "responsibility of an *I* for a *Thou*" (Buber 1986, 29) and a "*presumptive responsiveness* to emergent situations" (Connolly 2013, 135). Shared responsibility emerges from a "matrix of social relationships and the dynamics of internal dialogue that enable and inform action" (Harmon 1995, 129). We must develop "collective responsibility" and "reciprocal modification" in our actions (Follett 2013b, 75).

The notion of mutual answerability is often linked to both Catholic and Protestant Christian stewardship theology, in which humankind is charged with responsibility to care for, sustain, and make better all of creation within its reach (Hefner 1993; Rhodes 1987; Thistlethwaite 2005). Similarly, "process theology calls us to accept a world in which we must bear responsibility" (Mesle 1993, loc. 1119). However, the characteristics of Stewardship are moral and ethical rather than sectarian and are found in broadly diverse cultural traditions and religions. It is a concept that is applied to social, economic, and environmental issues, alike. Drawing from a broader literature (Atherton 2000; Block 1993; Carter 2002; Graves and Addington 2003; Greenleaf 1982; Hall 1990; Harries 1992; Jenkins 2003; Kearns 1996 Morro 1932; Senge 1990; Simpson 1999; Stackhouse 1987; Weiming 1996; Williams 1999; Woodlock and Young 2001), Stewardship is understood as an internal, intrinsic motivation that stems from both philosophical commitments and experience.

Stewards make prudent and careful judgments that consider tradition, present conditions, and the future. Furthermore, stewards exhibit trustworthy behavior that is guided by the community's shared moral principles and definition of the common good. From these characteristics, it becomes evident that Stewardship is a motivation, an attitude, and an act of both deciding and doing. As a motivation and attitude, Stewardship stems from ***reverent interconnectivity***. As an act, Stewardship reflects respect for the community's determining process and resulting ***emergent principles***. This public ethic can be exercised by anyone and everyone. As Bohm (2004) argues, "If people would do this in government or in business or internationally, our society would work differently" (45).

Integrative pathways

An Integrative synthesis must generate pathways that are easily traversed by those holding other positions. In the case of ethics, Stewardship must provide concepts that sufficiently meet fundamental principles within the other ethical frameworks, or at least create a basis for shared understandings. As shown in Figure 9.1, we imagine the shared characteristics shown in Table 9.2 as pathways into a dynamic synthesis that is always open to contestation and change.

Going back to our discussion of dialectic synthesis in the chapter's introduction, we know that a dialectical synthesis must include understandings of both *Right* and *Good* as well as both *external criteria* and *internal motivations*. Within ***reverent interconnectivity***, *Right* and *Good* are redefined as relational and mutually determinant; ends and means are no

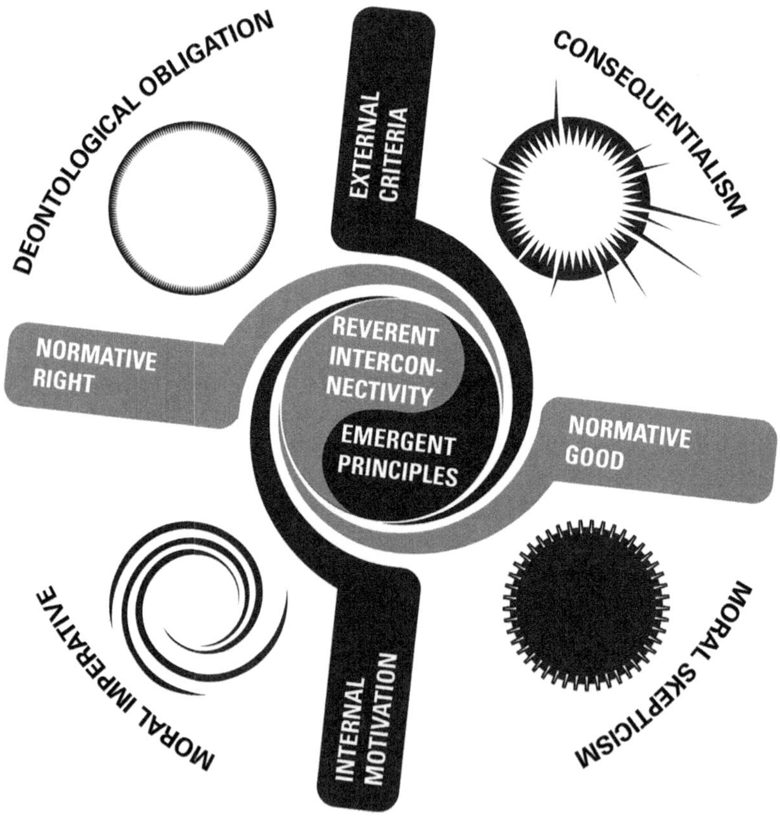

Figure 9.1 Integrative pathways for Stewardship

longer distinct. Mutual care redefines both self- and group-interest as relational-interest, while relational mindfulness nurtures mutual care through ongoing reflection. Combining *external criteria* and *internal motivations*, moral guidelines must synthesize the will of the individual and the will of the group. The participative determining process of integration through which ***emergent principles*** are developed identifies the group as the fundamental ethical unit in which local groups consider mutual impact globally. Because ***emergent principles*** are established through a participatory determining process, integration of individual preferences is pursued if not always attained.

However, the primary concerns of each distinct ethical position must also be addressed in order establish a starting point for dialogue with the Integrative perspective, as shown in Table 9.2.

Deontological Obligation seeks to procedurally enforce a universal morality, combining externally imposed criteria of what is Right. The ***emergent principles*** developed in the determining process of integration provide guidelines for action and foster a sense of loyalty to mutual obligation, while the relational mindfulness of ***reverent interconnectivity*** provides a sense of Right action. Consequentialism seeks individual and societal progress through the pluralist pursuit of Good. ***Reverent interconnectivity*** ensures consideration

Table 9.2 Integrating ethical concerns

Ideal-Type	***Characteristics***	***Primary Concern***	***Synthesis Solution***
Deontological Obligation	*external criteria, normative Right*	Enforced universal morality or Right as Law	***Emergent principles*** foster a sense of loyalty to guidelines for action; ***Reverent interconnectivity*** provides a sense of Right action
Consequentialism	*external criteria, normative Good*	Individual and societal progress through pursuit of the Good	***Reverent interconnectivity*** promotes relational-interests through mutual care; ***Emergent principles*** allow for moral progress
Moral Imperative	*internal motivation, normative Right*	Self-regulated desire to act in accordance with what is Right in each situation	***Emergent principles*** foster a sense of loyalty; ***Reverent interconnectivity*** generates mutual care for the generalized and particular other
Moral Skepticism/ Relativism	*internal motivation, normative Good*	Agency in determining what is Good	***Reverent interconnectivity*** protects individual agency; ***Emergent principles*** are generated through a participative process

of relational-interests of individual and group through mutual care. The process of crafting ***emergent principles*** creates a sense of moral contract into which individuals enter while allowing for ethical progress through renegotiation of the guiding principles. The Moral Imperative demands a self-imposed desire to act in accordance with what would be Right for anyone in each given situation. The determining process of integration provides ***emergent principles*** to which individuals have a sense of loyalty. ***Reverent interconnectivity*** generates mutual care for the generalized and particular other, providing a universal Golden Rule for anyone in the situation. Ethical Skepticism and Relativism wish to protect autonomy and agency in the process of determining Good while rejecting externally imposed norms. ***Reverent interconnectivity*** protects each individual's agency. The participative determining process ensures individual voice in the creation of ***emergent principles*** while the associated mutual obligation of others protects the individual. In sum, the ethic of Stewardship provides guidance for active, intentional co-creation toward the flourishing of all life. As will be discussed further in the remaining chapters of this section, these characteristics transform the meaning of political, economic, and administrative theory.

Notes

1 Habermasian communicative rationality is misaligned with the assumptions of Relational Becoming. Communicative action (Habermas 1998a, c) is a highly rational approach to deliberation that relies on predetermined understandings of right and is heavily weighted toward argumentation and persuasion. It is not designed for building consensus through mutual responsiveness and often results in compromise or *de facto*, if not overt domination (Kim and Kim 2008; Mansbridge et al. 2006; Bartels 2013).

2 This study included extensive interview data from female and male children, adolescents, and adults.

3 As an example, the government of New Zealand recognizes the entirety of the Whanganui River and its tributaries as an indivisible, living whole, both in terms of physical and metaphysical aspects (Cullinan 2014).

10 Political theory

Radical Democracy

The dignity of the human being is of both planetary and cosmic dimensions. The appearance of human beings on Earth is one of the stages in the history of the Universe. The recognition of the Earth as our home is one of the imperatives of transdisciplinarity. Every human being is entitled to a nationality, but as an inhabitant of the Earth is also a transnational being. The acknowledgement by international law of this twofold belonging, to a nation and to the Earth, is one of the goals of transdisciplinary research.

– (Article 8 of the Charter of Transdisciplinarity, Nicolescu 2002, 150)

Political ideologies, political leaders, and the political process itself are often blamed for the crisis of sustainability. Politics determines which values will prevail in society as whole, or in a given public policy decision (Patterson 2008). Driven by the dominant values of recent history, both governments and governance fail to mitigate the pressing social, economic, and environmental crises we confront. Violent conflict has not abated, we have not avoided economic catastrophes, and environmental disasters continue to become more frequent and extreme. Therefore, the crises of sustainability and government are inextricably linked; we must re-conceptualize the political theories informing governance practices in order to better respond to the wicked problems we confront.

In this context, the global governed have grown increasingly distrustful of institutions that fail to mitigate or prevent this crisis of sustainability. While republican and parliamentary systems offer "nominal democracy," critics argue that even these systems "mock the promise of deeper democratic practices" (Prugh 2015, 138). As Follett (1998) laments, "We have not yet tried democracy" (3) – *true* democracy. Members of the public increasingly claim political systems and parties inadequately represent them and that governance is too heavily influenced by corporate or ruling class interests. Social movements have taken up the demand for direct involvement across a range of issues (e.g., environmentalism, post-anarchism, prison abolition, alter-globalization, indigenous land sovereignty, food sovereignty, etc.) – this is "a time of uprisings, movements and moments against economic crises and the politics of representation" (Sitrin and Azzellini 2012, 15).

Most fundamentally, political theory concerns itself with the relationship between the individual and group. Contemporary crises demand "a redefinition of peoples' relationship with their society" (Lemus and Barkin 2013, 6). To transform how power operates (Mueller 2011), we must "transform *relationships* between individuals and groups so that none dominates others" (Thayer 1981, 42). Catlaw (2007b) argues this calls for a "politics of the subject" (192) that "commits to a presupposition of *radical difference*" (193) and collapses "our conventional categories of public and private, the political and the social, market and polis" (195). This approach transforms modes of association and organizational structures to foster self-governance throughout society.

Considering the global context, some argue self-governance must take a new form – "the cosmopolitan model of democracy" (Held 1992, 33). This has implications for moral, legal, institutional, and interactional aspects of governance as they impact individual rights (Pogge 1992). Morally, all persons stand in relation to one another and should therefore, as global citizens, enjoy the same legal standing. Institutional rules and practices – international law – should ensure rights and responsibilities, guided by a public ethic of Stewardship. As Habermas (1998b) argues, global law and democratic procedures for deliberative discourse should protect against potential moral fundamentalism. Because networks of power are found in all societal sectors – public, private, and civic – cosmopolitan democracy would demand principles of self-determination and justice across all three domains. To achieve this outcome, Held (1992) recommends establishing: (1) international systems of law for economic and environmental regulation, protection of human rights, and peacekeeping; (2) more democratic and just forms of civil and political organization; and (3) cooperative patterns of ownership and possession.

While we do not adopt cosmopolitan ideas indiscriminately, many of its reconfigurations of the political economy generally fall under the rubric of Radical Democracy. As noted in the Preface, Radical Democracy moves sovereignty from parties and elected representatives to actual citizens[1] (i.e., community members). Thus, Radical Democracy is differentiated from classical conservative liberalism, modern liberalism, and communitarian approaches to democracy which emphasize social contract (Tønder and Thomassen 2005b). Specifically, Radical Democracy is distinguished from its liberal counterparts based on its reliance on participatory rather than representative practices (Simons 2005).

Similar to Radical Democracy, collaborative governance approaches seek to *transform* government by further democratizing it (Jun 2002). Boyte (2005, 536) elucidates the radically democratic promise of governance networks quite well:

> Governance intimates a paradigm shift in the meaning of democracy and civic agency – that is, who is to address public problems and promote the general welfare? The shift involves a move from citizens as simply voters, volunteers, and consumers to citizens as problem solvers and cocreators of public goods; from public leaders, such as public affairs professionals and politicians, as providers of services and solutions to partners, educators, and organizers of citizen action; and from democracy as elections to democratic society. Such a shift has the potential to address public problems that cannot be solved without governments, but that governments alone cannot solve, and to cultivate an appreciation for the commonwealth. Effecting this shift requires politicizing governance in nonpartisan, democratizing ways and deepening the civic, horizontal, pluralist, and productive dimensions of politics.

We contend that in order to achieve these objectives, we must resolve the dialectics at play in political theory. As shown in Table 10.1, the relational dialectic in the horizontal axis considers whether governing institutions exhibit a *centralized structure* based on group sovereignty or a *decentralized structure* based on individual sovereignty. In other words, political form follows the function of political power. Unitary and republican institutions are hierarchical, while federated or un-centered institutions are pluralist. The process dialectic on the vertical axis considers the relative strength of governing *authority* as *moderate*

Table 10.1 Dialectical political theory

	Centralized Structure	***Decentralized Structure***
Moderate Authority	Classical Conservative Liberalism	Modern Liberalism
Strong Authority	Socialism	Individualist Anarchism

(Source: adapted from Stout and Love 2016)

or *strong*. In both forms of liberalism, authority is claimed by the state and authorized by the citizenry through a social contract established by either hierarchical demand (Classical Conservative Liberalism) or pluralist competition (Modern Liberalism).[2] It is the voluntary nature of the social contract that moderates the political authority allocated to either group or individual. In Socialism the authority of the group is intensified through a natural order, while in Individualist Anarchism, the authority of the individual is intensified through a natural sovereignty.

An Integrative approach would need to restructure governing institutions to synthesize *centralized structure* and *decentralized structure*. An un-centered, ***self-organizing confederalism*** would produce deeply nesting and broadly inclusive interconnected loci of governing, from the neighborhood to the global level of analysis (Follett 1998). While pluralism is accommodated, the self-organizing, relational approach is neither coercive nor competitive. Therefore, a political form of ***power-with*** equalizes the authority granted to both individuals and the group in governing processes.

The egalitarian mode of relational coexistence found in the ethic of Stewardship demands new organizational forms and institutional rules of engagement (Buber 1971). Drawing from classical Greek political theory, Ramos (1981) and White (1990) call this approach to self-governance *isonomy* which means equal (iso) arrangement, distribution, or management (nomos). Similarly, Day (2001) argues that a poststructuralist reinterpretation of Proudhon's "federative heteronomy" built through social contract provides an opportunity for Radical Democracy. The suffix *nomos* indicates that the structure has no ruler as implied by *archy* or *cracy* – it is egalitarian and self-organizing and enables its members to pursue self-actualization free from superimposed prescriptions. However, acknowledging that politics is a process of arranging power and that democracy seeks to ground that power in the people – in a form of "radical political subjectivity" (Newman 2011, 61) – we prefer the label Radical Democracy.

The equitable impulse of Radical Democracy is reflected in the language used to describe new social movements and new politics, including " 'autonomous', 'anti-authoritarian' or 'horizontal' " (Gordon 2007, 33). Indeed, equity is one of the primary tenets in contemporary organizing, where people "organize on a flatter plane . . . using the tools of direct democracy and direct action" (Sitrin 2005, 3). This most aligns with certain approaches to social anarchism that affirm relational and inclusive practices of self-governance (Jeppesen 2011; Dixon 2014). This has been described as a politics rooted in "something generic like self-governing or self-conducting of conduct" (Catlaw 2007b, 15) where government is understood as a relational "whole a-making" (Follett 2013c, 102). Underlying these efforts is a recognition of the centrality of power relationships to shape outcomes (Smucker 2014). Therefore, Radical Democracy follows "post-anarchist" tenets (Rousselle and Evren 2011) and seeks to *transform* political power and its institutions both structurally and procedurally, at both macro- and micro-political levels. Rather than a reform of the state, or a revolution to claim the seat of power, Radical Democracy is a transformation of the state's governing authority and structures.

This understanding is reflected in the notion that the personal is political (Combahee River Collective 1995; Hanisch 1970; Lorde 2007). In this sense, democracy is a process that is acted out anew in our everyday interactions (Rawlings and Catlaw 2011). Contemporary social movements recognize "the power of transforming daily relations" (Sitrin 2005, 162) by calling out and resisting the patriarchal, racist, colonialist, nativist, heteronormative, cisnormative, ableist, and other forms of constraint in all areas of human activity, while also affirming a positive direction for future action (Grosz 2010). This requires the formulation of "functional, human-scale alternatives that can affirmatively foster citizen initiative, participation, and innovation: 'strong democracy' that has everyday meaning and impact" (Bollier 2016, 14).

Radical Democracy also considers the attitude with which one engages in civic life. While the degree of direct participation in a democratic republic has been contested since the founding of the United States, all agreed it "could survive only if animated by a spirit of virtue and concern for the public good" (Bellah et al. 1985, 253). These ethical expectations of "civic stewardship" (Dupré 2002) are seen in indigenous traditions that inspired a number of American founding fathers (Young 2000).[3] For example, in Blackfoot culture, to achieve the status of "persons," individuals must "act reciprocally, generously, and with a mind toward the community" (Lokensgard 2010, 79). As often seen in contemporary communitarian and social capital literature (Barber 1998; Etzioni 1993, 1996; Gardner 1991; Putnam 2000), citizenship implies "a certain duty or obligation on the part of the citizen to contribute to the betterment of the community" (Denhardt and Denhardt 2003, 53). This conception reflects Bookchin's (2015a) communalist understanding of citizenship as active participation in political life. Citizens "must come to view themselves as vital coproducers of public goods and that their full dignity as citizens entails becoming ever more responsible, skilled, and effective as producers of those goods" (Sirianni 2009, 44).

To enable this type of citizenship, as noted in architecture, form follows function. In the case of Radical Democracy, we must build a structure for self-governing authority and its associated roles and activities. We must design institutions accordingly, and those institutions, in turn, will foster Radical Democracy. Therefore, where to start the explanation presents a causal dilemma. Because we are following the structure of Relational Becoming, we begin with form and follow with the explanation of function.

Self-organizing confederalism

A radically democratic structure must enable the "dialectical development of independence and dependence into a more richly articulated form of interdependence" (Bookchin 2015d, loc. 1444). ***Self-organizing confederalism*** provides a political *structure* that synthesizes *centralization* and *decentralization* through *un-centering*. As noted in Chapter 4, decentralization retains ultimate authority at the center, while un-centering generates multiple centers of nonhierarchical authority (Cleveland 2000; Dubnick and Meehan 2004). This approach generates interconnected "spheres of authority (SOAs) that are not necessarily consistent with the division of territorial space and are subject to considerable flux" (Rosenau 1999, 295). Unlike federalism, which is built from the top down and in which states "*confine, restrict, and essentially suppress local democratic institutions and initiatives*" (Bookchin 2015d, loc. 885), confederation is built from the ground up. Because confederation creates multiple loci of political authority, the unifi*ed* state as an object is transformed to a unify*ing* state as a governing process that proceeds "from the Many to the One" (Follett 1998, 284).

Attention to organizing structures is critical to enable this form of interconnection. Radicalism "is about creating new forms of organization . . . creating and enacting horizontal networks instead of top-down structures like states, parties or corporations; networks based on principles of decentralized, non-hierarchical consensus democracy" (Graeber 2002, 70). These networks are also "based on principles of connection, heterogeneity, multiplicity and non-linearity" (Gordon 2007, 33). They have been described as "relational constellations" (Hernes 2008, 67) and "rhizomatic . . . assemblages" (Deleuze and Guattari 1987, 8) with "interpenetration of group and group" (Follett 1998, 249). This aligns with Kooiman's (2001, 2003) description of governance networks as structural assemblages that utilize intersubjective agreement.

Self-organizing confederalism describes "collectively managed, and directly democratic communities" that are networked as "confederated municipalities" (Bookchin 2002, 10) – autonomous local communities that are loosely bound together into a system of government. This is similar to what Ostrom (2010) calls "polycentric governance systems" that combine local authority for responsiveness, but within shared guidance and constraints. Although these descriptions sound somewhat chaotic, "extensive empirical research confirms that some of the most stable, resilient forms of governance are distributed, self-organized, and collaborative" (Bollier 2016, 18).

This multiscalar structure loosely binds autonomous local communities together into a system of government, building from the micro (neighborhood) to the macro (global). Because all units are self-governing, this structure ensures that it remains nonhierarchical and that macro-level assemblies do not hold authority over micro-level groups. Following the principle of subsidiarity, decisions are made by political units at the scale and scope appropriate to the issue at hand, while considering the effects on other levels of analysis. Rather than a "single monolithic social contract," multiple "functional contracts" are created (Wachhaus 2014, 585) – there are no "fixed boundaries" (Gordon 2007, 33). However, to maintain legitimacy, all levels must also be active and interpermeating in this process, with "representatives from the smallest units to the larger and larger" (Follett 1998, 251). In this way, delegates serve as "linking pins" connecting groups within the network (Likert 1967, 50).

To build up to confederation at the global level while protecting the sovereignty of individuals and localities, confederation must begin at the micro-political level because popular sovereignty needs smaller units to be exercised properly (Mouffe 2005). Pogge (1992, 58) advises:

> Persons should be citizens of, and govern themselves through, a number of political units of various sizes, without any one political unit being dominant and thus occupying the traditional role of state. And their political allegiance and loyalties should be widely dispersed over these units: neighborhood, town, county, province, state, region, and world at large. People should be politically at home in all of them, without converging upon any one of them as the lodestar of their political identity.

Self-organizing confederalism thus begins at the most micro levels. For instance, Prugh and Renner (2014) argue "all governance begins with individuals-in-communities" (249). From this perspective, confederation builds "from the smallest neighborhood group to the city, the state, the nation" (Follett 1998, 284). This "multilevel 'constitutional process'"

(Ansell 2011, 61) is aligned with Addams (1964), Follett (1998), and Bookchin (2002), all of whom recommend neighborhoods as the starting point for Radical Democracy. Similarly, Thomas Jefferson devised a "ward republic," arguing that there is no way to make a republic democratic "except by founding it at the grassroots level," with any system of representation emanating through direct democracy exercised in community (Hart 2002, 102).

Neighborhoods are where day-to-day life is lived and where we find the most immediately felt needs. They are where people live, work, learn, worship, and play – they can also provide "vital spaces where people congregate to discuss political as well as social issues" (Bookchin 2015f, loc. 951). Local issues – environmental degradation, social and economic inequities, health, sanitary conditions, education – have the potential to bring people together in a common effort (Bookchin 2015f). Direct participation in these "small local groups" provides the "continuous political activity which ceaselessly creates the state" (Follett 1998, 11). From this perspective, politics is a function that generates nodes – points that resonate together – to help actualize relationships of interdependence (Jun 2011). The state retains a role of "legitimate collective action" (Connolly 2013, 70), but it is a "plastic state" (Follett 1998, 314) or "relational State" that is "articulated in an associational (or federative) manner" (Donati 2014, 112). Government, therefore, remains valuable as "an ensemble of institutions designed to deal with the problems of consociational life in an orderly and hopefully fair manner" (Bookchin 2015a, loc. 395).[4]

This form of confederalism allows for autonomy while unifying ever-broader groups in a dynamic manner: a "Commune of communes" (Bookchin 2015f, loc. 940). Rodrik (2000) argues that instituting global federalism is a logical way to improve the outcomes of globalization. Similarly, Barber (2013) calls for a form of libertarian municipalism, arguing that it fosters a "globalization that is public rather than private, democratic not hegemonic, egalitarian rather than monopolistic" (12).[5] However, to create constellations large enough to accommodate broadly shared issues and large-scale social action, these governance nodes must be interconnected; in this way, all of society is interconnected at the macro-level through nesting overlaps that begin at the micro-level (Buchanan 2002; Granovetter 1973). Ideally, confederal political regions are defined by shared issues, such as geographic proximity within natural resource commons like watersheds and foodsheds, and as these shared issues change, so will the structures of governance used to address them (Barber 2013). ***Self-organizing confederalism*** can therefore "maintain the ecological integrity of a region" (Bookchin 2015c, loc. 1609) while "scaling up of the principles and techniques of collaborative problem solving to matters of national and global concern" (Cohen 2008, 505).

Self-organizing confederalism has become a key factor in generating social change through confederated social movements (Holt-Giménez and Shattuck 2011); however, they are not a recent innovation of utopian imaginary. In Israel, individual kibbutzim form their own collectives but exist as part of a larger federation (Blasi 2009). Some Native American systems of confederation still reflect "no absolute authority, no coercive enforcement of decisions, no hierarchy, and no separate ruling entity" (Alfred 1999, 56). Therefore, Day (2001) argues "Native American political theory represents a distinct and relevant option to both self-government and sovereignty on the nation-state model" (187).

Power-with

Politics is most commonly associated with garnering the power to influence or make decisions that affect all members of a group: "Who is to decide what are the ends of society?"

(Follett 2013c, 192). Politics determines *who* is given authority and the scope of *what* they can decide. Power is therefore manifest in the relationship between the individual and the group, which in turn determines political sovereignty and institutions of governance. Thus, any discussion of political theory and praxis must include an examination of how power is defined and exercised.

To clarify, Follett (2013c) rhetorically queries, "What is the central problem of social relations? It is the question of power" (xiii). She argues, "the relation of whole to parts is the core of any of our present political problems" (111). Confederalism is therefore not purely about structure – it is about how power is embedded in that structure. To assess this, Follett (1919) urges us to consider "the modes of association through which we are to act within these different pluralities" (584). This is necessary whether we consider the relation of group to individual, or a collective to subgroups. Radical Democracy requires attending to the power dynamics in these relatings; the dialectic of placing either *moderate* or *strong* governing *authority* with either the group or the individual must be resolved through synthesis rather than domination (Carr and Zanetti 1999). This is achieved through the development of ***power-with*** (Follett 2003f).

The egalitarian character of Radical Democracy demands the dismantling of dominating power relations and preventing their recurrence in politics. Power is typically described as a static, limited resource or capacity that is distributed in a zero-sum game. Political power is either doled out to representatives through elections or taken by divine right or force. This view of power is found in all of the primary approaches to governance. In each case, those who hold power have the authority to make decisions for and about those who have less power. Thus, power is often referred to as "power-over" which conveys the "ability of the powerful to affect the actions and thought of the powerless" (Gaventa 2006, 24). Not surprisingly, then, power-over reinforces the political tension between individual and group, as well as competition amongst individuals and groups (Foucault 1990).

In contrast, Radical Democracy reimagines power. Carrying forward assumptions from Relational Becoming, unilateral power is replaced by relational power (Loomer 1976a, b) and coercive power is replaced by persuasive power (Mesle 2008). Drawing on an ethic of Stewardship, this form of power must be egalitarian in character. The notion of rule (*kratia*) – as ruling *over* – must be eliminated from politics. Ruling *with* fits the social condition and identity of Ensembling individuality as well as the intersubjective process of Integral Knowing and the public ethic of Stewardship. ***Power-with*** thus redefines power as emergent and synergistic, as well as socially situated and generative (Antliff 2011). It is a "synergy which can emerge through partnerships and collaboration with others, or through processes of collective action and alliance building" (Gaventa 2006, 24). More specifically, power is generated through co-creative acts of self-expression (Follett 2013c). Rather than focusing on differentials across individuals, ***power-with*** considers what is produced by the group as a whole and celebrates everyone's contribution: "More than anything, creating a different power means neither being submissive to another person or forcing your ideas upon them, but being inclusive" (Sitrin 2005, 165). ***Power-with*** therefore has expansive potential rather than static limits – when more people are involved, more power is developed.

This reconceptualization of power also transforms the notion of liberty. In power-over conceptions, negative liberty means freedom from coercion or domination by others while positive liberty relies on the power of the state to ensure rights and opportunities. In ***power-with*** conceptions, however, liberty is the freedom to become, to engage, or to influence others (Dewey 1993b) – political action is co-creative. As Follett (2013g) explains, "this self-generated control does not coerce" (88) because "the more power I have over myself the more capable I am of joining fruitfully with you and with you developing power in the new unity thus formed [by] our two selves" (Follett 2013c, 189–190). Gaventa (2006) describes this freedom as "power 'to' " or "the capacity to act, to exercise agency and to realise the potential of rights, citizenship or voice" (24). It is a form of " 'relational' autonomy' " (Donati 2014, 59) in which "freedom and control *penetrate each other*, and thus remain *interdependent, inter-penetrated, and interactive*" (34).

This egalitarian understanding of power is reflected in pagan worldviews that describe beings in "a dynamic partnership or colloquium of potential equals" (York 2003, 162). Similarly, some Native American cosmologies hold, "We are no better or worse than any of our relations, because the metaphysics of respect (interdependency) sustaining our fundamental relations with Mother Earth are relations of equality" (Verney 2004, 135). We "express 'a natural democracy,' in which humans are related and interdependent with plants, animals, stones, water, clouds, and everything else" (Cajete 2004, 46).

Power-with has also been cogently linked to feminist theory and activism (Banerjee 2008) as well as "affirmative" postmodern theory. For instance, Boje and Rosile (2001) argue this approach avoids the dualistic trap of "all-or-nothing" understandings of power. Similarly, Adorno (1998) describes this as "differentiation without domination" (247) – a foundation for social relationship that is not based on force or threat (Carr and Zanetti 1999). Describing the horizontalist social movements emerging in Argentina, Sitrin (2005) notes "A core part of this rejection includes a break with the idea of 'power-over' " (3). Contemporary social movements seek to create an "alternative power . . . an emancipatory, liberating power" (162). Thus, ***power-with*** is the only "genuine authority" in social relations (Follett 2013a, 46).

Cooperative sovereignty

The assumption of ***power-with*** redefines the meaning of political sovereignty. Generically, sovereignty means the right of an entity to govern or rule itself without external interference. Wherever power lies, so does sovereignty. Because sovereignty is grounded in the individual-in-their-groups, ***power-with*** explicitly rejects any notion of the state as sovereign. Political authority must remain within each person in a manner that cannot be alienated or externalized. Radically democratic sovereignty is thus a "power 'within' " which "often refers to gaining the sense of self-identity, confidence and awareness that is a precondition for action" (Gaventa 2006, 24).

Sovereign individuals cannot give away or lend their sovereignty to another person, institution, or organization. Therefore, sovereignty cannot be conferred to the state, however it is established. Power is "neither given, nor exchanged, nor recovered, but rather exercised, and . . . it exists only in action" (Foucault 1980, 89). Based on this characteristic alone, ***power-with*** appears to call for political anarchy, meaning that no form of political coercion, including majoritarianism, can be ethically justified (Willoughby 1930). Yet, as persons-in-communities, neither can sovereignty be legitimately exercised autonomously. The relational character of ***power-with*** ensures that while sovereignty resides within the individual, that person engages in self-governance with others. To be legitimate, the state must be *composed* of the individuals who hold sovereignty through direct participation in governance, rather than aggregating sovereignty into an abstract mass – the People or *demos*.

Conceived in this way, sovereignty "is not a property or right bestowed on, or removed from, individuals by others but a capacity or potentiality to act" (Grosz 2010, 152). Sovereignty is therefore an active process that "emphasizes people building power together to decide their own circumstances collectively" (Dixon 2014, 79). In other words, sovereignty is generated and wielded together – a relational or "coöperative sovereignty" (Follett 1998, 316). Pogge (1992) argues that such a "dispersal of sovereignty" (61) would improve peace and security, reduce oppression, and increase economic, environmental, and social justice.

Multiscalar citizenship

Cooperative sovereignty necessarily transforms citizenship. Traditionally, a citizen is an individual sanctioned by the sovereign state as a party to the social contract. Those deemed non-citizens are therefore excluded from political decision making processes. This notion of citizenship is problematic for a global, egalitarian, deterritorialized political theory. The juridical connotation must be eliminated and citizenship must be redefined through membership in many communities, at scales from local to global, rather than through legal status in a particular jurisdiction (Follett 1998). This fosters a sense of citizenship in which "our loyalty is neither to imaginary wholes nor to chosen wholes" (Follett 1919, 579) but which "interweaves citizenship in a state . . . and societal citizenship" (Donati 2014, 112).

This multiscalar citizenship is not a claim for a homogenized universal community or substantive political identity – it is a claim that no community is valid if it excludes any particular type of person or group (Prozorov 2014a). Equality made universal means there can be no hierarchical ordering of people (i.e., citizen, legal resident, undocumented immigrant). This concept can be seen in the rallying cry of the contemporary immigrant rights movement, No One Is Illegal (2003). Multiscalar citizenship therefore demands our understanding of "how power, privilege, and group-based inequalities structure individual and group life" so we might take responsibility "for redressing inequalities and promoting social justice" (Nagda and Maxwell 2011, 5).

Delegate representation

With political authority located in the individual sovereign citizen, the less representation the better. Ideally, political participation occurs without proxy – all who are affected by the situation lend their voice to the process. Practically, such active participation requires: time to participate; access to information needed; participatory agenda setting, issue framing, formulation of policy alternatives, and decision making; fair procedures; consensus decisions; and just outcomes (Box 1998). Given the demanding nature of active citizenship, the practicalities of direct participation remain a challenge – realistically, not everyone can engage in every deliberation that affects them. This limitation is often the justification for systems of representative democracy (Dahl 1998); however, representation as it is conceived and implemented in liberalism is highly problematic (Catlaw 2007b). No manner of descriptive, symbolic, or substantive forms of representation recommended by liberal democracy will ever suffice (Kelly 1998), particularly if they are imposed through a method of power-over. Instead, representation must be structured in a way that fosters ***power-with***, so that all individuals retain their authentic voice and agency in the political process. Farmer (2005) calls this a "citizen-ing" (191) of governance, in which participation is not measured in terms of quantity, but rather quality (Schattschneider 1960). This means authentic self-governance, where active, direct participation is central, rather than a "mere governmental contrivance" (Addams 1964, 221).

At the very local level, most individuals are able to "represent" themselves through direct participation. In larger groups, facilitated dialogue and deliberation employs small breakout groups for effective work with delegate reporting for scaling up (Institute of Cultural Affairs 2011; Kaner et al. 1996; NCDD 2010; Weisbord and Janoff 2000). As decision making is scaled up to larger groups, however, even this approach becomes impractical. While communications technology can enable aggregation, groups too large in scale for actual interaction require representation.

In most democracies, representatives act as autonomous trustees who may or may not take ideas from their constituents into consideration (Mill 1873). In contrast, delegates report constituent opinions and advocate for them in the political process. As the situation evolves, delegates maintain active communication with constituents, employing humility and "political modesty" (Mueller 2011, 91). Follett (2013c) identifies four characteristics that fit effective delegation: (1) representatives seek integrative agreement; (2) representatives keep in touch with constituents as the situation changes; (3) keeping in touch includes both conceptual and material understanding; and (4) representation is an egalitarian, functional relationship guided by the needs of the situation.

As stewards, delegates are judged by the criterion of responsiveness to ensure individual sovereignty is maintained. Delegates are specifically mandated, recallable, and accountable to their various assemblies and are authorized only "for the purpose of coordinating and administering the policies formulated by the assemblies themselves" (Bookchin 2015d, loc. 1406). This kind of responsive and fluid representation is found in the spokescouncils of many contemporary social movements (Dixon 2014; Sitrin and Azzellini 2014).

While Radical Democracy calls for direct participation where practicable and delegate-style representation where not, in light of Relational Becoming, some note must be made about those who cannot engage in the political process. For example, it is generally accepted that intellectual capacity and maturity plays a role in determining the degree to which participation is feasible (White 1990). Yet, all must be included to the greatest degree possible, whether it is through actual engagement, delegate representation, or advocate representation. Furthermore, consideration must also be extended beyond humanity. As Bennett (2005) argues, "because their modes of embodiment differ, humans and nonhumans cannot participate equally or in the same way in political affairs" (145). Thus, delegate representation requires a creative rethinking of how advocacy for future generations, nonhumans, and places proceeds.[6]

Participatory policy making

The process of politics is often described as determining who gets what, when, and how (Lasswell 1950). The purpose of policy making is to identify collective interests and determine how to respond to them. It includes iterative processes to identify problems and opportunities, explore possible responses, and come to decisions about what to do. As noted above, "the main concern of politics is *modes of association*" (Follett 1998, 147) – who participates and how do they decide? Where sovereignty is held by active citizens, the political process of making public policy moves into their hands, thereby synthesizing "(1) effective participatory process, and (2) effective authoritative process" (White 1990, 212). Institutions of governance must be "*inhabited by active citizens*" (Stivers 1990, 247).

For comparison, in the power-over paradigm, modes of association are predominantly hierarchical (authoritative domination) or competitive (pluralist majoritarianism). In contrast, policy making *by* the people must use procedures beyond traditional representative and ballot box practices (Barber 1984; Green 1999; Mansbridge 1980; Pateman 1970; Pranger 1968; Sandel 1996). This reflects the long-held ideal that democratic consent should be given through cooperative explanation and persuasion, rather than force (Morstein Marx 1946). This type of self-organizing process "generates 'win-win' outcomes, potentially for all" (Archer 2015, 12). Inclusive participation "can mobilize the talents and energies of large numbers of people whose interests are directly at stake in the issues they confront" (Prugh 2015).

However, who is at the table determines how an issue is defined (Hoppe 2011), and "if our present mechanical government is to turn into a living, breathing, pulsing life, it must be composed of an entire citizenship educated and responsible" (Follett 1998, 168). Participatory policy making requires that "all people in a society can participate in the decisions that affect their lives" (Wang 2012, 121). Furthermore, while participants must also include the "usual suspects" among stakeholders, the overall composition and process cannot enable experts or majorities to dominate dialogue and deliberation. As noted by Cobb Jr. (1981) "preservation and enhancement of these separate flows of personal experiences should be the purpose of all the political and economic structure of society" (19). Those affected by the policy and those engaged in implementing the policy must be enabled to co-create "a genuine collective will" (Follett 1998, 152) "conceived as an *emergent*, biocultural formation" (Connolly 2013, 127) in which "majority and minority ideas may be so closely interwoven that we are truly ruled by the will of the whole" (Follett 1998, 147).

As Follett (2003g) explains, "One of the fundamental differences between consent and participation is that consent . . . comes at the end of or after the process. Participation . . . should begin with the beginning of the process" (223). Participation must therefore be deeply embedded in the policy making process in which both the collective will and consent are developed through "the method of integration" (Follett 2013c, 178). Although "not all differences . . . can be integrated" (163), this approach to participatory decision making is the most fruitful in pursuit of win-win solutions (Evans 2000; Harmon 2006; Shields 2005; Stivers 2000a, 2008; Thayer 1981).

The integrative process in participatory policy making employs aspects of both Integral Knowing's approach to finding intersubjective agreement and Stewardship's process for determining emergent principles. Integration requires careful attention to issues of power and vigilance to ensure that decisions are not made through domination or compromise, whether through coercion or voluntary submission. Facilitation is necessary to ensure that power-over dynamics are diffused and to foster a productive ***power-with*** learning environment. This includes attention to power grounded in socioeconomic and organizational position, as well as expertise (Follett 2013c). Therefore, integration requires a willingness of parties to engage with others in a cooperative process that accommodates constructive and creative conflict, while not being adversarial. In dialogue, as opposed to debate, participants recognize "that many people have pieces of the answer and that together they can craft a solution" (Yankelovich 1999, 39).

Participatory policy making uses consensus-oriented dialogue and deliberation for "facilitating fruitful synergies between the processes of fact-finding and will-forming" (Van Buuren and Nooteboom 2010, 134). The integrative process recognizes that knowledge, values, and political interests build upon one another in formulating policy positions, drawing together processes of generating intersubjective agreement and emergent principles. Therefore, to build collective will, policy making must begin with *sharing* causal and normative beliefs (Sabatier 1988) in addition to joint fact-finding. In virtually any group, sharing policy positions will reveal differences of opinion, or at least nuanced differences within a shared position. Therefore, the interpretation of difference as "constructive conflict" (Follett 2003b, 30) is crucial in policy making. The integrative method is a "post-oppositional" approach to conflict resolution that moves beyond either/or possibilities "to develop creative compromise or generate innovative hybrid perspectives that draw from strikingly different views" (Keating 2013, 7).

To enable productive exploration and to avoid the pitfall of policy polarization, the process of *disintegration* brings conflicting views into conversation with one another, generating creative confrontation that reveals new possibilities (Follett 2003b). Policy positions are typically composed of a desire, an idea about how to fulfill the desire, and a passion to make it happen. To enable integration, desired policy goals must be split from proffered policy tools; desires might be composed of experiential need or normative belief, while policy methods might be informed by both causal knowledge and normative belief. Therefore, the various components of differing policy positions must be broken apart in dialogue to identify the underlying motivations.

Decoupling driving normative concerns from *a priori* policy preferences allows consensus building and conflict resolution through "exploration, listening, learning, invention, proposals, [and] creative work" (Forester 2009, 491). Differences in causal beliefs are resolved through the process of coming to intersubjective agreement. However, differences in normative beliefs require the deliberative, consensus-oriented process of *revaluation* to identify commonalities in experience, values, and desires. While determining emergent principles is a starting point for this process, policy making also requires a careful examination of the experiences of those affected by the policy, power imbalances, and outcome tradeoffs to achieve "a revaluation of interests" (Follett 2013c, 171) among participants. Follett (2013c) notes that such revaluation can also occur in response to changes in the situation, changes in oneself, and new sources of knowledge. This reflective process of goal analysis at the individual, organizational, and network level is recommended as a strategy to assist in achieving shared purpose (Vangen and Huxham 2012).

Through the combination of integrative fact-finding and will-formation, a *synthesis* policy position can be formulated. The degree to which it represents an integrative outcome is measured by the degree to which initial positions or perspectives are transformed through the process and whether the decisions made influence subsequent policy and action (Pogrebinschi 2013). Furthermore, an integrative policy position achieves multiple interests without harm or tradeoffs among them. The goal is "not compromise, not betrayal of commitments, not giving up but *crafting practical options that work for both* [all] *parties*" (Forester 2009, 491).

The benefits of this radically democratic approach to participatory policy making are both practical and ethical in nature. In terms of effectiveness, an inclusive, participatory process brings many perspectives to bear on the situation. Because "each person is a unique locus of intrinsic value and a unique contributor to society" (Cobb Jr. 1981, 19), the integrative method ensures that we obtain the innovative "plus values" of differing perspectives (Follett 2013c, xiv). "By integrating these interests you get the increment of the unifying" (45–46) – what we would now call synergistic effects. These creative innovations enable a break from expert-dominated path dependency and incrementalism (Lindblom and Woodhouse 1993). Integration yields qualitatively better outcomes because all aspects of the situation are considered and nothing is lost through domination or compromise, because "when we compromise; something is always lost" (Follett 2003g, 214).

Ethically, those affected by the policy at hand have voice and agency in the process of integration. Through engagement in all stages, the policy making process "is fraught with active power and force; it affirms and accomplishes" (Follett 1998, 82). Through direct participation, "positions *are* taken, identities *are* asserted, injustices *are* addressed, and conceptual and logistical spaces *are* occupied" and "serve to open up and cultivate possibilities for social change" (Bertalan 2011, 218). Therefore, participatory policy making "synthesizes the conceptions of freedom and non-freedom" (Follett 2013c, 289) because restraint is not domination when it is genuinely self-generated and self-imposed as an active member of the whole – "the course of action decided upon is what we all together want" (Follett 1998, 25).

Finally, integrative policy decisions are longer lasting than when exclusion, avoidance, domination, or compromise are used to come to agreement through hierarchical domination or pluralist competition (Follett 2003b, 2013c). Because originating disagreements remain, these decision-making options yield "temporary and futile" results that are "merely a postponement of the issue" and therefore produce a "sham reconciliation" (Follett 2013c, 156). In contrast, the integrative participatory process ensures both longevity and effectiveness because a sense of ownership and loyalty is developed through coproduction. Acting in accordance is ensured not through mere consent or the binding authority of law or contract, "but in the fact that it has been produced by the community" (130). As such, "nothing will ever truly settle differences but synthesis" (Follett 1998, 114).

To achieve these benefits, however, sufficient time must be invested in the policy making process: "Patient decision-making translates into wisdom and common commitment when every voice is heard" (van Gelder, Korten, and Piersanti 2011, 13). As noted in the collaborative governance literature, the time allotted to complex policy issues within formal governance processes is typically between two and four years, while many citizen participation efforts are only a matter of months (Hoppe, van de Graaf, and Besseling 1995). This means deliberations are brought to premature closure. This apparent aversion to participatory policy making may be due to its relational character. Whether through legislative processes or on the front lines of administration, governance actors engage in "public encounters" (Bartels 2013) with citizens in their various community and economic roles. It has been well-argued that such encounters are most productive when they are egalitarian and authentically participatory (King, Feltey, and Susel 1998). These relational in-betweens can be understood as a democratic way of doing and being together (Rawlings and Catlaw 2011). However, these encounters are not necessarily pleasant or easy. Indeed, as Young (2000) notes, participatory encounters allow for "more disruptive modes of expression such as protest, emotional outbursts, or personal stories" (Bartels 2013, 477). We argue that this is a necessary cost of doing public business – the "emotional labor" (Guy, Newman, and Mastraci 2008) necessary to obtain the constructive, creative potential of difference and conflict (Follett 2003b).

Radical Democracy

To enable Radical Democracy, government must become a system of ***self-organizing confederalism*** that operates according to the principle of subsidiarity. These changes transform the state into a mechanism that facilitates coordinated effort among groups from the most local to the global scope. These institutions foster ***power-with*** – a generative and synergistic sum co-produced in the political process. This reconceptualization of power fundamentally transforms sovereignty as an inherent capacity within individuals who exist as responsible persons-in-community, multiscalar citizens of local to global political units. In carrying forward the ethic of Stewardship, Radical Democracy can also be understood as a "politics of care" (Hummel and Stivers 1998, 36) or "*política afectiva*" (Sitrin and Azzellini 2012, 68). This concept is rooted in care not only for self and neighbors but for future generations and the global ecosystem. Citizens exercise their sovereignty through inclusive and impactful participation in the policy making process, wherein interests are integrated through dialogue and deliberation. Where representation is necessitated by practicalities, delegates are temporarily appointed with communicative procedures in place to ensure legitimacy.

Together, ***self-organizing confederalism*** and ***power-with*** produce what Thayer (1981) called "structured nonhierarchical social interaction" (A-38), an organizing style for generating the collective will and taking collective action that employs participatory practice, consensus decision rules, and interlocking coordination. He drew heavily from Follett, who called the democratic social contract a "fiction" (Follett 1998, 162), arguing a "genuine unity" (Follett 2003h, 189) can only be generated through an inclusive, egalitarian, dynamic process of "***unifying***" among sovereign but relational citizens (195). Therefore,

> democracy must be conceived as a process, not a goal. We do not want rigid institutions, however good. We need no 'body of truth' of any kind, but the will to will, which means the power to make our own government, our own institutions, our own expanding truth.
>
> (Follett 1998, 99)

Similarly, Derrida (2005) argues that democracy is a promise that never arrives (Stanisevski 2011). It must remain open to criticism, resistance, and change in order to explore new horizons of both form and function.

For Radical Democracy to become "a way of life" (Dewey 1993a, 241), "an activity to be exercised every moment of the time" (Follett 1998, 335), ***self-organizing confederalism*** and ***power-with*** must be applied to all social groups, including neighborhoods, occupational groups, and even families. Radical Democracy recognizes that "true democracy" (156) involves "complex citizenship that operates by valorizing the principle of relationality applied to all of society's spheres" (Donati 2014, 113). From a relational process perspective, the separation of societal sectors (political, social, economic) is artificial – governing is a process that cuts across human activity and does not entail permanent social roles (Follett 1998). As Arendt (1998) notes, "wherever you go, you will be a *polis*" (198). Indeed, "democracy, if it [is] to mean anything at all, must be played out in the concrete realities of what it means to be a human being" (Gawthrop 1989, 194).

While such a transformation may not be quick, it is certainly possible. Thus, as discussed in Chapter 13, we must look to a prefigurative politics characterized by "the desire to express chosen ends in the means used to achieve them" (Day 2011, 102). We must change micro-relations in order to transform macro-structures of confederation. We must "maintain a constant awareness of interpersonal dynamics and the way in which they might reflect social patterns of exclusion" as we are "planning and carrying out campaigns, projects and direct actions" (Gordon 2007, 41).

Integrative pathways

An Integrative synthesis must generate pathways that are easily traversed by those holding other positions. In the case of political theory, Radical Democracy must provide concepts that sufficiently meet fundamental principles within the other political theories, or at least create a dialogical basis for creating shared understandings. As illustrated in Figure 10.1, we imagine the shared characteristics shown in Table 10.2 as pathways into a dynamic synthesis that remains open to contestation and change.

Going back to our discussion of dialectical synthesis in the chapter's introduction we know that Radical Democracy must not structure institutions through either *centralization* or *decentralization*. ***Self-organizing confederalism*** un-centers units of political decision making according to the principal of subsidiarity from local to global scope, allocating *authority* in a manner that synthesizes the relatively *moderate authority* of group hierarchy (Classical Conservative Liberalism) and pluralist competition (Modern Liberalism) as well as the relatively *strong authority* of unitary collectivism (Socialism) and no governance whatsoever (Individualist Anarchism). ***Power-with*** reconceives authority, making it an egalitarian, generative capacity that is exercised through the participatory process of integration. However, the primary concerns of each distinct position need to be addressed in order establish a starting point for dialogue with the Integrative perspective, as shown in Table 10.2.

Classical Conservative Liberalism is primarily concerned with ensuring social order and political stability by wielding centralized political authority that is moderated by electoral representation. ***Self-organizing confederalism*** provides relatively stable mechanisms for coordination from the local to the global scope, while ***power-with*** maintains democratic

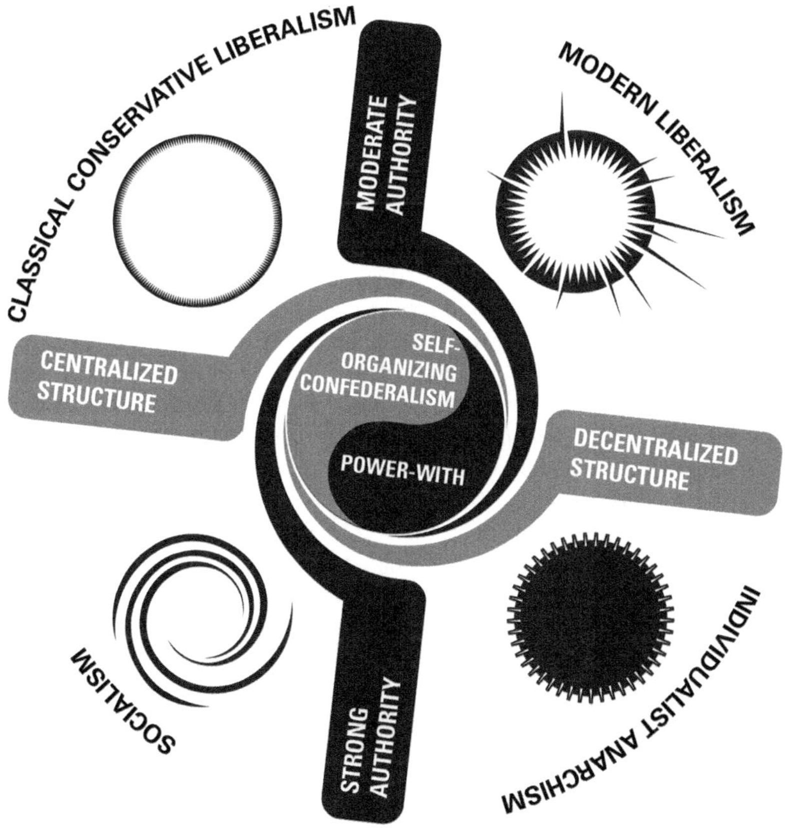

Figure 10.1 Integrative pathways for Radical Democracy

Table 10.2 Integrating political concerns

Ideal-Type	*Characteristics*	*Primary Concerns*	*Synthesis Solution*
Classical Conservative Liberalism	*moderate centralized authority*	Social order and stability	***Self-organizing confederalism*** provides relatively stable mechanisms for coordination; ***Power-with*** maintains democratic political authority
Modern Liberalism	*moderate decentralized authority*	Checks and balances within pluralist choice and competition	***Self-organizing confederalism*** includes all concerned parties; ***Power-with*** fosters integration through participatory policy making
Socialism	*strong centralized authority*	Equality within social unity	***Self-organizing confederalism*** ensures equality among interlocking groups; ***Power-with*** ensures equal political authority among individuals
Individualist Anarchism	*strong decentralized authority*	Freedom from coercion	***Self-organizing confederalism*** ensures all have a voice in structure and operations; ***Power-with*** retains individual sovereignty and prevents coercion in policy making

political authority. While delegates within these confederations may be more fluid, the participatory policy making process and structure of confederalism itself provides relative stability. Modern Liberalism is primarily concerned with decentralizing political units to moderate authority through the checks and balances of federalism, while providing efficient mechanisms for the resolution of conflicting interests and citizen choice and voice. The structure of ***self-organizing confederalism*** allows for the use of representation at meso- and macro levels of decision making in order to foster efficiency while retaining maximum interactive participation. ***Power-with*** employs participatory policy making and addresses diverse interests through constructive conflict and the integrative method. Socialism is primarily concerned with fostering a sense of social unity and equality. ***Self-organizing confederalism*** employs network horizontalism and subsidiarity to ensure unity among interlocking groups. ***Power-with*** ensures equal political authority among all sovereign citizens that is not coopted by delegates. Individualist Anarchism is concerned with maintaining each person's autonomy and freedom from coercion. ***Self-organizing confederalism*** ensures that every individual has voice and agency in how confederated groups are formed and operate. ***Power-with*** ensures that sovereignty remains with the individual. The integrative process of participatory policy making prevents coercion by synthesizing freedom and control.

Notes

1 We again note *citizen* is a problematic term in deterritorialized political theory due to its connotations of legal status. We define citizens as *group members*, whatever the level of analysis may be.

2 This distinction between Classical Conservative Liberalism and Modern Liberalism is drawn from Clark (1998). The former infuses liberalism with a deference to traditional values enforced by the state, while the latter emphasizes negative liberty achieved through small government and free markets.
3 Young (2000) points out that the Native American Iroquois Confederacy, or League of Peace and Power, reflected cooperative governance among independent nations. This was an inspiration to Benjamin Franklin and influenced the US Articles of Confederation.
4 While we embrace much of Bookchin's (2015a) thinking, certain aspects do not align with Integrative Governance. For example, he insists upon the Enlightenment ideal of "rationality" and "soundly objective premises." He eschews the notion of consensus, assuming such a practice can only lead to endless argumentation, stymying action. Further, he denies the value of including nonhuman beings and places in relationality, suggesting that this cheapens the value of citizenship. Finally, he uses the term "decentralized" rather than un-centered and calls for a "stateless" society rather than transforming the form and function of the state.
5 While we appreciate Barber's discussion of confederalism, his specific proposal is not fully confederal in that he does not challenge the existing institutions of representative democracy.
6 As an example, New Zealand has granted legal personhood to the Whanganui River in response to Maori tribal advocacy. This agreement recognizes the entirety of the river and its tributaries as an indivisible, living whole, both in terms of physical and metaphysical aspects (Cullinan 2014). Similarly, some countries are acknowledging the rights of future generations in pursuit of intergenerational justice (Ebel and Rinke 2014).

11 Economic theory

Coopetition

The development of a transdisciplinary economy is based on the postulate that the economy must serve the human being and not the reverse.

– (Article 12 of the Charter of Transdisciplinarity, Nicolescu 2002, 150)

Economic policies are often identified as central drivers of the crisis of sustainability. Economic systems determine rules for ownership and production as well as mechanisms for distribution. During the Progressive Era, George (1929) noted that in the (still) prevailing political economy, progress was measured primarily in terms of material advancement and accumulation produced through market competition and government regulation. Limited to either liberalism or socialism, political systems thus set competition for profit against state socialism as an either-or choice resulting in welfare-state compromises. The underlying shared assumption of never-ending progress through quantitative growth is unsustainable socially, economically, and environmentally. These approaches result in unequal distribution of income, wealth, and access to fundamental resources. These inequalities foment social crises, while the environmental destruction driven by the profit motive fuels environmental crises.

As noted in Chapter 1, much of the global political economy is now rooted in free market ideology, considering little beyond material wealth. Material progress is achieved through competition among economic actors, the monetized value of which is aggregated into calculations such as the Gross Domestic Product of a nation. This perspective assumes that we compete over scarce resources while simultaneously pursuing endless quantitative growth and expansion. Furthermore, without adequate community regulation of financial institutions, processes of financialization have overrun the system; finance serves finance (Collins 2015). For instance, in the wake of the Global Financial Crisis of 2008, efforts have focused on reestablishing stability of the system *as configured*, rather than addressing underlying causes of the collapse and related issues of wealth disparities, growing indebtedness, and poverty (Palley 2014). Therefore, financial institutions must be redesigned to serve the economy, the environment, and the people's needs, not the reverse.

Donati (2014) argues that the economic crash of 2008 and its aftermath result from the dominant systems of political economy (45). Connolly (2013) suggests we are at potential turning point in political economy quite similar to where the physical sciences stood over a century ago as the Newtonian system began to collapse. There is a growing movement to find the "Next System" (Alperovitz, Speth, and Guinan 2015) – a political economy that supports an Earth community as opposed to a human empire (Korten 2006). We need a new understanding of materialism to make "a realistic assessment of solutions to the major problems of climate change, global inequality, and warfare that face the world today" (Edwards 2010, 297).

Neoliberalism, the dominant economic mode, privileges global governance networks and capital flows while minimizing aspects of the welfare state and collectively planned economies. Connolly (2013) argues that while the current system is set up as a massive orthodoxy, we might rather explore a heterodoxy of innumerable interacting, self-organizing systems. The umbrella of "heterodox economics" includes a collection of alternative economic logics that challenge the assumptions of neoclassical economics (Lee 2009). These approaches are emerging because "the *modus operandi* of the production, distribution and the exploitation of resources must be compatible with the democratic process and a common framework of action" (Held 1992, 36). Many of these schools of thought begin with the assumption of interrelationship, particularly among economic actors (Davis 2003).

Some argue economic transformation can come from within by changing the terms of engagement – focusing on exchange dynamics among market actors in economic systems. This transformed system need not be seen as marginal and weak, nor merely defined in reference to that which it seeks to replace (Tønder 2005). By building grassroots economic methods, we can "'hollow out' capitalism" (Gordon 2007, 36) and displace it with a new system. Bookchin (2015f, loc. 1153) argues that

> global capital, precisely because of its very hugeness, can only be eaten away at its roots. . . . It must be eroded by the myriad millions who, mobilized by a grassroots movement challenge global capital's sovereignty over their lives and try to develop local and regional economic alternatives to its industrial operations.

If we redefine property and capital as social products, we can reactivate the political in order to reinvent our economy (Critchley 2005). Initiatives like the Next System Project, the Solidarity Economy Network, and the New Economy Coalition are forwarding this agenda. Rather than addressing economics from a purely macro perspective, these groups argue that we can bring about political and social transformation through situated everyday practices, attending to "the character of everyday life and lived space . . . and by attending to its relationship to the ordering of the city, region, state, and international system" (Edwards 2010, 297). These "'new' critical materialists situate citizens, ideas, and values . . . within the fields of material forces and power relations that reproduce and circumscribe their existence and coexistence" (Coole and Frost 2010, 28). Everyday practices exist in reciprocal relation with global systems – they are mutually impacting. Thus, "every economy – local to global – is embedded within society and within the living world" (Raworth 2017, 244). This micro-macro praxis means our micro-level interactions eventually transform the economic system writ large; this enables simultaneous resistance of the existing political economy while affirming alternatives.

As shown in Table 11.1, our Governance Typology presents two dialectics at play in common approaches to economic theory. On the horizontal relational axis, we consider whether the economy is organized by institutions external to economic exchange, or internally organized by economic actors themselves. *External regulation* refers to some degree of government intervention in economic activities while *internal regulation* refers to economic actors freed from government intervention to one degree or another. On the vertical

Table 11.1 Dialectical economic theory

	External Regulation	*Internal Regulation*
Moderate Authority	Welfare State	Market Exchange
Strong Authority	Collective Planning	Self-Sufficiency and Barter

(Source: adapted from Stout and Love 2016)

process axis, we consider whether the *regulation* of the economy is relatively *weak* or *strong*, regardless of whether government or economic actors are responsible for that task.

As a synthesis position, Integrative Governance must structure economic institutions that draw together the relatively moderate ideals of external regulation (Welfare State) and internal regulation (Market Exchange) as well as the stronger ideals of mandated mutualism (Collective Planning) and no planning or coordination at all (Self-Sufficiency and Barter). What we generically label Coopetition synthesizes *external* and *internal regulation*, interlocking markets and communities from the local to global scope through relational ***commoning*** (Bollier 2016). Producers and consumers support one another's pursuits with an eye toward global flourishing, while competing to advance the best outcomes – an approach to qualitative progress through cooperative competition. The ***power-with*** concept of ***cooperation*** allocates neither *moderate* nor *strong* regulatory *authority* to either government or economic actors. Instead, all situated actors contribute to the self-organizing coordination of economic production and exchange.

According to Polanyi (1944), economic logics include market, redistribution, and reciprocity. Markets are systems of exchange between producers and consumers. Redistribution relies on the state to transfer wealth to the needy. In our terms, the choices have vacillated between Collective Planning/Welfare State models and a Market Exchange system seeking ever greater freedom from regulation and increasing Self-Sufficiency and Barter (Stout and Love 2016). Orthodoxies that emphasize either market or redistribution have led to devastating results in modern times (Laville 2013); none of these approaches have produced sustainable economic outcomes. "We need another economic logic" (Donati 2014, 50).

As explained by Polanyi (1944), the logic of reciprocity establishes voluntary social and economic relations among free and equal citizens. Similarly, Ramos (1981) argues for a "para-economic paradigm" of "mutuality-oriented systems" which operates under substantive rather than purely instrumental values (162). Extending the logic of mutuality and reciprocity beyond constraining self-interest and the market, ***relationality*** transforms individualist assumptions by democratizing the market itself. Following this logic, ***commoning*** draws upon the relational ethic of Stewardship in all economic relationships, while ***cooperation*** generates ***power-with*** in all economic activities.

Economic history reveals voluntary reciprocity in the most ancient forms of human association (Marques 2013). In the early Greek translations of the Bible, the term for stewardship was *oikonomia*, which also means "managing the household by providing basic resources for sustaining its members" (Atherton 2000, 45). While the term economics is derived from this meaning, the concept also carries forward "the earlier, broader concept of the political economy, relating to the whole process of creating and distributing wealth" (45). Thus, "embedded in the deeper and broader meanings of the term 'stewardship' is the notion of an institutional arrangement" (Stackhouse 1987, xiii); and, conversely, the notion of stewardship is embedded within the concept of economics. Stewardship therefore can be a guideline for the institutional rules of political economy within all sectors of society, helping to ensure that resources are managed in a manner that achieves social and economic justice and environmental wellbeing.

In Western society, stewardship in economics dwindled as capitalism became increasingly dominant (McMurty 2013), but it re-emerged as a counterhegemonic movement among tradespeople in the eighteenth century; mutual aid associations of peasants and workers in the nineteenth century; and, unions, mutual insurance and finance companies, cooperatives, and nonprofit organizations in the twentieth century (Laville 2013). Unfortunately, over the most recent decades, many nonprofit and third sector reciprocity organizations have also become imbued with the individualist and hierarchical characteristics of liberal capitalist markets and state redistribution (Desmarais 2007; Laville 2013; Marques 2013; McMurty 2013).

However, principles of reciprocity can be found in social movements' pursuit of distributivism (McConkey and Lawler 2003), mutualism and communalism (Bookchin 2015a), "social economics" or "solidarity economics" (Allard, Davidson, and Matthaei 2008), the "cooperative commonwealth" (Nembhard 2014, 54), and the activities of "commoners" around the world (Bollier 2016). These relational approaches achieve the synthesis sought between individual competition and collective control, offering a third alternative to capitalism and state socialism (Cheney 2001; Greenberg 1986; Rothschild and Whitt 1986). In fact, George (1929), Follett (1998), and Ramos (1981) all highlight the distinction specifically, even while noting sentiments that the "ideal of socialism is grand and noble" (George 1929, 321). State socialisms, however, are merely stronger forms of hierarchical power that do not democratize the economy (Follett 1998; Thayer 1981). Similarly, few contemporary radicals hold to the notion of state ownership as the best solution for the unification of labor and capital (Rothschild and Whitt 1986).

Instead, these approaches draw ideas from collectivism as well as social anarchism. The former focuses on the common ownership (but not in the form of a coercive state) of all means of production, including land, with equitable distribution of all that is produced (Morris 1993); the latter proposes a society composed of federated, democratic, self-managing communes with cooperative use and regulation of the means of production, including land (Puente 1985). For example, Bookchin (2015f) calls for the confederalization of the economy – maintaining as much economic control at the local level as possible, engaging in shared decision making and action where material interests overlap. This approach focuses on producing and buying locally (food, goods, services), community-based enterprise networks, and recognition of traditionally unremunerated activities that are essential to the community (e.g., caregiving). Rather than tying this effort solely to workers (in the traditional sense), it becomes a community-wide effort that joins together producers and consumers in solidarity, while also moving property into collective control or ownership. Communalism thus offers a "reconstructive vision of a fundamentally different society – directly democratic, anticapitalist, ecological, and opposed to all forms of domination" (Bookchin and Taylor 2015, loc. 99).

While some argue that social, economic, and environmental sustainability will be achieved only by "replacing competition with cooperation, and profit-seeking with relationships based on sharing and mutual concern" (Bookchin 2015d, loc. 786), we contend that we must reinterpret competition according to the ethic of Stewardship. The assumptions and methods of ***commoning*** and ***cooperation*** do not *eliminate* competition, but instead move it into a holistic system in which individuals and groups understand they can be more successful through mutual support than if working toward market domination alone. From this perspective, competition is "the search for the best solutions in a contest which is not detrimental to the other participants but stimulates each participant to contribute his/her best effort toward achieving the same common goal" (Donati 2014, 106). We are more likely to succeed in eliminating shared challenges such as scarcity, hunger, and poverty through cooperation than in competition with one another for protection against them. We are collectively in competition with the wicked problems of sustainability.

The combination of cooperation and competition has occasionally re-emerged as "co-opetition" (Cherington 1913; Hunt 1937) which seeks a cooperative synergism that creates and adds value to all participants, rather than pursuing pure competitive advantage over others (Padula and Dagnino 2008). This is similar to the logic behind "collaborative advantage" (Vangen and Huxham 2012). While intergroup coopetition was originally conceptualized as a regional or industry cluster phenomenon, in light of the crisis of sustainability we confront, we argue that we must expand the "region" to the global context (Henton, Melville, and Walesh 2004). Furthermore, Coopetition must be infused with the ethic of Stewardship in order to avoid slipping into individualistic competitive games (Padula and Dagnino 2008).

Considering such a solidarity-infused Coopetition, Dee Hock (2000), founder of VISA International, uses the term *chaordic* to describe the necessity of integrating the chaos of competition and the order of cooperation. He argues, "The organization of the future will be the embodiment of *community* based on *shared purpose* calling to the *higher aspirations of people*" (as quoted in Cleveland 2000, 293). This approach to associational behavior seeks a collaborative assessment of "what enables human beings to thrive" (Raworth 2017, 37) – through cooperation rather than purely competitive exchange (McSwite 1997).

This chapter explores what such an alternative economic system might look like. We must consider "how resources are to be acquired, produced, allocated, and distributed" (Bookchin 2015b, 3108). Therefore, in the following sections, we consider the implications of ***commoning*** for the meaning of progress in a relational world and our understanding of economic actors in this context, and how ***cooperation*** is used as the process for coordinating resource use, production, and exchange in that system.

Commoning

Commoning is at once an ethic, an economic paradigm, and a set of social practices that include various acts of mutual support and the administration required to maintain them (Bollier 2016). This approach to solidarity economics acknowledges and embraces a conscious project of ethical social transformation (Marques 2013). Economic structures and moral considerations must come together for efficient and holistic social progress (Ramos 1981) that ensures "the betterment of the whole not just the few" (Timney 2001, 26). The ethic of Stewardship makes visible both the hand of the market and the hand of regulation, reconnecting the manner in which moral sentiments (Smith 2000a) guide exchange (Smith 2000b). In this section, we focus on the relational aspects of a self-regulating economy.

As with Radical Democracy, a causal dilemma is created by separating relational process concepts for discussion. The ***power-with*** ethic associated with ***cooperation*** prefigures the relational understanding of ***commoning***. Economic systems grounded in reciprocity relations are often referred to as "social economics" or "solidarity economics" (Allard, Davidson, and Matthaei 2008), both of which are linked to an ethic of mutual aid, participatory democracy at community levels of action, and a relational understanding of individualism (McMurty 2013). From this perspective, economic activity is not something that can exist as a separate sphere of interaction, because "they are so inextricably interwoven as to be conceptually and analytically inseparable" (Parker 1995, 283). In this formulation, all institutions would operate under the rules of cooperation, reciprocity, and mutuality through which both instrumental and substantive values are co-determined and pursued. This approach employs "a ***network-like logic*** which is forced to make the different societal spheres more co-operative, or at least to follow a mutually non-destructive competition logic, within a world-system's global sustainability project" (Donati 2014, 55).

Once goods and services are ready for use, markets are systems for distributing them through various forms of exchange. To ensure these actors are guided by an ethic of Stewardship, we must transform our assumptions about resource use and associated property rights, as well as the relationship between producers and consumers. We adopt the term ***commoning*** (Bollier 2016) to describe these relationships; this synthesizes ***external*** and ***internal*** mechanisms of ***regulation***, because all forms of economic activity are relationally determined by situated economic actors. Markets are reconnected to people and place, re-embedding the economy within society and making it answerable to the people.

This is not a new concept. It is reflected in explanations of mutualism based on observation of nineteenth century mutual aid societies and worker cooperatives (Proudhon 1969) – conceived of as "'reciprocal service'" based on cooperation (Follett 2003d, 133). Today, common pool resources are managed cooperatively "between similarly-situated persons" (Nelson 2006, 206) for mutual benefit. In short, shared situations deepen the drive toward cooperation. Depending upon the degree of mutual impact and varying understandings of the concept of "us," these shared situations may be found at any level of analysis; people are just as likely to engage in mutual aid globally as they are locally, as evidenced in philanthropy, volunteerism, and cooperative associations of various types. As examples, local buying movements put consumers and producers in solidarity with shared community values (BALLE 2002), as do fair trade movements for consumers and producers across global communities (Fair Trade USA 2016).

When markets are reconnected to people and place, the fullness of actual human experience can be engaged. As evolutionary biologists note, cooperation is an innate human drive – one that is equal to the competitive urge for survival in the processes of natural selection (Gould 1992). This assumption that humankind is capable of "cooperating in the enterprise of life" (Christ 2003, 85) is timeless. For instance, Marcus Aurelius argued that "We are made for co-operation – like feet, like hands, like eyelids, like the rows of the upper and lower teeth" (quoted in George 1929, 330). Similarly, in his examination of the evidence of cooperation in nonhuman animals, in pre-feudal societies, medieval cities, and modern times alike, Kropotkin (1902) concluded that cooperation and mutual aid are the most important factors in the evolution of species and the ability to survive.

Assuming that we hold the world of which we are a part in common changes every aspect of economic theory. In the following subsections, we will explore how it transforms our understanding of progress and profit, economic actors as people, property rights of place, and how they come together in sustainable relationships of production, consumption, and finance.

Qualitative progress

The meaning of progress is the cornerstone on which any political economy rests – what is the goal we pursue in the use, production, and distribution of resources? ***Commoning*** seeks to generate collective goods and public benefits in the commons, as opposed to draining the commons for private gain (Bollier 2016). In terms of material progress, this means focusing on *qualitative* improvements to do more with less, with the caveat that these efforts be undertaken through sustainable methods as opposed to industrial and technological approaches that ultimately deplete natural resources.

This has been described as "doughnut economics" in which the economy is bounded – we must produce enough to meet the needs of every person, but not more than is environmentally sustainable (Raworth 2017, 22). As examples, renewable energy production maximizes the use of natural resources without depleting them (Colombo, Bologna, and Masera 2013); agroecology rebuilds and conserves soils for sustained production (Holt-Giménez 2006); smart growth policies densify urban areas to reduce commuting distances and conserve open space for both human and wildlife use (Smart Growth America 2016); low growth, no growth, and degrowth proposals focus on reducing – rather than expanding – economic production to achieve sustainability (Daly and Cobb Jr. 1994; Victor and Jackson 2015).

However, material progress is not the only aim of an economy. We also seek a more robust and authentic form of experience that produces complex value, including needs of community, engagement, and relationship which cannot be reduced to material transaction (Thayer 1981). Transformed economic methods generate "relational goods" that provide multidimensional value based on "their 'mode of production'" (Donati 2014, 94) and the "particular social subjects" (95) who produce them together.[1] Relational goods have the following properties:

> They are not 'things' but consist of social relations that have a *sui generis* reality; they are produced and enjoyed *together* by those who participate in them; the good that they entail is an *emergent effect* which redounds to the benefit of participants as well as of those who share in its repercussions from the outside, without any single subject's having the ability to appropriate it for him/herself. Relational goods have an intrinsically democratic character in that they distinguish themselves from bureaucratic organizations (such as the public administration) that act on command and generate goods that redound to their surrounding community's benefit (whether territorial or not). They are not particularistic and closed goods.
>
> (Donati 2014, 92)

From this conceptualization of relational goods, it follows that social capital is broadened beyond its traditional instrumental value grounded in atomistic individualism (see for example, Bourdieu 1986; Coleman 1990; Granovetter 1973; Putnam et al. 1983). Social capital facilitates value production in the other forms of community capital: natural, cultural, human, political, financial, built (Flora and Flora 1993). Additionally, organizational capital reflects the contribution of social capital to all types of groups (Chrislip 2002).

However, for social capital to function in this way, actors must have dispositions of trust, reciprocity, mutualism, and cooperation. Motivations for cooperation are not factors of convenience or sentiment, but are rooted in "the sense of well-being that individuals derive from the relation" (Donati 2014, 97–98). If we are brought up understanding ourselves in a natural state of relation and anticipating abundance and reciprocity, we have a starting place for building social capital because relation itself is valued. These affective dimensions are what reinforce norms of cooperation. If the cultural situation supports this mode of association, trustworthiness and mutualism are generally borne out in experience. Through positive experiences, generalized reciprocity is strengthened reflexively. Thus, the more social capital is used, the more it grows.

Relationality and Stewardship further require we consider both qualitative and quantitative end values to measure progress. Such indicators are typically codified under the rubric of quality of life: "Life as it is worth living, in fulfillment, health, vitality, joy, and the abiding awareness that every day you live you have made the world a little better" (Diwan 2000, 315). Stated differently, "What we care about is the ***productive*** life, and the first test of the productive power of the collective life is its nourishment of the individual" (Follett 2013c, xiii). This requires more than fulfilling physiological and safety needs; human beings need creative self-actualization as well as a sense of belonging and respect from others (Maslow 1943) and this means we must expand economic space to foster a more multidimensional life (Ramos 1981). As Thomas Jefferson noted, happiness must be found in both private and public expression (Stivers 2008) – neither economic nor political nor civic action can be reduced to material transaction (Thayer 1981).

To re-humanize life, rather than dividing the work of life into small isolated slices, individuals should be enabled to engage in a variety of life's activities in the course of a given day – industry or enterprise, craft, food cultivation, child rearing, etc. (Bookchin 2015d). This diversity enables greater happiness because "play, as useless idling, does not give us joy. Work, as drudgery, does not give us joy. Only creating gives us joy" (Follett 1998, 101). The "function" of work is

> at least threefold: to give man a chance to utilise and develop his faculties; to enable him to overcome his ego-centredness by joining with other people in a common task; and to bring forth the goods and services needed for a becoming existence.
>
> (Schumacher 2010, 58)

Through group work, we develop our capacities to co-create and it is through co-creation that we experience joy in our lives (Follett 2013c). This then becomes

> the chief function, the real service, of business: to give an opportunity for individual development through the better organization of human relationships . . . every activity of man should add to the intangible values of life as well as to the tangible.
>
> (Follett 2003d, 141)

The intangible indicators found at both intrapersonal and interpersonal levels of analysis are the measures of ***relational***, as opposed to ***material***, wealth. From this perspective, "relational wealth emanates from our interconnections with other human beings. It gives us inner strength and emotional security and defines our quality of life" (Diwan 2000, 305). Indicators like the Human Development Index and Social Progress Index are therefore offered as replacements for the monetized Gross National Product (GNP) approach (UNDP 1999). For example, The Kingdom of Bhutan began using a Gross National Happiness Index in 1972 (Shekhawat 2008). From these perspectives, the notion of growth is meant "in the qualitative rather than the quantitative sense . . . purposes which will include more of those fundamental values for which most of us agree we are really living" (Follett 2003e, 268).

Relational wealth circles back to material concerns by defining human livelihood in a way that emphasizes the interdependence between people and their natural surroundings (Polanyi 1977). To develop a vision for sustainable economies we must "think routinely of ourselves and our economies as nested subsystems that are embedded in the global ecosystem, unviable apart from it" (Prugh 2015, 133). This balanced perspective of social, economic, and environmental sustainability is found in Buddhist economics (Bell 2006;

Daniels 2007; Nelson 2006; Schumacher 2010), Gandhian economics (Diwan 2000), feminist economics (Barker and Kuiper 2003; Mansbridge 1990), pragmatist economics (Follett 1998; George 1929, 1941), "eco-nomics" (Timney 2001), and ecological economics (Daly and Cobb Jr. 1994). These approaches combine self-development and expression, holistic mutual interest, and cooperation in production and consumption that does not deplete natural resources. In this sense progress should be measured by the degree to which our institutions further mutual aid (Kropotkin 1902).

From this holistic perspective, economic actors consider the implications of their actions for people, place, and profits, as well as toward qualitative, rather than purely quantitative progress. This complex understanding of progress is relational in nature – in terms of material relations between humankind and the Earth as well as social and economic relations among human beings. This new economic logic sees resource use, production, distribution, and consumption as activities within social relations, as opposed to isolated transactions between disinterested entities. These characteristics contribute to achieving both local and global sustainability in that they are attentive to: (1) intergroup conflicts that cause social strife; (2) imbalances in resource distribution that cause economic crises; and (3) production and consumption methods that cause negative impacts on the environment (Diwan 2000).

Socioeconomic actors

The ***reverent interconnectivity*** of Stewardship that informs ***commoning*** jettisons the self-interested utilitarian assumptions of *homo economicus* (Mill 2000), replacing this one-dimensional actor with the holistically relational *homo socio-economicus* (Buchanan 2002; Davis 2003). This synthesis concept rejects both "the non-relational, autonomous extreme" of atomistic individualism, as well as "the overly connected, dependent extreme" of collectivism (Nelson 2006, 205). For actual humans (as opposed to those designed for economic modeling), multiple values guide economic decisions and actions, and self-interest is redefined. Due to ***relationality***, "there is no fully separate self whose interests do not of necessity include others" (Sampson 1988, 20). In this view, "self-interest rightly understood" (Tocqueville 2000) means one's own interests are complex and interconnected with those of others (Dewey 1957). *Homo socio-economicus* acts as an Ensembling individual within a socioeconomic community.

The relational character of ***commoning*** and qualitative progress thus places economic actors into relation with their environment, reconceiving the economy as a naturally connective, enmeshed, and interactive system that builds from localized collectives outward to the global stage (Timney 2001). These "individuals-in-relation" and the households and firms comprising them, are "profoundly inter-knit with the sustenance and change of the natural environment" (Bell 2006, 210). In other words, socioeconomic actors must be mindful of the social, economic, and environmental implications of their actions, whether directed toward production or consumption.

Common ownership and use

All production begins with the use of natural and human resources. The tendency of modern Western technoscience to objectify all of nature has been called *resourcing* – transforming all places, nonhuman life, and objects into resources subject to appropriation (Sofoulis 1988). As the ongoing practice of slavery attests, this understanding also extends to humans (Fisher 2013). Taking the ownership of humans to be immoral at face value, Relational Becoming extends this wariness of private ownership to all others (e.g., fauna, flora, and places), as all things have some form of agency. To the extent that we can apply the notion of ownership, all of creation falls within the purview of co-ownership, for which we are all stewards.

Due to the limited availability of natural resources, the fear of scarcity and overconsumption led to enclosure and control of land (Hardin 1968). Both private and state ownership generates what George (1929) called "the land problem" (Dewey 1927) in which lords of the land are equally lords of the people who rely upon that land to reside or produce a living.[2] Moving land and its associated resources into community ownership as a collective resource prevents land ownership from siphoning off earnings and wealth from laborers/ capitalists without benefit.[3] This notion of common ownership of land has been presented as "usufruct" or the temporary right of one to use another's property (Sementelli 2007)[4] "based entirely on one's needs and citizenship in a community rather than one's proprietary, vocational, or professional interests" (Bookchin 2015e, loc. 2364).

From a ***commoning*** perspective, the boundaries of private and shared property become permeable and flexible in order to support interconnected mutual needs while conserving common assets in perpetuity (Barnes 2006). Land and natural resource use would thus be guided by all individuals within a given community with scale (local to global) dependent on the scope of use. Users would have only temporary rights to shared resources for living or production purposes according to rules determined by the co-owners. All proceeds from such use would be distributed among the entire community (George 1929).

Many argue that these practices of ***commoning*** will redress the environmental crises we now face and ensure a more sustainable future while producing greater social and economic equity (Bollier 2016) by adopting enabling laws that recognizes commons as holding legal status (Bollier and Weston 2014). Nascent practices can be found in the common ownership of mineral rights in the Alaska Permanent Fund (Barnes 2006) and even the notion of owning and trading rights to carbon emissions in order to reduce them (Gore 2006). International commons law already exists in the manner in which oceans, Antarctica, and outer space are being treated (Milun 2011).

More directly, the ***commoning*** practice of community land cooperatives (George 1929) continues in today's nonprofit community land trusts (CLTs) in which the land is owned by the trust, while use rights, buildings, and improvements are owned by the tenants (Greenstein and Sungu-Eryilmaz 2007). Some approaches, such as "commune enterprises" in Latin America (Sitrin and Azzellini 2012, 43), place land and enterprises in community ownership controlled by citizen assemblies and managed by their delegates through confederal councils (Bookchin 2015c).

Finally, some sharing economy practices extend the commons into the social and cultural products of community life (On the Commons 2016). An increasing number of peer-to-peer sharing and commons property licensing move human knowledge and creativity into the commons to accelerate collective progress (The Foundation for P2P Alternatives 2017), while acknowledging the rights of cultural groups to control the use of their traditions and heritage (Farah and Tremolada 2015).

Precedent for ***commoning*** reaches back to historical roots of commons law in Anglo-European villages as well as indigenous cultures (Milun 2011). Moving forward, special categories of ownership both within and between nations could be created that are neither public nor private, but are rather held in common. Furthermore, special categories of personhood could be created for nonhuman beings and places.[5] Interestingly, there are cultures that have never lost this understanding of the commons. For example, the best-known efforts in cooperative economics are led by indigenous communities (Martínez

Torres and Rosset 2010). This reflects a "cosmic economy of sharing" (Bird-David 1999, 29) in which all existence is related to as "a friend, a relative, a parent who shares resources with them" (31).

Relational production and consumption

The relational practices of ***commoning*** also transform production and consumption. In this context, rather than dividing producers and consumers or owners and workers, both individuals and firms have a "relational nature" and a "need for friendly and cooperative relationships" that are intrinsically motivating (Pirson and Turnbull 2011, 103). Producers strive to meet the needs of their consumers and will seek to work with one another to do so, while competing to produce the very best product or service they can (Follett 2003d). Enterprises composed of worker-owners eliminate the conflict between labor and capital that generates deep wealth disparities and more equal distribution of profits naturally causes business "to assume the co-operative form, since the more equal diffusion of wealth would unite capitalist and laborer in the same person" (George 1929, 468).

As far back as the Knights of Labor in the 1800s, workers have advocated for the replacement of the capitalist wage system by worker cooperatives (Krimerman and Lindenfeld 1992). Since then, there have been recurring waves of cooperativism during periods of general social change (Rothschild 2000; Rothschild and Whitt 1986). Today, worker cooperatives (USFWC 2016) and workplace democracy enterprises provide "a unique forum in which to explore and experiment with the ideals of justice, sustainability, and democracy" (Krimerman and Lindenfeld 1992, 215).

However, cooperatives are not the only form of incorporation that pursues social, economic, and environmental justice. Public benefit corporations exist in many states in the US (Cordes 2014). Incorporation documents for these businesses detail how the organization will benefit all stakeholders, including its own workers, customers, suppliers, the local community, and the global context in general – annual audits of all stated objectives must be made public. Similarly, some civic and social entrepreneurs engage in mutual aid through nonprofit and voluntary action (Goldsmith, Georges, and Burke 2010; Henton, Melville, and Walesh 1997), or by establishing social enterprises that are designed to address actual unmet social needs through a market-driven approach (Social Enterprise Alliance 2016).

This convergence of shared purpose demonstrates how previously understood "sectors" are moving closer to one another philosophically and in practice. Even public goods are increasingly acknowledged to be relational in character. For example, the term "co-production" describes the necessity of service providers and clients working together to achieve desired outcomes (Boyle and Harris 2009). Follett (1998) calls this type of dynamic unity "coöperative collectivism" (161).

On the consumption side of the economy, cooperative associations moderate differentials between price and demand by leveling the playing field between consumers and producers (Euro Coop n.d.) – to be truly collaborative, however, these must be more than membership buying clubs that cut costs through economies of scale and wholesale pricing. Similarly, the sharing economy's collaborative consumption shifts traditional private ownership to shared ownership through mutual lending (Botsman and Rogers 2011).

This solidarity business model joins worker-owners and consumers in "multi-stakeholder" cooperative association to achieve balance in production and consumption (Lund n.d.). Community Supported Agriculture (CSAs) provide example; growers and consumers join into mutualistic arrangements that provide a stable and secure source of income to growers through guaranteed sales, while consumers share the risk of crop success at harvest (Local Harvest 2016). This framework also provides a mechanism for traditionally non-remunerated work – such as care work and other "life-sustaining activities" (Eisler 2007, xxi) – to be brought into the system of exchange. These approaches constitute "prosumer economics," in which members of cooperative systems are both laborer and owner in production and cooperative traders in consumption (Toffler 1984). They are whole economic and social beings who engage in the creation and exchange of resources, products, and services – including those which are non-remunerated – in pursuit of a just and sustainable quality of life.

Relational finance

Traditionally, the role of finance is to provide enterprise investment, homeowner mortgages, insurance services, savings instruments, and financial transaction services. However, cooperative enterprises often do not fit the financing protocols of this commercial banking system. Self-organizing systems of finance apply ***commoning*** logic to pooled capital resources. In some cases, they are designed to localize and cooperatize the producer-consumer relationship. For example, community and complementary currencies provide localized exchange outside the monetary system, as do direct and electronic barter systems (e.g., Bitcoin) (Bindewald, Nginamau, and Place 2013). Those using the existing monetary system work through mechanisms like membership credit unions (NCUA 2016) and cooperative lending circles (Poyaoan 2013). Microfinance from these types of sources has proven to be one of the most effective strategies for realizing economic potential for those in poverty, while invigorating local economies (Barber 2013) – this method is used by the Grameen Bank in Bangladesh, the Los Angeles Microfinance Network, and the Bay Area Opportunity Fund.

Community-owned institutions like the Bank of North Dakota also work within the traditional financial system (Public Banking Institute 2016). Civic banks of these types are preferred funders for municipal enterprises and land purchases (Bookchin 2015c). Similarly, Community Development Financial Institutions (CDFIs) move traditional finance out of the conventional lending market by allowing for higher risk, generally paired with capacity building technical assistance (FSRI 2012). These institutions reduce debt at high interest rates, protect against predatory lending practices, build resiliency by keeping assets in the community, and maintain stability in global financial crises.

Community wealth building strategies allow people to "join together through some form of public, community, or employee-owned business to meet local needs and thereby regain a measure of local economic democracy and control" (Alperovitz 2014, 195). These strategies include community development corporations (CDCs), community land trusts (CLTs), social enterprises, employee-owned enterprises, and producer and consumer cooperatives. All of these organizational strategies include financial components in that they pool capital in ways that build local wealth and opportunity while retaining profits in the community.

Cooperation

Just as ***commoning*** changes how resources are owned and used as well as how producers and consumers are related, the activities undertaken throughout the processes of resource management, production, and consumption must change. Rather than *external regulation* by the state or *internal regulation* by competing economic actors, communities of economic actors engage in cooperative self-regulation. The central consideration in ***cooperation*** "is whether the contributions of individuals can be fruitfully united" (Follett 2013c, xiii).

Cooperation is based on a "*partnership* or mutual respect system" as opposed to a "*domination* or top-down control system" (Eisler 2007, xviii). Self-organizing and self-regulating producers engage in interlocking local, regional, and global markets in "the free, federated grouping of the workers" (Goldman 1913, 6). Following Radical Democracy, workplace democracy replaces hierarchy with direct participation (Greenberg 1986; Rothschild and Whitt 1986; Zwerdling 1980) that moves beyond representational democracy (Pinchot and Pinchot 1993, 72). In genuinely participative processes, workers must have significant input into key decisions about what is produced, how it is produced, and how the proceeds from production are distributed to democratize an organization (Benello 1992; Eylon 1998; Melman 2001). Such input requires substantive ownership through either worker cooperatives or employee stock ownership plans (ESOPs).[6]

Perhaps the most noted exemplar is the Mondragon Worker Cooperatives in the Basque region of Spain. Founded in 1956 as a confederation of worker cooperatives, there are now over 150 cooperatives with more than 33,000 worker-owners around the world, all of whom contribute to collective governance (Cheney 2001). Following the principle of subsidiarity, the system incorporates both direct and delegate forms of democracy for the highest level of participation practicable at all levels of decision making, from each individual co-op to a collective coordinating body called the Cooperative Congress. The entire system is operated according to ten principles: (1) open admission; (2) democratic organization; (3) sovereignty of labor; (4) the instrumental and subordinate character of capital; (5) participatory management; (6) wage solidarity; (7) inter-cooperation; (8) social transformation; (9) universality through external solidarity; and (10) cooperative and professional education (Ormaechea 2001). This model has been implemented in other regions, including the Evergreen Cooperatives Initiative in Cleveland (Capital Institute 2011) which links anchor institutions, worker cooperatives, and community-based financing for "economic inclusion and building a local economy from the ground up" (Evergreen Cooperatives 2016).

Cooperatives use democratic participation to identify a shared vision of progress and to determine mechanisms for utilizing and distributing resources in a way consistent with that vision. Equitability is achieved by fairly distributing resources and profits while conserving and reinvesting in collective resources. In this sense, ***cooperation*** follows the communist mantra: "From each according to his ability, to each according to his needs" (Marx 2008, 27). However, rather than depending on centralized control, distribution of resources is local and situation-dependent (Schumacher 2010). Community Land Trusts (CLTs) embrace such principles of financial mutuality in their operating agreements (Swann 1972). For example, to maintain ongoing housing affordability while enabling members to build equity through home ownership, the appreciation of property value is shared between the CLT and the member upon transfer of ownership.

Other types of commons follow similar operating principles: "Commoners negotiate their own rules of access and use, assign responsibilities and entitlements, set up monitoring systems to identify and penalize free riders, among other acts to maintain the commons" (Bollier 2016, 5). Winner of a Nobel Prize in Economics, Elinor Ostrom made a life's work of studying such common pool resource management around the world (see for example, Ostrom 1990). While her research focused solely on the negotiations around shared resource use as opposed to other dimensions of cooperation, her findings consistently show that self-organized management is successful and sustainable. Within an integrated system where the commons are "understood as a living social system of creative agents" (Bollier 2016, 6), people who rely on shared natural resources can work out the values, rules, and traditions necessary to sustain all in response to ongoing system changes.

While the role of "government" in today's political economy would be to create the conditions that facilitate cooperative collective action, including enabling policies and laws (Bollier 2016), it is also possible for public organizations to take on the economic role of managing joint resources (Sementelli 2007). In this case, "government would change its character, and would become the administration of a great co-operative society. It would become merely the agency by which the common property was administered for the common benefit" (George 1929, 455–457). Circling back to aim of ***commoning***, "association in equality" frees human creativity toward fruitful ends rather than dissipating it in power struggles (George 1929, 508). Only when the will to cooperate is unimpeded by competition and coercion can a civilization be said to truly advance.

Regardless of who is charged with facilitating, in ***cooperation*** organizations employ ***integrative collaboration***, as explained in Chapter 12. While the focus in that chapter is on *intra*-organizational coordination, ***cooperation*** merely transfers those same operating principles to *inter*-organizational coordination as well. Integration is therefore "the method of social progress" (97) because differences are integrated in a manner that is unique to each context in ever broadening social circles. From this perspective, progress can be measured as a continuous widening of the area of association and cooperation that yields a political economy "radiant with hope" (George 1929, 559).

Toward this end, ***cooperation*** builds on the integrative method outlined in previous chapters in an effort to coordinate the production and exchange of resources between various economic actors. As a reminder, "the method of integration" (Follett 2013c, 178) includes a relational disposition, a cooperative style of relating, a participatory mode of association, and an integrative approach to decision making and action (Stout and Love 2017). The decision making process follows the four steps of *sharing*, *disintegration*, *revaluation*, and *synthesis*.

The economic application of integration begins with the *sharing* of information. ***Cooperation*** includes the sharing of visions for qualitative progress, considering local and global flourishing, human and nonhuman. Sharing must draw forward information about available resources, processes of production, and systems of exchange. Because this sharing occurs within an ethic of Stewardship, possibilities are guided by considerations of sustainability.

Once various understandings of progress and assessments of availability and limitations of resources are offered, *disintegration* can occur. Here, participants seek to identify the values underlying visions of flourishing and progress by identifying ***emergent principles.*** Fact claims regarding resource availability and limits are broken apart to understand the perspectives and values therein, applying the process of intersubjective agreement. Suggestions for organizing production, exchange, and distribution apply the process of participatory policy making to identify underlying interests and power dynamics. Once these elements have been broken down to their core claims and values, *revaluation* allows participants in the economy to reassess these goals and processes and address differences in perspectives that still remain. All considerations within the revaluation process are shaped by the ethic of Stewardship. *Revaluation* at each level yields the possibility for *synthesis* in determinations for vision, production, and exchange.

The interplay between *sharing*, *disintegration*, *revaluation*, and *synthesis* that make up the process of ***cooperation*** occur in iterative process – an ever-evolving situation means that conceptions of flourishing, knowledge regarding resources, and mechanisms for production and exchange are deeply interrelated. For instance, as we learn more about the impacts of human activity on the climate and resultant social and environmental upheaval through the process of intersubjective agreement, this new knowledge impacts both ideas of progress and policy solutions.

Coopetition

Coopetition repositions economic relationships within the larger sphere of social life for a complete theory of radically democratic political economy, reflecting the assertion that "democratic control of the economy is both desirable and possible" (Simons 2005, 151). Coopetition infused with an ethic of Stewardship produces ***commoning*** relationships engaging in ***cooperation*** in competition with shared challenges in the pursuit of flourishing for all. Its generative principles replace self-interest with mutual interest, the assumption of scarcity with an expectation of abundance, fear of competition with mutual care and the trust it engenders, and dominating hierarchy and strategic competition with self-organizing cooperation. Such an economy would include: (1) common ownership and stewardship of natural resources; (2) the merging of capital and labor through cooperative enterprise; (3) the linkage of producers and consumers through cooperative association; (4) the collaboration of lenders and borrowers in community finance; and (5) participative coordination of resource use, exchange, and distribution.

These types of efforts appear to be coalescing around the core economic sectors that sustain life – land ownership, food production, water rights, caregiving, energy production, and home and small business finance. These are the arenas in which we find burgeoning social, cooperative, and mutually owned enterprises. Community land trusts and agricultural cooperatives put land into common ownership for current and future mutual benefit. Farming cooperatives, farmers markets, Community Supported Agriculture (CSAs), food distribution systems (hubs), and consumer cooperatives interconnect local food systems to provide the highest sustainable levels of nutrition, affordability, and profit. Water rights activists are working to ensure that critical fresh water sources are protected from commodification and that fisheries are protected for future generations. Caregiving cooperatives and social enterprise are taking child, elder, and other types of home care back from corporate, for-profit systems. Community-based systems are reclaiming energy production through distributed solar and wind power production to lower utility rates and reinvest profits as social enterprises. Community Development Financial Institutions, public banks, cooperative credit unions, and lending circles are taking back home and business finance from multinational financial institutions.

Through these tactics, the common good is transformed; "Each person's interest is realized *together* with that of others, not *in opposition* to it (as happens with the private good) nor *apart* from others' interest (as happens with the public good)" (Donati 2014, 101). Such a society is thought to promote: (1) greater efficiency through inclusiveness and less waste of talent; (2) social order without individual repression; and (3) enhanced human rights and quality of life through egalitarian relationships (Schumacher 2010). However, acknowledging that material want quickly erodes solidarity (Bookchin 2015b), it is important to consider the ability of Coopetition to build and sustain material wealth. Because cooperatives pool both risk and equity, and community financing lowers both risk and interest rates, savings and surplus are reinvested rather than siphoned off.

Through cooperative associations of worker-owners and consumers, all of whom have complex loyalties to communities at various geographic scales, attention will be held on people, place, and profit as both material and relational wealth is produced. This triple bottom line typically results in greater sustainability across social, economic, and environmental dimensions – allowing individuals and nations to work together in competition with problems or in collaboration with opportunities to address the crisis of sustainability confronting humanity today. These cooperative associations free human creativity toward fruitful ends rather than dissipating it in power struggles (George 1929). To redress the social and environmental crises we face, we must escape the economic dialectic of hierarchy and competition, of centralized state control and laissez-faire markets.

In sum, an economic system based on Coopetition offers great promise in producing sustainable economic outcomes, while fostering stronger social relations and conservation of environmental resources. Five general principles found in solidarity economics are necessary to overcome the crisis of sustainability we now confront:

1 autonomy in governance, including self-management;
2 solidarity among community members and with other communities cooperating in a similar process;
3 self-sufficiency in so far as it is feasible, given the resource endowment and ecological conditions;
4 productive diversification for trade with other communities and in the market; and finally,
5 sustainable management of regional resources (Lemus and Barkin 2013, 3).

When infused with a sense of solidarity, Coopetition holds a promise of "'holistic' or integrated development" that is of significant interest to the international development community (UNRISD 2012; IATFSSE 2014) as well as the alternative globalization movement (Marques 2013).

Integrative pathways

An Integrative synthesis must generate pathways that are easily traversed by those holding other positions. Coopetition must provide concepts that sufficiently meet fundamental principles within the other economic systems, or at least create a dialogical basis for shared understandings. As illustrated in Figure 11.1, we imagine the shared characteristics shown in Table 11.2 as pathways into a dynamic synthesis that is always open to contestation and change.

Going back to our discussion of dialectical synthesis in the chapter's introduction we know that to accommodate the basic assumptions of the other ideal-types, Coopetition must synthesize *external* and *internal* economic *regulation* as well as relatively *moderate* and *strong* regulatory *authority*. Coopetition synthesizes *external* and *internal regulation* by interlocking markets and communities from the local to global scope through relational ***commoning*** (Bollier 2016). The ***power-with*** concept of ***cooperation*** allocates neither *moderate* nor *strong authority* to government or economic actors. Instead, all situated actors contribute to the self-organizing coordination of economic production and exchange.

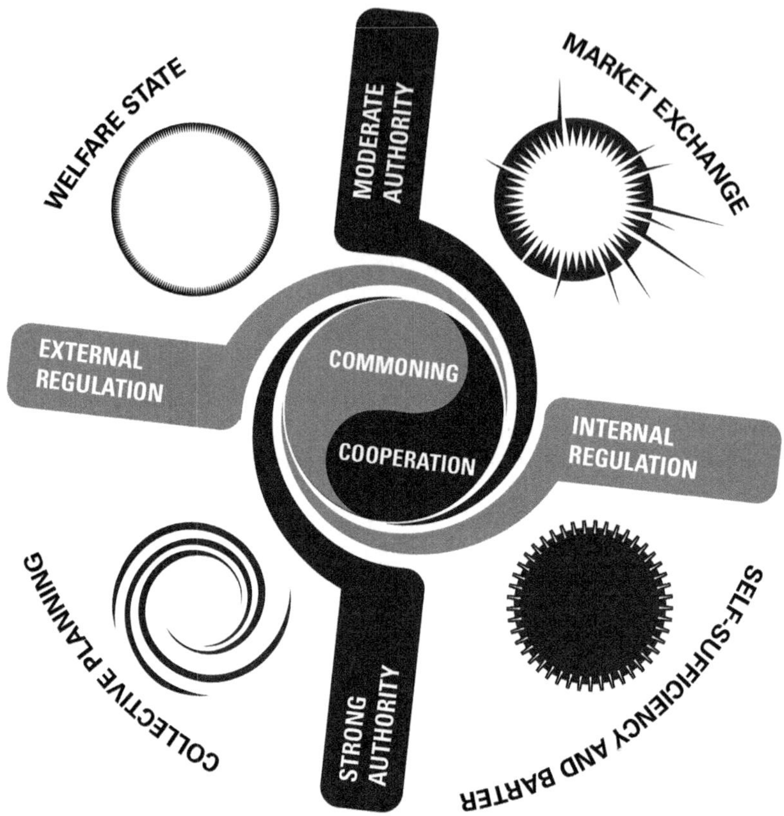

Figure 11.1 Integrative pathways for Coopetition

The primary concerns of each distinct position also need to be addressed to establish a starting point for dialogue with the Integrative perspective, as shown in Table 11.2.

The Welfare State system is primarily concerned with maintaining economic stability and ensures this through moderate redistribution of resources. Coopetition accomplishes stability by moving key elements of production (land and capital) into community ownership within the process of ***commoning*** and determining use and distribution of resources through ***cooperation***. The Market Exchange system is primarily concerned with increasing production and profits and does so by minimizing government regulation and encouraging market competition. Coopetition promotes qualitative improvements to production through ***commoning*** and maximizes value for all through ***cooperation***. Collective Planning is primarily concerned with the equitable distribution of resources. Coopetition ensures equity through producer and consumer cooperatives within ***commoning*** relationships guided by Stewardship, along with ***cooperation*** to determine equitable distribution of value. Self-Sufficiency and Barter systems seek to maximize individual utility and enjoyment. ***Commoning*** produces material and relational value, including non-remunerated work, while ***cooperation*** maintains a sense of agency in the economic system.

Table 11.2 Integrating economic concerns

Ideal-Type	***Characteristics***	***Primary Concerns***	***Synthesis Solution***
Welfare State	*external institution, moderate regulation*	Redistribution of resources to maintain stability	***Commoning*** ensures community ownership of land, natural resources, and finance; ***cooperation*** determines use and distribution of value
Market Exchange	*internal institution, moderate regulation*	Increasing production and profits	***Commoning*** promotes qualitative improvements to production; ***cooperation*** maximizes value for all
Collective Planning	*external institution, strong regulation*	Equitable distribution of resources	***Commoning*** ensures producer and consumer cooperatives guided by Stewardship; participative ***cooperation*** determines equitable distribution of value
Self-Sufficiency and Barter	*internal institution, strong regulation*	Maximized individual utility and enjoyment	***Commoning*** produces material and relational value, including non-remunerated work; ***cooperation*** maintains agency

Notes

1 Like Ramos (1981), despite his pursuit of relational understandings of social action, Donati keeps spheres of activity separate, rather than seeking a relational approach within all sectors of society.

2 Henry George (1929) was a Progressive Era public intellectual that Dewey ranked with Plato as a social philosopher, noting that George's ideas had greatly influenced his own thinking (1927). George's 1880 book, *Progress and Poverty, the Remedy: An Inquiry into the Causes of Industrial Depressions and the Increase of Want with Increase of Wealth*, presents groundbreaking work on the problem of social, economic, and environmental justice in a liberal democratic, capitalist society. Subsequent Georgists established the ongoing and influential Lincoln Institute of Land Policy.

3 George (1929) grounds his argument in theism, but natural law can be reinterpreted without references to a deity.

4 Thomas Jefferson brought up the question of the use and ownership of common resources, recommending the concept of usufruct (Sementelli 2007). While in use since the 1600s, meaning the legal use of someone else's property, the term usufruct comes from the Medieval Latin terms "use" and "fruits." In this case, using the fruits of the commons.

5 As noted in Chapter 9, the government of New Zealand recognizes the legal rights of the Whanganui River and its tributaries as an indivisible, living whole, both in terms of physical and metaphysical aspects (Cullinan 2014).

6 ESOPs transfer shares to employees with each year of employment until all shares have been distributed. However, not all operate under democratic governance practices.

12 Administrative theory

Facilitative Coordination

> Rigor, opening *and* tolerance *are the fundamental characteristics of the transdisciplinary attitude and vision.* Rigor *in argument, taking into account of all existing data, is the best defense against possible distortions.* Opening *involves an acceptance of the unknown, the unexpected and the unpredictable.* Tolerance *implies acknowledging the right to ideas and truths opposed to our own.*
>
> – (Article 14 of the Charter of Transdisciplinarity, Nicolescu 2002, 151)

In order to resolve the crisis of government that has allowed social, economic, and environmental crises to develop and perpetuate, both political and economic life must be administered in a different manner; a transformation is required to support relational process practices. For example, Bollier (2016) describes commoning as a "systemic way to reclaim social, ecological, and ethical values for managing our shared wealth" (9). "Green governance" is an approach based on collective rights-based principles, as opposed to individualistic property rights principles (Bollier and Weston 2013, 2014). Its practices include internal regulation within specific commons associations and larger but still self-governing laws and institutions that enable commons identification and ownership. This can be initiated through amendments to existing legal strategies to accommodate organizing forms appropriate to specific types of commons (i.e., local, regional, international and geological, atmospheric, or biological).

We argue that this is precisely the goal of Integrative Governance – reintegrating social, economic, and environmental domains in a more ethical manner that is both locally and globally responsive. However, as explained in Chapter 3, this cannot be achieved through a new management approach applied within existing conventional organizations – it requires a paradigmatic transformation in administrative structure, process, and function. These three elements shape both internal organizational relationships and those between the organization and its environment. For example, public administration theory considers the relationships among administrators, between politicians and administrators, and between citizens and both politicians and public administrators (Stout 2013). Scholars of humanistic organization theory view the people in these roles as more than rational actors; they also have a "relational nature" and the "need for friendly and cooperative relationships" (Pirson and Turnbull 2011, 103). Thus, hierarchical and principal-agent organizational theories must be replaced with concepts fitting Relational Becoming and Ensembling individuality.

As shown in Table 12.1, our Governance Typology presents two dialectics at play in common approaches to administrative theory. On the horizontal axis, the relational dialectic is between structuring administration via *hierarchical organization* versus *matrix*

Table 12.1 Dialectical administrative theory

	Hierarchical Organization	***Matrix Organization***
Moderate Discretion	Orthodox Administration	New Public Service
Strong Discretion	New Public Administration	New Public Management

(Source: adapted from Stout and Love 2016)

organization.[1] Within these organizations, following the power dynamics of political theory, the vertical process dialectic is about the *relative strength* of *administrative discretion* within the organization. While we draw from for-profit and nonprofit management theory to develop the Integrative ideal-type, in light of our focus on governance, we identify central ideas around which schools of public administration thought cluster, acknowledging that such groupings are by no means ideal-typical in nature, but rather hybrids that lend themselves more or less to the four primary approaches to governance.

Orthodox Administration serves a centralized, hierarchical state directed by the political elite. Administrative discretion is minimized to ensure legitimacy through the political system. (These relationships are mirrored in the board of directors and staff of private organizations.) New Public Administration serves within a centralized government; however, administrative authority is maximized through broad discretion to ensure good outcomes via expertise and minimized political corruption. New Public Service assumes a decentralized government in which both political leaders and administrators are guided by pluralist policy making procedures that ideally moderate administrative discretion through citizen participation. New Public Management assumes a highly decentralized government that relies heavily on the private sector through load shedding of public functions or contracting out for services, giving strong administrative discretion to private economic actors.

Mirroring the political structure of ***self-organizing confederalism*** as well as the economic structure of ***commoning***, Integrative organizational systems are characterized as ***responsive networks***. Each functional unit within an organization is a network, while the organization as a whole is a network of networks. Organizations interact with one another in social and economic systems in a network, including both confederal governing organizations and solidarity economics organizations. Following Radical Democracy's understanding of ***power-with***, positional differentials of *moderate* and *strong discretion* no longer hold meaning. To enable effective collective thinking and doing both within groups and between groups, ***integrative collaboration*** employs situational authority, emergent leadership that evokes and enables the best contribution from all group members, and the integrative process to foster cooperation and coordination. Together, the administrative function of Facilitative Coordination replaces both hierarchical administration and matrix-style management within an organization; the administrative function retains significance, but without command or arbitrary authority.

Proponents of this administrative approach in governance fully recognize that this is a transitional moment in history – one in which midwifery is needed to usher in these transformations (Stivers 2000b). To achieve robust progress across social, economic, and environmental dimensions, public administration can use its existing role to advocate for change. Such theories describe "self-conscious administrators who are critically aware of the political-economic context" (Adams et al. 1990, 233), who work to "break down the barriers" between government and its constituents (Box and Sagen 1998, 159) as proactive, emancipative facilitators of "citizen governance" (Box 1998). Administration must become "a differentiated function of the political body specialized in making sure that social processes do not create poverty and exclusion but, rather, wealth and social cohesion through the production of relational goods" (Donati 2014, 111). As Saint Simon argued, "The time will come when the art of governing men will disappear. A new art will take its place, the art of administering things" (quoted in Rocker 2004, 10).

To understand and enable Facilitative Coordination, we consider the various aspects of administrative theory and how they must be transformed or redefined: (1) the organizing style used to guide behavior; (2) the political authority delegated to administrators; (3) the scope of administrative action; (4) the criteria of proper administrative behavior; and (5) the approach to administrative decision making (Stout 2013). Together, these concepts shape the administrative function in governance and prescribe administrators' actions in practice.

We find Integrative interpretations of these aspects of administrative theory in "transformational public service," which employs citizen engagement in the pursuit of social and economic justice; it is "collaborative, humanistic, emancipatory, inclusive and diverse" (King and Zanetti 2005, xi). Integrative concepts can also be found in "anti-administration," an imaginative, morally reflective, and multi-epistemological approach that considers administration to be a loving art that relies on thinking as play and justice as seeking (Farmer 2005). In "a politics of the subject": (1) neither unity nor atomism are acceptable; (2) radical difference must be accommodated within dynamic compositions; (3) becoming occurs through generative, situational processes; (4) governing is a process that cuts across human activity; (5) governing does not entail permanent social roles; and (6) governing focuses on facilitating the process (Catlaw 2007b, 192). The Collaborative Tradition of public administration theory (Stout 2013) weaves together the classical pragmatism promoted by Stivers (2008) with these more contemporary proposals, thus describing an approach that has been present, albeit marginalized, since public administration emerged as a distinct field of study and practice (Stout 2010a).

While some suggest these are new ideas, calling such a synthesis both "post-individualistic" and "post-holistic" (Donati 2014, 6), a compelling pragmatist proposal can be found at the turn of the last century in Mary Follett's work (Stout and Love 2015a). Follettian thought is an excellent source from which to generate Integrative administrative theory because she draws from both political and organizational theory to frame the manner in which integrative process permeates all social action; she is uniquely positioned to close the theoretical gap in collaborative governance between instrumental and democratic objectives. Indeed, Follett is not only a key theorist of political theory, management, negotiation, and social work, she is recognized as a founder of the field of public administration (Fry and Raadschelders 2014). Many scholars use her theories to inform public engagement in collaborative governance (see for example, Elías and Alkadry 2011; King 2011; King, Feltey, and Susel 1998; King and Zanetti 2005; Stivers 2000a; Stout 2013), and to augment our understandings of interrelations within networks (Gehani and Gehani 2007).

Follett (1998) argues coordination is the role of the "new State" in "true democracy" (156), but affirms a place for expertise in decision making. Even communalists wish to see experts involved in advising citizens' assemblies in policy making and maintaining responsibility for administration (Bookchin 2015f). However, administrators must be experts on tap, not on top; "A decentered ego allows practitioners . . . to see themselves as facilitators . . . not as experts" (King and Zanetti 2005, 116). As facilitators, practitioners can support collaboration among all governance actors – expert administrators, politicians, and citizens

(Stout 2013). Citizens are viewed not only as volunteers and coproducers, but as co-learners alongside administrators and elected representatives, with administrators acting as facilitators of deliberation and stewards of the public trust (Roberts 2004).

In private sector organizational theory, we find proposals that reflect the same concepts, with the most systematic conceptualizations presented in sociocracy and Holacracy.[2] Sociocracy is an organizational system conceived in 1945 by Kees Boeke as a way to adapt Quaker egalitarian principles to secular organizations. His student, Gerard Endenburg, further developed the concept using his own business as a learning laboratory (Sociocracy For All n.d.). Sociocracy, or dynamic governance, is a whole systems governance method that makes collaboration, self-organization, and distributed authority practical and effective in any group application – public or private. However, groups must have an established shared purpose upon forming – this is what differentiates *socio*-cracy from *demo*-cracy.

Holacracy is "a new social technology for governing and operating an organization" (Robertson 2015, 12) or an organizational design and operations system that seeks "better ways of working together as humans" (Robertson 2014). Holacracy reflects a radically democratic, integrative process in practice. In fact, its ideas are tested against the question, "Does this integrate the core energies/strengths brought by all types of people, or bias towards just a subset?" (Robertson 2014). Following principles from the agile movement[3] in management theory, Holacracy employs self-organizing teams with the authority to make decisions in response to changing conditions, with transparency and communicative feedback throughout the organization. It is designed to achieve "governance *of* the organization, *through* the people, *for* the purpose" (Robertson 2015, 33). It entails pulling back from the day-to-day work to improve the structure and processes of the organization. Individuals and groups then work within those structures and processes to coordinate operations.

In the social movement literature, we find similar concepts in horizontalism, which advocates for an end to all hierarchies through the establishment, development, and maintenance of social structures that equitably distribute authority through self-organizing relationships (Sitrin 2007). These social movements frequently use general assemblies for the "intentional coming together in ways so that all can speak and be heard, and often, so decisions can be made" (Sitrin and Azzellini 2012, 52). By networking affinity groups and small general assemblies into larger spokescouncils, horizontalism is applied at all levels of decision making (Dixon 2014). This approach often uses consensus-based decision processes, but this is not a requirement. Decisions are made at the smallest scale possible to allow the greatest degree of direct participation. Engagement in deliberative encounters enables groups to pursue a shared purpose in an egalitarian fashion – in other words, without vertical, hierarchical power relationships.

In sketch, all of these conceptualizations promote "structured nonhierarchical social interaction" (Thayer 1981, A-38). Within networks of groups and organizations, administrative authority is transformed and decision making becomes an integrative, collaborative process in which leadership is emergent and responsive to the requirements of the situation at hand. Thus, the administrative function is transformed into one of facilitation and coordination of participative practice, one that relinquishes positional authority and replaces it with dynamic, situation-specific decisions and action. We break these concepts down, considering the manner in which organizational structure, authority, leadership, management, operating procedures, and the administrative function itself are transformed and redefined.

Responsive networks

The primary characteristic of Integrative relationships is their lack of hierarchical authority, once again reflecting the causal dilemma in the relational process concepts of Radical Democracy – they both start and end with power dynamics. The types of communicative, process-oriented practices described in Stewardship, Radical Democracy, and Coopetition "depend on the existence of those social and political institutions that allow for and foster . . . dialogue" (Bernstein 1976, 199). Therefore, all Integrative social and economic groups organize in the same fashion – nonhierarchically.

Within all groups, relationships are the fundamental unit of analysis – not the individual members. In other words, groups are a form of community as process (Follett 1919). These "relational constellations" of actor-networks (Hernes 2008, 67) "do not consist of stable nodes and links, but consist of relations that shape actors recursively . . . relations are formed and reformed to obtain a stabilized system that serves some purpose" (70). Thus, it is best to understand these interconnecting networks as open systems (von Bertalanffy 1975); each group is in an ongoing process of self-organizing while interrelating with its environment (Wheatley 2006).

Every group (family, community, organization, etc.) exists within networks that are interconnected with one another through overlapping memberships. For geographic communities, these groups nest within one another from the global to most local scope. Through crossover members, the boundaries between groups are porous; social groups and political, economic, and administrative organizations all interconnect in dynamic and fluid ways through their members. Futurist Alvin Toffler (1984) notes that we do not have the language to describe these organizing structures, suggesting that "ensembles" and "networks" are closer than "matrix" or "ad hoc" (264). We use the term ***responsive networks*** – an organizational *structure* that synthesizes *hierarchical* and *matrix* forms – to join the emergent assemblages of ***self-organizing confederalism*** with ***commoning***. This organizing style enables a type of collaboration that achieves both the stability associated with hierarchy and the flexibility associated with competition. These networks are emergent and responsive to the ongoing situation.

Responsive networks enable a type of collaboration that achieves both the stability associated with hierarchy and the flexibility associated with competition (Buchanan 2002; Weick 2001). Cleveland (2000) argues that decentralization maintains hierarchical control at the center, merely diffusing it somewhat through delegations of authority to lower levels. Therefore, nonhierarchical *un*centralization is what is required for global governance. Reflecting back on Anti-federalist ideals for democracy, he says, "the practical prospect for a workable world seems to lie in reinventing their nobody-in-charge concept for *global* application" (294). In this system, everyone must be partly in charge, which requires everyone to agree to shared norms and standards while maximizing each individual's freedom to use "common sense, imagination, and suasive skills" (296) to advance common purposes. Therefore, every group within the network holds its own authority, which is neither more nor less than any other group's.

However, this conflation of the term centralization with hierarchical authority is problematic. ***Self-organizing confederalism*** "is neither an individual nor a collective entity overshadowing the single agents/actors" (Donati 2014, 67). Instead, *central* functions simply support more functions than others. For example, in sociocracy (Endenburg 1998) and Holacracy (Robertson 2015), working groups are called *circles*, each of which has a particular functional domain and aim over which it has authority as well as responsibility and accountability – sub-circles (and sub-sub-circles) operate within a super-circle that is the organization.[4] A governance circle is placed at the center of the organization because it is an intergroup decision-making body for the super-circle made up of representatives from each operational sub-circle. However, responsibility "can only be met jointly" (Follett 2013b, 74); therefore, no hierarchy is indicated within the circular formations shown in Figure 12.1.

It has been argued that network relationships result in strong ties between those with a high level of overlapping membership and weak ties between those who are connected only through other groups (Granovetter 1973). Therefore, nonhierarchical network structures must be designed to ensure sufficient direct participation across groups to enable strong ties, supported by adequate transparency through communication and information between independent groups to support weak ties (Robertson 2015).

On this point, Gittell (2011) argues that "relational coordination theory" brings Follett's ideas of federated coordination up to date by considering conditions of reciprocal interdependence, uncertainty, and time constraints – the very same conditions cited as the conditions of governance networks. However, rather than suggesting that network structures displace existing hierarchical structures, she argues that relational processes can be redesigned to improve how strong ties within units are integrated with boundary-spanning weak ties, resulting in an overall system of robust, but flexible and dynamic relationships. We argue that while this is a reasonable transitional approach, ultimately, network members must eliminate hierarchical and competitive structures and their relational dynamics to fully enable the integrative and collaborative practices necessary for effective network operations. Therefore, this type of mutually responsible, nonhierarchical, interlocking network structure requires revised understandings of the administrative process and function.

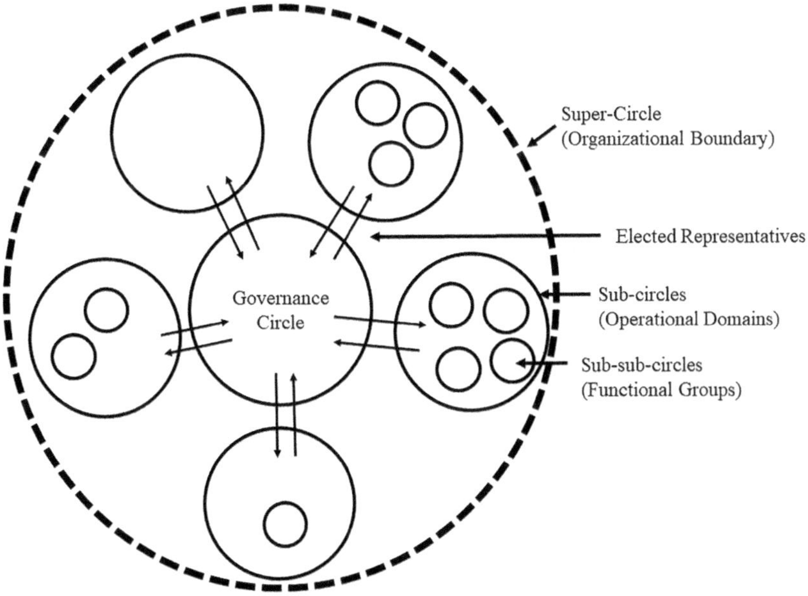

Figure 12.1 Responsive network organizational structure

Integrative collaboration

Administration and management are terms that connote dominion over some part of an organization, function, or the people within them. Therefore, these terms do not fit with Radical Democracy's concept of ***power-with*** or Coopetition's concept of ***cooperation***. We use the term ***collaboration*** because it means laboring together and a collaborator is defined as "a person who works jointly on an activity or project; an associate" (Oxford English Dictionary 2017). As noted in Chapter 3, we must add the adjective ***integrative*** to differentiate the term from how it is interpreted in most governance network literature.

Through the lens of Radical Democracy, ***integrative collaboration*** transforms *administrative discretion* and all aspects of the administrative process through ***power-with***, including authority, leadership, management, and operating procedures. All group members are understood as collaborators, enhancing both autonomy and mutuality among all group members. This form of active participation emphasizes self-organizing coordination of labor and reciprocal cooperation to achieve common goals across organizational boundaries. This is not only true in public organizations; in private organizations, workplace democracy opens the door to integrative process.

Situational authority

Within organizational settings, power is exercised through the authority to decide and determine action. In ***responsive networks***, authority cannot be exerted through hierarchical force because domination is neither ethically acceptable nor logistically feasible. Nor can authority function legitimately through pluralist competition. This means that administration must eschew both command and control and majority rules (Wheatley 2006). Following pragmatist visions of an engaged citizenry collectively solving public problems (Dewey 1957, 1999; Follett 1919, 1998, 2013c), ***situational authority*** means allowing the particulars of the situation at hand to dictate who should have authority over specific functions. Participative processes bestow decision-making authority and autonomy to all, while also demanding responsibility and accountability from all.

Under ***power-with***, positional governing authority in groups is relinquished and transferred to the collaborative process itself in order to foster dynamic, situation-specific decisions and action (White 1990). As explained in Holacracy, "uncovering purpose is a dynamic and continuing process" among all organizational members (Robertson 2015, 32). The integrative process enables collaborators to form a shared understanding of "the law of the situation" (Follett 2003f, 104), which includes intersubjective agreements about what is true, right, and good. Finding the law of the situation requires consideration of all physical and social factors, including future implications and those who are not actually present in the discussion. Knowing when this law has been found must be sensed by the group and re-evaluated as the situation evolves. Thus, authority is situationally determined both epistemologically and ethically, thereby rectifying power relationships in all social contexts: "If both sides obey the law of the situation, no *person* has power over another" (Follett 2003f, 105). Instead, each individual is engaged according to the unique expertise they can bring to bear on whatever the situation demands.

In Holacracy, this approach to authority is operationalized in a detailed, written constitution (Robertson 2015). Everyone in the organization is bound by the same transparency rules. Specifically, authority is granted to individuals and circles according to their functional domain. In accepting that domain of authority, the individual or circle takes on responsibility for the domain's purpose and accountability as a steward. While voting procedures are used to select individuals for particular roles, the process is preceded by dialogue and deliberation designed to find what the situation calls for. All roles and functions remain open to amendment in response to the organization's ever-changing situation, enabling a continuous evolution of the organization as an open system.

Included among the functional domains is governance of the organization as a whole. The governance circle is initially constituted through democratic voting procedures of all organizational members. In operations circles, a "lead link" role is appointed by the governing circle and helps ensure that the sub-circle is being attentive to the purpose, strategy, and needs of its broader context. A "delegate link" role is elected by the functional circle and helps ensure that the sub-circle's needs are represented and addressed by other circles through the governance circle. This "double link" structure builds confederation among circles that maintain communications and feedback while maintaining integrative autonomy. Also within each circle, a "facilitator" is elected and authorized to maintain the decision-making process defined in the organizational constitution. A "secretary" is elected and is accountable for recordkeeping and communications that meet the requirements of accountability and transparency throughout the organization. All other function-specific roles are initially appointed by the circle's leader and thereafter are accepted and amended through the decision making process.

In fulfilling the role accepted, each individual is expected to identify projects that benefit the role's domain of authority, identify and resolve issues that hinder the work, identify action steps needed for project completion, track projects and actions in a transparent manner, and prioritize time and resources in an effective manner that coordinates well with other roles. While most decisions are made in functional circle meetings, independent decisions are also accommodated due to time constraints, limited impact on resources beyond one's authority, and the judgment that it will resolve more issues than it might create. However, this type of autonomous action requires immediate follow up with the domain of authority infringed upon and a commitment to take restorative action if necessary. In sum, situational authority demands an intensive level of administrative responsibility from each organizational member.

Leadership as emergent and evoking

Leaders are often described as visionary individuals who establish the purpose groups will pursue. The tenets of Radical Democracy require purpose to be discovered and generated together, rather than by a particular individual. Yet, as Follett (1998) notes, "administrative responsibility and expert service are as necessary a part of genuine democracy as popular control is a necessary accompaniment of administrative responsibility" (175). The trick is combining both in an effective manner. "Emerging" is the term she uses to indicate how creative insight and foresight necessary for progress comes from anyone in an organization (Follett 2003e, 267).

Emergent leadership is a function that is dynamic and diffuse, allowing different individuals to emerge to fulfill what the situation demands – including both substantive knowledge and the ability to facilitate the integrative process. This emergent quality prevents the reification of authority inuring to a particular person, role, or organizational position, and promotes a sense of nonhierarchy. Follett (2013d) argues that leadership is a function that is dynamic and diffuse, "sometimes in one place and sometimes in another" (51); "one man is over another in some things and under him in others" (Follett 2003i, 286). She refers to this as "multiple leadership" (Follett 2003e, 251), a type of leadership that is "always open and negotiable" (Donati 2014, 68), with "the logic of selection" based on "situational needs that require the creation of new opportunities" (70). Thus, leadership must be invested in all, meaning each person leads something and everyone follows others "in service of the organization's purpose" (Robertson 2015, 22).

In this emergent formulation, "leadership is better seen as a capacity of the group, a resource which resides in the group and which must be activated in order for the group to fulfill its potential" (Denhardt 1981, 130). The freedom to speak up within the group ignites the passion and creativity of each member, enabling the group to take advantage of anyone who perceives "a specific gap between current reality and a sensed potential" (Robertson 2015, 5). This vastly augments agility and responsiveness within the organization, maximizing its potential and evolutionary capacity.

Management as enabling

The term management suggests a hierarchical arrangement – a leader who wields power over human and material resources in order to arrange them functionally. The term administration is little better, but at least allows an inference of service – administering – *to* others. In either case, the concepts are meant to describe how action is directed and controlled because there is a practical need for getting things done. This requires identifying shared problems and opportunities, analyzing possible responses, coming to decisions about what to do, taking action, and then evaluating how things went.

The leadership function of "evoking" (Follett 2003e, 267) draws out and develops strength in others to grow and contribute their best abilities, as emergent leaders themselves. Thus, management is redefined as a function that *enables* others to do their work well rather than directing and controlling the actions of others. The goal is "transformation . . . invention and creation . . . of women and men . . . at their potential best (to help them become better at what they are)" (Barber 1984, 25). Thus, management or administration becomes "the generic name of the group of tactical-support" (Catlaw 2007b, 203). This support function enables groups in the process of coming to shared understanding and agreement about collective action and then in coordinating joint undertakings. Although it is true that "enabling requires the ability to see the 'big picture'" (Waterhouse and Keast 2012, 568), even those with a very narrow functional scope must understand how that function fits into the whole. While each individual is responsible for their own work, they also share responsibility for the overall purpose; "Collective responsibility is not a matter of adding but of interweaving" (Follett 2013b, 75). Therefore, much of the enabling function consists of "interacting" (Follett 2003e, 267) – communicating and listening to ensure everyone understands their contribution to the organization's purpose.

While self-regulating groups are *autopoietic* (Weick 1979), these activities can be enabled by facilitated process. Those who are able to facilitate "the interweaving of all the experience concerned" garner the "legitimate authority" to do so (Follett 2003h, 204). Others propose "the alternative term of 'process minder'" (Mandell, Keast, and Chamberlain 2016, 336). At this point in time, facilitation of group process has become a well-crafted "technology of participation" (Institute of Cultural Affairs 2011). A plethora of creative techniques have been put forth by the IAP2 (2007) and the NCDD (2010). The *Facilitator's Guide to Participatory Decision-Making* (Kaner et al. 1996) has attained nearly canon-like status. In addition to application to all types of enterprise and nonprofit organizations, these techniques are found in the "thick" practices of public participation (Nabatchi and Leighninger 2015), as well as the operations of new social movements in general assemblies and spokescouncils (Graeber 2002).

As an example, Holacracy employs governance meetings and tactical meetings designed to enable decision making and coordination through specific process components within every circle. Within these meetings, the facilitator guides the integrative process but all individuals are expected to know the process and to address their own concerns through its rules. The facilitator minds the process by suppressing out-of-process behavior, similar to a referee in sports. Facilitators help keep the process moving quickly and effectively, emphasizing the goal of producing a workable decision that may be revisited at any time. The process is designed to enable "dynamic steering" which refers to "constant adjustment in light of real feedback, which makes for a more organic and emergent path" (Robertson 2015, 129). Teams can move quickly from discussion and planning to action and learning from the results, then return to further discussion and planning.

This type of enabling is critical in ***responsive networks*** because this intra-organizational function must be replicated for inter-organizational relationships in open systems (Weick 1979). These "boundary spanner" roles establish and facilitate relationships among organizations (Williams 2002). Donati (2014) calls this "relational steering" which is guided by "reciprocal action between agents/actors" (68) that determines stable patterns of interaction, agreed-upon rules of interaction, and shared understandings of purpose. This type of relational facilitation increases the importance of system integrators in administration, and therefore "relational competence" among administrators (Gittell 2011, 408).

Participative coordination

As Robertson (2015) notes, "operations is about getting work done – identifying outcomes to achieve, making specific decisions, allocating resources, taking actions, and coordinating those actions with others" (26). Of these activities, Follett argues "co-ordination, is certainly the crux of almost every problem the organization engineer or the business manager has to deal with" (Follett 2003h, 192). Coordination is an ongoing process through which the perspectives, expertise, and functions of all parties are interwoven. As noted in the discussion of situational authority, everyone is responsible for coordinating their efforts in a cooperative and fruitful manner; therefore, coordination is an emergent, participatory, and dynamic function.

In traditional approaches to management and administration, operating procedures that guide decision making and routinized action toward shared purposes are determined in advance by those in upper echelons of the organizational hierarchy. To enable ***integrative collaboration***, such *procedures* must become flexible and participative *processes.* In co-creative processes aimed toward getting something done, we still identify challenges, explore possible actions, make choices and plans, implement those actions, and then assess the results. In all types of organizational contexts, this has been conceived as the policy process – making, implementing, and evaluating policy. However, rather than a set of rational, formal, scientific techniques, the manner in which these processes are constructed and executed are transformed in order to produce a welcoming milieu for the participatory practices of Radical Democracy, which include finding intersubjective agreement, determining emergent principles, participatory policy making, participative cooperation, and participative coordination.

The iterative stages of identifying problems and opportunities, exploring possible responses, and coming to decisions about what to do are explained in the participatory policy making process of Radical Democracy. This process is equally applicable to all groups and organizations, whether formal or informal, when considering democracy as a way of life. Moving from policy making into the administrative function, we must add the process of implementing what was decided and evaluating how effective, efficient, ethical, and equitable the results are in order to inform new policy as the situation evolves. These administrative stages also employ a combination of Integral Knowing's process of coming to intersubjective agreement and Stewardship's process for determining emergent principles. Therefore, participative coordination utilizes the method of integration to facilitate implementation in all stages.

In what Follett (2003f) calls "functional unifying" (116), the coordination of complex activities toward the organizational purpose is accomplished through ongoing co-adaptation. Here, we will summarize briefly how these processes occur in administrative contexts *within* groups, as opposed to Coopetition's participative cooperation *among* groups. "Integrating" is the relational management task that helps individuals and groups coordinate efforts (Follett 2003e, 267). As explained in previous chapters, "the method of integration" (Follett 2013c, 178) includes a relational disposition, a cooperative style of relating, a participatory mode of association, and an integrative approach to decision making and action (Stout and Love 2017). The process follows the four steps of *sharing*, *disintegration*, *revaluation*, and *synthesis*. Using this process, the group can co-produce knowledge, shared principles, joint purpose, choice of method, operational techniques, and evaluative criteria and methods; in short, all the activities common to the policy process. Coordination of action also requires micro-processes of these activities on a day-to-day basis. Because all of these elements come together in administration, they can be taken as a whole, or broken apart in iterative phases of integration (Follett 2003b).

For example, the group may focus first on establishing joint purpose and evaluative criteria, as the two are linked in operational planning (Rossi, Lipsey, and Freeman 2004). This may require doubling back to the coproduction of knowledge and shared principles in order to align causal and normative beliefs (Sabatier 1988). Once the integrative process produces a shared understanding of the situation, aims, and evaluative criteria, the process moves into the choice of method, once again returning to issues of intersubjective agreement and emergent principles. Once integration produces agreement on the approach to be taken, the group must determine the operational tactics that will be employed. Again, this is likely to require some degree of doubling back. Finally, the process will repeat once more to determine the methods of evaluation that will be used to assess progress.

In each iteration, the participative processes of *sharing* through dialogue, *disintegrating* and *revaluating* ideas and proposals through deliberation, and *synthesizing* toward consensus agreements are followed to produce the best and most lasting results. By combining integrative dialogue and deliberation in each decision made, participants come to agreement in all considerations contributing to collective action. Due to the organic change in perspective that comes from open dialogue and deliberation, both common ground and new ideas are identified. Therefore integration coproduces innovative methods that can be at once more effective, efficient, ethical, and equitable.

While this may sound like an unwieldy or seemingly endless process, this is not the case for numerous organizations (Knuchel 2017; Robertson 2015). In short, the larger investment of time and human resources in the integrative process is rewarded by better outcomes, in both practical and ethical terms. Furthermore, as people become more familiar with and skilled in the process of integration, the time investment diminishes. The lessons learned by organizations using these methods contribute to increasingly detailed guidance for practice, making initiation even easier today than it was in the past.

For example, in sociocracy, dialogue and deliberation techniques are used in quick iterative rounds until consensus is achieved, which is properly understood in this approach as consent without objection rather than unanimous agreement (Endenburg 1998). As decisions are put into action, evaluation is used to revisit the work plan for iterative change and improvement on an ongoing basis. This evaluation may include feedback from other circles within the organization and beyond. Similarly, in Holocracy, actionable decisions are made within each organizational circle through consensus-oriented processes (Robertson 2015). An "integrative decision making process" (Robertson 2014, n.p.) is used that employs facilitated dialogue and deliberation methods. While the method is tailored to each type of meeting (governance versus operational), the process follows a common structure that is completed in rounds. In each round, every participant has the option to provide input or choose to pass during a series of steps: (1) check in to clear distractions; (2) handle administrative or logistical matters; (3) build the agenda; (4) complete integrative decision making for one agenda item at a time; and (5) offer closing reflections. The decision-making step follows a sub-process: (1) present a challenge or opportunity and a proposed response; (2) ask clarifying questions that are answered by the proposer, (3) offer reaction statements, (4) make objection statements and notation, (5) offer integration of amendments to resolve the objection, and (6) offer consent or repeat the objection round until integration is achieved.

In sum, participative coordination is an integrative process of unifying functions that is both self-organizing and enabled by facilitative structures, processes, and functions. The integrative process anticipates difference and embraces constructive conflict through: (1) sharing of perspectives, opinions, and positions; (2) collaborative discovery of facts and values; (3) revaluation of desires and methods through dialogue and integrative deliberation; (4) consensus-oriented decision making; and (5) coordinated action. Once engaged in action, ongoing dialogue and deliberation enables both process and outcomes evaluation for continuous improvement. These participatory practices foster a sense of collective responsibility and experientially founded commitment to functional coordination. It is through these interactive relationships that action is coordinated within groups (Follett 2013f).

Facilitative Coordination

To a large degree, Facilitative Coordination is a function for everyone in all groups, because everyone holds some level of responsibility for coordination.

> The creative act of building a consensus can be defined as the *primary act of citizenship* for each individual, wherever he or she is *now* – in schools, families, corporations, public agencies – or wherever affected by the decisions of one or more of them.
>
> (Thayer 1981, 38)

As applied to governance, the withering away of administrative hierarchy dissolves existing social roles of "politician," "administrator," "citizen," as well as organizational roles of "manager," and "worker," integrating all roles in a form of stewardship (Hall 1990; Kass 1990). In other words, administrators are "facilitators, educators, and co-participants, rather than deference-demanding experts or independently responsible decision makers" (Adams et al. 1990, 235–236). For these shared responsibilities to be effective, the skills of facilitation as well as participation in group process must be learned. Individuals in all walks of life will need to invest energy into "training which will give them the ability to act with others" (Addams 1964, 138). "Governance is about how we work – the pattern of how we organize" (Robertson 2015, 26) – if we want to improve the former, we must address the latter.

A group of scholars at the third Minnowbrook retreat in 2008 asked, "Is it possible to evolve fully from twentieth-century management techniques to relationally based, socially embedded, sector diminished (if not sectorless) relations?" (Bryer 2010, 279). Facilitative Coordination suggests the answer is affirmative. Regardless of sector, administration is radically democratic in nature, transforming and redefining all associated functions and concepts. Organizational structure is produced through ***responsive networks*** that are self-organizing and agile. Authority is driven by the evolving needs of the situation to focus efforts on the group purpose while drawing most effectively from the capacity of the group. Emergent leaders work to evoke the best from every group member and enable their activities. The management function becomes one of facilitation of the integrative processes involved in coordinating operations.

This approach to administration was exemplified in the settlement house movement which offered a relational and pragmatic alternative to thinking about public life, democracy, and the place of administration within it (Stivers 2000a). This method sought to improve living conditions and humanize processes to make government more accessible, caring, and connected to the people living in specific neighborhoods. The persona of social workers was one of autonomous neighbor – a person with discretionary judgment guided by caring and participatory relationships with fellow citizens.

The call for leadership based on the understanding that human motivation and development are generated by our relationships also reflects this approach (Uhl-Bien and Ospina 2012). Such relational leadership "requires a way of engaging with the world in which the leader holds herself/himself as always in relation with, and therefore morally accountable to others" (Cunliffe 2011, 1462). Building on more traditional human relations approaches to organizational behavior, the relational approach sees leadership as "a social influence process through which emergent coordination (e.g., evolving social order) and change (e.g., new approaches, values, attitudes, behaviors, ideologies) are constructed and produced" (Uhl-Bien 2006, 654). These concepts have also been attributed to women's approaches and experiences of leadership (Regan and Brooks 1995) as well as in servant leadership wherein "the servant-leader shares power, puts the needs of others first and helps people develop and perform as highly as possible" (Center for Servant Leadership 2016). More specifically, servant leaders employ listening, empathy, intuitive and imaginative awareness, conceptual insight, foresight, situational creativity, persistent but gentle persuasion, stewardship, developmental growth, and community building (Greenleaf 2002).

Facilitative leadership is thus an approach that seeks to bring out the best in others. Cufaude (2005) summarizes this approach in six themes. Facilitative leaders help groups build shared understandings, synthesize ideas, reflect, and learn together. They help the group determine its direction by asking and engaging its members – what some would call leading alongside or from behind (Bentley 1995). Facilitative leaders focus on both process (how work is being done) and product (what is being done). They enable difficult conversations and issues to surface for respectful, creative, and constructive resolution. They support learning and development both within individuals and the group to foster the highest levels of capacity and independence. Finally, facilitative leaders operate with restraint and minimize directive action. Perhaps most importantly, each of these tactics must be engaged with authenticity – with genuine care and a deep commitment to and faith in those following.

Considering these characteristics, it is not surprising that Block (1993) uses the term stewardship as an alternative to leadership – choosing service over self-interest. In this approach, leaders foster stewardship among all group members to enable deep responsibility and accountability among all. This means neither trying to take care of them like a benevolent parent, nor trying to control or direct them from a position of authority. Instead, by sharing power and engaging team members in decision making, administrative stewardship fosters a deep sense of care for both the organization's purpose and the people working together toward that shared aim.

While many techniques of Facilitative Coordination enjoy popularity in the management literature (i.e., humanistic, total quality, agile, lean, etc.), when applied within an existing hierarchically or competitively structured milieu, they prove to be ineffective because the relational dynamics are mismatched. However, this administrative approach is being implemented successfully by many for-profit and nonprofit organizations that have adopted Holacracy, sociocracy, or dynamic governance (Bockelbrink 2016; Holacracy One 2016; Knuchel 2017; Structure and Process 2016). These organizations combine the structure of ***responsive networks*** with the processes of ***integrative collaboration***, guided by the function of Facilitative Coordination to foster a holistic application of Integrative Governance.

Integrative pathways

An Integrative synthesis must generate pathways that are easily traversed by those holding other positions. In the case of administrative theory, Facilitative Coordination must provide concepts that sufficiently meet fundamental principles from other administrative theories, or at least create a dialogical basis for shared understandings. As illustrated in Figure 12.2, we imagine the shared characteristics shown in Table 12.2 as pathways into a dynamic synthesis that is always open to contestation and change.

Going back to our discussion of dialectical synthesis in the chapter's introduction we know that Facilitative Coordination must synthesize *hierarchical* and *matrix organization*. ***Responsive networks*** have the flexibility sought by matrix-style organizations, along with a distinct structure of authority held in the integrative process itself. This administrative structure eliminates the question of *weak* and *strong* levels of administrative discretion by granting a high degree of authority and autonomy to all organizational members, while demanding proportionate amounts of responsibility and accountability. Taken together, these concepts address the primary concerns of each distinct approach to administration, as shown in Table 12.2.

Orthodox Administration is concerned with ensuring accountability so that governance remains under the control of policy makers. ***Responsive networks*** include both governance and operations functions. ***Integrative collaboration*** ensures the governance team is composed of organizational members chosen by the membership of each functional domain,

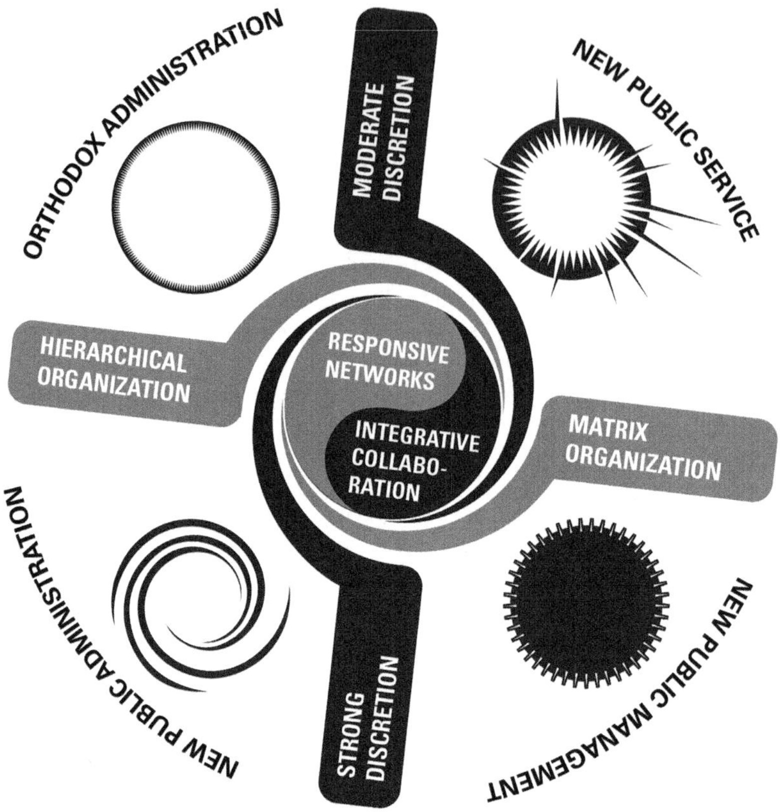

Figure 12.2 Integrative pathways for Facilitative Coordination

while leaders in each functional team are, in turn, appointed by the governance team. All organizational members and teams must maintain sufficient transparency to maintain accountability for their responsibilities. New Public Service seeks to empower all governance actors in the policy making and implementation process. ***Responsive networks*** include all governance actors and ***integrative collaboration*** ensures that all organizational members are engaged in policy making, implementation, and evaluation – directly within functional domains and indirectly through both delegates to the governance function and feedback to transparency mechanisms. New Public Administration seeks to ensure equitable and ethical processes and outcomes through a large amount of administrative discretion. The non-hierarchical structure of ***responsive networks*** distributes full authority according to functional domains, while ***integrative collaboration*** authorizes emergent leaders and ***emergent principles*** as the situation demands. New Public Management seeks to ensure efficient and effective methods and outcomes through a large amount of administrative discretion. Facilitative Coordination achieves these outcomes through ***responsive networks*** and ***integrative collaboration***, fostering emergent leadership that evokes and enables creativity and excellence in others to produce the efficiencies and effectiveness sought through privatization and contracting out.

Table 12.2 Integrating administrative concerns

Ideal-Type	*Characteristics*	*Primary Concerns*	*Synthesis Solution*
Orthodox Administration	*hierarchical organization, moderate discretion*	Accountability to policy makers	***Responsive networks*** include both governance and operations functions; ***Integrative collaboration*** ensures participative leadership and transparency
New Public Service	*matrix organization, moderate discretion*	Responsiveness among governance actors	***Responsive networks*** include all governance actors; ***Integrative collaboration*** ensures all organizational members are engaged in policy making, implementation, and evaluation
New Public Administration	*hierarchical organization, strong discretion*	Responsibility for equity and ethics	***Responsive networks*** distribute full authority according to functional domains; ***Integrative collaboration*** authorizes emergent leaders and ***emergent principles*** as the situation demands.
New Public Management	*matrix organization, strong discretion*	Responsibility for efficiency and effectiveness	***Responsive networks*** and ***integrative collaboration*** support emergent leadership that evokes and enables creativity and excellence in others

Notes

1 We acknowledge a change in terminology from previous versions of the Governance Typology.
2 Holacracy is appropriated from sociocracy with registered trademarks and marketed as a consulting product with required certifications and licensure for anyone who wants to teach others the practice. On the other hand, sociocracy training and consulting is offered by Sociocracy for All volunteers on a sliding scale basis or through the Sociocracy Consulting Group.
3 The agile movement started in the software industry with the signing of the *Manifesto for Agile Development* (Breck et al. 2001). It outlined four core values stressing relationships and collaboration between software designers and customers, further elaborated in 12 principles for agile practice that reflect principles of Coopetition.
4 Holacracy draws its name from Arthur Koestler's 1967 book *The Ghost in the Machine* in which he describes a *holon* as an autonomous whole that is part of a series of nested holons, all of which are interconnected in *holarchy* (Robertson 2015, 38).

Part III

Illustration and affirmation of Integrative Governance

To fully understand the structural arrangements, dispositions, and processes necessary to achieve collaborative advantage requires extending the realm of empirical enquiry to study networks that are actually operating in that fashion. Therefore, in Part III, we begin establishing the fact that collaborative governance networks using an Integrative Governance approach, either in part or completely, do in fact exist.

Imagining the ideal-type as a system, Chapter 13 explores some of the new social movements, considering what might drive them to exercise Integrative Governance. We provide more in-depth analysis of a global food movement that reflects the characteristics of Integrative Governance, from ontology to administration. These examples demonstrate that this approach is not utopian, but rather a living, prefigurative practice that is growing in this historical moment of transition and transformational change.

Chapter 14 ends the book with an affirmation of Integrative Governance, arguing that in response to the crises noted in Part I, "change must be both fundamental and rapid because of the speed with which phenomena such as climate change are closing the window of opportunity" (Cullinan 2014, 74). We reiterate the characteristics of Integrative Governance and explore the integrative pathways that are possible in conversation with those holding other positions in our Governance Typology. From this foundation of potential translation and integration, we make a transdisciplinary call to scholars to embrace, affirm, and profess Integrative Governance within social, political, and economic institutions as they interact globally. We invite scholars to engage in prefigurative praxis through theoretically informed action research and to participate in the difficult work of paradigmatic change.

13 Finding the will to integrate

> *We are men and women of the earth, we are those who produce food for the world. We have the right to continue being peasants and family farmers, and to shoulder the responsibility of continuing to feed our peoples. We care for seeds, which are life, and for us the act of producing food is an act of love. Humanity depends on us, and we refuse to disappear.*
>
> – (*La Vía Campesina 2008*)

As demonstrated by any serious consideration of the interlocking crises of sustainability described in Chapter 1, factors once considered isolated from, or externalities to, specific market functions are now understood as impacting social, economic, and environmental systems through synergistic declines, cascading effects, and feedback loops within and across dimensions (Renner 2015). We are increasingly aware that implications are never isolated. The ecological movement has had a particularly strong influence on the convergence of contemporary social movements due to the inescapably global nature of environmental impacts and their relationship to capitalism and militarism (Gordon 2007). As climate change accelerates, the social and economic implications become impossible to ignore.

Governance networks have not mitigated – let alone reversed – the trajectories of these crises. In recent decades, responses have vacillated between authoritarian regulation of social issues and neoliberal deregulation of economic and environmental issues, meanwhile creating a democratic deficit in the global market economy (Keohane and Nye 2003). As more people are brought into an ever-widening communications and economic community, the driving market ethic of self-interest is fracturing all other forms of community (Beck and Beck-Gernsheim 2001; Smadja 2000).

The current civil war in Syria and resultant refugee crisis is just one example of the interlocking implications. Explanations often point to the public protests inspired by the spreading Arab Spring in 2011, and the resultant violent crackdown by the Assad regime (Aljazeera 2017; BBC News 2016) – a social crisis in response to state oppression. However, the roots of this social crisis are also environmental and economic. In the 1970s, in response to economic crisis, Syria adopted agricultural advances that required extensive drilling of wells, leading to a depletion of groundwater reserves (Kelley et al. 2015; Wendle 2016, Mar.). In 2006, the region faced the worst three-year drought on record (Kelley et al. 2015), creating extreme food insecurity and economic collapse (Wendle 2016, Mar.). Roughly 1.5 million people migrated from rural farming regions to urban areas resulting in "illegal settlements, overcrowding, poor infrastructure, unemployment, and crime" (Kelley et al. 2015) – the government ignored these issues, exacerbating the hardships faced by the rural refugees. In response to these conditions, initially peaceful protests in Syria were met with deadly crackdowns by the Assad regime (Aljazeera 2017; BBC News 2017). Today, over 5 million people have fled Syria and another 6.3 million remain displaced within the country (High Commissioner for Refugees 2017b). Such phenomena are not isolated; globally, there are roughly 65.6 million displaced people, 22.5 million refugees, and 10 million stateless individuals (High Commissioner for Refugees 2017a).

Overwhelming challenges like these have the potential to paralyze public action. In response to such wicked problems, "one may even sometimes have a sense of being confronted by difficulties beyond the possibility of resolution by human intelligence and co-operative endeavor" (Bohm 2004, 70). Yet, there is reason for hope – "we have the technology, know-how and financial means to end extreme poverty in all of its forms should we collectively choose to make it happen" (Raworth 2017, 233). However, we must act quickly before ecological catastrophe, total economic collapse, or world war closes the window of opportunity.

Recognizing interconnections among wicked problems has brought increased awareness of our global interdependence as humans living within mutually influencing economies and ecosystems. Increasingly, there is a felt sense of interdependence, even while political leaders attempt to fan the flames of populist nationalism to build their bases of support. Thus, "we witness both a contraction and an expansion of what it means to be a citizen" (Donati 2016, 41) – engendering a new sense of solidarity, even within cultures that have embraced atomistic individualism or statist collectivism for generations. An open-ended "we" perspective is reflected in the concept of planetary jurisprudence, an approach that "seeks to guide humans to pursue their own well-being by contributing to the health, beauty, and integrity of the Earth communities within which they live" (Cullinan 2014, 73). This awakening provides "the impetus or pressure to improve governance" to make "communities sustainable places" (Prugh and Renner 2014, 249).

We insist that Integrative Governance, as a system of genuinely collaborative global networks grounded in local co-creation, is our best option for meeting the challenges we face. The assumptions of Relational Becoming drive home the reality that our interdependence *has always been the case*. This ontological lens allows us to understand these dynamic interconnections and gives the philosophical grounding for institutions and practices that respond to issues of sustainability and foster care for the world. These assertions require going "far beyond the realm of technological adaptations" (Renner 2015, 17) and "risk upsetting the very foundations of how we see the world" (Kaufman 2003, 12). Despite this challenge, we argue the stakes are so high that we have arrived at a moment when deep, global, transformational change is essential.

However, we also agree that in order to persuade people to adopt novel ideas and approaches, proponents of paradigm change must "explore its possibilities, and show what it would be like to belong to the community guided by it" (Kuhn 1996, 159). As noted in Part I, collaborative governance networks display some characteristics of Integrative Governance; however, these efforts are limited in number and insufficiently address power dynamics. Therefore, they do not meet the tenets of inclusive and impactful participation. We suggest that myriad contemporary social movements provide more robust examples of Integrative Governance in action. A study of 87 countries found 59 such movements in 2006 and 112 during the first half of 2013. In that timeframe, there were 488 protests on economic justice and austerity policies, 376 protests on the failure of political representation, 311 protests on environmental justice, and 311 protests on human rights (Renner and Prugh 2014). These kinds of direct actions appear to be increasing. Clearly, there is something to be learned from this growing phenomenon. As Dean (2017) suggests in regard to

Occupy London, "examining its operating procedures can illuminate the practices typical of this mode of participation" (9).

The need for affirmation

While new social movements hold promise for learning about the philosophical assumptions and practices of Integrative Governance, we do not adopt them wholesale. We have explored elsewhere how resistance and reform movements typically shift governance approaches back and forth along a continuum that never escapes the underlying philosophical assumptions that feed social, economic, and environmental crises (Stout and Love 2016). Simply put, political economies based on a tension between freedom (individualism) and control (collectivism) "*are not sustainable as long-term systems*" (Donati 2014, 45). Yet, as discussed in Part I, these hierarchical and pluralistic assumptions continue to shape most understandings of reality and how we relate to one another, including most collaborative governance networks.

Resistance efforts often seek solidarity with like-minded individuals who speak out against prevailing social, economic, environmental, and political conditions. This fuels an agonistic (or antagonistic) pluralism wherein groups ("us") avoid or attack those who adhere to different political positions or worldviews ("them"). As a result, reform attempts are rife with unproductive conflict – these conflicts become amplified rather than seeking out commonalities across our differences in ways that can lead to integration and meaningful system change. Thus, these efforts can often "subtly reinforce the very systems against which we struggle" (Keating 2013, 3).

It is important to note, however, that oppositional forms of critique have not been without benefit. They have generated social theory (i.e., Marxism, structuralism, post-structuralism, postmodernism, etc.) that provides critical perspectives for identifying and deconstructing power dynamics and hegemonic norms inherent in sociopolitical institutions – *including within social movements themselves.* However, while these critiques have spurred social action in the form of refusal, resistance, and even revolution, they have also largely failed to resolve underlying issues. For instance, Marxism uncovered the detrimental impacts of classism and yet Leninist socialist revolutions often installed an elite Vanguard of "correct line" politics to lead the way (Dixon 2014, 60), thereby maintaining hierarchical power. In other words, the oppressed simply adopted the methods of the oppressor as they claimed the seat of power. Likewise, while postmodern philosophy opens up and makes visible spaces for contemporary social movements to articulate "a more radical critique of centralized power, industrial civilization, white supremacy, patriarchy, heteronormative/ity and multiple other oppressions" (Adams 2011, 124–125), the dark side of postmodernism fragments community with extreme individualism (Boje 2006).

Disintegration is indeed a critical component of integration; yet, ending with deconstruction leaves us with nothing to build upon. For this reason, Bookchin (2015b) dismisses reform efforts rooted in protest: "A politics of mere protest, lacking programmatic content, a proposed alternative, and a movement to give people direction and continuity" is insufficient for systemic change (2895). Those involved in community action have made similar observations: "But about the process of construction? How much have we advanced on that front?" (Pedro Magaña Guerrero, former national peasant leader, UNORCA, quoted in Desmarais 2007, 135). We must follow with affirmative revaluation and synthesis – "a politics of social innovation" (Bookchin 2015a, 3235).

Integrative Governance provides the theory and method to visualize new possibilities for the political economy, understand the philosophical commitments necessary to achieve those possibilities, and act in ways that move us toward those ends. From a relational process perspective, we can re-conceptualize global collaborative governance networks as "the beginning of a new vision for humanity" (Carlsson and Ramphal 1995, 6) – one that points to "the potential of human creativity and co-operation" (27). Such affirmation provides for more effective social action (Fraser and Nicholson 1988). These approaches "are not just efforts at reforming democracy, they are democracy in action" (Barber 2013, 224). The emerging "aim is not . . . to liberate some 'essential self' by throwing off the burden of government and the State, but to develop the self in creative and voluntary relations with others" (Marshall 1993, 642–643). This transforms society while transforming participants themselves. Such attempts to "restructure the entire society" (Bookchin 1994a, 4) through "*displacement* and *replacement*" (Day 2011, 101) of the political and economic system require multilevel structural transformation – a global movement of multiple broad-based social movements (Cox 1995).

Systemic change, however, cannot be built from one universal vision for political economy; to effectively forge a new political economy on a global scale, it must build from the micro to the macro. As opposed to claiming power over others, the "will to power" (Nietzsche 1968) is more accurately understood as "activities of creative relation and becoming" (Connolly 2013, 165). Many contemporary social movements employ micro-political action across groups, borders, and societal spheres to transform macro-political systems globally. These micro-politics bring situation-responsive integrative practices into the actual functions of governance throughout society – in communities, governments, and markets. This approach is perhaps best described as *prefigurative politics*: "the embodiment, within the ongoing political practice of a movement, of those forms of social relations, decision-making, culture, and human experience that are the ultimate goal" (Boggs 1977, 100). In simple terms, a prefigurative politics is one wherein the methods used to engage reflect and manifest the vision sought (Dixon 2014). Rather than mimicking the dominating structure of existing political institutions (e.g., centralized authority, representative democracy, etc.), prefigurative social movements utilize counterhegemonic resistance alongside the affirmative co-creation of new institutions rooted in "new values" (Breines 1989, 55). This approach heeds Emma Goldman's (2012) caution, "the *means* used to *prepare* the future becomes its *cornerstone*" (403) and Audre Lorde's (2007) reminder that the master's tools cannot dismantle the master's house.

Prefigurative politics recognizes that neither the system being critiqued nor the goals toward which we strive are static; as the situation evolves, integrative processes will yield shifting ideals. Many draw inspiration from the Zapatista Liberation movement's slogan, "*preguntando caminamos*" (walking we ask questions) (Dixon 2014, 20) – a reminder that "even deep structural change such as revolution is not an act but a process" (Sitrin and Azzellini 2012, 116) which must avoid reification of values or structures (Day 2011). Political and economic activists alike argue that "we make the road by walking" (Horton and Paulo 1990) and "we build the road as we travel" (Morrison 1991). This open-ended and emergent approach is critical to keeping Radical Democracy central and to remain flexible and responsive to situational context.

As Bookchin (2015b) argues, "Such a revolutionary movement needs a distinctive body of tactics designed to expand the scope of any issue" (3040). Thus, while prefigurative politics entails a critical distrust of hierarchy and centralization, movement-building requires organization of some kind (Dixon 2014). In short, "Activists need to build flexible and democratic leadership structures" (Tugal 2014, 3) that are "enduring, structured, and broadly programmatic" (Bookchin 2015b, 3050). We suggest Integrative Governance provides a suitable approach.

While prefigurative politics is utopian, it is not naïve. Those who engage in its practices are deeply aware of existing systems of privilege and oppression, power imbalances in the political economy, and the need for ongoing resistance ***alongside*** affirmation of an alternative understanding of reality, humanity, and governance – to be "in the world but not of it" (Dixon 2014, 125). Community members, practitioners, activists, and theorists must put forward affirmative visions of how to create institutions and mechanisms of governance while simultaneously refusing and reforming the dominant institutions that continue to hold political and economic power. It is a vision of an "enacted utopia" in which "*we already are free while fighting for freedom*" (Žižek 2002, 559).

Nascent practices of Integrative Governance

Ken Wilber (2011, loc. 1611) suggests,

> We are awaiting the new global founding Fathers and Mothers who will frame an integral system of governance that will call us to our more encompassing future, that will act as a gentle pacer of transformation for the entire spiral of human development.

Dixon (2014) argues that social movements are actively answering this call "with powerful visions and practical possibilities for action" (2) for "a rich democratic vision" (3). We concur; there are a number of social movements around the world advancing affirmative visions, living those ideals, and using communications technology to coordinate efforts and integrate purposes and actions. Studies of governance failures point to the remedies of public participation (Geall and Hilton 2014) and grassroots organizing (Bartosiewicz and Miley 2014; Tugal 2014).

Many grassroots social movements eschew hierarchy and redefine relationships of leadership and power (Attrache 2014; Dixon 2014; Sitrin 2005). These movements are often characterized as "anti-globalization" (Evren 2011, 1), or the "alternative globalization" movement (Gordon 2007, 30). While there is no universally accepted label, this umbrella includes myriad movements associated with economic and social justice, ecology and food sovereignty, land and water rights, feminism, indigenous rights, anti-capitalism, anti-corporate globalization, anti-neoliberalism, anti-war, and pro-grassroots movements. These movements broadly share three characteristics: (1) an objection to domination in all forms; (2) an ethos of prefigurative politics in direct action; and (3) an open-ended orientation to an evolving present (Gordon 2007, 30). This has been described as "another politics" (Dixon 2014) – one aligned with an understanding of postmodern anarchism (Call 2002) drawn from Nietzsche, Foucault, and Deleuze, and classical as well as post-anarchism (Evren 2011; Rousselle and Evren 2011). Contemporary social movements, and their direct actions, are also grounded in social anarchism's principles of mutual aid, voluntary association, and egalitarian or consensus-based decision making (Graeber and Grubacic 2004; Jeppesen 2011).

Seeking to understand the context that gives rise to these movements, Tejerina et al. (2013) identify two driving motivations: demands for meaningful participatory democracy; and calls to rectify increasing wealth gaps. We add two additional provocations: resistance to persistent oppression and state violence based on race, ethnicity, religion, sexual orientation, gender identity, or similar characteristics; and rejection of policies and practices that further climate change and environmental degradation. While we consider the manner in which these movements instantiate characteristics of Integrative Governance elsewhere (Love and Stout 2018), here, we focus on the food sovereignty movement in particular.

Metaphorically, food production is a strong illustration of relational process. As Bookchin (2015d, loc. 1329) notes, gardening enables food to become

> more than a form of material nutrient. The soil one tills, the living things one cultivates and consumes, the compost one prepares all unite in an ecological continuum to feed the spirit as well as the body, sharpening one's sensitivity to the nonhuman and human world around us.

Furthermore, it is a favored metaphor for understanding our relational condition and its corollary responsibilities. As Dewey (1999) artfully describes, "to gain an integrated individuality, each of us needs to cultivate his own garden. But there is no fence about this garden: it is no sharply marked-off enclosure. . . . Our garden is the world" (83). Similarly, Liu and Hanauer (2011) explain that not only are we gardeners, we are also "organisms within the greater garden, each affecting the next. We form each other. We are bound up in each other's choices. We are not separate" (53).

More practically, agricultural production affects everyone on the planet, including not only our food but also a wide variety of the material resources upon which we rely. As agroecologist Eric Holt-Giménez says, "Successful social movements are formed by integrating activism with livelihoods. These integrated movements create the sustained social pressure that produces political will – the key to changing the financial, governmental and market structures that presently work against sustainability" (Food First 2016). Studying the growing social movements within the global food system allows us to consider efforts that are utilizing Integrative Governance to build a new political economy.

Furthermore, we believe this sector of the political economy is best able to illustrate the impact of governance approaches on social, economic, and environmental considerations because it engages all three directly and thus illustrates their interdependence. It is also frequently the sector where impacts are first noticed: "The first indication of the string of global crises we have seen in the last few years (food, fuel, finance, and climate) was seen in the food system" (Nicholson 2011, loc. 500). Today, "behind the façade of economic progress, industrial models for agricultural development are clearly in social and environmental crisis" (Holt-Giménez 2006, 179). This "current global food crisis" (Holt-Giménez 2009, 142) is the combined product of industrialization of agriculture, neoliberal trade policies of the WTO, and economic restructuring and land reform demanded by the World Bank and IMF.

In brief, to address the social crises of economic disparity and global hunger, global governance networks fostered the Green Revolution – the vast industrialization of agriculture based on genetically modified monocultures, nitrogen fertilizers, biocides, water irrigation (such as damming up rivers and depleting groundwater aquifers), and mass production methods applied to both plant and animal agriculture. These technologies were promised to increase food production; however, these approaches have led to deforestation, polluted waterways (Halden and Schwab 2008; Mallin and Cahoon 2003; Tilman et al. 2002), soil nutrient depletion (Gardner 2015; Halden and Schwab 2008), and a scarcity of both fresh water and arable land (Gardner 2015; Hawken, Lovins, and Lovins 1999; Shiva 2015).

Further, agricultural and industrial practices wreak havoc on biodiversity at local, regional, and global levels (Desmarais 2007; Mies and Shiva 2014). Climate change has further exacerbated these problems, causing significant sustained droughts that have led to mass migrations to cities, civil wars, and political refugees.

In sum, the global food crisis is directly implicated in and affected by economic, environmental, and social crises. Thus, food sovereignty movements provide both a meaningful place to begin to address these crises and a viable illustration of a globalized network of local movements that engage in practices of refusal and reform, as well as affirmation of an alternative system. As argued by Subcomandante Marcos, what the indigenous peasant farmers in Chiapas have learned

> about non-hierarchical decision-making, decentralized organizing and deep democracy holds answers for the non-indigenous world as well – if only it were willing to listen . . . these free spaces, born of reclaimed land, communal agriculture, resistance to privatization, will eventually create counter-powers to the state simply by existing as alternatives.
>
> (Klein 2004, 21)

The food sovereignty or farmer-to-farmer movement is well-established and arguably the most advanced example of Integrative Governance through collaborative governance networks:

> A dynamic global food movement has risen up to confront the corporate assault on our food. Around the world, local food justice activists have taken back pieces of their food systems through local gardening, organic farming, community-supported agriculture, farmers markets, and locally owned processing and retail operations. Food sovereignty advocates have organized for land reform, the end of destructive global-trade agreements, and support for family farmers, women, and peasants.
>
> (Holt-Giménez 2011b, loc. 411)

La Vía Campesina (LVC) is "an international federation for smallholder-peasant-fisher-pastoralist organizations" (Holt-Giménez 2011a, 318). This network reaches across diverse global regions, even though they confront differing agricultural challenges and nation-state contexts. The network includes about 164 organizations in 73 countries in Africa, Asia, Europe, and America, representing an estimated 200 million peasant farmers. However, they also engage many other non-member farmer groups through regional and international assemblies. Furthermore, previous regional network incarnations have disbanded or morphed into others, such as the Movimiento Campesino a Campesino (MCAC) in Central America becoming the Farmer-to-Farmer Agroecological Movement (MACAC) in Cuba (Sosa et al. 2013).

Moving outward in scale to networks that engage in policy advocacy, LVC is also one of the 11 global organizations constructing the International Planning Committee for Food Sovereignty (IPC), an autonomous and self-organized global platform of 800 organizations and 300 million small-scale food producers, rural workers, and grassroots/community-based social movements (Juarez et al. 2015). Moving inward in scale, this complex, interlocking and nesting configuration is replicated within and among its network members due to the complex nature of overlapping purposes shared with other social movements at local, national, regional, and international levels.

Most important to our inquiry, the shared purposes of this network mirror the utilitarian and democratic aims of collaborative governance networks: solving the wicked problem of environmental sustainability while pursuing social and economic justice (Juarez et al. 2015). Over the past 20 years, LVC has become one of the most important social movements in the world by calling into question the entire system of economic production and reproduction as viewed through the lens of rural farmers. LVC has raised awareness of the unsustainable design and implementation of agricultural technology (GMOs, direct seeding, etc.) and the type of food it produces, the undermining of local markets and farmer livelihoods by free trade, and the oppression of peasant and indigenous people by the states in which they reside. They have shown the world how rural families produce the low-wage workers demanded by industry while transnational corporations take their land in government-supported land grabs. They tap into the local knowledge of peasant farmers and peer-to-peer sharing across countries and continents through regional and global networks (Juarez et al. 2015, 22). Together, these reform and affirmation efforts have not only strengthened re-indigenization efforts and supported peasant farmers locally, they have succeeded in potent resistance against the global political economy that has threatened their existence.

LVC participants have consistently shared a common methodology for transforming agricultural production. Rather than using the expert-led, top-down scientific dissemination approaches of agricultural extension, outreach agents learn from the local indigenous people, engage in experimentation *together* to develop sustainable agricultural methods, and then work together to develop and share knowledge with other farmers. While NGO and government Extension agents provide the necessary logistical resources, the farmers themselves learn with and from one another. Using simple, inexpensive agroecology principles and practices, smallholder recovery efforts often result in 100–200 percent yield increases or more, enabling family farmers to move from subsistence into market trade (Holt-Giménez 2006). The social result is a thick, people-centered network of farmers, agronomists, and NGOs.

In the course of pursuing this utilitarian purpose, democratic aims are also advanced – as hunger is overcome and economic agency is built, political agency follows. Like Paulo Freire's popular education work in South America in the 1960s and 1970s, these agricultural learning communities easily accommodate critical pedagogy, which enables people to question their historical and social situation and become active subjects in the creation of a democratic society. Within a short period of time, these interconnecting groups began to advance land and territory rights, agrarian reform, sustainable rural agriculture, biodiversity and protection of genetic resources, food sovereignty, gender parity, and the human rights of young people, migrant workers, and rural folk forced to relocate to urban areas. As an autonomous, radically pluralist and multicultural movement, it continues to evolve through nationally, regionally, and locally responsive strategies. However, the farmer-to-farmer methodology and core aims of social, economic, and environmental justice and sustainability remain constant.

Clearly, LVC and its many interlocking networks are deeply engaged in governance. While they employ the methods of the dominant system at the intersections – the counter-hegemonic resistance and refusal commonly associated with social movements along with pluralistic policy advocacy in traditional governance networks – they also engage in affirmational practices within the networks themselves in efforts to transform or displace the dominant system. In fact, this counterhegemonic agenda has generated sufficient strength to become the target of push back. LVC's confrontations with the World Bank and the IMF have resulted in the withdrawal of foundation and government support from member organizations, as well as the creation of an NGO called the International Land Coalition, which frames discourse about the land and food sovereignty from a market perspective (Juarez et al. 2015). Therefore, we believe it is the type of case most informative for learning about collaborative governance networks and Integrative Governance within the current milieu.

While we cannot analyze in detail the example of La Vía Campesina (LVC), its predecessors, and its affiliated movements, even using secondary sources of official organizational documents and existing ethnographies and case studies, we find ample illustration of every element of Integrative Governance, from Relational Becoming to Facilitative Coordination. *The dual utilitarian and democratic purposes of farmer-to-farmer networks are nicely illustrated in the* stick figure human diagram MCAC uses to explain its mission: The movement works with two hands, one for production of food and one for protection of the environment. It walks on the two legs of innovation and solidarity. In its heart, "it believes in love of nature, family, and community, and it 'sees' with a vision of campesino-led, sustainable agricultural development" (Holt-Giménez 2006, 104). In this simple teaching tool, MCAC demonstrates many of the conceptual elements of Integrative Governance.

The *shared love of nature and solidarity* and respect for each person's capacity for *innovation* speaks to a deep understanding of Relational Becoming within interdependent environmental and social systems. In Latin America, the farmer-to-farmer movement is grounded in an indigenous worldview – the Kaqchikel Mayan "cosmovision" of an interconnected universe in which human beings play a conscious role in reflection and development (quoted in Holt-Giménez 2006, 46). As one LVC youth explains, "We cannot address climate change unless we treat nature and humans as one. What happens to her happens to us, and so the exploitation of Mother Earth is the exploitation of us as human beings and vice versa" (La Vía Campesina 2017, 43).

Ensembling individuality is reflected in a *shared love of nature, family, and community* that demonstrates the importance of the person-in-community, which includes an identity that is interlinked with both others and place. "For farmers land is life, therefore, their struggle goes beyond the sense of ownership and is part of a more complex system of life in which the land is fundamental to the construction of rural identity" (Juarez et al. 2015, 30). It is this intertwining identity that generates the political "struggle for 'the land' . . . understood in broad, shared, common terms, and both a means of production and a way of life" (24).

Integral Knowing is evident in a shared *commitment to common sense innovation* and *sustainable agricultural development.* Knowledge is built collaboratively within a community of practice that includes ancestral knowledge, farmers, and Extension technicians. In farmer-to-farmer learning exchanges, knowledge is shared through discussion, teaching demonstrations, exhibitions, experiential practice, and even games, songs, poetry, skits, and folktales (Holt-Giménez 2006; Sosa et al. 2013).

There is a clear *reverence for the entire ecosystem – people, animals, and land* that aligns with the tenets of Co-Creationism. As one Nicaraguan farmer says, "Agroecology is not just a collection of practices. Agroecology is a way of life" (171). Its worldview is described as "a feminine perspective of the world of fertility and social reproduction of humanity in egalitarian and just conditions" (Stédile and Martines de Carvalho 2011, loc. 758), what LVC members describe as a "life project" in resistance to the "death project" pursued by the agro-industrial complex (Juarez et al. 2015, 48).

Those in the farmer-to-farmer movement value mutual respect and mutual aid; their sense of Stewardship is described as a moral obligation to pay it forward in solidarity. One Nicaraguan farmer explains, "I told my son, we have soil for many years here. I will die, and this soil will be yours. He understood the value of the land. . . . I work with two hands: protection and production" (quoted in Holt-Giménez 2006, 116). For the most part, farmer-to-farmer promoters work as volunteers. "Why? Because, personally, I was convinced that our work was an opportunity and that I was learning more new things each day and that sharing this with other campesinos was a tremendous experience. I was enchanted with life!" (quoted in Holt-Giménez 2006, 56).

Radical Democracy is evident in the commitment to ***farmer-led development*** that moves sovereignty to individuals, and LVC's status as an international ***network of organizations*** is a ***self-organizing confederalism***. Furthermore, farmer-to-farmer movements practice prefigurative politics: "to change ourselves, we need to change our world. To change our world, we need to change ourselves. Both are necessary. Both are difficult" (Patel 2007, 309). Farmer-to-farmer networks are governance actors that engage in policy making by bringing peasants into formal decision making processes, and engage in coproduction of sustainability policy outcomes through member adoption of agroecology methods (Juarez et al. 2015).

Farmer-led food production within an ethic of solidarity reflects many characteristics of Coopetition. The "campesinado's culture of mutual aid" (Holt-Giménez 2006, 112) includes sharing of both knowledge and resources in a solidarity economy. One Kaqchikel promoter even describes it as an "ideology of working with other campesinos" (quoted in Holt-Giménez 2006, 53). At a larger scale, The Mons Declaration (1996) seeks to "bring about an agricultural development which is ecologically sustainable, socially just and which allows the producer real access to the wealth which s/he generates day in day out" (71). LVC thus seeks economic transformation by "reconstituting farmers as key actors in the form of production and proposing a more equitable distribution of the income of the land" (Juarez et al. 2015, 23).

As a movement, both formal organizations and informal groups within LVC utilize Facilitative Coordination to one degree or another. One farmer's union technician explains the leadership style:

> Sometimes, being participatory means being sufficiently humble to just stand aside. Just be quiet and let people make their own mistakes and learn. Often, in good faith, we want to run and help. In order to be a proactive movement, people have to feel things as their own and get involved and think and reflect. It is a process.
>
> (quoted in Holt-Giménez 2006, 67)

In terms of functional coordination, the MACAC network in Cuba has three specified functions: promoter, facilitator, and coordinator (Sosa et al. 2013). All enjoy a high level of autonomy in fulfilling their duties, while working collaboratively in the fulfilling the mission of the movement.

Considering these examples, it is clear that not only are food sovereignty movements and farmer-to-farmer networks operating from an Integrative Governance paradigm, the framework itself is useful in studying the characteristics of *collaboration*. The framework is also useful for identifying instances of ***misalignment***. Because the farmer-to-farmer movement is operating within a global political economy that emphasizes hierarchy and competition, and in which experience in effective collaboration is often lacking and self-interest has been a matter of survival, the existence of some misalignments are neither surprising nor fatal to the prospect of Integrative Governance. By viewing these challenges within the provided theoretical framework, the underlying tensions between philosophy and practice can be identified and techniques for addressing them articulated.

Therefore, the ideal-type overcomes the barriers previously identified in the collaborative governance network literature: it is useful in studying more appropriate cases of collaborative governance; the ideal-type is grounded in philosophies associated with collaborative dynamics; and the framework itself is constructed from transdisciplinary sources beyond the narrow sources used in governance network theory. It therefore provides a robust theoretical basis from which to craft instruments of empirical analysis to inform both theory building and practice.

14 Affirming Integrative Governance

The transdisciplinary vision is resolutely open insofar as it goes beyond the field of the exact sciences and demands their dialogue and their reconciliation with the humanities and the social sciences as well as with art, literature, poetry and spiritual experience.

– (Article 5 of the Charter of Transdisciplinarity, Nicolescu 2002, 149)

This book has extended our argument that none of the traditional approaches to governance can achieve global acceptance, nor have they been able to prevent the crises of sustainability we face on social, economic, and environmental fronts. The most recent attempts to establish collaborative governance networks that cross both borders and sectors have failed to prove themselves more effective than traditional nation-state and international efforts – in fact, some of these governance networks fuel the fires of discontent within the world's citizenry by creating democratic deficit rather than gain. Thus, we see an increasing loss of legitimacy in all forms of governance. People the world over demand more direct participation in the matters that affect their lives.

We have argued that collaborative governance networks, while on the right track, are still conceptualizing and enacting collaboration through either hierarchical collectivist or competitive individualist lenses, contributing to both utilitarian and democratic governance failures. In theory building to improve collaborative advantage, scholars are studying poor examples of collaboration through the wrong normative lenses, while largely drawing from an insular disciplinary literature that is philosophically mismatched to collaboration.

In response, we have reconceptualized governance in a transdisciplinary manner and carefully explicated an integrative approach drawing broadly from multiple disciplines and worldviews. We claim that Integrative Governance offers a potentially more effective approach because its philosophy and practices can help transform both social and economic domains of life, while ensuring considerations of environmental impact and justice. Its characteristics can be found in many contemporary movements that transcend jurisdictional borders across these domains. Thus, an integrative approach is a better fit for the pursuit of sustainability in a context of global governance and holds more promise for networks at all scales. Its open, participatory, and dynamic practices may help build global consensus on how to address economic and environmental crises, while also expanding political voice, agency, and equity among the global governed. Its systemic approach is malleable and adaptable enough to accommodate the unique character and needs of each interlocking group, just as human DNA binds us together as a species and yet allows vast diversity in expression. In sum, we argue that Integrative Governance has the potential to produce more fruitful outcomes and global acceptance. While it may not flourish within the confines of currently dominant institutions, it can work very well beyond them, as shown in Chapter 13.

To reiterate, Relational Becoming grounds a public philosophy and ethic different from those of classical conservative liberalism, modern liberalism, communitarianism, and contemporary extensions thereof. It also differs from collectivist socialism and individualist anarchism. The assumption of material interconnectivity and relational individualism transcends the dialectical trap of hierarchy versus competition set up by all forms of collectivism and individualism. Instead, Integrative Governance offers a relational, open, self-organizing, egalitarian process for developing knowledge and reasoning together toward what is right and good. This ethic of mutuality and responsive stewardship provides a logically coherent foundation for collaborative governance practices such as participatory planning and policy making toward social and economic justice, as well as collaborative implementation through coproduction. Therefore, it is logically very similar to what is proposed as the ideal for collaborative governance networks. Both challenge the status quo governance approaches, suggesting a paradigmatic shift.

Because the practices associated with Integrative Governance have been successfully demonstrated in nontraditional spaces, we do not hesitate to make a public declaration of its characteristics and our intentions to promote its potential. Even as we confront disciplinary expectations of scholarly neutrality and warnings against polemic, we dare to affirm Integrative Governance and withhold critique until it is tried and studied in greater depth and with the confident spirit of pragmatic experimentation.

Fostering translational integration

Many may ask, "Why would I accept or adopt Integrative Governance?" This question presents the problem of how to foster the attitudinal shift required to "*will the common will*" (Follett 1998, 49). Rosenau (1999) argues that ontologies and paradigms change in response to either normalization of cumulated anomalies resulting from transformations in the conditions of existence or the introduction of new technologies that enable people to perceive circumstances in a new way – both of which are at play in our current situation. As illustration, he suggests that the contemporary moment is one in of "*fragmegration*" which attempts to hold "globalizing and localizing forces" in productive tension (293). We suggest he is describing the simultaneous movements from what we call Holographic Governance (which seeks unity) and Fragmented Governance (which seeks autonomy) into Integrative Governance (which seeks agency within an integrative group process).

We contend this movement toward Integrative Governance is possible because it is a *synthesis* perspective; furthermore, there is sufficient commonality to enable a movement from *any* of the primary approaches to governance into Integrative Governance. However, we must reiterate that on at least two key characteristics, the four primary approaches to governance fundamentally disagree with one another; they are either collectivist or individualist and either static or dynamic. Each approach generates pathologies, because they are either/or options that disregard opposing concepts. As examples, too much group control in Hierarchical Governance leads to a sense of bondage, while too much independent choice in Atomistic Governance leads to a sense of social isolation.

These either/or dialectics are resolved by the synthesis of both/and, which is a third alternative that resolves paradoxes through dialogue. "The task is to take elements that seem in themselves mutually opposed and mutually exclusive and to transform them into a novel contrast that gains richness and intensity through inclusion of the best of both" (Cobb Jr.

1990, 154). Therefore, the actual work of integration is still required – meanings must be transformed by those who hold them.

As shown in Figure 14.1, bringing driving concerns and values forward creates a dialogical pathway for movement from each of the primary governance approaches into Integrative Governance. Indeed, this is a core feature of Follett's (1924) explanation of the method of integration – we must get underneath fully formulated positions to core desires in order to find common ground for generating a new synthesis position that meets all of those desires.

Translating this process into the language of collaborative governance networks (Keast 2016), Holographic Governance seeks consolidation of efforts (unity), Hierarchical Governance seeks coordination of efforts (order), Atomistic governance seeks cooperation (choice), and Fragmented Governance seeks competition (autonomy). Integrative Governance seeks collaboration through integrative processes that achieve coordination through self-organizing efforts and cooperation through a sense of mutuality.

We have begun this translational, integrative process in Part II through explorations in each chapter that illustrate how integrative concepts can resolve dialectical tensions between other ideal-typical concepts through synthesis. Integrative Governance pursues the desires held by proponents of the other governance approaches, addresses their fears, and resolves the resulting pathologies through transformational assumptions and practices (Stout and Love 2016). In other words, each integrative concept achieves the *aims* of the other conceptions, but through a different *method*.

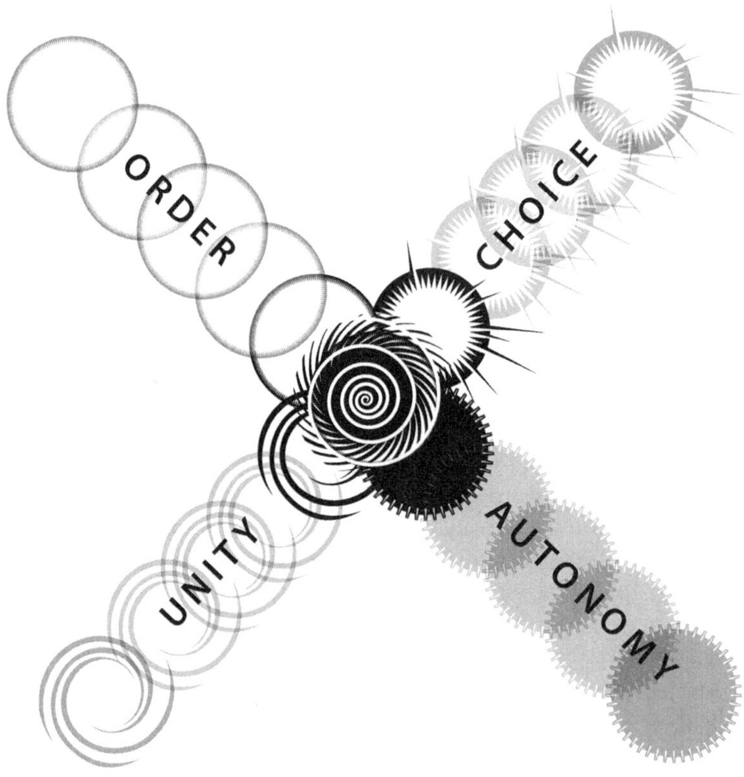

Figure 14.1 Integrative pathways for Integrative Governance

The fundamental concern of Hierarchical Governance is maintenance of *order* to avoid conflict within the group. The approach is fundamentally hierarchical – something or someone must design and provide command and control to order society. This is demonstrated by its static cosmological hierarchy directed by a divine power; clearly defined social roles, status, and identity; universal Truth and Right determined by a higher power as interpreted by elite leaders; and a political system that maintains and regulates all sectors of society.

The fundamental concern of Atomistic Governance is preventing control, ensuring freedom of *choice* in the pursuit of happiness. This is demonstrated by its individualistic and pluralistic ontology; the lack of predetermined social roles and identity; a humanistic trust in the capacity of every human being to learn and know through observation and to individually determine what is Good; and a political economy that enables pluralist competition and majority rule to define the collective Good in all sectors of society.

The fundamental concern of Holographic Governance is maintaining *unity* among all members of society to avoid conflict. This is demonstrated by its sense of collective identity; individuals are one not only with the social group but with the universe and the divinity enfolding it all; the intuitive understanding of what is Right for the betterment of all and the inherent motivation to pursue it; and a political economy guided by equal, interchangeable members of the group.

The fundamental concern of Fragmented Governance is ensuring *autonomy* in resistance to social construction. This is demonstrated by its adamant refusal of all forms of essentialism whether they are of an ontological, psychological, sociological, epistemological, or ethical nature; and the preference for a fiercely individualistic political economy that enables the pursuit of an ever-changing set of personal preferences.

In dialogue with Hierarchical and Atomistic Governance, Integrative Governance accommodates *order* and *choice* through an ongoing participatory, self-organizing, unifying process within networks that interlock across scales. In dialogue with Holographic and Fragmented Governance, Integrative Governance accommodates both *unity* and *autonomy* through respect for difference and agency within a social condition of interdependence.

In essence, Integrative Governance enables us to achieve both order/unity (collectivism) and choice/autonomy (individualism) through self-organizing interdependence. Furthermore, it allows for moments of harmony and stability (stasis) within change (dynamism). Therefore, it resolves the primary dialectical tensions undergirding the other approaches in our Governance Typology. Furthermore, through its relational process approach, the tenets of Integrative Governance remain open to contestation and integrative amendment. This is necessary to prevent affirmation from becoming colonizing or hegemonic, demanding that everyone conform to either a static logic or one imposed and controlled by others.

Daring to affirm

Despite the cynicism evident in the literature that collaborative governance networks don't generate a paradigm shift (Hill and Lynn 2005), aren't a cure-all for governance problems (Imperial 2005), and won't produce some sort of utopian bliss (Agranoff and McGuire 2011), we believe the need for better approaches to governance outweighs the risk that Integrative Governance will not work within the existing political economy. Paradigm shifters must attend to "*possibilities* in relation to the contemporary *need* for them more than political probabilities" (Connolly 2005, 253) and "have faith that the new paradigm will succeed" (Kuhn 1996, 158). As discussed in Chapter 13, prefigurative practice demonstrates alternative possibilities, enticing others into the new system until its influence displaces the previous system – while simultaneously resisting the oppressive power imbalances within the existing political economy. This is an approach that is ambitious, but not naïve.

We invite other scholars and practitioners to join us on these translational, integrative pathways to build the consensus necessary to embrace, affirm, and profess Integrative Governance within social, political, and economic institutions as they interact globally. We are not alone in this call – many others suggest that the conceptual elements of relational process ontology prefigure a better way forward for individual and societal progress. We "belong to a growing contingent who think that a perspective defined by active examination of becoming can make positive contributions to explorations of spirituality, economic, political action, poetic experience, and ethics" (Connolly 2011, 8). To borrow from political theorist and philosopher Charles Taylor (1989), those of us resisting traditional governance approaches are taking on "the exploration of order through personal resonance" (511), rather than disciplinary canons. We agree that such a project demands

> a radical reappraisal of the contours of the subject, a reassessment of the possibility and texture of ethics, an examination of new domains of power and unfamiliar frames for imagining justice, and an exploration of the sources, quality, and dimensions of agency.
>
> (Coole and Frost 2010, 37)

We have cited our companions in this endeavor throughout Part II, but like us, many speak to the risks involved as a scholar in the project of affirmation of alternative paradigms. While political praxis "is certainly easier said than done" (Prozorov 2014b, 128), an affirmational stance is more appealing to a growing number of scholars. In this regard, we agree with Braidotti (2010) that "political thinkers of the postsecular era need to be visionary, prophetic, and upbeat. . . . This is the horizon of sustainable futures" (216–217); it is work that requires a sense of hope as "a sort of 'dreaming forward,' . . . a powerful motivating force grounded in our collective imaginings" (217). Howe (2006) argues that it is time to "appeal to people's sense of integrity and hope" (427) and affirm that which is desirable. Unfortunately, this is precisely the type of stance that mainstream scholars attack as utopian and naïve.

First, there is the charge that fears of crises are overstated and proposed changes are therefore overly extreme. Proponents of the status quo claim we can solve our problems through incremental improvements to techniques and technologies. However, the crises of sustainability we face "makes it imperative for us to come to terms with the present in new, fundamental ways" (Braidotti 2013, 186). As management systems theorist Peter Senge (2004, xiv) notes,

> I would call David Bohm an extreme *realist*. He knew that no society has ever faced the sort of global predicament we face, and that we are not likely to muddle through without radical changes in our way of being – together.
>
> (emphasis added)

To respond effectively to the global crisis of sustainability, we must base governance on principles of the newest scientific advancements.

Second, there is the criticism that assumptions about interconnection at an ontological level are delusional. However, "A world of becoming has considerable evidence on its side" (Connolly 2011, 6), as detailed in Chapter 5. It is those who suggest interconnection is a simple matter of cause and effect due to growth in human population, markets, and technology to a global scale who are proven wrong by ongoing advancements in the physical and biological sciences. As these discoveries show, we are, and have always been, interconnected on both physical and metaphysical levels – a sentiment shared by a number of new perspectives in the humanities as well as many indigenous cultures. Given the preponderance of evidence and belief on the side of relational process, those who cling to an atomistic, rationalist view of the world are those more appropriately characterized as misguided. In fact, proponents of transdisciplinary studies argue that if we do not reconnect the physical and the metaphysical, we cannot hope to resolve the crises of sustainability we currently face (Nicolescu 2002).

Third, there is the criticism that legitimate social scientists only have two choices: to remain neutral and objective in analyzing the facts and provide recommendations based on those findings, or provide critique of either ideas or behaviors. In other words, the business of making normative claims and propositions is the domain of the humanities. Social scientists are to stay out of spiritual and moral affairs, unless it is to uphold established traditions and laws – or risk being defined "as enemies of God, science, or both" (Connolly 2011, 108). Alternatively, they can critique such ideas, but not proffer alternatives beyond received traditions. These "acceptable" choices have only been reinforced by the postmodern turn in social theory in which deconstruction and skepticism are regarded highly, while affirmative postmodern philosophy (Rosenau 1992) or constructive postmodern philosophy (Griffin 2007) are typically dismissed (Stout and Love 2016).

It could be argued, then, that the social sciences themselves are complicit in the failures of governance to prevent the global crises we now confront. If we are to survive and thrive, we must find "the pathway *out* of nihilism towards the positive transformation of worlds" (Prozorov 2014a, 36). Such generative praxis consists of: "existential gratitude, periodic suspension, creative political action, and reflective recoil" (Connolly 2011, 168). In plain terms, affirmation requires a sense of attachment to existence – sustained cynicism and skepticism are unproductive. Pausing on occasion to contemplate the meaning of existence provides inspiration for innovative action, while care for the implications motivates periodic reflection. This constructive stance enables pragmatic experimentation and evaluation. Through such back and forth, "creativity and critique proceed together in the quest for affirmative alternatives" (Braidotti 2013, 165).

The need for such creativity is clear; in our role as social scientists we are often called upon to make recommendations for beneficial social change. In response, many of us are attempting to conceptualize "the social relations and subsequently governing structures and practices that are rooted in a different political ontology" (Catlaw 2005, 471) – one that generates "a new creative synthesis" (Christ 2003, 224) that will enable transformation rather than reform of existing practice. However, because of the academic barriers we face in such research agendas, we need a fundamental restructuring of scholarship. We cannot operate within the commodified "university as a chain-production unit mass-producing academic good" (Braidotti 2013, 173).

Calls for transdisciplinary study and affirmation are on the rise across disciplines – humanities and the social and physical sciences alike. There are an increasing number of "theorists who want to relate their conceptual endeavours to a broader and more integrated array of social criticism and proposals for change" (Gordon 2007, 47). Appeals are coming from feminism, cross-cultural research of all types, ecology movements, postmodern social theory, and anarchist political theory (Sampson 1986). For example, Donati (2014) calls for "the mobilisation for a relational society" (142). This requires all of us – scholars and non-academics alike – to "inhabit" the many roles we play "in more militant, visible, creative and inspirational ways" (Connolly 2011, 144) – ways that combine "critique with creativity, putting the 'active' back into 'activism'" (Braidotti 2013, 11).

This call has not been absent in public administration. King and Zanetti (2005) describe "transformational administration" in a manner compatible with what is presented herein. It is also quite fitting to the "Arendt-Follett model of government" (Stivers 2008, 116), post-traditional, anti-administration (Farmer 2005), a politics of the subject (Catlaw 2007b), "Government is Us 2.0" (King 2011), Follettian governance (Stout and Staton 2011), and the Collaborative Tradition of public administration (Stout 2006, 2009a, 2009b, 2013). All acknowledge a transformational moment in which we are crafting the practices of Integrative Governance and applying them *within the existing structures of government* to effect change.

This is where the transdisciplinary inclusion of non-expert knowledge, action research, and political praxis come into play, "at the tangled overlap" of a practitioner's thoughtful reflection on action and a scholar's deconstruction and critique of recursive social life (Miller and King 1998, 57). This tangled overlap includes *all* voices. Through participatory approaches to action research, scholars are encouraged to collaborate with non-academic institutions and activists: "It takes all three in tandem – in their theistic and nontheistic forms – to press for pluralism, equality, and ecological sensitivity" (Connolly 2010, 197). In doing so, scholars may come "from the academy" but must stop "writing *for* the academy" (Rousselle 2011, viii).

This is not just a matter of scholars reaching out to those in other sectors; technological advances in social media have broken down traditional mechanisms of intellectual gatekeeping through a democratization of public speech. Voices that were once marginalized are now engaging in potent political and social commentary, forming communities of discourse, and shaping everything from mainstream news coverage, to social movements, to political campaigns. As discussed in Chapter 13, this transdisciplinary mix of public intellectuals is becoming increasingly prevalent and impactful.

Reflecting back to Chapter 3, we argue that failure to achieve collaborative advantage is caused in part by the failure of collaborative governance network scholars to look in the right places for theory building and to learn about new skills. As Kuhn (1996) suggests, paradigmatic shifts require innovative approaches: "Led by a new paradigm, scientists adopt new instruments and look in new places. Even more important, during revolutions scientists see new and different things when looking with familiar instruments in places they have looked before" (111). As with transdisciplinary studies, we need to adopt an aim of doing this – if we want to understand collaboration, we need to look to new *instruments* as we have in Part II. If we want a more robust understanding than theory alone can provide, we must look to new *places* for empirical evidence – this means drawing from non-expert wisdom and learning with nontraditional collaborative networks, as we have in Chapter 13.

Thankfully, there are excellent examples of transdisciplinary study that are doing so, from whom we can learn and on whose work we can build. For example, the TRANSIT project is guided by a vision to "*increase the impact and potential of transformative social innovation that can empower people and facilitate change for sustainable development in society*" and uses an iterative process of theory building through empirical analysis of existing collaborative networks in a variety of settings (TRANSIT 2014a, b). A key underlying question across these case studies is, "What forms of governance facilitate transformative social innovation?" To date they have studied and produced reports on 20 different kinds of networks, with a wide range of foci such as social entrepreneurship, alternative economies, sustainability initiatives, and food systems. This work focuses on four driving research questions examining:

(1) development of local groups and transnational networks; (2) types of social innovation that emerge; (3) the empowerment and disempowerment of actors; and (4) identifying other emergent issues that help understand the dynamics of social innovation.

Advancing Integrative Governance theory and practice

Because Integrative Governance is grounded in a worldview that is unfamiliar to those held by the globally dominant societies, it will require a great deal of explanation, experimentation, evaluation, and integrative amendment to garner acceptance. Political theorist David Ray Griffin (2007, loc. 1043) calls for a worldview

> that is deeply ecological; one that is pragmatic, in the sense of providing a livable guide for action; one that can be commended, because of its coherence and relative adequacy, is at least not obviously false; and one that, as part of the evidence for its relative adequacy, can reconcile tensions between other positions, doing justice to the elements of truth in each.

While we have made an attempt to meet these evaluative criteria, to generate a more robust understanding of Integrative Governance requires "dialogue with people in different disciplines and even sub-disciplines. If we want to approach the fullest truth of which we are capable, we need dialogue with as many perspectives as possible" (Griffin 2007, loc. 1545). We have brought a wide array of ideas into conversation with one another, yet, perhaps we have missed something in our definition. We need comrades from other disciplines and cultures to join us. Much more theory-building work is needed in terms of: (1) transdisciplinary contributions to the conceptual elements of Integrative Governance as a framework; (2) operationalization of its practices for study; and (3) inductive empirical research of effective collaborative action.

First, we hope that scholars from other disciplines will take on the challenge of clarifying, expanding, and amending Integrative Governance as a theoretical framework. Furthermore, we invite them to reframe our definition of the object of study as "Governance in contexts of social, economic, and environmental interconnectedness." We believe this research agenda is in the spirit of the Charter adopted at the 1994 First World Congress of Transdisciplinarity, and likewise invite all who are "interested in promoting progressive national, international, and transnational measures to ensure the application" and development of Integrative concepts "in everyday life" (Nicolescu 2002, 151).

Second, we will continue to use the ideal-type of Integrative Governance as an evaluative tool against which to measure practice as tested in a secondary case study (Stout and Love 2018). We intend to continue our work to operationalize integrative characteristics and practices to enhance empirical research at various levels of individual and group experience. While we have drawn heavily from Mary Follett who developed her integrative method from community-based practice and we have drawn from our own experiences in community development and social services practice, further detail is required for both study and skill-building instruction. Toward that end, we have presented a preliminary evaluative logic model based on Follett's concepts (see Stout, Bartels, and Love 2014, 2018), but we need to take a similar approach to develop the indicators of Integrative Governance.

Our contention, given this combination of theoretical inquiry and practical experience, is that governance networks that more closely resemble indicators of Integrative Governance will achieve better results in both utilitarian and democratic measures. To test this hypothesis, we will employ the Integrative Governance ideal-type as an analytical framework in primary qualitative case studies to assess how each situation illustrates its implementation. Using the Integrative Governance framework across studies will enable robust meta-analysis that can inform continued theory building and operationalization.

Indeed, case study and meta-analyses thereof are the most prominent types of research in public administration (Cleary 2000, 1992; Kaag 2008; Kolb 1996; Krupp 1961; Maddock and Mcalpine 2006; Neumann 1996; Perry and Kraemer 1986; Raadschelders 1999; White and Adams 1994). However, not all are analytical in a methodological sense, which we hope to rectify. Weber (1949) recommends the ideal-type method as the preferred approach to case study: "Only through ideal-typical concept-construction do the viewpoints with which we are concerned in individual cases become explicit. Their peculiar character is brought out by the *confrontation* of empirical reality with the ideal-type" (110). In our view, this is a pragmatic proposition for theory building that will balance deductive and inductive inquiry.

Third, as *professors*, we will continue to "confess, or declare openly, and therefore publicly" our calling (Barrett 1958, 4). At minimum, these ideas affect our contributions to curriculum design, course content, and pedagogical approaches. As argued by others, "schools of public administration and public affairs owe it to future public managers and administrators to provide better training in these processes. These skills are essential to effective functioning in the new horizontal and networked governance structures" (Bingham, Nabatchi, and O'Leary 2005, 555). Additionally, as we know from the prefigurative praxis of social movements, "The way to create a new world is to take steps *to* create it, to live the life we want to live" (Ackelsberg 2012, 3). Therefore, as faculty members and consulting practitioners, we will also use the ideal-type of Integrative Governance as guidance in institutional design and operational dynamics, as well as evaluative indicators against which to measure our practice.

In other words, we will organize where we work by seeking to instantiate Integrative Governance through our own collaborative praxis, even within the most hierarchical and competitive of contexts – the academy. In doing so, we fully acknowledge that not only is letting go of control unsavory to power holders, we are not generally *prepared* to act in a collaborative manner. This will likely be a long row to hoe, but we are committed to building the road as we walk it with our colleagues.

Onward the revolution!

We are not alone as we work to advance Integrative Governance. We must reach out to others to form a transcontinental "network of communication among all our struggles," in order to affirm an "international order of hope, for a new, just, and dignified peace" (EZLN 1996). In this endeavor, "We are the network, all of us who speak and listen" (EZLN 1996) – all of us who dare to affirm and enact these principles in our professional research, writing, and teaching, as well as in our personal and civic lives. We have no doubt that the philosophical assumptions and practices embedded in Integrative Governance are "something which can, potentially, produce a revolution" (Bohm 2004, 108).

Whether we see this endeavor as transformational reform or system replacement, perhaps it is time for another revolution, another turn in an ongoing spiral of societal progress (Stout 2009b) – "a participatory evolution" (Bookchin 2015d, loc. 1454). Two centuries ago, the Anti-federalists proclaimed a crisis during the founding of the United States and the break from autocratic, feudal society to build one that would be more participatory and democratic (Storing 1981). A century later, Progressives declared a crisis in the conditions created by the industrial revolution and corrupt politics, initiating the expert-led "administrative state" (Waldo 1984). After yet another century, critical theorists of public administration pointed out that this political economy had led us into a cul-de-sac of hierarchy and competition (Thayer 1981). In each century of modern democracy, we have been presented with an opportunity to fully embrace its radical tenets, to release our fears of self and others and step into self-governance without trepidation (Stout 2010a). Perhaps each time we come back to this moment, we come closer to actually doing so.

While often critiqued as a utopian curmudgeon, Thayer was, perhaps, the first governance theorist (Catlaw 2008; Stout 2007a). He argued that an organizational transformation would emerge through a withering away of domination and competition due to increasing network configurations and boundary permeations.

> When the organizational revolution has run its course, and when societies have been transformed as they must be if we are to survive, the world of organizations will be one of innumerable small face-to-face groups characterized by openness, trust, and intensive interpersonal relations.
>
> (Thayer 1981, 5)

What would remain are social functions rather than social sectors, organizations, and static roles defined by employment. All would be responsible for the co-creative functions of citizenship in relationships free from domination.

While Thayer did not offer an instruction manual for this transformation of the political economy and Follett's Progressive era critique simply provided guidelines for how to function in a radically democratic manner in day-to-day practice, many others – cited herein – have continued both theoretical development and experimentation in practices that reflect their descriptions of Radical Democracy as a means to in the political economy. Many such scholars are cited herein, and as discussed in Chapter 13, Radical Democracy is practiced by contemporary social movements as a "prefigurative" (Boggs 1977) as opposed to strategic (Smucker 2014) approach to social change. Radical Democracy does not seek to claim the seat of power – it seeks to transform power itself through ***power-with*** processes in ***self-organizing confederalism***.

At present, we once again collectively ponder, "If the older democracies confront and overcome their challenges in the twenty-first century, they just might transform themselves, at long last, into truly advanced democracies" (Dahl 1998, 188). Despite the "dark times" we are witnessing (Stivers 2008), we are hopeful. In response to the fragmentation of the postmodern social condition and ongoing economic crisis, we see a partisan and populist retrenchment into nationalism and authoritarian tendencies. However, rather than feeding into escalating tensions, some are seeking to understand the underlying fears and desires in order to find integrative common ground. This approach is reflected in what Keating (2013) refers to as "listening with raw openness" (53).

Nonetheless, considering the fact that Mary Follett introduced many of the concepts of Integrative Governance in 1918, some may feel that the desired paradigm shift will never come. Many scholars are understandably cynical about the slow uptake of collaborative governance networks, suggesting it is not ever likely to represent a paradigmatic change (Hill and Lynn 2005). However, paradigm shifts do not happen overnight, or even over a few decades. Fundamental assumptions must be re-imagined, explicated in detail, disseminated, and accepted by a sufficient number to produce a tipping point toward the "new normal." As Kuhn (1996) explains, normal science "often suppresses fundamental novelties because they are necessarily subversive of its basic commitments" (5) and because new phenomena "are often not seen at all" (24). How can those expecting methodological individualism and self-interested, rational behavior even recognize anomalies of relational thinking and behavior? We do our best to fit what we see into the boxes we know until we can no longer ignore the incongruencies. We have transformed the physical sciences through complexity theory. Now we must do the same for all of the social sciences and the practices that rely upon them.

Even more apropos to our endeavor, Kuhn (1996) likens scientific revolutions to political revolutions because they both ensue when "existing institutions have ceased adequately to meet the problems posed by an environment that they have in part created" (92). As we argued in Part I, this is particularly true of the linkages between governance theory, governance practices, and the crises of sustainability. As noted in studies of government coproduction with citizens and corporate social responsibility, everyone must contribute to the common good. We cannot construct our societies wholly around atomistic individualism and self-interested behavior and then expect government alone to ensure the common good.

We recognize the present revolution is particularly frightening to both scientists who crave certainty and stability and political leaders who are loathe to relinquish control. To shift the paradigm, we must "effect transformation of the ontological underpinnings of the terms in which world order is conceived and the meaning of existence is articulated" (Stewart-Harawira 2005b, 3) – these are high stakes indeed. Yet, considering the new scientific discoveries surveyed herein, "a conceptual shift, 'tectonic' in its implications has taken place. We ground things, now, on a moving earth" (Marcus 1986, 22); such process-oriented syntheses do not hold "any absolute truth" (Rocker 2004, 15). Thus, Relational Becoming produces a fundamental "rupture and transformation" (Coole and Frost 2010, 36). Indeed, "this transformation in character cannot merely be appended to the current forms of society, but would demand a thoroughgoing transformation of the entire societal system in order to be realized" (Sampson 1986, 90). Relational process requires a complete transformation of governmentality, or the conduct of conduct, throughout all social spheres as conceptualized by Foucault (1991) (see also, Catlaw 2007c; Stout 2010a).

This assumption of uncertainty is much more difficult to embed culturally than replacing one certain order with another. Despite the risks involved, for the sake of surviving and thriving, we must summon the courage to embrace these governance practices. As Father Leone tells Superman in *Man of Steel*, "Sometimes, you have to take a leap of faith first. The trust part comes later" (Snyder 2013). To redirect the disastrous trajectory we seem to be on, we believe it is time to take that leap, despite fears that are quite justifiable.

Paradigms provide us maps of reality by which to navigate as well as the rules for altering them. Politically speaking, these dynamic and open-ended scientific principles are reflected in prefigurative social movements that seek a "utopia unnamed" (Vahabzadeh 2002, 315) – they have "no definite terminus nor . . . fixed goal" (Rocker 2004, 15). Unlike previous eras that promoted "unitary blueprints" for society, the new project is "based on diversity and perpetual experimentation" (Gordon 2007, 43) and "advances the vision of an ever increasing wholeness, fullness and richness of differentiation and subjectivity" (Bookchin 1994b, 20). We must seek a new society whose institutions are continually open to contestation and ensure an integrative response that alters the society, as opposed to its contestants. We must admit the "unlimited perfectibility of social arrangements and human living conditions" and push onward (Rocker 2004, 15).

However, democracy as a way of life cannot be realized through coercive methods – even from well-meaning vanguards. Radical Democracy is something that must emerge and expand organically within our own daily lives, from individual to individual, group to group, throughout society. We must foster integrative collaboration "by practising it with the first person we meet; by approaching every man with the consciousness of the complexity of his needs, of the vastness of his powers" (Follett 1998, 160). These urgings echo the anarchistic principle of "prefigurative politics (i.e., modes of organization that consciously resemble the world you want to create)" (Graeber and Grubacic 2004, 2). If we want a democratic world, we must adopt an approach that will enable us to organize and act democratically and start doing so – everywhere. This is not a Pollyanna endeavor – it is a project of "utopistics," of imagining a historically *possible* future based on nascent evidence (Wallerstein 1998, 65) and then *acting* accordingly. Clichéd or not, it is *being* the change we wish to see in the world. As those in La Vía Campesina would say, *Adelante!*

References

Abram, David. 1988. "Merleau-Ponty and the voice of the earth." *Environmental Ethics* 10 (2):101–120.

Acevedo, Nicole. 2017, March 27. " 'We cannot hide': Sanctuary cities join forces in first meeting of its kind." *NBC News*. www.nbcnews.com/news/latino/we-cannot-hide-sanctuary-cities-join-forces-first-meeting-its-n739681.

Ackelsburg, Martha. 2012. Preface. In *Queering anarchism: Addressing and undressing power and desire*, edited by C.B. Daring, J. Rogue, Deric Shannon, and Abbey Volcano, 1-4. Oakland, CA: AK Press.

Adams, Guy B., Priscilla V. Bowerman, Kenneth M. Dolbeare, and Camilla M. Stivers. 1990. "Joining purpose to practice: A democratic identity for the public service." In *Images and identities in public administration*, edited by Henry D. Kass and Bayard L. Catron, 219–240. Thousand Oaks, CA: Sage Publications.

Adams, Jason. 2011. "The constellation of opposition." In *Post-anarchism: A reader*, edited by Duane Rousselle and Sureyyya Evren, 117–138. London: Pluto Press.

Addams, Jane. 1964. *Democracy and social ethics*. Cambridge, MA: Harvard University Press. Original edition, 1902.

Adler, Margot. 1986. *Drawing down the moon*. Boston: Beacon Press.

Adorno, Theodor W. 1973. *Negative dialectics*. New York: Seabury Press.

Adorno, Theodor W. 1998. *Critical models: Interventions and catchwords*. Translated by H. Pickford. New York: Columbia University Press. Original edition, 1963.

Agarwal, Renu, and Willem Selen. 2009. "Dynamic capability building in service value networks for achieving service innovation." *Decision Sciences* 40 (3):431–475.

Agranoff, Robert. 2003. *Collaborative public management: New strategies for local governments*. Washington, DC: Georgetown University Press.

Agranoff, Robert. 2004. "Intergovernmental and network administration, accountability, and performance: Symposium introduction." *Public Performance & Management Review* 31 (3):315–319.

Agranoff, Robert. 2005. "Managing collaborative performance: Changing the boundaries of the state?" *Public Performance & Management Review* 29 (1):18–45.

Agranoff, Robert. 2006. "Inside collaborative networks: Ten lessons for public managers." *Public Administration Review* 66 (Supplemental):56–65.

Agranoff, Robert. 2007. *Managing within networks: Adding value to public organizations, public management and change series*. Washington, DC: Georgetown University Press.

Agranoff, Robert. 2008. "Enhancing performance through public sector networks: Mobilizing human capital in communities of practice." *Public Performance & Management Review* 31 (3):320–347.

Agranoff, Robert, and Michael McGuire. 1998. "Multinetwork management: Collaboration and the hollow state in local economic policy." *Journal of Public Administration Research and Theory* 8 (1):67–91.

Agranoff, Robert, and Michael McGuire. 1999. "Managing in network settings." *Policy Studies Review* 16 (1):19–41.
Agranoff, Robert, and Michael McGuire. 2001. "Big questions in public network management research." *Journal of Public Administration Research and Theory* 11 (3):295–326.
Agranoff, Robert, and Michael McGuire. 2011. "The limitations of public management networks." *Public Administration* 89 (2):265–284.
Albert, Michael, Leslie Cagan, Noam Chomsky, Robin Hahnel, Mel King, Lydia Sargeant, and Holly Sklar. 1986. *Liberating theory.* Boston: South End Press.
Alcoff, Linda. 1994. "Cultural feminism versus post-structuralism: The identity crisis in feminist theory." In *Culture/ power/ history: A reader in contemporary social theory*, edited by Nicholas B. Dirks, Geoff Eley and Sherry B. Ortner, 96–122. Princeton, NJ: Princeton University Press.
Alexander, Christopher, Sara Ishikawa, Murray Silverstein, Max Jacobson, Ingrid Fiksdahl-King, and Shlomo Angel. 1977. *A pattern language: Towns, buildings, construction.* Oxford: Oxford University Press.
Alfred, Taiaiake. 1999. *Peace, power, righteousness: An indigenous manifesto.* Oxford: Oxford University Press.
Aljazeera. 2017. "Syria's civil war explained from the beginning." Aljazeera, Last Modified September 27, accessed September 27, 2017. www.aljazeera.com/news/2016/05/syria-civil-war-explained-160505084119966.html.
Allard, Jenna, Carl Davidson, and Julie Matthaei, eds. 2008. *Solidarity economy: Building alternatives for people and planet.* Chicago: ChangeMaker Publications.
Allen, William, Bridget Anderson, Nicholas Van Hear, Madeleine Sumption, Franck Düvell, Jennifer Hough, Lena Rose, Rachel Humphris, and Sarah Walker. 2017. "Who counts in crises? The new geopolitics of international migration and refugee governance, geopolitics." *Geopolitics*:1–27.
Allies Against Slavery. 2015. "About allies against slavery." Allies Against Slavery, accessed November 26, 2017. www.alliesagainstslavery.org/mission/.
Allison, Graham T. 1971. *The essence of decision: Explaining the Cuban missile crisis.* Boston: Little Brown.
Alperovitz, Gar. 2013. *What then must we do? Straight talk about the next American revolution.* White River Junction, VT: Chelsea Green Publishing.
Alperovitz, Gar. 2014. "The political-economic foundations of a sustainable system." In *State of the world 2014: Governing for sustainability*, edited by Lisa Mastny, 191–202. Washington, DC: Worldwatch Institute.
Alperovitz, Gar, James Gustave Speth, and Joe Guinan. 2015. "The next system project: New political-economic possibilities for the 21st century." In *NSP Report.* Washington, DC: Next System Project.
Alter, Catherine, and Jerald Hage. 1993. *Organizations working together.* Thousand Oaks, CA: Sage Publications.
Anderson, Kym. 2000. "The future agenda of the WTO." In *From GATT to WTO: The multilateral trading system in the new millenium*, edited by WTO Secretariat, 7–35. Boston: Kluwer Law International.
Ansell, Chris, and Alison Gash. 2008. "Collaborative governance in theory and practice." *Journal of Public Administration Research and Theory* 18 (4):543–571.
Ansell, Christopher. 2011. *Pragmatist democracy: Evolutionary learning as public philosophy.* Oxford: Oxford University Press.
Antliff, Allan. 2011. "Anarchy, power and post-structuralism." In *Post-anarchism: A reader*, edited by Duane Rousselle and Süreyyya Evren, 160–167. New York: Pluto Press.
Anzaldúa, Gloria. 1987. *Borderlands/La frontera: The new mestiza.* San Francisco: Aunt Lute Books.
Anzaldúa, Gloria. 2004. "La concienda de la mestiza: Towards a new consciousness." In *Oppression, privilege, and resistance: Theoretical perspectives on racism, sexism, and heterosexism*, edited by Lisa Heldke and Peg O'Connor, 739–751. Boston: McGraw-Hill.

Archer, Margaret S. 1995. *Realist social theory: The morphogenic approach*. New York: Press Syndicate of the University of Cambridge.
Archer, Margaret S., ed. 2015. *Generative mechanisms transforming the social order*. New York: Springer.
Arendt, Hannah. 1977. *On revolution*. Harmondsworth, UK: Penguin. Original edition, 1963.
Arendt, Hannah. 1998. *The human condition*. Chicago: University of Chicago Press. Original edition, 1958.
Arendt, Hannah. 2005. *The promise of politics*. New York: Schocken Books.
Argyris, Chris, and Donald A. Schön. 1978. *Organizational learning: A theory of action perspective*. Reading, MA: Addison-Wesley.
Arnstein, Sherry. 1969. "A ladder of citizen participation." *Journal of the American Institute of Planners* 35 (3):216–224.
ASEAN, Association of Southeast Asian Nations. n.d. "ASEAN member states." Association of Southeast Asian Nations, accessed July 15, 2017. http://asean.org/asean/asean-member-states/.
Atherton, John. 2000. *A public theology for a global context*. London: Society for Promoting Christian Knowledge.
Atleo, Umeek E. Richard. 2005. *Tsawalk: A Nuu-chah-nulth worldview*. Seattle: University of Washington Press.
Attrache, Ghaleb. 2014. "Introduction to power & prefiguration forum." *Berkeley Journal of Sociology* 58:1.
Aurobindo, Sri. 1957. *The synthesis of yoga*. Pondicherry, India: Aurobindo Ashram Press.
Babikova, Zdenka, Lucy Gilbert, Toby J. A. Bruce, Michael Birkett, John C. Caulfield, Christine Woodcock, John A. Pickett, and David Johnson. 2013. "Underground signals carried through common mycelial networks warn neighbouring plants of aphid attack." *Ecology Letters* 16 (7):835–843.
Badiou, Alain. 2000. *Deleuze: The clamor of being*. Translated by Louise Burchill. Minneapolis: University of Minnesota Press.
Badiou, Alain. 2005. *Being and event*. Translated by Norman Madarasz. Albany, NY: State University of New York Press.
Badiou, Alain. 2009. *Logics of worlds: Being and event II*. Translated by Albert Toscano. New York: Continuum.
Baker, Peter. 2017, January 23. "Trump abandons trans-pacific partnership, Obama's signature trade deal." *New York Times*. www.nytimes.com/2017/01/23/us/politics/tpp-trump-trade-nafta.html.
BALLE, Business Alliance for Local Living Economies. 2002. "Home page." Business Alliance for Local Living Economies, accessed May 18, 2016. https://bealocalist.org/.
Banerjee, Amrita. 2008. "Follett's pragmatist ontology of relations: Potentials for a feminist perspective on violence." *Journal of Speculative Philosophy* 22 (1):3–11.
Bang, Henrik, and Anders Esmark. 2009. "Good governance in the network society: Reconfiguring the political from politics to policy." *Administrative Theory & Praxis* 31 (1):7–37.
Barad, Karen. 2007. *Meeting the universe halfway: Quantum physics and the entanglement of matter and meaning*. Durham, NC: Duke University Press.
Barber, Benjamin R. 1984. *Strong democracy: Participatory politics for a new age*. Berkeley: University of California Press.
Barber, Benjamin R. 1998. *A place for us: How to make civil society and democracy strong*. New York: Hill and Wang.
Barber, Benjamin R. 2013. *If mayors ruled the world: Dysfunctional nations, rising cities*. New Haven, CT: Yale University Press.
Bardach, Eugene. 2001. "Developmental dynamics: Interagency collaboration as an emergent phenomenon." *Journal of Public Administration Research and Theory* 11 (2):149–164.
Barker, Drucilla K., and Edith Kuiper. 2003. *Toward a feminist philosophy of economics, economics as social theory*. New York: Routledge.

Barnes, Peter. 2006. *Capitalism 3.0: A guide to reclaiming the commons.* San Francisco: Barrett-Koehler.
Barrett, William. 1958. *Irrational man: A study in existential philosophy.* New York: Double Day Anchor Books.
Bartels, Koen P. R. 2012. "The actionable researcher: Cultivating a process-oriented methodology for studying administrative practice." *Administrative Theory & Praxis* 34 (3):433–455.
Bartels, Koen P. R. 2013. "Public encounters: The history and future of face-to-face contact between public professionals and citizens." *Public Administration* 91 (2):469–483.
Bartels, Koen P. R. 2015a. *Communicative capacity: Public encounters in participatory theory and practice.* Bristol, UK: Policy Press.
Bartels, Koen P. R. 2015b. "Gaining grip on neighborhood practices: Fostering integrative collaborative dynamics in street level work." International Conference on Public Policy, Milan, Italy, July 1–4.
Bartels, Koen P. R. 2016. "Doing what's necessary: How encounters in practice shape and improve interactive governance." In *Critical reflections on interactive governance: Self organization and participation in public governance*, edited by Jurian Edelenbos and Ingmar van Meerkerk, 352–375. Cheltenham, UK: Edward Elgar.
Bartels, Koen P. R. 2018. "Encounters with an open mind: Innovative neighbourhood work in Amsterdam." In *From austerity to abundance? Creative approaches to coordinating the common good*, edited by Margaret Stout. Bingly, UK: Emerald Publishing.
Barthes, Roland. 1972. "Jeunes chercheurs." *Communications* 19:1–5.
Bartosiewicz, Petra, and Marissa Miley. 2014. "The too-polite revolution: Understanding the failure to pass U.S. climate legislation." In *State of the world 2014: Governing for sustainability*, edited by Lisa Mastny, 115–128. Washington, DC: Worldwatch Institute.
Barzelay, Michael. 2001. *The new public management: Improving research and policy dialogue.* Berkeley: University of California Press.
Basso, Keith H. 1996. *Wisdom sits in places: Landscape and language among the Western Apache.* Albuquerque: University of New Mexico Press.
Bastien, Betty. 2004. *Blackfoot ways of knowing: The worldview of the Siksikaitsitapi.* Calgary, Alberta, Canada: University of Calgary Press.
BBC News. 2016. "Syria: The story of the conflict." BBC News, accessed September 27, 2017. www.bbc.com/news/world-middle-east-26116868.
BBC News. 2017. "Syria profile – Timeline." BBC News, accessed September 15, 2017. www.bbc.com/news/world-middle-east-14703995.
Beck, Don, and Chris Cowan. 1995. *Spiral dynamics: Mastering values, leadership, and change.* Cambridge, MA: Blackwell Publishers.
Beck, Ulrich, and Elisabeth Beck-Gernsheim. 2001. *Individualization: Institutionalized individualism and its social and political consequences.* Vol. 13. Thousand Oaks, CA: Sage Publications.
Beeman, Chris, and Sean Blenkinsop. 2008. "Might diversity also be ontological? Considering Heidegger, Spinoza and indigeneity in educative practice." *Encounters on Education* 9 (Fall):95–107.
Bell, Michael. 2006. "Toward an ecology of spirit." In *Business within limits: Deep ecology and Buddhist economics*, edited by Zsolnai Laszlo and Knut Johannessen Ims, 269–318. Bern, Switzerland: Peter Lang AG.
Bellah, Robert N., Richard Madsen, William M. Sullivan, Ann Swidler, and Steven M. Tipton. 1985. *Habits of the heart: Individualism and commitment in American life.* New York: Harper & Row.
Benello, C. George. 1992. *From the ground up.* Boston: South End Press.
Benhabib, Seyla. 1992. *Situating the self: Gender, community and postmodernism in contemporary ethics.* New York: Routledge.
Benhabib, Seyla. 2006. *Another cosmopolitanism, the Berkeley tanner lectures.* Oxford: Oxford University Press.

Ben-Jacob, Eshel, Yoash Shapira, and Alfred Tauber. 2011. "Smart bacteria." In *Chimeras and consciousness: Evolution of the sensory self*, edited by Lynn Margulis, Celeste A. Asikainen and Wolfgang E. Krumbein, 55–62. Cambridge, MA: MIT Press.

Bennett, Jane. 2001. *The enchantment of modern life: Attachments, crossings, and ethics*. Princeton, NJ: Princeton University Press.

Bennett, Jane. 2005. "In parliament with things." In *Radical democracy: Politics between abundance and lack*, edited by Lars Tønder and Lasse Thomassen, 133–148. New York: Manchester University Press.

Bentley, Trevor. 1995. *Facilitation: Providing opportunities for learning*. New York: McGraw-Hill.

Berger, Peter L., and Thomas Luckmann. 1966. *The social construction of reality: A treatise in the sociology of knowledge*. Garden City, NY: Anchor Books.

Bergson, Henri. 1913. *Matter and memory*. Translated by Nancy Margaret Paul and W. Scott Palmer. London: George Allen & Co., Ltd. Original edition, 1896.

Bergson, Henri. 2001. *Time and free will: An essay on the immediate data of consciousness*. Translated by F. L. Pogson. 3rd ed. Mineola, NY: Dover Publications. Original edition, 1913.

Bergson, Henri. 2007. *The creative mind: An introduction to metaphysics*. Mineola, NY: Dover Publications. Original edition, 1946.

Bergson, Henri, and Arthur Mitchell. 1920. *Creative evolution*. London: Palgrave Macmillan. Original edition, 1911.

Bernstein, Richard J. 1976. *The restructuring of social and political theory*. Philadelphia: University of Pennsylvania Press.

Bernstein, Richard J. 1991. *The new constellation: The ethical-political horizons of modernity/postmodernity*. Cambridge, MA: MIT Press. Reprint, third.

Berry, Frances S., Ralph S. Brower, Sang Ok Choi, Wendy Xinfang Goa, HeeSoun Jang, Myungjung Kwon, and Jessica Word. 2004. "Three traditions of network research: What the public management research agenda can learn from other research communities." *Public Administration Review* 64 (5):539–552.

Bertalan, Hilton. 2011. "When theories meet: Emma Goldman and 'post-anarchism'." In *Post-anarchism: A reader*, edited by Duane Rousselle and Sureyyya Evren, 208–230. London: Pluto Press.

Bevir, Mark. 2010. *Democratic governance*. Princeton, NJ: Princeton University Press.

Bevir, Mark. 2012. *Governance: A short introduction*. Oxford: Oxford University Press.

Beyer, Christian. 2013. "Edmund Husserl." In Stanford encyclopedia of philosophy, edited by Edward N. Zalta. http://plato.stanford.edu/archives/sum2013/entries/husserl Accessed: Jan. 11, 2016

Biernacki, Lorillai. 2014. "Introduction: Panentheism outside the box." In *Panentheism across the world's traditions*, edited by Lorillai Biernacki and Philip Clayton. Oxford: Oxford University Press.

Bindewald, Leander, Maria Nginamau, and Christopher Place. 2013. *Validating complementary and community currencies as an efficient tool for social and solidarity economy networking and development: The deployment of theory of change approach and evaluation standards for their impact assessment*. Geneva: United Nations Non-Governmental Liaison Service.

Bingham, Lisa Blomgren. 2008. "Legal frameworks for governance and public management." In *Big ideas in collaborative public management*, edited by Lisa Blomgren Bingham and Rosemary O'Leary, 247–269. Armonk, NY: M.E. Sharpe.

Bingham, Lisa Blomgren. 2009. "Collaborative governance: Emerging practices and the incomplete legal framework for public and stakeholder voice." *Journal of Dispute Resolution* (2):269–325.

Bingham, Lisa Blomgren, Tina Nabatchi, and Rosemary O'Leary. 2005. "The new governance: Practices and processes for stakeholder and citizen participation in the work of government." *Public Administration Review* 65 (5):547–558.

Bingham, Lisa Blomgren, and Rosemary O'Leary, eds. 2008. *Big ideas in collaborative public management.* Armonk, NY: M.E. Sharpe.
Bingham, Lisa Blomgren, Rosemary O'Leary, and Christine Carlson. 2008. "Frameshifting: Lateral thinking for collaborative public management." In *Big ideas in collaborative public management*, edited by Lisa Blomgren Bingham and Rosemary O'Leary, 3–16. Armonk, NY: M.E. Sharpe.
Bingham, Lisa Blomgren, Jodi Sandfort, and Rosemary O'Leary. 2008. "Teaching managers to collaborate in networks." In *Big ideas in collaborative public management*, edited by Lisa Blomgren Bingham and Rosemary O'Leary, 270–285. Armonk, NY: M.E. Sharpe.
Bird-David, Nurit. 1992. "Beyond 'The Original Affluent Society': A culturalist reformulation." *Current Anthropology* 33 (1):25–47.
Bird-David, Nurit. 1999. " 'Animism' revisited: Personhood, environment, and relational epistemology." *Current Anthropologist* 40 (Supplement):S67–S91.
Bixler, R. Patrick, Dara M. Wald, Laura A. Ogden, Kirsten M. Leong, Erik W. Johnston, and Michele Romolini. 2016. "Network governance for large-scale natural resource conservation and the challenge of capture." *Frontiers in Ecology and the Environment* (April):165–171.
Blasi, Joseph. 2009. *The communal experience of the kibbutz.* New Brunswick: Transaction Publishers.
Block, Peter. 1993. *Stewardship: Choosing service over self-interest.* San Francisco: Berrett-Koehler Publishers.
Bockelbrink, Bernhard. 2016. "Sociocratic organizations around the globe." Evolving Collaboration, accessed August 5, 2016. http://evolvingcollaboration.com/who-is-using-sociocracy/.
Boffey, Daniel. 2017. "Mayors of 7,400 cities vow to meet Obama's climate commitments." *The Guardian*, June 28, accessed September 17, 2017. www.theguardian.com/environment/2017/jun/28/global-covenant-mayors-cities-vow-to-meet-obama-climate-commitments.
Bogason, Peter. 2001. "Postmodernism and American public administration in the 1990s." *Administration & Society* 33 (2):165–193.
Bogason, Peter, and Juliet A. Musso. 2006. "The democratic prospects of network governance." *American Review of Public Administration* 36 (1):3–18.
Boggs, Jr., Carl. 1977. "Marxism, prefigurative communism, and the problem of workers' control." *Radical America* 11 (6):99–122.
Bohm, David. 1980. *Wholeness and the implicate order.* London: Routledge & Kegan Paul.
Bohm, David. 2004. *On dialogue.* New York: Routledge.
Bohr, Niels. 1996. "Complementarity: Bedrock of the quantal description." In *Foundations of quantum physics II (1933–1958)*, edited by Jørgen Kalckar, Niels Bohr, Léon Rosenfeld, Erik Rüdinger and Finn Aaserud, 249–432. Amsterdam: Elsevier Science.
Boik, John. 2013, February 5. "Can local currencies help advance global sustainability?" *The Guardian.*
Boje, David M. 2006. "What happened on the way to postmodern? Part II." *Administrative Theory & Praxis* 28 (4):479–494.
Boje, David M., and Grace Ann Rosile. 2001. "Where's the power in empowerment? Answers from Follett and Clegg." *Journal of Applied Behavioral Science* 37 (1):90–117.
Bollier, David. 2016. "Commoning as a transformative social paradigm." In *New systems.* Washington, DC: The Next System Project.
Bollier, David, and Burns H. Weston. 2013. *Green governance: Ecological survival, human rights, and the law of the commons.* Cambridge: Cambridge University Press.
Bollier, David, and Burns H. Weston. 2014. "Advancing ecological stewardship via the commons and human rights." In *State of the world 2014: Governing for sustainability*, edited by Lisa Mastny, 91–104. Washington, DC: Worldwatch Institute.
Bonewits, Isaac. 2007. "Defining paganism: Paleo-, meso-, and neo-." Neopagan, accessed July 12, 2015. www.neopagan.net/PaganDefs.html.

Bookchin, Debbie, and Blair Taylor. 2015. "Introduction." In *The next revolution*, edited by Debbie Bookchin and Blair Taylor, loc. 81–224. Brooklyn, NY: Verso.
Bookchin, Murray. 1994a. "The ecological crisis, socialism, and the need to remake society." *Society and Nature* 2 (3):1–10.
Bookchin, Murray. 1994b. *The philosophy of social ecology: Essays on dialectical naturalism*. 2nd ed. Montreal: Black Rose Books.
Bookchin, Murray. 2002. "Theses on libertarian municipalism." In *The anarchist papers*, edited by Dimitrios Roussopoulos, 9–22. Montreal: Black Rose Books.
Bookchin, Murray. 2015a. "The communalist project." In *The next revolution*, edited by Debbie Bookchin and Blair Taylor, loc. 230–733. Brooklyn, NY: Verso. Original edition, 2002.
Bookchin, Murray. 2015b. "The future of the left." In *The next revolution*, edited by Debbie Bookchin and Blair Taylor, loc. 2487–3297. Brooklyn, NY: Verso. Original edition, 2002.
Bookchin, Murray. 2015c. "Libertarian municipalism: A politics of direct democracy." In *The next revolution*, edited by Debbie Bookchin and Blair Taylor, loc. 1524–1724. Brooklyn, NY: Verso. Original edition, 1991.
Bookchin, Murray. 2015d. "The meaning of confederalism." In *The next revolution*, edited by Debbie Bookchin and Blair Taylor, loc. 1282–1516. Brooklyn, NY: Verso. Original edition, 1990.
Bookchin, Murray. 2015e. "Nationalism and the 'National Question'." In *The next revolution*, edited by Debbie Bookchin and Blair Taylor, loc. 1905–2398. Brooklyn, NY: Verso. Original edition, 1993.
Bookchin, Murray. 2015f. "A politics for the twenty-first century." In *The next revolution*, edited by Debbie Bookchin and Blair Taylor, loc. 913–1279. Brooklyn, NY: Verso. Original edition, 1998.
Botsman, Rachel, and Roo Rogers. 2011. *What's mine is yours: How collaborative consumption is changing the way we live*. New York: Harper Collins.
Bourdieu, Pierre. 1986. "The forms of capital." In *Handbook of theory and research for the sociology of education*, edited by John Richardson, 241–258. New York: Greenwood.
Bowker, John. 1997. "Karma." In *The concise oxford dictionary of world religions*. Oxford: Oxford University Press.
Box, Richard C. 1998. *Citizen governance: Leading American communities into the 21st century*. Thousand Oaks, CA: Sage Publications.
Box, Richard C., ed. 2004. *Public administration and society: Critical issues in American governance*. Armonk, NY: M. E. Sharpe.
Box, Richard C., Gary S. Marshall, B. J. Reed, and Christine M. Reed. 2001. "New public management and substantive democracy." *Public Administration Review* 61 (5):608–619.
Box, Richard C., and Deborah A. Sagen. 1998. "Working with citizens: Breaking down barriers to citizen self-governance." In *Government is us: Public administration in an anti-government era*, edited by Cheryl Simrell King, Camilla Stivers and Collaborators, 158–174. Thousand Oaks, CA: Sage Publications.
Boyle, David, and Michael Harris. 2009. *The challenge of co-production*. London: NESTA Foundation.
Boyte, Harry C. 2005. "Reframing democracy: Goverance, civic agency, and politics." *Public Administration Review* 65 (5):536–546.
Bradford, Colin I., and Wonhyuk Lim. 2011. *Global leadership in transition: Making the G20 more effective and responsive*. Washington, DC: Brookings Institution.
Bradley, Quintin. 2012. "A 'performative' social movement: The emergence of collective contentions within collaborative governance." *Space and Polity* 16 (2):215–232.
Brady, F. Neil. 2003. "'Publics' administration and the ethics of particularity." *Public Administration Review* 63 (5):525–534.
Braidotti, Rosi. 2006. *Transpositions: On nomadic ethics*. Cambridge, MA: Polity Press.

Braidotti, Rosi. 2010. "The politics of 'life itself' and new ways of dying." In *New materialisms: Ontology, agency, and politics*, edited by Diana Coole and Samantha Frost, 201–218. Durham, NC: Duke University Press.

Braidotti, Rosi. 2013. *The posthuman*. Cambridge, MA: Polity Press.

Breck, Kent, Mike Beedle, Arie van Bennekum, Alistair Cockburn, Martin Fowler, James Grenning, Jim Highsmith, Andrew Hunt, Ron Jeffries, Jon Kern, Brian Marick, Robert C. Martin, Steve Mellor, Ken Schwaber, Jeff Sutherland, and Dave Thomas. 2001. "Manifesto for agile development." Agilemanifesto, accessed August 8, 2016. http://agilemanifesto.org/.

Breines, Wini. 1989. *Community and organization in the new left, 1962–1968: The great refusal*. New Brunswick, NJ: Rutgers University Press.

Brigg, Morgan. 2007. "Biopolitics meets terrapolitics: Political ontologies and governance in settler-colonial Australia." *Australian Journal of Political Science* 42 (3):403–417.

Briggs, John, and F. David Peat. 1999. *Seven life lessons of chaos: Spiritual wisdom from the science of change*. New York: Harper Perennial.

Brooks, Michael P. 2002. *Planning theory for practitioner*. Chicago: American Planning Association.

Brown, A. J. 2002. "Collaborative governance versus constitutional politics: Decision rules for sustainability from Australia's South East Queensland forest agreement." *Environmental Science and Policy* 5:19–32.

Brown, Charles, and Ted Toadvine, eds. 2003. *Eco-phenomenology: Back to the Earth itself*. Albany, NY: State University of New York Press.

Brown, Joseph Epes. 2007. *The spiritual legacy of the American Indian: Commemorative edition with letters while living with Black Elk, perrenial philosophy*. Bloomington, IN: World Wisdom.

Brown, Kerry A., and Robyn L. Keast. 2003. "Community-government engagement: Community connections through networked arrangements." *Asian Journal of Public Administration* 25 (1):107–132.

Brown, Tim. 2011. "Why social innovators need design thinking." *Stanford Social Innovation Review*, accessed July 11, 2017. https://ssir.org/articles/entry/why_social_innovators_need_design_thinking.

Bryer, Thomas A. 2009. "Explaining responsiveness in collaboration: Administrator and citizen role perceptions." *Public Administration Review* 69 (2):271–283.

Bryer, Thomas A. 2010. "Review: The collaborative public manager: New ideas for the twenty-first century." *Administrative Theory & Praxis* 32 (2):274–279.

Bryson, John M., Barbara C. Crosby, and Laura Bloomberg. 2014. "Public value governance: Moving beyond traditional public administration and the new public management." *Public Administration Review* 74 (4):445–456.

Buber, Martin. 1986. *I and thou*. Translated by Ronald Gregor Smith. 1st ed. New York: Scribner Classics. Original edition, 1937.

Buchanan, Mark. 2002. *Nexus: Small worlds and the groundbreaking science of networks*. Vol. 1. New York: W.W. Norton.

Bucko, Raymond A. 1998. *The Lakota ritual of the sweat lodge: History and contemporary practice*. Omaha: University of Nebraska Press.

Bullard, Robert. 2004. "Environment and morality: Confronting environmental racism in the United States." United Nations Research Institute for Social Development, accessed November 26, 2017. www.unrisd.org/80256B3C005BCCF9/search/543B2B250E64745280256B6D005788F7.

Burkhart, Brian Yazzie. 2004. "What Coyote and Thales can teach us: An outline of American Indian epistemology." In *American Indian thought*, edited by Anne Waters, 15–33. Malden, MA: Blackwell Publishing.

Burrell, Gibson, and Gareth Morgan. 2005. *Sociological paradigms and organizational analysis*. Burlington, VT: Ashgate.

Bust, Homer. 2005. "We were all indigenous, and can again become . . . " *Green Anarchy* 19 (Spring):2–3.

C40. 2017. "About." C40, accessed July 25, 2017. www.c40.org/about.

C40, and ARUP. 2017. *Deadline 2020: How cities will get the job done*. London.

Cajete, Greg, John Mohawk, and Julio Valladolid Rivera. 2008. "Re-indigenization defined." In *Original instructions: Indigenous teachings for a sustainable future*, edited by Melissa K. Nelson, 252–264. Rochester, NY: Bear & Company.

Cajete, Gregory. 2004. "Philosophy of native science." In *American Indian thought*, edited by Anne Waters, 45–57. Malden, MA: Blackwell Publishing.

Call, Lewis. 2002. *Postmodern anarchism*. Lanham, MD: Lexington Books.

Campaign Zero. n.d. "Campaign Zero: We can end police violence in America." Campaign Zero, accessed July 25, 2017. www.joincampaignzero.org/.

Capital Institute. 2011. *Field guide to investing in a resilient economy*. Greenwich, CT: Capital Institute.

Capra, Fritjof. 1983. *The turning point: Science, society, and the rising culture*. New York: Bantam Books. Original edition, 1982.

Capra, Fritjof. 1999. *The Tao of physics: An exploration of the parallels between modern physics and eastern mysticism*. Boston: Shambhala Publications, Inc.

Carlsson, Ingvar, and Shridath Ramphal. 1995. *Our global neighborhood: The report of the commission on global governance*. Oxford: The Commission on Global Governance.

Carlsson, Lars. 2000. "Policy networks as collective action." *Policy Studies Journal* 28 (3):502–520.

Carr, Adrian, and Lisa A. Zanetti. 1999. "Metatheorizing the dialectic of self and other." *American Behavioral Scientist* 43 (2):324–345.

Carson, Kevin A. 2006. *Studies in mutualist political economy*. North Charleston, SC: Booksurge LLC.

Carson, Rachel. 2002. *Silent spring*. Boston: Houghton Mifflin Company.

Carter, Jimmy. 2002. "Challenges for humanity a beginning." *National Geographic* 201 (2):2–3.

Cassidy, John. 2017. "Donald Trump's new world disorder." *The New Yorker*, January 24, accessed September 17, 2017. www.newyorker.com/news/john-cassidy/donald-trumps-new-world-disorder.

Castaneda, Carlos. 1971. *The teachings of Don Juan: A Yaqui way of knowledge*. New York: Simon and Schuster. Original edition, 1968.

Castaneda, Carlos. 1973. *A separate reality: Further conversations with Don Juan*. New York: Simon and Schuster.

Castellano, Marlene Brandt. 2000. "Updating aboriginal knowledge." In *Indigenous knowledges in global contexts: Multiple readings of our world*, edited by George J. Sefa Dei, Budd L. Hall and Dorothy Golden Rosenberg, 21–36. Toronto: University of Toronto Press.

Castells, Manuel. 2000. *The rise of network society*. 2nd ed. London: Blackwell.

Catlaw, Thomas J. 2005. "Constitution as executive order: The administrative state and the political ontology of we the people." *Administration & Society* 37 (4).

Catlaw, Thomas J. 2007a. "The effect of affect: Fear, order, and government." 20th Annual International Conference of the Public Administration Network, Harrisburg, PA.

Catlaw, Thomas J. 2007b. *Fabricating the people: Politics & administration in the biopolitical state*. Tuscaloosa, AL: University of Alabama Press.

Catlaw, Thomas J. 2007c. "From representations to compositions: Governance beyond the three-sector society." *Administrative Theory & Praxis* 29 (2):225–259.

Catlaw, Thomas J. 2007d. "Political economy interview." Tempe, AZ, January-February.

Catlaw, Thomas J. 2008. "Frederick Thayer and the structural transformation of the public sphere." *Administration & Society* 40 (4):358–383.

Catlaw, Thomas J. 2009. "Governance and networks at the limits of representation." *American Review of Public Administration* 39 (5):478–498.

Center for Servant Leadership, Robert K. Greenleaf. 2016. "What is servant leadership?" Robert K. Greenleaf Center for Servant Leadership, accessed August 4. www.greenleaf.org/what-is-servant-leadership/.

Chacón, Justin Akers, and Mike Davis. 2006. *No one is illegal: Fighting violence and state repression on the U.S.-Mexico border*. Chicago: Haymarket Books.

Chalmers, David B. 1996. *The conscious mind: In search of a fundamental theory*. Oxford: Oxford University Press.

Chen, Bin. 2008. "Assessing interorganizational networks for public service delivery: A process-perceived effectiveness framework." *Public Performance & Management Review* 31 (3):348–363.

Cheney, George. 2001. "Mondragon cooperatives." *Social Policy* 32 (2):4–9.

Cherington, Paul Terry. 1913. *Advertising as a business force: A compilation of experience records, Associated Advertising Clubs of America*. New York: Doubleday.

Chernus, Ira. 2016. *Monsters to destroy: The neoconservative war on terror and sin*. New York: Routledge.

Chisholm, Hugh. 1911. "Krause, Karl Christian Friedrich." In *Encyclopedia britannica*, edited by Hugh Chisholm. Cambridge: Cambridge University Press.

Chrislip, David D. 2002. *The collaborative leadership fieldbook: A guide for citizens and civic leaders*. San Francisco: Jossey-Bass.

Christ, Carol P. 2003. *She who changes: Reimagining the divine in the world*. New York: Palgrave Macmillan.

Clark, Barry. 1998. *Political economy: A comparative approach*. 2nd ed. Westport, CT: Praeger Publishers.

Cleary, Robert E. 1992. "Revisiting the doctoral dissertation in public administration: An examination of the dissertations of 1990." *Public Administration Review* 52 (1):55–61.

Cleary, Robert E. 2000. "The public administration doctoral dissertation reexamined: An evaluation of the dissertations of 1998." *Public Administration Review* 60 (5):446–455.

Cleveland, Harlan. 1993. *Birth of a new world: An open moment for international leadership*. San Francisco: Jossey-Bass.

Cleveland, Harlan. 2000. "Donald C. Stone lecture: The future is uncentralized." *Public Administration Review* 60 (4):293–297.

Clifford, James. 1986. "Introduction: Partial truths." In *Writing culture: The poetics and politics of ethnography*, edited by James Clifford and George E. Marcus, 1–26. Berkeley: University of California Press.

Cobb Jr., John B. 1965. *A Christian natural theology based on the thought of Alfred North Whitehead*. Philadelphia: The Westminister Press.

Cobb Jr., John B. 1981. "The political implications of Whitehead's philosophy." In *Process philosophy and social thought*, edited by John B. Cobb, Jr. and W. Widick Schroeder, 11–28. Chicago: Center for the Scientific Study of Religion.

Cobb Jr., John B. 1990. "Two types of postmodernism: Deconstruction and process." *Theology Today* 47 (2):149–158.

Cobb Jr., John B. 1993. "Process theism." In *Process theology: A basic introduction*, edited by C. Robert Mesle, loc. 1888–2101. St. Louis: Chalice Press.

Cobb Jr., John B. 2002. *Postmodernism and public policy*. Albany, NY: State University of New York Press.

Cobb Jr., John B. 2007. "Person-in-community: Whiteheadian insights into community and institution." *Organization Studies* 28 (4):567–588.

Cobb Jr., John B. 2008. *Whitehead word book*. Claremont, CA: P&F Press.

Cobb Jr., John B., and David Ray Griffin. 1976. *Process theology: An introductory exposition*. Louisville, KY: Westminster Press.

Cockburn, Alistair, and Jeffrey St. Clair. 2000. *Five days that shook the world: Seattle and beyond*. London: Verso.

Coen, David, and Mark Thatcher. 2008. "Network governance and multi-level delegation: European networks of regulatory agencies." *Journal of Public Policy* 28 (1):49–71.
Cohen, Amy J. 2008. "Negotiation, meet new governance: Interests, skills, and selves." *Law & Social Inquiry* 33 (2):503–562.
Cohen, Cathy J. 1997. "Punks, bulldaggers, and welfare queens: The radical potential of queer politics?" *GLQ* 3:437–465.
Coleman, James Samuel. 1990. *Foundations of social theory.* Cambridge, MA: Belknap Press of Harvard University Press.
Coles, Romand. 2005. "The wild patience of radical democracy: Beyond Žižek's lack." In *Radical democracy: Politics between abundance and lack*, edited by Lars Tønder and Lasse Thomassen, 68–85. New York: Manchester University Press.
Collins, Patricia Hill. 1990. *Black feminist thought: Knowledge, consciousness, and the politics of empowerment. Perspectives on gender.* Vol. 2. Boston: Unwin Hyman.
Collins, Mike. 2015. "Wall Street and the financialization of the economy." *Reinventing America*, accessed September 16. www.forbes.com/sites/mikecollins/2015/02/04/wall-street-and-the-financialization-of-the-economy/#42f14c815783.
Colombo, Emanuela, Stefano Bologna, and Diego Masera, eds. 2013. *Renewable energy for enleashing sustainable development.* Cham, Switzerland: Springer International Publishing.
Combahee River Collective. 1995. "A black feminist statement." In *Words of fire: An anthology of African-American feminist thought*, edited by Beverly Guy-Sheftall, 232–240. New York: The New Press.
Commonwealth Foundation. 1999. *Citizens and governance: Civil society in the new millennium.* London: CIVICUS.
Connelly, David R., Jing Zhang, and Sue R. Faerman. 2008. "The paradoxical nature of collaboration." In *Big ideas in collaborative public management*, edited by Lisa Blomgren Bingham and Rosemary O'Leary, 17–35. Armonk, NY: M.E. Sharpe.
Connolly, William E. 2005. "Immanence, abundance, democracy." In *Radical democracy: Politics between abundance and lack*, edited by Lars Tønder and Lasse Thomassen, 239–255. New York: Manchester University Press.
Connolly, William E. 2010. "Materialities of experience." In *New materialisms: Ontology, agency, and politics*, edited by Diana Coole and Samantha Frost, 178–200. Durham, NC: Duke University Press.
Connolly, William E. 2011. *A world of becoming.* Durham, NC: Duke University Press.
Connolly, William E. 2013. *The fragility of things: Self-organizing processes, neoliberal fantasies, and democratic activism.* Durham, NC: Duke University Press.
Considine, Mark, and Jenny M. Lewis. 2003. "Bureaucracy, network, or enterprise? Comparing models of governance in Australia, Britain, the Netherlands, and New Zealand." *Public Administration Review* 63 (2):131–140.
Cook, S., D. Noam, and Hendrik Wagenaar. 2012. " Navigating the eternally unfolding present: Toward an epistemology of practice." *The American Review of Public Administration* 42 (1):3–38.
Cooke, Bill, and Uma Kothari, eds. 2004. *Participation: The new tyranny?* London: Zed Books.
Coole, Diana. 2010. "The intertia of matter and the generativity of flesh." In *New materialisms: Ontology, agency, and politics*, edited by Diana Coole and Samantha Frost, 92–115. Durham, NC: Duke University Press.
Coole, Diana, and Samantha Frost. 2010. "Introducing the new materialisms." In *New materialisms: Ontology, agency, and politics*, edited by Diana Coole and Samantha Frost, 1–43. Durham, NC: Duke University Press.
Cooper, Andrew F., and Andrew Schrumm. 2011. "Reconciling the Gs: The G8, the G5, and the G20 in a world of crisis." In *Global financial crisis: Global impact and solutions*, edited by Paolo Savona, John J. Kirton and Chiara Oldani, 229–244. Burlington, VT: Ashgate.
Cooper, Terry L., Thomas A. Bryer, and Jack W. Meek. 2006. "Citizen-centered collaborative public management." *Public Administration Review* 66 (Special Issue):76–88.

Cordes, Colleen. 2014. "The rise of triple-bottom-line businesses." In *State of the world 2014: Governing for sustainability*, edited by Lisa Mastny, 203–214. Washington, DC: Worldwatch Institute.
Cordova, V. F. 2004. "The We and the I." In *American Indian thought*, edited by Anne Waters, 173–187. Malden, MA: Blackwell Publishing.
Council, U. S. National Research. 1999. *Our common journey: A transition towards sustainability*. Washington, DC: National Academy Press.
Cox, Robert W. 1995. "Critical political economy." In *International political economy: Understanding global disorder*, edited by Bjorn Hetne, 30–52. Halifax, Nova Scotia: Fernwood Publishing.
Crenshaw, Kimberle. 1989. "Demarginalizing the intersection of race and sex: A black feminist critique of antidiscrimination doctrine, feminist theory and antiracist politics." *University of Chicago Legal Forum* 43 (6):139–167.
Critchley, Simon. 2005. "True democracy: Marx, political subjectivity and anarchic meta-politics." In *Radical democracy: Politics between abundance and lack*, edited by Lars Tønder and Lasse Thomassen, 219–235. New York: Manchester University Press.
Crossley, Nick. 2011. *Towards relational sociology*. New York: Routledge.
Crow, Michael M., and William B. Dabars. 2015. *Designing the new American university*. Baltimore, MD: Johns Hopkins University Press.
Csikszentmihalyi, Mihaly. 1990. *Flow: The psychology of optimal experience*. New York: Harper Collins.
Cufaude, Jeffrey. 2005. "The art of facilitative leadership: Maximizing others' contributions." *Systems Thinker* 15 (10):2–5.
Cullinan, Cormac. 2014. "Governing people as members of the earth community." In *State of the world 2014: Governing for sustainability*, edited by Lisa Mastny, 72–81. Washington, DC: Worldwatch Institute.
Culp, John. 2013. "Panentheism." In *Stanford encyclopedia of philosophy*, edited by Edward N. Zalta. http://plato.stanford.edu/archives/spr2013/entries/panentheism/ Access Date: Dec 18, 2013
Cunliffe, Ann L. 2011. "Relational leadership." *Human Relations* 64 (11):1425–1449.
Dahl, Robert A. 1998. *On democracy*. New Haven, CT: Yale University Press.
Daly, Herman E., and John B. Cobb Jr. 1994. *For the common good: Redirecting the economy toward community, the environment, and a sustainable future*. 2nd ed. Boston: Beacon Press.
Daly, Mary. 1973. *Beyond God the father: Toward a philosophy of women's liberation*. Boston: Beacon Press.
Damasio, Antonio. 2010. *Self comes to mind: Constructing the conscious brain*. New York: Pantheon Books.
Daniels, Christopher P. 2012. "All my relations: A process-indigenous study in comparative ontology." Doctor of Philosophy, Religious Studies, University of Calgary.
Daniels, Peter. 2007. "Buddhism and the transformation to sustainable economies." *Society and Economy* 29 (2):155–180.
Darity, Jr., William, and Jessica Gordon Nembhard. 2000. "Racial and economic inequality: The international record." *The American Economic Review* 90 (2):308–311.
Davies, Jonathan S. 2005. "Local governance and the dialectic of hierarchy, market, and network." *Policy Studies* 26 (3/4):311–335.
Davies, Jonathan S. 2009. "The limits of joined-up government: Towards a political analysis." *Public Administration* 87 (1):80–96.
Davis, Angela. 1990. *Women, culture, & politics*. New York: Vintage Books.
Davis, John B. 2003. *The theory of the individual in economics: Identity and value. Advances in social economics*. New York: Routledge.
Day, Richard J. F. 2001. "Who is this we that gives the gift? Native American political theory and the western tradition." *Critical Horizons* 2 (2):173–201.

Day, Richard J. F. 2011. "Hegemony, affinity and the newest social movements: At the end of the 00s." In *Post-anarchism: A reader*, edited by Duane Rousselle and Sureyyya Evren, 95–116. London: Pluto Press.
Dean, Rikki John. 2017. "Beyond radicalism and resignation: The competing logics for public participation in policy decisions." *Policy & Politics* 45 (2):213–230.
deLeon, Peter. 1992. "The democratization of the policy sciences." *Public Administration Review* 52 (2):125–129.
deLeon, Peter. 1997. *Democracy and the policy sciences.* Albany, NY: State University of New York Press.
Deleuze, Gilles. 1991. *Bergsonism.* Translated by Hugh Tomlinson and Barbara Habberjam. New York: Zone Books.
Deleuze, Gilles. 1992. *The fold: Leibniz and the Baroque.* Translated by Tom Conley. Minneapolis: University of Minnesota Press.
Deleuze, Gilles. 1994. *Difference and repetition.* Translated by Paul Patton. New York: Columbia University Press.
Deleuze, Gilles. 2001. *Pure immanence: Essays on a life.* Translated by Anne Boyman. New York: Zone Books.
Deleuze, Gilles, and Félix Guattari. 1983. *Anti-oedipus: Capitalism and schizophrenia.* Minneapolis: University of Minnesota Press.
Deleuze, Gilles, and Félix Guattari. 1987. *A thousand plateaus: Capitalism and schizophrenia.* Translated by Brian Massumi. New York: Continuum.
Deloria Jr., Vine. 1999. *Spirit and reason.* Golden, CO: Fulcrum Publishing.
Denhardt, Robert B. 1981. *In the shadow of organization.* Lawrence, KS: Regents Press of Kansas.
Denhardt, Janet Vinzant, and Robert B. Denhardt. 2003. *The new public service: Serving, not steering.* New York: M. E. Sharp.
Derrida, Jacques. 1976. *Of grammatology.* Baltimore, MD: Johns Hopkins University Press.
Derrida, Jacques. 1981. *Dissemination.* Translated by Barbara Johnson. London: The Athlone Press.
Derrida, Jacques. 2005. *Rogues: Two essays on reason.* Stanford, CA: Stanford University Press.
Descartes, Rene. 1980. *Discourse on method, and meditations on first philosophy.* Translated by Donald Cress. Indianapolis: Hackett Publishing.
Desmarais, Annette Aurélie. 2007. *La Vía Campesina: Globalization and the power of peasants.* Halifax: Fernwood Publishing.
Dewey, John. 1927. "An appreciation of Henry George." School of Cooperative Individualism, accessed December 22, 2008. www.cooperativeindividualism.org/dewey_on_henry_george.html.
Dewey, John. 1934. *A common faith.* New Haven, CT: Yale University Press.
Dewey, John. 1957. *The public and its problems.* Chicago: Swallow Press. Original edition, 1927.
Dewey, John. 1958. *Experience and nature.* Mineola, NY: Dover Publications.
Dewey, John. 1993a. "Creative democracy: The task before us." In *The political writings*, edited by Debra Morris and Ian Shapiro, 240–245. Indianapolis: Hackett Publishing. Original edition, 1939.
Dewey, John. 1993b. "Philosophies of freedom." In *The political writings*, edited by Debra Morris and Ian Shapiro, 133–141. Indianapolis: Hackett Publishing. Original edition, 1928.
Dewey, John. 1999. *Individualism old and new.* Amherst, NY: Prometheus Books. Original edition, 1930.
Didonna, Fabrizio. 2009. "Introduction: Where new and old paths to dealing with suffering meet." In *Clinical handbook of mindfulness*, edited by Fabrizio Didonna, 1–14. New York: Springer Science and Business Media.
Dilthey, Wilhelm. 1988. *Introduction to the human sciences: An attempt to lay a foundation for the study of society and history.* Detroit: Wayne State University Press. Original edition, 1883.

Dimock, Marshall E. 1937. *Modern politics and administration: A study of the creative state.* New York: American Book Company.
Diwan, Romesh. 2000. "Relational wealth and the quality of life." *Journal of Socio-Economics* 29 (4):305–340.
Dixon, Chris. 2014. *Another politics: Talking across today's transformative movements.* Berkeley: University of California Press.
Donahue, John D., and Richard J. Zeckhauser. 2011. *Collaborative governance: Private roles for public goals in turbulent times.* Princeton, NJ: Princeton University Press.
Donati, Pierpaolo. 2011. *Relational sociology: A new paradigm for the social sciences.* New York: Routledge.
Donati, Pierpaolo. 2013. "The added value of social relations." *Italian Journal of Sociology of Education* 5 (1):19–35.
Donati, Pierpaolo. 2014. *Transcending modernity: The quest for a relational society.* Bologna: University of Bologna, Cesis-Department of Sociology and Business Law.
Donati, Pierpaolo. 2016. "On the social morphogenesis of citizenship: A relational approach." *Società Mutamento Politica* 7 (13):41–66.
Douglas, Mary. 1996. *Natural symbols: Explorations in cosmology.* New York: Routledge. Original edition, 1970.
Drees, William B. 1990. *Beyond the big bang: Quantum cosmologies and God.* Chicago: Open Court Publishing.
Dryzek, John S. 1982. "Policy analysis as a hermeneutic activity." *Policy Sciences* 14 (4):309–329.
Dryzek, John S. 1989. "Policy sciences of democracy." *The Journal of the Northeastern Political Science Association* 22 (1):97–118.
Dryzek, John S. 1990. *Discursive democracy: Politics, policy, and political science.* Cambridge: Cambridge University Press.
Dryzek, John S. 1993. "Policy analysis and planning: From science to argument." In *The argumentative turn in policy analysis and planning*, edited by Frank Fischer and John Forester, 213–232. Durham, NC: University of North Carolina Press.
Dryzek, John S. 2000. *Deliberative democracy and beyond: Liberals, critics, contestations.* Oxford: Oxford University Press.
Dryzek, John S. 2007. "Networks and democractic ideals: Equality, freedom, and communication." In *Theories of democratic network governance*, edited by Eva Sørensen and Jacob Torfing, 262–273. New York: Palgrave Macmillan.
Du Bois, W. E. B. 2003. *The souls of black folk.* New York: Barnes & Noble Classics.
Dubnick, Melvin J., and Elizabeth M. Meehan. 2004. "Integrative governance in Northern Ireland." In *Working paper.* Belfast, Ireland: Queen's University.
Dudley, Larkin S. 1996. "Fencing in the inherently governmental debate." In *Refounding democratic public administration: Modern paradoxes, postmodern challenges*, edited by Gary Wamsley and James F. Wolf, 68–91. Thousand Oaks, CA: Sage Publications.
Duncan, Brent. 2008. "Dynamic needs: Discovering holistic-dynamic needs beneath a rigid pyramid." *Perspective* (August/September):14–17.
Dunne, David, and Roger Martin. 2006. "Design thinking and how it will change management education: An interview and discussion." *Academy of Management Learning & Education* 5 (4):512–523.
Dupré, Judith. 2002. "s." *ENR: Engineering News-Record* 248 (8):27–29.
Duranti, Alessandro. 2010. "Husserl, intersubjectivity and anthropology." *Anthropological Theory* 10 (1):1–20.
Durkheim, Emile. 1964. *The division of labor in society.* Translated by G. Simpson. New York: Free Press of Glencoe.
Eagleton, Terry. 2003. *After theory.* New York: Basic Books.
Earth Day Network. 2017. "The history of Earth Day." Earth Day Network, accessed July 25, 2017. www.earthday.org/about/the-history-of-earth-day/.

Easwaran, Eknath. 2007. "Introduction." In *The Bagavad Gita*. Canada: Nilgiri Press.
Ebel, Antoine, and Tatiana Rinke. 2014. "Listening to the voices of young and future generations." In *State of the world 2014: Governing for sustainability*, edited by Lisa Mastny, 82–90. Washington, DC: Worldwatch Institute.
Edelenbos, Jurian. 2005. "Institutional implications of interactive governance: Insights from Dutch practice." *Governance: An International Journal of Policy, Administration, and Institutions* 18 (1):111–134.
Edelenbos, Jurian, and Ingmar van Meerkerk. 2016. "Introduction: Three reflecting perspectives on interactive governance." In *Critical reflections on interactive governance: Self organization and participation in public governance*, edited by Jurian Edelenbos and Ingmar van Meerkerk, 1–28. Cheltenham, UK: Edward Elgar.
Edelenbos, Jurian, and Erik-Hans Klijn. 2007. "Trust in complex decision-making networks: A theoretical and empirical exploration." *Administration & Society* 29 (1):25–50.
Edwards, Jason. 2010. "The materialism of historical materialism." In *New materialisms: Ontology, agency, and politics*, edited by Diana Coole and Samantha Frost, 281–298. Durham, NC: Duke University Press.
Eggers, William D., and Shalabh Kumar Singh. 2009. *The public innovator's playbook: Nurturing bold ideas in government*. Cambridge, MA: Ash Institute for Democratic Governance and Innovation.
Eichengreen, Barry. 1993. "Epilogue: Three perspectives on the Bretton Woods System." In *A retrospective on the Bretton Woods system: Lessons for international monetary reform*, edited by Michael D. Bordo and Barry Eichengreen, 621–658. Chicago: University of Chicago Press.
Eisler, Riane. 2007. *The real wealth of nations: Creating a caring economics*. Oakland, CA: Berrett-Koehler Publishers.
Elías, María Verónica. 2010. "Governance from the ground up: Rediscovering Mary Parker Follett." *Public Administration and Management* 15 (1):9–45.
Elías, María Verónica, and Mohamad G. Alkadry. 2011. "Constructive conflict, participation, and shared governance." *Administration & Society* 43 (8):869–895.
Ellwood, Robert S., and Harry Partin. 1987. *Religious and spiritual groups in modern America*. 2nd ed. New York: Pearson.
Elson, Anthony. 2017. *The global financial crisis in retrospect: Evolution, resolution, and lessons for prevention*. New York: Palgrave Macmillan.
Emerson, Kirk. 2009. "Synthesizing practice and performance in the field of environmental conflict resolution." In *The collaborative public manager: New ideas for the twenty-first century*, edited by Rosemary O'Leary and Lisa Blomgren Bingham, 215–231. Washington, DC: Georgetown University Press.
Emerson, Kirk, and Tina Nabatchi. 2015. *Collaborative governance regimes*. Washington, DC: Georgetown University Press.
Emerson, Kirk, Tina Nabatchi, and Stephen Balogh. 2012. "An integrative framework for collaborative governance." *Journal of Public Administration Research and Theory* 22 (1):1–29.
Emirbayer, Mustafa. 1997. "Manifesto for a relational sociology." *American Journal of Sociology* 103 (2):281–317.
Endenburg, Gerard. 1998. *Sociocracy: The organization of decision-making*. Delft, The Netherlands: Eburon.
Epperly, Bruce G. 2014. *Process theology: Embracing adventure with God*. Kindle ed., Topical Line Drives. Gonzalez, FL: Energion Publications.
Etzioni, Amitai. 1993. *The spirit of community: The reinvention of American society*. New York: Simon & Schuster.
Etzioni, Amitai. 1996. *The new golden rule: Community and morality in a democratic society*. New York: Basic Books.
Euro Coop. n.d. *Consumer co-operatives: Democracy, development, employment*. Brussels: Euro Coop.

Evans, Karen G. 1998. "Governance, citizenship, and the new sciences: Lessons from Dewey and Follett on realizing democratic administration." Doctor of Philosophy Dissertation, Public Administration and Public Affairs, Virginia Polytechnic Institute and State University.

Evans, Karen G. 2000. "Reclaiming John Dewey: Democracy, inquiry, pragmatism, and public management." *Administration & Society* 32 (3):308–328.

Evergreen Cooperatives. 2016. "About us." Evergreen Cooperatives, accessed August 8. www.evgoh.com/about-us/.

Evren, Süreyyya. 2011. "Introduction: How new anarchism changed the world (of opposition) after Seattle and gave birth to post-anarchism." In *Post-anarchism: A reader*, edited by Duane Rousselle and Süreyyya Evren. New York: Pluto Press.

Eylon, Dafna. 1998. "Understanding empowerment and resolving its paradox: Lessons from Mary Parker Follett." *Journal of Management History* 4 (1):16.

Eze, Michael Onyebuchi. 2008. "What is African communitarianism? Against consensus as a regulative ideal." *South African Journal of Philosophy* 27 (4):386–399.

EZLN, Ejército Zapatista de Liberación Nacional. 1996. *Second declaration of la realidad (reality) for humanity against neoliberalism.* Zapatista Army of National Liberation. http://plato.stanford.edu/archives/spr2013/entries/panentheism/

Access Date: Dec 18, 2013

Faber, Roland, Henry Krips, and Daniel Pettus. 2010. *Event and decision: Ontology and politics in Badiou, Deleuze, and Whitehead.* Newcastle: Cambridge Scholars.

Fair Trade USA. 2016. "Home page." Fair Trade USA, accessed May 18. https://fairtradeusa.org/.

Farah, Paolo Davide, and Riccardo Tremolada. 2015. "Conflict between intellectual property rights and human rights: A case study on intangible cultural heritage." *Oregon Law Review* 94 (1):125–176.

Farazmand, Ali. 1994. "The new world order and global public administration: A critical essay." In *Public administration in the global village*, edited by Jean-Claude Garcia-Zamor and Renu Khatot. Westort, CT: Praeger.

Farmer, David John. 2005. *To kill the king: Post-traditional governance and bureaucracy.* Armonk, NY: M. E. Sharpe.

Farmer, David John. 2010. *Public administration in perspective: Theory and practice through multiple lenses.* Armonk, NY: M.E. Sharpe.

Favreau, Marc, ed. 2011. *A people's history of World War II: The world's most destructive conflict, as told by the people who lived through it.* New York: The New Press.

Feldman, Martha S., and Anne M. Khademian. 2002. "To manage is to govern." *Public Administration Review* 62 (5):541–554.

Ferré, Frederick. 1998. *Knowing and value: Toward a constructive postmodern epistemology.* Albany, NY: State University of New York Press.

Fischer, Frank. 1993. "Citizen participation and the democratization of policy expertise: From theoretical inquiry to practical cases." *Policy Sciences* 26 (3):165–187.

Fischer, Frank. 2003. *Reframing public policy: Discursive politics and deliberative practices.* Oxford: Oxford University Press.

Fischer, Frank, and John Forester, eds. 1993. *The argumentative turn in policy analysis.* Durham, NC: Duke University Press.

Fisher, Max. 2013. "This map shows where the world's 30 million slaves live. There are 60,000 in the U.S." *The Washington Post*, October 17, WorldViews, accessed September 17, 2016. www.washingtonpost.com/news/worldviews/wp/2013/10/17/this-map-shows-where-the-worlds-30-million-slaves-live-there-are-60000-in-the-u-s/?utm_term=.e64bec4569a7.

Fisher, Roger, and William Ury. 1991. *Getting to yes: Negotiating agreement without giving in.* 2nd ed. New York: Houghton Mifflin Company.

Flannery, Nathaniel Parish. 2017. "Explainer: What is UNASUR?" Council of the Americas, accessed July 15, 2017. www.as-coa.org/articles/explainer-what-unasur.

Flint Rising. 2017. "About the flint rising coalition." Flint Rising, accessed November 26. http://flintrising.com/about/.

Flora, Cornelia, and Jan L. Flora. 1993. "Entrepreneurial social infrastructure: A necessary ingredient." *Annals of the American Academy of Political and Social Science* 529 (September):48–58.

Flyvbjerg, Bent. 2001. *Making social science matter: Why social inquiry fails and how it can succeed again.* Translated by Steven Sampson. Cambridge: Cambridge University Press.

Foderaro, Lisa W. 2014, September 21. "Taking a call for climate change to the streets." *New York times.* www.nytimes.com/2014/09/22/nyregion/new-york-city-climate-change-march.html.

Follett, Mary Parker. 1919. "Community is a process." *Philosophical Review* 28 (6):576–588.

Follett, Mary Parker. 1924. *Creative experience.* New York: Longmans, Green and Co. Original edition, 1924.

Follett, Mary Parker. 1998. *The new state: Group organization the solution of popular government.* University Park, PA: Pennsylvania State University Press. Original edition, 1918.

Follett, Mary Parker. 2003a. "Business as integrative unity." In *Dynamic administration: The collected papers of Mary Parker Follett*, edited by Henry C. Metcalf and Lyndall Urwick, 71–94. New York: Routledge. Original edition, 1942.

Follett, Mary Parker. 2003b. "Constructive conflict." In *Dynamic administration: The collected papers of Mary Parker Follett*, edited by Henry C. Metcalf and Lyndall Urwick, 30–49. New York: Routledge. Original edition, 1942.

Follett, Mary Parker. 2003c. "The giving of orders." In *Dynamic administration: The collected papers of Mary Parker Follett*, edited by Henry C. Metcalf and Lyndall Urwick, 50–70. New York: Routledge. Original edition, 1942.

Follett, Mary Parker. 2003d. "How must business management develop in order to possess the essentials of a profession?" In *Dynamic administration: The collected papers of Mary Parker Follett*, edited by Henry C. Metcalf and Lyndall Urwick, 117–131. New York: Routledge. Original edition, 1942.

Follett, Mary Parker. 2003e. "Leader and expert." In *Dynamic administration: The collected papers of Mary Parker Follett*, edited by Henry C. Metcalf and Lyndall Urwick, 247–269. New York: Routledge. Original edition, 1942.

Follett, Mary Parker. 2003f. "Power." In *Dynamic administration: The collected papers of Mary Parker Follett*, edited by Henry C. Metcalf and Lyndall Urwick, 95–116. New York: Routledge. Original edition, 1942.

Follett, Mary Parker. 2003g. "The psychology of consent and participation." In *Dynamic administration: The collected papers of Mary Parker Follett*, edited by Henry C. Metcalf and Lyndall Urwick, 210–229. New York: Routledge. Original edition, 1942.

Follett, Mary Parker. 2003h. "The psychology of control." In *Dynamic administration: The collected papers of Mary Parker Follett*, edited by Henry C. Metcalf and Lyndall Urwick, 183–209. New York: Routledge. Original edition, 1942.

Follett, Mary Parker. 2003i. "Some discrepancies in leadership theory and practice." In *Dynamic administration: The collected papers of Mary Parker Follett*, edited by Henry C. Metcalf and Lyndall Urwick, 270–294. New York: Routledge. Original edition, 1942.

Follett, Mary Parker. 2013a. "The basis of authority." In *Freedom and co-ordination: Lectures in business organization by Mary Parker Follett*, edited by Lyndall Urwick, 34–46. Abingdon: Routledge.

Follett, Mary Parker. 2013b. "Co-ordination." In *Freedom and co-ordination: Lectures in business organization by Mary Parker Follett*, edited by Lyndall Urwick, 61–76. Abingdon: Routledge.

Follett, Mary Parker. 2013c. *Creative experience.* Peabody, MA: Martino Fine Books.

Follett, Mary Parker. 2013d. "The essentials of leadership." In *Freedom and co-ordination: Lectures in business organization by Mary Parker Follett*, edited by Lyndall Urwick, 47–60. Abingdon: Routledge.

Follett, Mary Parker. 2013e. "The giving of orders." In *Freedom and co-ordination: Lectures in business organization by Mary Parker Follett*, edited by Lyndall Urwick, 16–33. Abingdon: Routledge.

Follett, Mary Parker. 2013f. "The illusion of final authority." In *Freedom and co-ordination: Lectures in business organization by Mary Parker Follett*, edited by Lyndall Urwick, 1–15. Abingdon: Routledge.

Follett, Mary Parker. 2013g. "The process of control." In *Freedom and co-ordination: Lectures in business organization by Mary Parker Follett*, edited by Lyndall Urwick, 77–89. Abingdon: Routledge.

Food First. 2016. "Staff: Eric Holt-Giménez." Food First, accessed August 5, 2016. https://foodfirst.org/team/eric-holt-gimenez/.

Ford, Lewis S. 1977. "An appraisal of Whiteheadian nontheism." *Southern Journal of Philosophy* 15 (1):27–35.

Forester, John. 1981. "Toward a critical theory of planning and administrative practice." *Administration & Society* 13 (2):161–205.

Forester, John. 1989. *Planning in the face of power.* Berkeley: University of California Press. Reprint, 1988.

Forester, John. 1999a. "Dealing with deep value differences." In *The consensus building handbook: A comprehensive guide to reaching agreement*, edited by Lawrence Susskind, Sarah McKearnan and Jennifer Thomas-Larmer, 463–493. Thousand Oaks, CA: Sage Publications.

Forester, John. 1999b. *The deliberative practitioner: Encouraging participatory planning processes.* Cambridge, MA: MIT Press.

Forester, John. 2009. *Dealing with differences: Dramas of mediating public disputes.* Oxford: Oxford University Press.

Foucault, Michel. 1977. "Nietzsche, genealogy, history." In *Language, counter-memory, practice: Selected essays and interviews*, edited by D. F. Bouchard. Ithaca: Cornell University Press.

Foucault, Michel. 1978. *The history of sexuality.* Vol. I. New York: Pantheon Books.

Foucault, Michel. 1980. *Power/knowledge: Selected interviews and other writings, 1972–1977.* Translated by Colin Gordon, John Mepham, Kate Soper and Leo Marshall. New York: Pantheon Books.

Foucault, Michel. 1985. *The history of sexuality: The use of pleasure.* Vol. II. New York: Pantheon Books.

Foucault, Michel. 1986. *The history of sexuality: The care of the self.* Vol. III. New York: Pantheon Books.

Foucault, Michel. 1990. *The history of sexuality: An introduction.* New York: Penguin Books.

Foucault, Michel. 1991. "Governmentality." In *The Foucault effect: Studies in governmentality*, edited by Graham Burchell, Colin Gordon and Peter Miller, 87–104. Chicago: University of Chicago Press.

The Foundation for P2P Alternatives. 2017. "About." The Foundation for P2P Alternatives, accessed September 16, 2017. https://p2pfoundation.net/the-p2p-foundation/about-the-p2p-foundation.

Fox, Charles J., and Hugh T. Miller. 1995. *Postmodern public administration: Toward discourse.* Thousand Oaks, CA: Sage Publications.

Frankenberry, Nancy. 2011. "Feminist philosophy of religion." In *Stanford encyclopedia of philosophy*, edited by Edward N. Zalta. https://plato.stanford.edu/archives/win2011/entries/feminist-religion/ Access date: Nov 7, 2013

Franks, Benjamin. 2011. "Post-anarchism: A partial account." In *Post-anarchism: A reader*, edited by Duane Rousselle and Süreyyya Evren, 168–180. New York: Pluto Press.

Fraser, Nancy, and Linda Nicholson. 1988. "Social criticism without philosophy: An encounter between feminism and postmodernism." *Theory, Culture & Society* 5:373–394.

Frawley, David. 2010. *Mantra Yoga and primal sound: Secrets of seed (bija) mantras.* Twin Lakes, WI: Lotus Press.

Frederickson, H. George. 1971. "Toward a new public administration." In *Toward a new public administration: The Minnowbrook perspective*, edited by Frank Marini, 309–331. Scranton, OH: Chandler.
Freire, Paolo. 2011. *Pedagogy of the oppressed*. Translated by Donaldo Macedo. New York: Continuum. Original edition, 1970.
Fromm, Erich. 1997. *On being human*. London: The Continuum International Publishing Group Ltd.
Fry, Brian R., and Jos C. N. Raadschelders. 2014. *Mastering public administration: From Max Weber to Dwight Waldo*. 3rd ed. Washington, DC: CQ Press.
FSRI, Forum for Sustainable and Responsible Investment. 2012. *Report on socially responsible investing trends in the United States*. Washington, DC: The Forum for Sustainable and Responsible Investment.
Fung, Archon. 2003. "Recipes for public spheres: Eight institutional design choices and their consequences." *Journal of Political Philosophy* 11 (3):338–367.
Fung, Archon. 2004. *Empowered participation: Reinventing urban democracy*. Princeton, NJ: Princeton University Press.
Fung, Archon. 2006. "Varieties of participation in complex governance." *Public Administration Review* 66:66–75.
Furman, Gail C. 2004. "The ethic of community." *Journal of Educational Administration* 42 (2):215–235.
Gadamer, Hans-Georg. 2013. *Truth and method*. Translated by Joel Weinsheimer and Donald G. Marshall. New York: Bloomsbury Academic.
Gallese, Vittorio. 2003. "The manifold nature of interpersonal relations: The quest for a common mechanism." *Philosophical Transactions: Biological Sciences* 358 (1431):517–528.
Gardner, Gary. 2015. "Mounting losses of agricultural resources." In *State of the world 2015: Confronting hidden threats to sustainability*, edited by Lisa Mastny, 65–78. Washington, DC: Island Press.
Gardner, Howard. 1983. *Frames of mind: The theory of multiple intelligences*. New York: Basic Books.
Gardner, John. 1991. *Building community*. Washington, DC: Independent Sector.
Garza, Alicia. 2014, October 7. "A herstory of the #BlackLivesMatter movement by Alicia Garza." *Feminist Wire*.
Gaventa, John. 2006. "Finding the spaces for change: A power analysis." *IDS Bulletin-Institute of Development Studies* 37 (6):23–33.
Gawthrop, Louis C. 1989. "The search for a new reality." *Public Administration Review* 49 (2):194–195.
Gazley, Beth. 2010. "Why *not* partner with local government? Nonprofit managerial perceptions of collaborative disadvantage." *Nonprofit and Voluntary Sector Quarterly* 39 (1):51–76.
Geall, Sam, and Isabel Hilton. 2014. "China's environmental governance challenge." In *State of the world 2014: Governing for sustainability*, edited by Lisa Mastny, 129–137. Washington, DC: Worldwatch Institute.
Gehani, R. Ray, and Rashmi Gehani. 2007. "Mary Parker Follett's constructive conflict: A 'psychological foundation of business administration' for innovative global enterprises." *International Journal of Public Administration* 30 (4):387–404.
Gemenne, François. 2015. "Migration as a climate adaptation strategy." In *State of the world 2015: Confronting hidden threats to sustainability*, edited by Lisa Mastny, 117–126. Washington, DC: Island Press.
George, Henry. 1929. *Progress and poverty, the remedy: An inquiry into the causes of industrial depressions and the increase of want with increase of wealth*. New York: Random House. Original edition, 1879.
George, Henry. 1941. *The science of political economy*. New York: Robert Schalkenbach Foundation. Original edition, 1897.

Gergen, Kenneth J. 2009. *Relational being: Beyond self and community*. Oxford: Oxford University Press.

Giddens, Anthony. 1984. *The constitution of society: Outline of the theory of structuration*. Berkeley: University of California Press.

Gilligan, Carol. 1982. *In a different voice*. Cambridge, MA: Harvard University Press.

Gilligan, Carol. 1995. "Hearing the difference: Theorizing connection." *Hypatia* 10 (2):120–127.

Gittell, Jody Hoffer. 2011. "New directions for relational coordination theory." In *Oxford handbook of positive organizational scholarship*, edited by Kim S. Cameron and Gretchen M. Spreitzer, 400–411. Oxford: Oxford University Press.

Goa, David J. 2005. *Mantra: Hearing the divine in India and America*. New York: Columbia University Press.

Goldman, Emma. 1913. *Syndicalism: The modern menace to capitalism*. New York: Mother Earth Publishing Association.

Goldman, Emma. 2007. *Anarchism and other essays*. Charleston, SC: BiblioBazaar.

Goldman, Emma. 2012. "Afterword to My Disillusionment in Russia." In *Red Emma speaks: An Emma Goldman reader*, edited by Alix Kates Shulman, 383–404. Amherst, NY: Humanity Books.

Goldsmith, Stephen, Gigi Georges, and Tim Glynn Burke. 2010. *The power of social innovation: How civic entrepreneurs ignite community networks for good*. New York: Wiley.

Goldstein, Jeffrey. 1999. "Emergence as a construct: History and issues." *Emergence: Complexity and Organization* 1 (1):49–72.

Goleman, Daniel. 1995. *Emotional intelligence: Why it can matter more than IQ*. New York: Bantam Books.

Goleman, Daniel. 2011. *Working with emotional intelligence*. New York: Bantam Dell.

Goodin, Robert E. 1996. *The theory of institutional design*. Cambridge: Cambridge University Press.

Goodwin, Brian. 2001. *How the leopard changed its spots: The evolution of complexity*. Princeton, NJ: Princeton University Press.

Gordon, Uri. 2007. "Anarchism reloaded." *Journal of Political Ideologies* 12 (1):29–48.

Gore, Al. 2006. *An inconvenient truth*. New York: Rodale Books.

Gould, Stephen Jay. 1992. *Ever since Darwin: Reflections in natural history*. New York: W. W. Norton & Company.

Graber, Lena, and Nikki Marquez. 2016. *Searching for sanctuary: An analysis of America's counties and their voluntary assistance with deportations*. Washington, DC: Immigrant Legal Resource Center.

Graeber, David. 2002. "The new anarchists." *New Left Review* 13 (January-February):61–73.

Graeber, David, and Andrej Grubacic. 2004. "Anarchism, or the revolutionary movement of the twenty-first century." *Z-Net, the Spirit of Resistance Lives*, 1–5, accessed February 23, 2010. http://www.zcommunications.org/anarchism-or-the-revolutionary-movement-of-the-twenty-first-century-by-david-graeber

Graham, Daniel W. 2002. "Heraclitus and Parmenides." *Presocratic Philosophy: Essays in Honour of Alexander Mourelatos*:27–44.

Graham, Daniel W. 2008. "Heraclitus." In *Stanford encyclopedia of philosophy*, edited by Edward N. Zalta. https://plato.stanford.edu/archives/fall2008/entries/heraclitus/ Access date: April 8, 2010

Granovetter, Mark S. 1973. "The strength of weak ties." *The American Journal of Sociology* 78 (6):1360–1380.

Graves, Clare W. 1970. "Levels of existence: An open system theory of values." *Journal of Humanistic Psychology* November.

Graves, Stephen R., and Thomas G. Addington. 2003. *Behind the bottom line: Powering business life with spiritual wisdom*. San Francisco: Jossey-Bass.

Gray, Barbara. 1989. *Collaborating: Finding common ground for multiparty problems*. San Francisco: Jossey-Bass.

Gray, Philip C. L. 2001. "Christian stewardship: What God expects from us." *Lay Witness*, September.

Green, Judith M. 1999. *Deep democracy: Community, diversity, and transformation*. New York: Rowman & Littlefield Publishers.

Greenberg, Edward S. 1986. *Workplace democracy: The political effects of participation*. Ithaca, NY: Cornell University Press.

Greenleaf, Robert K. 1982. *Servant as leader*. Indianapolis, IN: Robert K. Greenleaf Center.

Greenleaf, Robert K. 2002. *Servant leadership: A journey into the nature of legitimate power and greatness*. 25th Anniversary ed. Mahwah, NJ: Paulist Press.

Greenstein, Rosalind, and Yesim Sungu-Eryilmaz. 2007. "Community land trusts: A solution for permanently affordable housing." *Land Lines*:8–13.

Griffin, David Ray. 1997. *Parapsychology, philosophy, and spirituality: A postmodern exploration*. Albany, NY: State University of New York Press.

Griffin, David Ray. 2001. *Reenchantment without supernaturalism: A process philosophy of religion*. Ithaca: Cornell University Press.

Griffin, David Ray. 2004. "Panentheism: A postmodern revelation." In *In whome we live and move and have our being*, edited by Philip Clayton and Arthur Peacocke, 36–47. Grand Rapids, MI: William B. Eerdmans.

Griffin, David Ray. 2007. *Whitehead's radically different postmodern philosophy: An argument for its contemporary relevance*. Albany, NY: State University of New York Press.

Griffin, David Ray. 2008. *Unsnarling the world-knot: Consciousness, freedom, and the mind-body problem*. Eugene, OR: Wipf & Stock Publishers.

Griffin, David Ray, William A. Beardslee, and Joe Holland. 1989. *Varieties of postmodern theology*. Albany, NY: State University of New York Press.

Grof, Stanislav. 1975. *Realms of the human unconscious: Observations from LSD research*. New York: Viking Press.

Grosz, Elizabeth. 2010. "Feminism, materialism, and freedom." In *New materialisms: Ontology, agency, and politics*, edited by Diana Coole and Samantha Frost, 139–157. Durham, NC: Duke University Press.

Guggenheim, Davis. 2006. *An inconvenient truth*. United States: Paramount Classics.

Guy, Mary E., Meredith A. Newman, and Sharon H. Mastraci. 2008. *Emotional labor: Putting the service in public service*. Armonk, NY: M.E. Sharpe.

Gyekye, Kwame. 1995. *An essay on African philosophical thought: The Akan conceptual scheme*. Revised ed. Philadelphia: Temple University Press.

Gyekye, Kwame. 1997. *Tradition and modernity: Philosophical reflections on the African experience*. Oxford: Oxford University Press.

H.B.C. 2016. "What are sanctuary cities?" *The Economist*, November 22.

Haack, Susan. 2009. *Evidence and inquiry: A pragmatist reconstruction of epistemology*. Amherst, NY: Prometheus Books.

Haas, Mark L., and David W. Lesch. 2013. "Introduction." In *The Arab Spring: Change and resistance in the Middle East*, edited by Mark L. Haas and David W. Lesch. Boulder, CO: Westview Press.

Haas, Peter M. 1992. "Introduction: Epistemic communities and international policy coordination." *International Organization* 46 (1):1–35.

Haas, Tanni, and Stanley Deetz. 2000. "Between the generalized and the concrete other: Approaching organizational ethics from feminist perspectives." In *Rethinking organizational and managerial communication from feminist perspectives*, edited by Patrice Buzzanell, 24–46. Thousand Oaks, CA: Sage Publications.

Habermas, Jürgen. 1998a. *Between facts and norms*. Cambridge, MA: MIT Press.

Habermas, Jürgen. 1998b. *The inclusion of the other: Studies in political theory*. Cambridge, MA: MIT Press.

Habermas, Jürgen. 1998c. *On the pragmatics of communication.* Edited by Maeve Cooke, *Studies in contemporary German social thought.* Cambridge, MA: MIT Press.

Hajer, Maarten, and Hendrik Wagenaar. 2003. "Introduction." In *Deliberative policy analysis: Understanding governance in the network society*, edited by Maarten Hajer and Hendrik Wagenaar, 1–30. Cambridge: Cambridge University Press.

Hajnal, Peter I. 2007. *G8 System and the G20: Evolution, role and documentation.* Aldershot, UK: Ashgate.

Halden, Rolf U., and Kellog J. Schwab. 2008. *Environmental impact of industrial farm animal production. Pew commission on industrial farm animal production.* Washington, DC: Pew Commission on Industrial Farm Animal Production.

Hales, Steven D., and Timothy A. Johnson. 2003. "Endurantism, perdurantism and special relativity." *The Philosophical Quarterly* 53 (213):524–539.

Hall, Douglas John. 1990. *The steward: A biblical symbol come of age.* New York: Friendship Press.

Hall, Stuart. 1998. "Notes on deconstructing the 'popular'." In *Cultural theory and popular culture: A reader*, edited by John Storey, 442–453. Essex: Pearson Education Limited.

Hanisch, Carol. 1970. "The personal is political." In *Notes from the second year: Women's liberation, major writings of radical feminists*, edited by Shulamith Firestone and Anne Koedt, 76–78. New York: Radical Feminism.

Haraway, Donna. 1988. "Situated knowledges: The science question in feminism and the privilege of partial perspective." *Feminist Studies* 14 (3):575–599.

Hardin, Garrett. 1968. "The tragedy of the commons." *Science* 162 (3859):1243–1248.

Hardt, Michael, and Antonio Negri. 2000. *Empire.* Cambridge, MA: Harvard University Press.

Hardt, Michael, and Antonio Negri. 2005. *Multitude: War and democracy in the age of empire.* Reprint ed. New York: Penguin Books.

Harmon, Michael M. 1981. *Action theory for public administration.* New York: Longman.

Harmon, Michael M. 1990. "The responsible actor as 'tortured soul': The case of Horatio Hornblower." In *Images and identities in public administration*, edited by Henry D. Kass and Bayard L. Catron, 151–180. Thousand Oaks, CA: Sage Publications.

Harmon, Michael M. 1995. *Responsibility as paradox: A critique of rational discourse on government.* Thousand Oaks, CA: Sage Publications.

Harmon, Michael M. 2006. *Public administration's final exam: A pragmatist restructuring of the profession and the discipline.* Tuscaloosa, AL: University of Alabama Press.

Harries, Richard. 1992. *Is there a gospel for the rich? Christian obedience in capitalist world.* New York: Mowbray.

Hart, David K. 1989. "A partnership in virtue among all citizens: The public service and civic humanism." *Public Administration Review* 49 (2):101–105.

Hart, Gary. 2002. *Restoration of the republic: The Jeffersonian ideal in the 21st-century.* Oxford: Oxford University Press.

Hartley, Jean. 2006. *Innovation and its contribution to improvement: A literature review for policy-makers, policy advisors, managers and academics.* London: Department of Communities and Local Government.

Hartley, Jean, Eva Sørensen, and Jacob Torfing. 2013. "Collaborative innovation: A viable alternative to market competition and organizational entrepreneurship." *Public Administration Review* 73 (6):821–830.

Hartshorne, Charles. 1984. *Omnipotence and other theological mistakes.* Albany, NY: State University of New York Press.

Harvey, Graham. 2011. *Contemporary paganism: Religions of the earth from druids and witches to heathens and ecofeminists.* 2nd ed. New York: New York University Press.

Hawken, Paul. 2007. *Blessed unrest: How the largest social movement in history is restoring grace, justice, and beauty to the world.* New York: Penguin Books.

Hawken, Paul, Amory Lovins, and L. Hunter Lovins. 1999. *Natural capitalism: Creating the next industrial revolution.* New York: Little, Brown and Company.

Hayden, Tom, ed. 2002. *The Zapatista reader.* New York: Thuder's Mouth Press.

Healey, Patsy. 1997. *Collaborative planning: Shaping places in fragmented societies.* Hampshire, UK: Palgrave Macmillan.

Healey, Patsy. 2003. "The communicative turn in planning theory and its implications for spatial strategy formation." In *Readings in planning theory*, edited by Scott Campbell and Susan S. Fainstein, 237–255. Malden, MA: Blackwell Publishers.

Heclo, Hugh. 1978. "Issue networks and the executive establishment." In *The new American political system*, edited by Anthony King, 87–124. Washington, DC: American Enterprise Institute.

Hefner, Philip. 1993. *The human factor: Evolution, culture and religion theology and the sciences.* Minneapolis: Fortress Press.

Hegel, Georg W. F. 1977. *Phenomenology of spirit.* Translated by Arnold V. Miller. Oxford: Clarendon Press. Original edition, 1807.

Heidegger, Martin. 1992. *Parmenides.* Translated by Andre Schuwer and Richard Rojcewicz. Bloomington, IN: Indiana University Press.

Heidegger, Martin. 1996. *Being and time.* Translated by J. Stambaugh. Albany, NY: State University of New York Press.

Heidegger, Martin. 2012. *The event.* Translated by Richard Rojcewicz. Bloomington, IN: Indiana University Press.

Held, David. 1992. "Democracy: From city-states to a cosmopolitan order?" *Political Studies* 50:10–39.

Hendriks, Carolyn M. 2008. "On inclusion and network governance: The democratic disconnect of Dutch energy transitions." *Public Administration* 86 (4):1009–1031.

Henry, Ella, and Henry Pene. 2001. "Kaupapa Maori: Locating indigenous ontology, epistemology and methodology in the academy." *Organization: The Interdisciplinary Journal of Organization, Theory, and Society* 8 (2):234–242.

Henton, Doug, John Melville, Terry Amsler, and Malka Kopell. 2005. *Collaborative governance: A guide for grantmakers.* Menlo Park, CA: The William and Flora Hewlett Foundation.

Henton, Douglas, John G. Melville, and Kimberly Walesh. 1997. *Grassroots leaders for a new economy: How civic entrepreneurs are building prosperous communities.* San Francisco: Jossey-Bass.

Henton, Douglas, John G. Melville, and Kimberly Walesh. 2004. *Civic revolutionaries: Igniting the passion for change in America's communities.* San Francisco: Jossey-Bass.

Hernes, Tor. 2008. *Understanding organization as process: Theory for a tangled world.* Vol. 2, *Routledge studies in management, organisation and society.* New York: Routledge.

Herranz Jr., Joaquín. 2008. "The multisectoral trilemma of network management." *Journal of Public Administration Research & Theory* 18 (1):1–31.

Hertting, Nils, and Evert Vedung. 2012. "Purposes and criteria in network governance evaluation: How far does standard evaluation vocabulary takes us?" *Evaluation* 18 (1):27–46.

High Commissioner for Refugees. 2017a. "Figures at a glance." High Commissioner for Refugees, accessed September 15, 2017. www.unhcr.org/en-us/figures-at-a-glance.html.

High Commissioner for Refugees. 2017b. "Syria emergency." High Commissioner for Refugees, accessed September 2, 2017. www.unhcr.org/en-us/syria-emergency.html.

Hill, Carolyn J., and Laurence E. Lynn, Jr. 2005. "Is hierarchical governance in decline? Evidence from the empirical research." *Journal of Public Administration Research & Theory* 15:173–195.

Hisschemöller, Matthijs, and Robert Hoppe. 1995. "Coping with intractable controversies: The case for problem structuring in policy design and analysis." *Knowledge and Policy* 8 (4):40–60.

Hock, Dee. 2000. *Birth of the chaordic age.* Oakland, CA: Berrett-Koehler Publishers.

Holacracy One. 2016. "What companies are using holacracy?" Holacracy One, accessed August 5. http://wiki.holacracy.org/index.php?title=FAQ.

Holm, Wayne, Irene Silentman, and Laura Wallace. 2003. "Situational Navajo: A school-based, verb-centered way of teaching Navajo." In *Nurturing native languages*, edited by Jon

Reyhner, Octaviana V. Trujillo, Roberto Luis Carrasco and Louise Lockard, 25–52. Flagstaff, AZ: Northern Arizona University.
Holt-Giménez, Eric. 2006. *Campesino a campesino: Voices from Latin America's farmer to farmer movement for sustainable agriculture.* Oakland, CA: Food First Books.
Holt-Giménez, Eric. 2009. "From food crisis to food sovereignty: The challenge of social movements." *Monthly Review* 61 (3):142–156.
Holt-Giménez, Eric. 2011a. "Food security, food justice, or food sovereignty?: Crises, food movements, and regime change." In *Cultivating food justice: Race, class, and sustainability*, edited by Alison Hope Alkon and Julian Agyeman, 311–330. Cambridge, MA: MIT Press.
Holt-Giménez, Eric. 2011b. "Introduction: Food movements unite! Strategies to transform our food systems." In *Food movements unite! Strategies to transform our food systems*, edited by Samir Amin. Oakland, CA: Food First Books.
Holt-Giménez, Eric, and Annie Shattuck. 2011. "Synopsis: Food movements unite! Making a new food system possible." In *Food movements unite! Strategies to transform our food systems*, edited by Samir Amin. Oakland, CA: Food First Books.
hooks, bell. 1990. *Yearning: Race, gender, and cultural politics.* Boston: South End Press.
Hoppe, Robert. 2011. "Institutional constraints and practical problems in deliberative and participatory policy making." *Policy & Politics* 39 (2):163–186.
Hoppe, Robert, Henk van de Graaf, and Erik Besseling. 1995. "Successful policy formulation processes: Lessons from fifteen case experiences in five Dutch departments." *Acta Politica* 30 (2):153–188.
Horton, Myles, and Freire Paulo. 1990. "We make the road by walking: Conversations on education and social change." In *We make the road by walking: Conversations on education and social change*, edited by Brenda Bell, John Gaventa and John Peters. Philadelphia, PA: Temple University Press.
Howe, Louis E. 2006. "Enchantment, weak ontologies, and administrative ethics." *Administration & Society* 38 (4):422–446.
Hughes, Stan. 2010. *Medicine seeker.* Nashville, IN: NorLightsPress.
Hull, Gloria T., Patricia Bell Scott, and Barbara Smith, eds. 1982. *All the women are white, all the blacks are men, but some of us are brave.* Old Westbury, NY: The Feminist Press.
Hummel, Ralph P., and Camilla Stivers. 1998. "Government isn't us: The possibility of democratic knowledge in representative government." In *Government is us: Public administration in an anti-government era*, edited by Cheryl Simrell King, Camilla Stivers and Collaborators, 28–48. Thousand Oaks, CA: Sage Publications.
Hunt, Rockwell D. 1937. "Co-opetition." *Los Angeles Times*, November 20, A, 4.
Huntington, Samuel P. 1996. *The clash of civilizations and the remaking of world order.* New York: Simon and Schuster.
Husserl, Edmund. 1982. *General introduction to a pure phenomenology.* Translated by F. Kerston. Boston: Kluwer. Original edition, 1931.
Husserl, Edmund. 1989. *Ideas pertaining to a pure phenomenology and to a phenomenological philosophy: Second book.* Translated by Richard Rojcewicz and André Schuwer. Boston: Kluwer Academic Publishers. Original edition, 1912.
Hutchins, Edwin. 2010. "Cognitive ecology." *Topics in Cognitive Science* 2:705–715.
Hutchins, Edwin. 2014. "The cultural ecosystem of human cognition." *Philosophical Psychology* 27 (1):34–49.
Huutoniemi, Katri. 2014. "Introduction: Sustainability, transdisciplinarity, and the complexity of knowing." In *Transdisciplinary sustainability studies: A heuristic approach*, edited by Katri Huutoniemi and Petri Tapio, 1–20. New York: Routledge.
Huxham, Chris. 1996. "Collaboration and collaborative advantage." In *Creating collaborative advantage*, edited by Chris Huxham, 1–18. Thousand Oaks, CA: Sage Publications.
Huxham, Chris. 2000. "The challenge of collaborative governance." *Public Management: An International Journal of Research and Theory* 2 (3):337–358.

Huxham, Chris, and David MacDonald. 1992. "Introducing collaborative advantage: Achieving inter-organizational effectiveness through meta-strategy." *Management Decision* 30 (3):50–56.

Huxham, Chris, and Siv Vangen. 2000. "Ambiguity, complexity and dynamics in the membership of collaboration." *Human Relations* 53 (6):771–806.

Huxley, Julian. 1964. "The new divinity." In *Essays of a humanist*, 218–226. London: Chatto & Windus.

IAP2, International Association for Public Participation. 2007. *Spectrum of public participation*. Thornton, CO: International Association for Public Participation.

IATFSSE, Inter-Agency Task Force on Social and Solidarity Economy. 2014. *Social and solidarity economy and the challenge of sustainable development*. Geneva: United Nations.

ICRC, International Committee of the Red Cross. n.d. "Resolutions of the Geneva International Conference, Geneva, 26–29 October 1863." International Committee of the Red Cross, accessed July 15, 2017. https://ihl-databases.icrc.org/applic/ihl/ihl.nsf/Treaty.xsp?documentId=5120E889210B512AC12563CD002D65DD&action=openDocument.

Immerwahr, Daniel. 2015. *Thinking small: The United States and the lure of community development*. Cambridge, MA: Harvard University Press.

Imperial, Mark T. 2005. "Using collaboration as a governance strategy: Lessons from six watershed management programs." *Administration & Society* 37 (3):281–320.

Innes, Judith E., and David E. Booher. 1999. "Consensus building and complex adaptive systems: A framework for evaluating collaborative planning." *Journal of the American Planning Association* 65 (4):412–423.

Innes, Judith E., and David E. Booher. 2003. "The impact of collaborative planning on governance capacity." In *Working paper*. Berkeley: Institute of Urban and Regional Development.

Institute of Cultural Affairs. 2011. "ICA certified top facilitator program." Institute of Cultural Affairs, accessed April 15, 2011. www.ica-usa.org/?page=topfacilitator.

IPCC, International Panel on Climate Change. 2014. "Summary for policymakers." In *Climate change 2014: Impacts, adaptation, and vulnerability. Part A: Global and sectoral aspects. Contribution of working group II to the fifth assessment report of the intergovernmental panel on climate change*, edited by C. B. Field, V. R. Barros, D. J. Dokken, K. J. Mach, M. D. Mastrandrea, T. E. Bilir, M. Chatterjee, K. L. Ebi, Y. O. Estrada, R. C. Genova, B. Girma, E. S. Kissel, A. N. Levy, S. MacCracken, P. R. Mastrandrea and L. L. White. Cambridge: Cambridge University Press.

Irfan, Umair. 2016, November 3. "Climate pledges will fall short of needed 2 degree C limit." *Scientific American*.

Ivanova, Maria. 2014. "Assessing the outcomes of Rio+20." In *State of the world 2014: Governing for sustainability*, edited by Lisa Mastny, 138–151. Washington, DC: Worldwatch Institute.

Jackson, Richard. 2005. *Writing the war on terrorism: Language, politics, and counter-terrorism*. New York: Manchester University Press.

James, William. 1890. *The principles of psychology*. New York: H. Holt and Company.

James, William. 1909. *A pluralistic universe*. New York: Longmans, Green.

James, William. 1955. *Pragmatism and four essays from the meaning of truth*. New York: Meridian Books. Original edition, 1907.

James, William. 1997. *The varieties of religious experience: A study in human nature*. New York: Simon & Schuster. Original edition, 1902.

Janssen, Ronald. 2010. *Greece and the IMF: Who exactly is being saved?* Washington, DC: Center for Economic Policy Research.

Jenkins, Willis. 2003. "Biodiversity and salvation: Thomasitic roots for environmental ethics." *Journal of Religion* 83 (3):401–420.

Jenkins-Smith, Hank C. 1990. *Democratic politics and policy analysis*. New York: Harcourt Brace.

Jeppesen, Sandra. 2011. "Things to do with poststructuralism in a life of anarchy: Relocating the outpost of post-anarchism." In *Post-anarchism: A reader*, edited by Duane Rousselle and Süreyyya Evren, 151–159. New York: Pluto Press.

Jessop, Bob. 2004. "Multi-level governance and multi-level meta-governance." In *Multi-level governance*, edited by Ian Bache and Matthew Flinders, 49–74. Oxford: Oxford University Press.

Johnson, Steven. 2001. *Emergence: The connected lives of ants, brains, cities, and software*. New York: Scribner.

Jojola, Ted. 2004. "Notes on identity, time, space, and place." In *American Indian thought*, edited by Anne Waters, 87–96. Malden, MA: Blackwell Publishing.

Joseph, Lawrence E. 1986. "Britain's whole earth guru." *The New York Times Magazine*, November 23.

Juarez, Paula, Bálint Balázs, Florencia Trentini, Anna Korzenszky, and Lucas Becerra. 2015. "WP4 case study report: La Via Campesina." In *Transformative social innovation theory*. Bernal, Argentina: National University of Quilmes.

Jun, Jong S. 2002. "New governance in civil society: Changing responsibility of public administration." In *Rethinking administrative theory: The challenge of the new century*, edited by Jong S. Jun, 297–307. Westport, CT: Praeger Publishers.

Jun, Nathan. 2011. "Reconsidering post-structuralism and anarchism." In *Post-anarchism: A reader*, edited by Duane Rousselle and Süreyyya Evren, 231–249. New York: Pluto Press.

Jung, Carl Gustav. 1923. *Psychological types*. Translated by H. Godwyn Baynes. New York Harcourt Brace and Company.

Jung, Carl Gustav. 1969. *The archetypes and the collective unconscious*. Princeton, NJ: Princeton University Press.

Jung, Carl Gustav. 1970. *Collected works of C. G. Jung*. Translated by Gerhard Adler and R. F. C. Hull. 2nd ed. Vol. Book 8. Princeton, NJ: Princeton University Press.

Jung, Carl Gustav. 1971. "Collected works." In *The portable Jung*, edited by Joseph Campbell. New York: Penguin Books. Original edition, 1930.

Jung, Carl Gustav. 2010. *Dreams*. Translated by R. F. C Hull. Princeton, NJ: Princeton University Press.

Kaag, John. 2008. "Women and forgotten movements in American philosophy: The work of Ella Lyman Cabot and Mary Parker Follett." *Transactions of the Charles S. Peirce Society* 44 (1):134–157.

Kaboolian, Linda. 1998. "The new public management: Challenging the boundaries of the management vs. administration debate." *Public Administration Review* 58 (3):189–193.

Kahne, Joseph. 1996. *Reframing educational policy: Democracy, community, and the individual, advances in contemporary educational thought series*. New York: Teachers College Press.

Kaner, Sam, Lenny Lind, Catherine Toldi, Sarah Fisk, and Duane Berger. 1996. *Facilitator's guide to participatory decision-making*. Gabriola Island, BC: New Society Publishers.

Kant, Immanuel. 1998. *Critique of pure reason*. Cambridge: Cambridge University Press.

Kass, Henry D. 1990. "Stewardship as a fundamental element in images of public administration." In *Images and identities in public administration*, edited by Henry D. Kass and Bayard L. Catron, 113–131. Thousand Oaks, CA: Sage Publications.

Kauffman, Stuart A. 1993. *The origins of order: Self-organization and selection in evolution*. Oxford: Oxford University Press.

Kauffman, Stuart A. 1995. *At home in the universe: The search for laws of self-organization and complexity*. Oxford: Oxford University Press.

Kauffman, Stuart A. 2010. *Reinventing the sacred: A new view of science, reason, and religion*. New York: Basic Books.

Kaufman, Cynthia. 2003. *Ideas for action: Relevant theory for radical change*. Boston: South End Press.

Kaufmann, Daniel, Aart Kraay, and Massimo Mastruzzi. 2009. *Governance matters VIII: Aggregate and individual governance indicators 1996–2008*. Geneva: The World Bank.

Kearney, Richard 2001. *The God who may be: A hermeneutics of religion*. Bloomington, IN: Indiana University Press.

Kearns, Laurel. 1996. "Saving the creation: Christian environmentalism in the United States." *Sociology of Religion* 57 (Spring):55–70.

Keast, Robyn L. 2016. "Why blue box thinking is not good for collaboration." In *Research raves*. Sydney: Southern Cross University School of Business and Tourism.

Keast, Robyn L., and Kerry A. Brown. 2002. "The government service delivery project: A case study of the push and pull of central government coordination." *Public Management Review* 4 (4):439–459.

Keast, Robyn L., and Myrna P. Mandell. 2013. "Network performance: A complex interplay of form and action." *International Journal of Public Administration* 18 (2):27–45.

Keast, Robyn L., Myrna P. Mandell, Kerry A. Brown, and Geoffrey Woolcock. 2004. "Network structures: Working differently and changing expectations." *Public Administration Review* 64 (3):363–371.

Keating, AnaLouise. 2013. *Transformation now! Toward a post-oppositional politics of change*. Chicago: University of Illinois Press.

Keller, Catherine. 2003. *Face of the deep: A theology of becoming*. New York: Routledge.

Kelley, Colin P., Shahrzad Mohtadi, Mark A. Cane, Richard Seager, and Yochanan Kushnir. 2015. "Climate change in the Fertile Crescent and implications of the recent Syrian drought." *Proceedings of the National Academy of Sciences* 112 (11):3241–3246.

Kelly, Rita Mae. 1998. "An inclusive democratic polity, representative bureaucracies, and the new public management." *Public Administration Review* 58 (3):201–208.

Keohane, Robert O., and Joseph S. Nye. 2000. "Introduction." In *Governance in a globalizing world*, edited by Joseph S. Nye and John D. Donahue, 1–41. Washington, DC: Brookings Institution.

Keohane, Robert O., and Joseph S. Nye. 2003. "Redefining accountability for global governance." In *Governance in a global economy*, edited by Miles Kahler and David Lake, 386–411. Princeton, NJ: Princeton University Press.

Kettl, Donald F. 2000. "The transformation of governance: Globalization, devolution, and the role of government." *Public Administraiton Review* 60 (6):488–497.

Kettl, Donald F. 2002. *The transformation of governance: Public administration for the twenty-first century America*. Baltimore, MD: Johns Hopkins University Press.

Kettl, Donald F. 2006. "Managing boundaries in American administration: The collaborative imperative." *Public Administration Review* 66 (s1):10–19.

Kickert, Walter J. M., Erik-Hans Klijn, and Joop F. M. Koppenjan. 1997. "Introduction: A management perspective on policy networks." In *Managing complex networks*, edited by Walter J. M. Kickert, Erik-Hans Klijn and Joop F. M. Koppenjan, 1–13. Thousand Oaks, CA: Sage Publications.

Kickert, Walter J. M., and Joop F. M. Koppenjan. 1997. "Public management and network management." In *Managing complex networks*, edited by Walter J. M. Kickert, Erik-Hans Klijn and Joop F. M. Koppenjan, 35–60. Thousand Oaks, CA: Sage Publications.

Kim, Joohan, and Eun Joo Kim. 2008. "Theorizing dialogic deliberation: Everyday political talk as communicative action and dialogue." *Communication Theory* 18 (1):51–70.

King, Deborah K. 1995. "Multiple jeopardy, multiple consciousness: The context of a black feminist ideology." In *Words of fire: An anthology of African-American feminist thought*, edited by Beverly Guy-Sheftall, 294–317. New York: The New Press.

King, Cheryl Simrell, ed. 2011. *Government is us 2.0*. Armonk, NY: M.E. Sharpe.

King, Cheryl Simrell, Kathryn M. Feltey, and Bridget O. Susel. 1998. "The question of participation: Toward authentic participation in public administration." *Public Administration Review* 58 (4):317–326.

King, Cheryl Simrell, and Lisa A. Zanetti. 2005. *Transformational public service: Portraits of theory in practice*. Armonk, NY: M. E. Sharpe.

Kirton, John J., Chiara Oldani, and Paolo Savona. 2011. "Introduction and analysis." In *Global financial crisis: Global impact and solutions*, edited by Paolo Savona, John J. Kirton and Chiara Oldani, 3–17. Burlington, VT: Ashgate.

Kirton, John J., and Radoslava N. Stefanova. 2017. *The G8, the United Nations, and conflict prevention.* London: Routledge.

Klein, Naomi. 2004. "The unknown icon." In *¡Ya Basta! Ten years of the Zapatista uprising: Writings of Subcomandante Insurente Marcos*, edited by Žiga Vodovnik, 15–22. Oakland, CA: AK Press.

Klickert, Walter J. M., Erik-Hans Klijn, and Joop F. M. Koppenjan. 1997. "Introduction." In *Managing complex networks: Strategies for the public sector*, edited by Walter J. M. Klickert, Erik-Hans Klijn and Joop F. M. Koppenjan. Thousand Oaks, CA: Sage Publications.

Klijn, Erik-Hans. 1996. "Analyzing and managing policy processes in complex networks: A theoretical examination of the concept policy network and its problems." *Administration & Society* 28 (1):90–119.

Klijn, Erik-Hans. 2001. "Rules as institutional context for decision making in networks: The approach to postwar housing districts in two cities." *Administration & Society* 33 (2):133–164.

Klijn, Erik-Hans, and Joop F. M. Koppenjan. 2000. "Public management and policy networks: Foundations of a network approach to governance." *Public Management* 2 (2):135–158.

Klijn, Erik-Hans, and Joop F. M. Koppenjan. 2016. *Governance networks in the public sector.* New York: Routledge.

Klijn, Erik-Hans, and Chris Skelcher. 2007. "Democracy and governance networks: Compatible or not?" *Public Administration* 85 (3):587–608.

Klingner, Donald E. 2004. "Globalization, governance, and the future of public administration: Can we make sense out of the fog of rhetoric surrounding the terminology?" *Public Administration Review* 64 (6):737–743.

Knitter, Paul F. 2002. *Introducing theologies of religions.* Maryknoll, NY: Orbis Books.

Knuchel, Francois. 2017. "Who (what organizations) is using sociocracy?" SociocracyUK, accessed August 5. http://sociocracyuk.ning.com/forum/topics/who-what-organisations-is-using-sociocracy.

Koestler, Arthur. 1967. *The ghost in the machine.* London: Hutchinson.

Kolb, Deborah M. 1996. "The love for three oranges or: What did we miss about Ms. Follett in the library?" *Negotiation Journal* 11 (4):339–348.

Koliba, Christopher, Jack W. Meek, and Asim Zia. 2011. *Governance networks in public administration and public polic.* New York: CRC Press, Taylor and Francis.

Kooiman, Jan. 2001. *Interactive governance.* London: Routledge.

Kooiman, Jan. 2003. *Governing as governance.* Thousand Oaks, CA: Sage Publications.

Koontz, Thomas. 2006. "Collaboration for sustainability? A framework for analyzing government impacts in collaborative-environmental management." *Sustainability: Science, Practice, & Policy* 2 (1):15–25.

Kopan, Tal. 2017, January 25. "What are sanctuary cities, and can they be defunded?" *CNN.* http://edition.cnn.com/2017/01/25/politics/sanctuary-cities-explained.

Kopkind, Andrew. 2002. "Opening shots." In *The Zapatista reader*, edited by Tom Hayden, 19–21. New York: Thuder's Mouth Press. Original edition, 1994.

Koppenjan, Joop, and Erik-Hans Klijn. 2004. *Managing uncertainties in networks.* London: Routledge.

Koppenjan, Joop F. M. 2007. "Consensus and conflict in policy networks: Too much or too little?" In *Theories of democratic governance*, edited by Eva Sørensen and Jacob Torfing. New York: Palgrave Macmillan.

Korten, David C. 2006. *The great turning: From empire to Earth community.* Bloomfield, CT: Kumarian Press.

Kouzmin, Alexander, Matthew T. Witt, Lance deHaven-Smith, and Kym Thorne. 2009. "Economic delusions and denial: Modernist and postmodernist strains." *Administrative Theory & Praxis* 31 (3):424–431.

Krimerman, Leonard I., and Frank Lindenfeld. 1992. *When workers decide: Workplace democracy takes root in North America.* Philadelphia, PA: New Society Publishers.

Kropotkin, Peter. 1902. *Mutual aid: A factor of evolution.* London: Peter Heinemann.

Krupp, Sherman R. 1961. *Pattern in organization analysis: A critical examination.* New York: Holt, Rinehart and Winston.
Kuhn, Thomas. 1996. *The structure of scientific revolutions.* 3rd ed. Chicago: University of Chicago Press.
La Vía Campesina. 2008. Declaration of Maputo: V International Conference of La Vía Campesina, Maputo, Mozambique, October 19–22.
La Vía Campesina. 2017. *Annual report 2016.* Harare, Zimbabwe: La Vía Campesina.
Lacan, Jacques. 1956. *The language of the self: The function of language in psychoanalysis.* Baltimore: Johns Hopkins University Press.
Laclau, Ernesto. 1996. *Emancipation(s).* London: Verso.
Laing, R. D. 2001. *The divided self: An existential study in sanity and madness.* Vol. 1, *R. D. Laing: Selected Works.* New York: Routledge. Original edition, 1964.
Lakoff, George. 2003. "Embodied mind, and how to live with one." In *The nature and limits of human understanding*, edited by Anthony Sanford. Dorsett, UK: T&T Clark International.
Lampmann, Erik. 2016. "Queerness and the next system: Opening up the discussion." http://thenextsystem.org/queerness-and-the-next-system-opening-up-the-discussion/?mc_cid=a9c2284e79&mc_eid=cab68c499e.
LAS, League of Arab States. 1945. Pact of the League of Arab States, March 22.
Lasswell, Harold D. 1950. *Politics: Who gets what, when, how.* New York: McGraw-Hill.
Latour, Bruno. 1993. *We have never been modern.* Translated by Catherine Porter. Cambridge, MA: Harvard University Press.
Latour, Bruno. 1999. *Pandora's hope: Essays on the reality of social studies.* Cambridge, MA: Harvard University Press.
Latour, Bruno. 2011. "Foreword." In *Thinking with Whitehead: A free and wild creation of concepts.* Cambridge, MA: Harvard University Press.
Lave, Jean, and Etienne Wenger. 1991. *Situated learning: Legitimate peripheral participation.* Cambridge: Cambridge University Press.
Laville, Jean-Louis. 2013. *The social and solidarity economy: A theoretical and plural framework.* Geneva: United Nations Research Institute for Social Development.
Leach, William D. 2006. "Collaborative public management and democracy: Evidence from western watershed partnerships." *Public Administration Review* (SI):100–112.
Leach, William D., and Neil W. Pelkey. 2001. "Making watershed partnerships work: A review of the empirical literature." *Journal of Water Resources Planning and Management* 127 (6):378–385.
Leach, William D., Neil W. Pelkey, and Paul A. Sabatier. 2002. "Stakeholder partnerships as collaborative policymaking: Evaluation criteria applied to watershed management in California and Washington." *Journal of Policy Analysis and Management* 21 (4):645–670.
Lee, Frederic. 2009. *A history of heterodox economics: Challenging the mainstream in the twentieth century.* New York: Routledge.
Lee, William R., ed. 2002. *Clare W. Graves: Levels of existence.* Santa Barbara, CA: ECLET Publishing.
Lemos, Maria Carmen, and Arun Agrawal. 2006. "Environmental governance." *Annual Review of Environment and Resources* 31:297–325.
Lemus, Blanca, and David Barkin. 2013. *Rethinking the social and solidarity economy in light of community practice.* Geneva: United Nations Research Institute for Social Development.
Levine, David P. 2011. *The capacity for civic engagement: Public and private worlds of the self.* Vol. 1. New York: Palgrave Macmillan.
Levy, Glen. 2009. "A brief history of the G-8." *Time.*
Likert, Rensis. 1967. *The human organization: Its management and value.* New York: McGraw-Hill.
Lindblom, Charles E. 2004. "The science of 'muddling through'." In *Classics in public administration*, edited by Jay M. Shafritz, Albert C. Hyde and Sandra J. Parkes, 177–187. Belmont, CA: Wadsworth/ Thompson Learning. Original edition, 1959.

Lindblom, Charles E., and Edward J. Woodhouse. 1993. *The policy-making process.* 3rd ed. Upper Saddle River, NJ: Prentice Hall.

Liu, Eric, and Nick Hanauer. 2011. *The gardens of democracy: A new American story of citizenship, the economy, and the role of government.* Seattle: Sasquatch Books.

Llinas, Rodolfo R. 2001. *I of the vortex: From neurons to self.* Cambridge, MA: MIT Press.

Lloyd, Genevieve. 1996. *Spinoza and ethics.* New York: Routledge.

Local Harvest. 2016. "About." Local Harvest, accessed July 15, 2017. www.localharvest.org/csa/.

Lokensgard, Kenneth Hayes. 2010. *Blackfoot religion and the consequences of cultural commoditization.* Burlington, VT: Ashgate.

Loomer, Bernard. 1976a. "Two conceptions of power." *Process Studies* 6 (1):5–32.

Loomer, Bernard. 1976b. "Two conceptions of power." *Criterion* 15 (1):7–29.

Lorde, Audre. 1995. "Age, race, class, and sex: Women redefining difference." In *Words of fire: An anthology of African-American feminist thought*, edited by Beverly Guy-Sheftall, 284–291. New York: The New Press.

Lorde, Audre. 2007. "The master's tools will never dismantle the master's house." In *Sister outsider: Essays and speeches*, edited by Audre Lorde, 110–114. Berkeley, CA: Crossing Press. Original edition, 1984.

Love, Jeannine M., and Margaret Stout. 2018. "Integrative governance: From theory to practice." Public Administration Theory Network, Cleveland, Ohio, June 1–3.

Lovelock, James E. 1972. "Gaia as seen through the atmosphere." *Atmospheric Environment* 6 (8):579–580.

Lovelock, James E. 1995. *The ages of Gaia: A biography of our living Earth.* New York: W.W. Norton & Company.

Lovelock, James E., and Lynn Margulis. 1974. "Atmospheric homeostasis by and for the biosphere: The Gaia hypothesis." *Tellus* 2 (1–2).

Lund, Margaret. n.d. *Solidarity as a business model: A multi-stakeholder cooperatives manual.* Kent, OH: Cooperative Development Center, Kent State University.

LVEJO, Little Village Environmental Justice Organization. 2014. "Mission & vision statement." Little Village Environmental Justice Organization, accessed November 26, 2017. http://lvejo.org/our-mission/mission-vision-statement/.

Lykes, M. Brinton. 1985. "Gender and individualistic vs. collectivist bases for notions about the self." *Journal of Personality* 53 (2):356–383.

Lyons, Nona Plessner. 1983. "Two perspectives: On self, relationships, and morality." *Harvard Educational Review* 53 (2):125–145.

MacAllister, James. 2011. "Nested communities." In *Chimeras and consciousness: Evolution of the sensory self*, edited by Lynn Margulis, Celeste A. Asikainen and Wolfgang E. Krumbein, 91–106. Cambridge, MA: MIT Press.

Maddock, Su, and Marion Mcalpine. 2006. "An inspiration for our time: Mary Parker Follett (1968–1933)." *The British Journal of Leadership in Public Services* 2 (2):44–48.

Madge, Clare. 1992. "Boundary disputes: Comments on sidaway (1992)." *Area* 25 (3):294–299.

Mallin, Michael A., and Lawrence B. Cahoon. 2003. "Industrial animal production: A major source of nutrient and microbial pollution." *Population and Environment* 24 (5):369.

Mandell, Myrna P. 1999. "Community collaborations: Working through network structures." *Policy Studies Review* 16 (1):42–64.

Mandell, Myrna P., and Robyn L. Keast. 2007. "Evaluating network arrangements: Toward revised performance measures." *Public Performance & Management Review* 30 (4):574–597.

Mandell, Myrna P., Robyn L. Keast, and Dan Chamberlain. 2016. "Collaborative networks and the need for a new management language." *Public Management Review* 19 (3):326–341.

Mannheim, Karl. 1997. *Ideology and utopia; an introduction to the sociology of knowledge, international library of psychology, philosophy and scientific method.* New York: Harcourt, Brace and Company. Original edition, 1936.

Mansbridge, Jane J. 1980. *Beyond adversary democracy.* New York: Basic Books.

Mansbridge, Jane J. 1990. *Beyond self-interest.* Chicago: University of Chicago Press.
Mansbridge, Jane J., Janette Hartz-Karp, Matthew Amengual, and John Gastil. 2006. "Norms of deliberation: An inductive study." *Journal of Public Deliberation* 2 (1):1–47.
Marchart, Oliver. 2005. "The absence at the heart of presence: Radical democracy and the 'ontology of lack'." In *Radical democracy: Politics between abundance and lack*, edited by Lars Tønder and Lasse Thomassen, 17–31. New York: Manchester University Press.
Marcus, George E. 1986. "Contemporary problems of ethnography in the modern world system." In *Writing culture: The poetics and politics of ethnography*, edited by James Clifford and George E. Marcus, 165–193. Berkeley: University of California Press.
Marett, Robert R. 1914. *The threshold of religion.* 2nd ed. London: Methuen & Co. Ltd. Original edition, 1909.
Margulis, Lynn. 1999. *Symbiotic planet: A new look at evolution.* New York: Basic Books.
Margulis, Lynn, Celeste A. Asikainen, and Wolfgang E. Krumbein, eds. 2011. *Chimeras and consciousness: Evolution of the sensory self.* Cambridge, MA: MIT Press.
Maroukis, Thomas C. 2012. *The peyote road: Religious freedom and the native American Church.* Norman, OK: University of Oklahoma Press.
Marques, Joana S. 2013. *Social and solidarity economy: Between emancipation and reproduction.* Geneva: United Nations Research Institute for Social Development.
Marshall, Peter. 1993. *Demanding the impossible: A history of anarchism.* London: Harper Perennial.
Martínez Torres, María Elena, and Peter M. Rosset. 2010. "La Vía Campesina: The birth and evolution of a transnational social movement." *Journal of Peasant Studies* 37 (1):149–175.
Marx, Karl. 1967. *Critique of Hegel's "Philosophy of right."* Cambridge: Cambridge University Press.
Marx, Karl. 2008. *Critique of the Gotha Program.* Rockville, MD: Wildside Press. Original edition, 1875.
Marx, Karl, and Friedrich Engels. 1998. *The communist manifesto: A modern edition.* New York: Verso. Original edition, 1848.
Maryboy, Nancy C. 2004. "Balancing the flux: A native woman's views of the language of spirituality." *ReVision* 26 (3):11–12.
Maslow, Abraham. 1943. "A theory of human motivation." *Psychological Review* 50 (3):370–396.
Maslow, Abraham H. 1968. *Toward a psychology of being.* 2nd ed. New York: D. Van Nostrand.
Maslow, Abraham Harold. 1987. *Motivation and personality.* Boston: Addison-Wesley Educational Publishers.
Mason, Edward S., and Robert E. Asher. 1973. *The world bank since Bretton Woods.* Washington, DC: The Brookings Institution.
Mathur, Navdeep, and Chris Skelcher. 2007. "Evaluating democratic performance: Methodologies for assessing the relationship between network governance and citizens." *Public Administration Review* 67 (2):228–237.
Maturana, Humberto R., and Francisco Varela. 1987. *Tree of knowledge.* Boston: Shambhala Publications.
May, Todd. 1994. *The political philosophy of poststructuralist anarchism.* University Park, PA: The Pennsylvania State University Press.
McCaffrey, David P., Sue R. Faerman, and David W. Hart. 1995. "The appeal and difficulties of participative systems." *Organization Science* 6 (6):693–627.
McConkey, Dale, and Peter Lawler. 2003. *Faith, morality, and civil society.* Lanham, MD: Lexington Books.
McCutcheon, Russell T. 2005. "Introduction." In *The insider/outsider problem in the study of religion: A reader*, edited by Russell T. McCutcheon, 15–22. London: Continuum.
McGuire, Michael. 2002. "Managing networks: Propositions on what managers do and why they do it." *Public Administration Review* 62 (5):599–609.
McGuire, Michael. 2006. "Collaborative public management: Assessing what we know and how we know it." *Public Administration Review* 66:33–43.

McMurty, John-Justin. 2013. *Prometheus, Trojan Horse, or Frankenstein? The social and solidarity economy as community creation, market wedge, or state monster*. Geneva: United Nations Research Institute for Social Development.
McSwite, O. C. 1997. *Legitimacy in public administration: A discourse analysis*. Thousand Oaks, CA: Sage Publications.
McSwite, O. C. 2006. "Public administration as the carrier of the new social bond." *Administrative Theory & Praxis* 28 (2):176–189.
Mead, George Herbert. 1967. *Mind, self & society from the standpoint of a social behaviorist*. Chicago, IL: The University of Chicago press.
Means, Robert. 1995. *Where white men fear to tread: The autobiography of Russell means*. New York: Macmillan Publishers.
Melman, Seymour. 2001. *After capitalism: From managerialism to workplace democracy*. New York: Alfred A. Knopf.
Merleau-Ponty, Maurice. 1968. *The visible and the invisible*. Translated by Alphonso Lingis. Evanston, IL: Northwestern University Press.
Merleau-Ponty, Maurice. 2012. *Phenomenology of perception*. Translated by Donald A. Landes. New York: Routledge. Original edition, 1945.
Mesle, C. Robert. 1993. *Process theology: A basic introduction*. Kindle ed. St. Louis: Chalice Press.
Mesle, C. Robert. 2008. *Process-relational philosophy: An introduction to Alfred North Whitehead*. West Conshohocken, PA: Templeton Foundation Press.
Metropolis. 2011. *Integrated urban governance: The way forward*. Berlin: Metropolis.
Meynhardt, Timo. 2009. "Public value inside: What is public value creation?" *International Journal of Public Administration* 32 (3–4):192–219.
Meynhardt, Timo, Peter Gomez, and Markus T. Schweizer. 2014. "The public value scorecard: What makes an organization valuable to society?" *Performance* 6 (1):2–9.
Mies, Maria, and Vandana Shiva. 2014. *Ecofeminism*. New York: Zed Books. Original edition, 1993.
Mill, John Stuart. 1873. *Considerations on representative government*. New York: Henry Holt and Company.
Mill, John Stuart. 2000. "Utilitarianism." In *What is justice? Classic and contemporary readings*, edited by Robert C. Solomon and Mark C. Murphy, 166–174. Oxford: Oxford University Press. Original edition, 1861.
Millar, Murray E., and Anne Abraham. 2006. *Towards the development of an integrative governance framework for the third sector: A theoretical review and analysis*. Adelaide: Navigating New Waters.
Miller, Jean Baker. 1984. "The development of women's sense of self." In *Work in progress papers*. Wellesley, MA: Wellesley College, The Stone Center.
Miller, Hugh T., and Cheryl Simrell King. 1998. "Practical theory." *American Review of Public Administration* 28 (1):43–60.
Miller, Hugh T., and Charles J. Fox. 2001. "The epistemic community." *Administration & Society* 32 (6):668.
Milun, Kathryn. 2011. *The political uncommons: The cross-cultural logic of the global commons*. Burlington, VT: Ashgate.
Milward, H. Brinton, and Keith G. Provan. 1998. "Measuring network structure." *Public Administration* 76 (Summer):387–407.
Milward, H. Brinton, and Keith G. Provan. 2000. "Governing the hollow state." *Journal of Public Administration Research and Theory* 10 (2):359–380.
Mirror, Mary Flaming Crystal. 2012. *Course of study series A*. Scottsdale, AZ: Deer Tribe Metis Medicine Society.
Mons Declaration. 1996. "Mons declaration." In *II International Conférence of the Vía Campesina*. Tlaxcala, Mexico.
Montuori, Alfonso. 2005. "Gregory Bateson and the challenge of transdisciplinarity." *Cybernetics and Human Knowing* 12 (1–2):147–158.

Montuori, Alfonso, and Gabrielle Donnelly. 2016. "The creativity of culture and the culture of creativity research: The promise of integrative transdisciplinarity." In *The Palgrave handbook of creativity and culture research*, edited by V. P. Glaveanu, 743–765. San Francisco: Palgrave.
Monture-Angus, Patricia. 1999. *Journeying forward: Dreaming first nations' independence*. Halifax: Fernwood Press.
Moore, Mark H. 1995. *Creating public value: Strategic management in government*. Cambridge, MA: Harvard University Press.
Moore, Mark, and Jean Hartley. 2008. "Innovations in governance." *Public Management Review* 10 (1):3–20.
Moraga, Cherríe. 2015. "Catching fire: Preface to the fourth edition." In *This bridge called my back: Writings by radical women of color*, edited by Cherrie Moraga and Gloria Anzaldúa, xv–xxvi. Albany, NY: State University of New York Press.
Morris, Brian. 1993. *Bakunin: The philosophy of freedom*. Montreal: Black Rose Books Ltd.
Morris, Randall C. 1991. *Process philosophy and political ideology: The social and political thought of Alfred North Whitehead and Charles Hartshorne*. Albany, NY: State University of New York Press.
Morrison, Roy. 1991. *We build the road as we travel*. Gabriola Island, BC: New Society Publishers.
Morro, William Charles. 1932. *Stewardship*. St. Louis: The Bethany Press.
Morstein Marx, Fritz. 1946. "The lawyer's role in public administration." *The Yale Law Journal* 55 (3):498–526.
Mouffe, Chantal. 2005. "For an agonistic public sphere." In *Radical democracy: Politics between abundance and lack*, edited by Lars Tønder and Lasse Thomassen, 123–132. New York: Manchester University Press.
Moynihan, Donald P. 2005. *Leveraging collaborative networks in infrequent emergency situations*. Washington, DC: IBM Center for the Business of Government.
Mueller, Tadzio. 2011. "Empowering anarchy: Power, hegemony and anarchist strategy." In *Post-anarchism: A reader*, edited by Duane Rousselle and Süreyyya Evren, 75–94. New York: Pluto Press.
Murdoch, Iris. 1992. *Metaphysics as a guide to morals*. New York: Penguin Books.
Nabatchi, Tina. 2010. "Addressing the citizenship and democratic deficits: The potential of deliberative democracy for public administration." *The American Review of Public Administration* 40 (4):376–399.
Nabatchi, Tina. 2012. "Putting the 'public' back in public values research: Designing participation to identify and respond to values." *Public Administration Review* 72 (5):699–708.
Nabatchi, Tina, and Matt Leighninger. 2015. *Public participation for 21st century democracy*. San Francisco: Jossey-Bass.
Nader, Ralph. 1993. "Introduction: Free trade & the decline of democracy." In *The case against free trade: GATT, NAFTA, and the globalization of corporate power*, edited by Ralph Nader and Jerry Brown, 1–12. San Francisco: Earth Island Press.
Næss, Arne. 1973. "The shallow and the deep, long-range ecology movement." *Inquiry* 16:95–100.
Nagda, Biren (Ratnesh) A., and Kelly E. Maxwell. 2011. "Deepening the layers of understanding and connection: A critical-dialogic approach to facilitating intergroup dialogues." In *Facilitating intergroup dialogues: Building bridges, catalyzing change*, edited by Kelly E. Maxwell, Biren (Ratnesh) A. Nagda and Monita C. Thompson, 1–22. Sterling, VA: Stylus.
NATO, North Atlantic Treaty Organization. 2017. "Collective defence – Article 5." North Atlantic Treaty Organization, accessed July 14, 2017. www.nato.int/cps/cn/natohq/topics_110496.htm.
NATO, North Atlantic Treaty Organization. 2017, June 2. "Funding NATO." North Atlantic Treaty Organization, accessed July 15, 2017. www.nato.int/cps/ro/natohq/topics_67655.htm.
NCDD, National Coalition for Dialogue and Deliberation. 2010. *Resource guide for public engagement*. Boiling Springs, PA: National Coalition for Dialogue and Deliberation.

NCUA, National Credit Union Administration. 2016. "What is a credit union?" National Credit Union Administration, accessed August 3, 2016. www.mycreditunion.gov/about-credit-unions/Pages/How-is-a-Credit-Union-Different-than-a-Bank.aspx.

Needham, Joseph. 1956. *Science and civilisation in China*. Vol. II. Cambridge: Cambridge University Press.

Nelson, Julie. 2006. "The relational firm: A Buddhist and feminist analysis." In *Business within limits: Deep ecology and Buddhist economics*, edited by Zsolnai Laszlo and Knut Johannessen Ims, 195–218. Bern, Switzerland: Peter Lang AG.

Nelson, Melissa K. 2015. "Re-indigenizing the people to the planet." *Earth Island Journal* 30 (3).

Nembhard, Jessica Gordon. 2014. *Collective courage: A history of African American cooperative economic thought and practice*. University Park, PA: Pennsylvania State University Press.

Neo-Paganism.com. 2015. "Neo-paganism." Neo-Paganism.com, accessed July 12, 2015. http://neo-paganism.com/.

Neufeldt, Victoria, ed. 1996. *Webster's new world college dictionary*. 3rd ed. New York: Macmillan.

Neumann, Francis X., Jr. 1996. "What makes public administration a science? Or, are its 'Big Questions' really big?" *Public Administration Review* 56 (5):409–415.

Newman, Saul. 2011. "Post-anarchism and radical politics today." In *Post-anarchism: A reader*, edited by Duane Rousselle and Süreyyya Evren, 46–68. New York: Pluto Press.

Nichol, Lee. 2004. "Foreword." In *On dialogue*, xv–xx. New York: Routledge.

Nicholson, Paul. 2011. "Food sovereignty: Alliances and transformation." In *Food movements unite! Strategies to transform our food systems*, edited by Samir Amin. Oakland, CA: Food First Books.

Nicolescu, Basarab. 2002. *Manifesto of transdisciplinarity*. Translated by Karen Claire Voss. Albany, NY: State University of New York Press.

Niebuhr, H. Richard. 1963. *The responsible self: An essay in Christian moral philosophy*. New York: Harper & Row.

Niebuhr, H. Richard. 1970. *Radical monotheism and western culture*. New York: Harper & Row. Original edition, 1943.

Nietzsche, Friedrich Wilhelm. 1968. *Will to power*. New York: Vintage Books. Original edition, 1901.

Nietzsche, Friedrich Wilhelm. 1969. *Thus spoke Zarathustra*. Translated by R. J. Hollingdale. New York: Penguin Classics.

Nietzsche, Friedrich Wilhelm. 1977. *Twilight of the idols; and the anti-Christ*. Translated by R. J. Hollingdale. Harmondsworth: Penguin.

Nishida, Kitaro. 1992. *An inquiry into the good*. New Haven, CT: Yale University Press. Original edition, 1911.

No One Is Illegal. 2003. "No one is illegal manifesto." No One Is Illegal UK, accessed August 7, 2016. www.noii.org.uk/no-one-is-illegal-manifesto/.

No One Is Illegal. n.d. "No one is illegal." No One Is Illegal, accessed July 16, 2017. www.nooneisillegal.org/.

noborder network. 2004. "About noborder.org." noborder network, accessed July 16, 2017. www.noborder.org/about.php.html.

Noddings, Nel. 2003. *Caring: A feminine approach to ethics and moral education*. 2nd ed. Berkeley: University of California Press.

North, Douglass Cecil. 1990. *Institutions, institutional change, and economic performance, the political economy of institutions and decisions*. Cambridge: Cambridge University Press.

Nowotny, Helga, Peter Scott, and Michael Gibbons. 2001. *Re-thinking science: Knowledge and the public in an age of uncertainty*. Cambridge, MA: Polity Press.

Nye, Joseph S., and John D. Donahue, eds. 2000. *Governance in a globalizing world*. Washington, DC: Brookings Institution.

OECD, Organization for Economic Co-operation and Development. 2017. "History." Organization for Economic Co-operation and Development, accessed July 19, 2017. www.oecd.org/about/history/.

Office of the Historian. 2017. "The league of nations." U.S. Department of State, Bureau of Public Affairs, accessed June 24, 2017. https://history.state.gov/milestones/1914-1920/league.
O'Leary, Rosemary, and Lisa Blomgren Bingham. 2009. *The collaborative public manager: New ideas for the twenty-first century, public management and change*. Washington, DC: Georgetown University Press.
Olsen, Jonathan, and John McCormick. 2017. *The European union: Politics and policies*. Boulder, CO: Westview Press.
On the Commons. 2016. "Home page." On the Commons. www.onthecommons.org/.
Oord, Thomas Jay. 2005. "The love racket: Defining love and *agape* for the love-and-science research program." *Zygon* 40 (4):919–938.
Open Spaces Society. n.d. "About us." Open Spaces Society, accessed July 25, 2017. www.oss.org.uk/who-we-are/about-us/.
Ormaechea, J. M. 2001. "Madragon's ten basic principles." *Social Policy* 32 (2):4–9.
Orr, David. 1992. *Ecological literacy: Education and the transition to a postmodern world*. Albany, NY: State University of New York Press.
Osborne, David, and Ted Gaebler. 1992. *Reinventing government: How the entrepreneurial spirit is transforming the public sector*. Reading, MA: Addison-Wesley.
Osborne, Stephen P. 2010. *The new public governance? Emerging perspectives on the theory and practice of public governance*. New York: Routledge.
Ostrom, Elinor. 1990. *Governing the commons: The evolution of institutions for collective action*. Cambridge: Cambridge University Press.
Ostrom, Elinor. 2010. "Beyond markets and states: Polycentric governance of complex economic systems." *American Economic Review* 100 (3):641–672.
O'Toole, Laurence J., Jr. 1997a. "Implementing public innovations in network settings." *Administration & Society* 29 (2):115–138.
O'Toole, Laurence J., Jr. 1997b. "The implications of democracy in a networked bureaucratic world." *Journal of Public Administration Research and Theory* 7:443–459.
O'Toole, Laurence J., Jr. 1997c. "Treating networks seriously: Practical and research-based agendas in public administration." *Public Administration Review* 57 (1):45–52.
O'Toole, Laurence J., Jr., and Kenneth J. Meier. 2004. "Desperately seeking Selznick: Cooptation and the dark side of public management in networks." *Public Administration Review* 64 (6):681–693.
Oxford English Dictionary. 2017. "Collaborator." In *English Oxford living dictionaries*. Oxford: Oxford University Press.
Padula, Giovanna, and Giovanni Battista Dagnino. 2008. "Untangling the rise of coopetition." *International Studies of Management and Organization* 37 (2):232–252.
Page, Stephen. 2003. "Entrepreneurial strategies for managing interagency collaboration." *Journal of Public Administration Research and Theory* 13 (3):311–339.
Page, Stephen. 2010. "Integrative leadership for collaborative governance: Civic engagement in Seattle." *The Leadership Quarterly* 21:246–263.
Palley, Thomas I. 2014. "Making finance serve the real economy." In *State of the world 2014: Governing for sustainability*, edited by Lisa Mastny, 174–180. Washington, DC: Worldwatch Institute.
Parker, Sir Peter. 1995. "Most quoted – least heeded: The five senses of Follett." In *Mary Parker Follett, prophet of management: A celebration of writings from the 1920s*, edited by Pauline Graham, 282–290. Washington, DC: Beard Books.
Parker, Rachel. 2007. "Networked governance or just networks? Local governance of the knowledge economy in Limerick (Ireland) and Karlskorna (Sweden)." *Political Studies* 55:113–132.
Parry, Glenn R. 2004. "Seed thoughts on dialogue." *ReVision* 26 (3):5–10.
Participatory Budgeting Project. 2017. "PB map & process list." Participatory Budgeting Project, accessed July 25, 2017. www.participatorybudgeting.org/pb-map/.

Patel, Raj. 2007. *Stuffed and starved: The hidden battle for the world food system.* Brooklyn: Melville House.

Pateman, Carole. 1970. *Participation and democratic theory.* Cambridge: Cambridge University Press.

Patterson, Thomas E. 2008. *We the people: A concise introduction to American politics.* 7th ed. Boston: McGraw-Hill.

Patton, Paul. 2005. "Deleuze and democratic politics." In *Radical democracy: Politics between abundance and lack*, edited by Lars Tønder and Lasse Thomassen, 50–67. New York: Manchester University Press.

Peat, F. David. 2002. *Blackfoot physics: An exploration of the native American universe.* Boston: Red Wheel/Weiser.

Peoples Climate March. 2014. "Peoples climate march, the story." Peoples Climate March, accessed July 25, 2017. http://2014.peoplesclimate.org/wrap-up/.

PERRO, Pilsen Environmental Rights and Reform Organization. n.d. "About our campaign." Pilsen Environmental Rights and Reform Organization, accessed November 26, 2017. https://pilsenperro.org/about/.

Perry, James L., and Kenneth L. Kraemer. 1986. "Research methodology in the *Public Administration Review*, 1975–1984." *Public Administration Review* 46:215–226.

Pierre, Jon, and Guy Peters. 2000. *Governance, politics and the state.* New York: St. Martin's Press.

Pinchot, Gifford, and Elizabeth Pinchot. 1993. *The end of bureaucracy and the rise of the intelligent organization.* San Francisco: Berrett-Koehler.

Pirson, Michael, and Shann Turnbull. 2011. "Toward a more humanistic governance model: Network governance structures." *Journal of Business Ethics* 99 (1):101–114.

Pogge, Thomas W. 1992. "Cosmopolitanism and sovereignty." *Ethics* 103:48–75.

Pogrebinschi, Thamy. 2013. "The squared circle of participatory democracy: Scaling up deliberation to the national level." *Critical Policy Studies* 7 (3):219–241.

Polanyi, Karl. 1944. *The great transformation: The political and economic origins of our time.* Boston: Beacon Press.

Polanyi, Karl. 1977. *The livelihood of man.* New York: Academic Press.

Polanyi, Michael. 1974. *Personal knowledge: Towards a post-critical philosophy.* Corrected ed. Chicago: University of Chicago Press. Original edition, 1958.

Polanyi, Michael. 2009. *The tacit dimension.* Chicago: University of Chicago Press. Original edition, 1966.

Pollan, Michael. 2001. *The botany of desire: A plant's-eye view of the world.* New York: Random House.

Popper, Karl R. 1940. "What is dialectic?" *Mind* 49 (196):403–426.

Powell, Walter W. 1990. "Neither market nor hierarchy: Network forms of organization." In *Research in organizational behavior*, edited by Barry M. Staw and Larry L. Cummings, 295–336. Greenwich, CT: JAI Press.

Poyaoan, Jassmin. 2013. "How lending circles create community resilience." *Economy.* www.shareable.net/blog/how-lending-circles-create-community-resilience.

Pranger, Robert J. 1968. *The eclipse of citizenship: Power and participation in contemporary politics.* New York: Holt, Rinehart and Winston.

Pressman, Jeffrey L., and Aaron Wildavsky. 1979. *Implementation: How great expectations in Washington are dashed in Oakland; or, why it's amazing that federal programs work at all, this being a saga of the economic development administration as told by two sympathetic observers who seek to build morals on a foundation of ruined hopes.* 2nd ed. Berkeley: University of California Press.

Prigogine, Ilya. 1981. *From being to becoming: Time and complexity in the physical sciences.* New York: W. H. Freeman & Co.

Proudhon, Pierre-Joseph. 1969. *Selected writings.* Translated by Elizabeth Fraser. 1st ed. New York: Anchor Books, Doubleday & Company.

Provan, Keith G., and H. Brinton Milward. 1991. "Institutional-level norms and organizational involvement in a service-implementation network." *Journal of Public Administration Research and Theory* 1 (4):391–417.

Provan, Keith G., and H. Brinton Milward. 2001. "Do networks really work? A framework for evaluating public-sector organizational networks." *Public Administration Review* 61 (4):414–443.

Provan, Keith G., and Patrick Kenis. 2008. "Modes of network governance: Structure, management, and effectiveness." *Journal of Public Administration Research and Theory* 18 (2):229–252.

Prozorov, Sergei. 2014a. *Ontology and world politics: Void universalism I.* Edited by Edkins Jenny and Nick Vaughan-Williams. 2 vols. Vol. 1, *Interventions.* New York: Routledge.

Prozorov, Sergei. 2014b. *Theory of the political subject: Void universalism II.* Edited by Edkins Jenny and Nick Vaughan-Williams. 2 vols. Vol. 1, *Interventions.* New York: Routledge.

Prugh, Tom. 2015. "Childhood's end." In *State of the world 2015: Confronting hidden threats to sustainability*, edited by Lisa Mastny, 129–140. Washington, DC: Island Press.

Prugh, Tom, and Michael Renner. 2014. "Call to engagement." In *State of the world 2014: Governing for sustainability*, edited by Lisa Mastny, 241–252. Washington, DC: Worldwatch Institute.

Public Banking Institute. 2016. "Mission." Public Banking Institute, accessed August 3, 2016. www.publicbankinginstitute.org/.

Puente, Isaac. 1985. *Libertarian communism.* Sydney, Australia: Monty Miller Press.

Pulitano, Elvira. 2003. *Toward a native American critical theory.* Lincoln, NE: University of Nebraska Press.

Purdy, Jill M. 2012. "A framework for assessing power in collaborative governance processes." *Public Administration Review* 72 (3):409–417.

Putnam, Robert D. 1994. *Making democracy work: Civic traditions in modern Italy.* Princeton, NJ: Princeton University Press.

Putnam, Robert D. 2000. *Bowling alone: America's declining social capital.* New York: Simon and Schuster.

Putnam, Robert D., Robert Leonardi, Rafaella Y. Nanetti, and Franco Pavoncello. 1983. "Explaining institutional success: The case of Italian regional government." *The American Political Science Review* 77 (1):55–74.

PwC, PricewaterhouseCoopers. 2008. *Integrated governance, risk, and compliance: Improve performance and enhance productivity in federal agencies.* Alexandria, VA: PricewaterhouseCoopers LLP.

Raadschelders, Jos C. N. 1999. "A coherent framework for the study of public administration." *Journal of Public Administration Research and Theory* 9 (2):281–303.

Ramachandran, V. S. 2012. *The tell-tale brain: A neuroscientist's quest for what makes us human.* New York: W. W. Norton & Company.

Ramos, Alberto Guerreiro. 1981. *The new science of organizations: A reconceptualization of the wealth of nations.* Toronto: University of Toronto Press.

Raphael, Melissa. 2000. *Introducing thealogy: Discourse on the Goddess.* Cleveland, OH: The Pilgrim Press.

Rasche, Andreas. 2010. "Collaborative governance 2.0." *Corporate Governance* 10 (4):500–511.

Rawlings, Kelly Campbell, and Thomas Catlaw. 2011. "Democracy as a way of life: Rethinking the places and practices of public administration." In *Government is us 2.0*, edited by Cheryl Simmrel King. Armonk, NY: M.E. Sharpe.

Raworth, Kate. 2017. *Doughnut economics: 7 ways to think like a 21st century economist.* White River Junction, VT: Chelsea Green Publishing.

Regan, Helen B., and Gwen H. Brooks. 1995. *Out of women's experience: Creating relational leadership.* Thousand Oaks, CA: Corwin Press, Inc.

Renner, Michael. 2015. "The seeds of modern threats." In *State of the world 2015: Confronting hidden threats to sustainability*, edited by Lisa Mastny, 3–17. Washington, DC: Island Press.

Renner, Michael, and Tom Prugh. 2014. "Failing governance, unsustainable planet." In *State of the world 2014: Governing for sustainability*, edited by Lisa Mastny, 3–19. Washington, DC: Worldwatch Institute.

Reuters. 2018, January 11. "U.S. will renegotiate NAFTA or pull out: Mnuchin." www.reuters.com/article/us-trade-nafta-usa/u-s-will-renegotiate-nafta-or-pull-out-mnuchin-idUSKBN1F02PN.

Rhodes, Lynn N. 1987. *Co-creation: A feminist vision of ministry*. Westminster: John Knox Press.

Rhodes, R. A. W. 1994. "The hollowing out of the state: The changing nature of the public service in Britain." *The Political Quarterly* 65 (2):138–151.

Rhodes, R. A. W. 1996. "The new governance: Governing without government." *Political Studies* 44 (4):652–667.

Rhodes, R. A. W. 1997a. "Foreword." In *Managing complex networks: Strategies for the public sector*, edited by Walter J. M. Klickert, Erik-Hans Klijn and Joop F. M. Koppenjan, xi–xv. Thousand Oaks, CA: Sage Publications.

Rhodes, R. A. W. 1997b. *Understanding governance: Policy networks, governance, reflexivity, and accountability*. Buckingham, UK: Open University Press.

Rico, Luis. 2011. "Cultural networks." In *Chimeras and consciousness: Evolution of the sensory self*, edited by Lynn Margulis, Celeste A. Asikainen and Wolfgang E. Krumbein, 259–266. Cambridge, MA: MIT Press.

Ritchie, Mark. 1993. "Agricultural trade liberation: Implications for sustainable agriculture." In *The case against free trade: GATT, NAFTA, and the globalization of corporate power*, edited by Ralph Nader and Jerry Brown, 163–192. San Francisco: Earth Island Press.

Rittel, Horst W. J. 1972. "On the planning crisis: Systems analysis of the 'first and second generations'." *Bedriftskonomen* 8:390–396.

Rittel, Horst W. J., and Melvin Webber. 1973. "Dilemmas in a general theory of planning." *Policy Sciences* 4 (2):155–169.

Rizzolatti, Giacomo. 2006. *Mirrors in the brain: How our minds share actions and emotions*. Translated by Frances Anderson. Oxford: Oxford University Press.

Roberts, Nancy. 2004. "Public deliberation in an age of direct citizen participation." *American Review of Public Administration* 34 (4):315–353.

Robertson, Brian J. 2014. "History of holacracy." August 8. https://blog.holacracy.org/history-of-holacracy-c7a8489f8eca#.q9c5tv2ly.

Robertson, Brian J. 2015. *Holacracy: The new management system for a rapidly changing world*. New York: Henry Holt and Company.

Rocker, Rudolf. 2004. *Anarcho-syndicalism: Theory and practice, working class series*. Oakland: AK Press. Original edition, 1938.

Rodrik, Dani. 2000. "Governance of economic globalization." In *Governance in a globalizing world*, edited by Joseph S. Nye and John D. Donahue, 347–366. Washington, DC: Brookings Institution.

Rogers, Carl R. 1961. *On becoming a person*. Boston: Houghton Mifflin.

Rogers, Ellen, and Edward P. Weber. 2010. "Thinking harder about outcomes for collaborative governance arrangements." *The American Review of Public Administration* 40 (5):546–567.

Roll, Stephen, and Nicole Thomas. 2014. "The legacy of Mary Parker Follett in contemporary scholarship." In *Mastering public administration: From Max Weber to Dwight Waldo*, edited by Brian R. Fry and Jos C. N. Raadschelders, 172–180. Washington, DC: CQ Press.

Rose, Nikolas. 2007. *The politics of life itself: Biomedicine, power and subjectivity in the twenty-first century*. Princeton, NJ: Princeton University Press.

Rosenau, James N. 1999. "Toward an ontology for global governance." In *Approaches to global governance theory*, edited by Martin Hewson and Timothy J. Sinclair, 287–301. Albany, NY: State University of New York Press.

Rosenau, Pauline Marie. 1992. *Postmodernism and the social sciences: Insights, inroads, and intrusions*. Princeton, NJ: Princeton University Press.

Rossi, Peter H., Mark W. Lipsey, and Howard E. Freeman. 2004. *Evaluation: A systematic approach*. 7th ed. Thousand Oaks, CA: Sage Publications.
Rothschild, Joyce. 2000. "Creating a just and democratic workplace: More engagement, less hierarchy." *Contemporary Sociology* 29 (1):195–213.
Rothschild, Joyce, and J. Allen Whitt. 1986. *The cooperative workplace: Potentials and dilemmas of organizational democracy and participation, the Arnold and Caroline Rose monograph series of the American Sociological Association*. Cambridge: Cambridge University Press.
Rousselle, Duane. 2011. "Preface." In *Post-anarchism: A reader*, edited by Duane Rousselle and Süreyyya Evren. New York: Pluto Press.
Rousselle, Duane, and Sureyyya Evren, eds. 2011. *Post-anarchism: A reader*. London: Pluto Press.
Rowlands, Jo. 1997. *Questioning empowerment: Working with women in Honduras*. Oxford, UK: Oxfam Publishing.
Ruccio, David F., and Jack Amariglio. 2003. *Postmodern moments in modern economics*. Princeton, NJ: Princeton University Press.
Ryan, Jim. 2004. "Divining grammar." *ReVision* 26 (3):28–30.
Ryan, Mark B. 2008. "The transpersonal William James." *Journal of Transpersonal Psychology* 40 (1):20–40.
Sabatier, Paul A. 1988. "An advocacy coalition framework of policy change and the role of policy-oriented learning therein." *Policy Sciences* 21 (2/3):129–168.
Sabatier, Paul A., ed. 1999. *Theories of the policy process: Theoretical lenses on public policy*. Boulder, CO: Westview Press.
Sabatier, Paul A., and Hank C. Jenkins-Smith. 1988. "Policy change and policy-oriented learning: Exploring an advocacy coalition framework." *Policy Sciences* 21 (2–3):123–127.
Sabatier, Paul A., and Hank C. Jenkins-Smith. 1999. "The advocacy coalition framework: An assessment." In *Theories of the policy process: Theoretical lenses on public policy*, edited by Paul A. Sabatier, 117–168. Boulder, CO: Westview Press.
Salamon, Lester M., ed. 2002. *The tools of government: A guide to the new governance*. Oxford: Oxford University Press.
Saldívar-Hull, Sonia. 2000. *Feminism on the border: Chicana gender politics and literature*. Berkeley: University of California Press.
Sampson, Edward E. 1986. "Individuation and domination: Undermining the Social Bond." Growth and Progress in Cross-Cultural Psychology: Eighth International Conference. Istanbul, Turkey.
Sampson, Edward E. 1988. "The debate on individualism: Indigenous psychologies of the individual and their role in personal and societal functioning." *American Psychologist* 43 (1).
Sandel, Michael. 1996. *Democracy's discontent*. Cambridge, MA: Belknap Press of Harvard University Press.
Saussure, Ferdinand de. 1960. *Course in general linguistics*. London: Peter Owen. Original edition, 1916.
Saward, Michael. 2003. *Democracy*. Cambridge, MA: Polity Press.
Scharpf, Fritz. 1993. "Coordination in hierarchies and networks." In *Games in hierarchies and networks: Analytical and empirical approaches to the study of governance institutions*, edited by Fritz Scharpf, 125–166. Boulder, CO: Westview Press.
Scharpf, Fritz W. 1997. *Games real actors play: Actor-centred institutionalism in policy research*. Boulder, CO: Westview Press.
Schattschneider, Elmer Eric. 1960. *The semisovereign people: A realist's view of democracy in America*. New York: Hold, Rinehart and Winston.
Schmidt, Mary R. 1993. "Grout: Alternative forms of knowledge and why they are ignored." *Public Administration Review* 53 (6):525–530.
Schneider, Anne Larason, and Helen Ingram. 1997. *Policy design for democracy*. Lawrence, KS: University Press of Kansas.

Schönig, Barbara, and Sebastian Shipper. 2016. "Introduction: Impacts of the global financial crisis on cities in Europe." In *Urban austerity: Impacts of the global financial crisis on cities in Europe*, edited by Sebastian Shipper and Barbara Schönig, 7–20. Berlin: Theater de Zeit.

Schreurs, Petra. 2000. "Enchanting rationality: An analysis of rationality in the Anglo-American discourse on public organization." Ph.D., Leiden University.

Schumacher, E. F. 2010. *Small is beautiful: Economics as if people mattered*. New York: Harper Perennial. Original edition, 1973.

Schutz, Alfred. 1967. *The phenomenology of the social world*. Translated by George Walsch and Frederick Lehnert. Evanston, IL: Northwestern University Press. Original edition, 1932.

SCI, Sustainable Cities Institute. 2013. "Welcome to the sustainable cities institute!". National League of Cities, accessed July 25, 2017. www.sustainablecitiesinstitute.org/.

Seligman, Martin E. P. 2002. *Authentic happiness: Using the new positive psychology to realize your potential for lasting fulfillment*. New York: The Free Press.

Seligman, Martin E. P., and Mihaly Csikszentmihalyi. 2000. "Positive psychology: An introduction." *American Psychologist* 55 (1):5–14.

Selznick, P. 1998. "Social justice: A communitarian perspective." In *The essential communitarian reader*, edited by Amitai Etzioni, 61–72. Oxford: Rowan and Littlefield Publishers Inc.

Sementelli, Arthur J. 2007. "Managing blurred environments: How usufruct can help address postmodern conditions." *Administration & Society* 38 (6):709–728.

Senge, Peter. 1990. *The fifth discipline: The art and practice of the learning organization*. New York: Doubleday.

Senge, Peter M. 2004. "Preface." In *On dialogue*, i–xiiii. New York: Routledge.

Seyle, D. Conor, and Matthew Wilburn King. 2014. "Understanding governance." In *State of the world 2014: Governing for sustainability*, edited by Lisa Mastny, 20–28. Washington, DC: Worldwatch Institute.

Sharp, E. B. 1980. "Toward a new understanding of urban services and citizen participation: The coproduction concept." *Midwest Review of Public Administration* 14 (2):105–118.

Shear, Michael D. 2017, June 1. "Trump will withdraw US from Paris climate agreement." *New York Times*. www.nytimes.com/2017/06/01/climate/trump-paris-climate-agreement.html.

Shekhawat, Prahlad. 2008. "Redefining progress: A report from the gross national happiness conference in Bhutan." In *Policy innovations for a fairer globalization*. New York: Carnegie Council for Ethics in International Affairs.

Shelburne, Walter A. 1988. *Mythos and logos in the thought of Carl Jung: The theory of collective unconscious in scientific perspective*. Albany, NY: State University of New York Press.

Sherburne, Donald W. 1966. *A key to Whitehead's process and reality*. New York: Macmillan.

Sherburne, Donald W. 1967. "Whitehead without God." *The Christian Scholar* L (3).

Shields, Patricia M. 2005. "Classical pragmatism does not need an upgrade: Lessons for public administration." *Administration & Society* 37 (4):504–518.

Shilling, Fraser M., Jonathan K. London, and Raoul S. Liévanos. 2009. "Marginalization by collaboration: Environmental justice as a third party in and beyond CALFED." *Environmental Science and Policy* 12 (6):694–709.

Shiva, Vandana. 2015. *Earth democracy: Justice, sustainability, and peace*. Berkeley, CA: North Atlantic Books.

Sidhu, Gretchen. 2007. *Intergovernmental negotiations and decision making at the United Nations: A guide*. United Nations.

Silvia, Chris. 2011. "Collaborative governance concepts for successful network leadership." *State and Local Government Review* 43 (1):66–71.

Silvia, Chris, and Michael McGuire. 2010. "Leading public sector networks: An empirical examination of integrative leadership behaviors." *Leadership Quarterly* 21:264–277.

Simons, Jon. 2005. "The radical democratic possibilities of popular culture." In *Radical democracy: Politics between abundance and lack*, edited by Lars Tønder and Lasse Thomassen, 149–166. New York: Manchester University Press.

Simpson, John H. 1999. "The search for community in America: Comments on 'Visions of the good society and the religious roots of American political culture'." *Sociology of Religion* 60 (1):41–45.

Sirianni, Carmen. 2009. *Investing in democracy: Engaging citizens in collaborative governance.* Washington, DC: The Brookings Institute.

Sitrin, Marina, ed. 2005. *Horizontalism: Voices of popular power in Argentina.* Oakland, CA: AK Press.

Sitrin, Marina. 2007. "Ruptures in imagination: Horizontalism, autogestion and affective politics in Argentina." *Policy & Practice: A Development Education Review* 5 (Autumn):43–53.

Sitrin, Marina, and Dario Azzellini. 2012. *Occupying language: The secret rendezvous with history and the present.* Brooklyn: Zuccotti Park Press.

Sitrin, Marina, and Dario Azzellini. 2014. *They can't represent us! Reinventing democracy from Greece to occupy.* London: Verso.

Skelcher, Chris. 2007. "Democracy in collaborative spaces: Why context matters in researching governance networks." In *Theories of democratic network governance*, edited by Eva Sørensen and Jacob Torfing, 25–46. Thousand Oaks, CA: Sage Publications.

Skelcher, Chris, Erik-Hans Klijn, Daniel Kübler, Eva Sørensen, and Helen Sullivan. 2007. "Explaining the democratic anchorage of governance networks: Evidence from four European countries." *Administrative Theory & Praxis* 33 (1):7–38.

Skelcher, Chris, Navdeep Mathru, and Mike Smith. 2005. "The public governance of collaborative spaces: Discourse, design, and democracy." *Public Administration* 83:573–596.

Skrbina, David. 2005. *Panpsychism in the West.* Cambridge: MIT Press.

Slave-Free Community Project. n.d. "About us." Slave-Free Community Project, accessed November 26, 2017. www.slavefreecommunityproject.com/our-mission.

Smadja, Claude. 2000. "Time to learn from Seattle." *Newsweek*, January 17.

Smart Growth America. 2016. *What is 'smart growth?'.* Washington, DC: Smart Growth America.

Smith, Adam. 2000a. "A theory of the moral sentiments." In *What is justice? Classic and contemporary readings*, edited by Robert C. Solomon and Mark C. Murphy, 144–147. Oxford: Oxford University Press. Original edition, 1759.

Smith, Adam. 2000b. "The wealth of nations." In *What is justice? Classic and contemporary readings*, edited by Robert C. Solomon and Mark C. Murphy, 148–151. Oxford: Oxford University Press. Original edition, 1776.

Smith, Maureen E. 2004. "Crippling the spirit, wounding the soul: Native American spiritual and religious suppression." In *American Indian thought*, edited by Anne Waters, 116–129. Malden, MA: Blackwell Publishing.

Smith, Mike, Navdeep Mathur, and Chris Skelcher. 2006. "Corporate governance in a collaborative environment: What happens when government, business, and civil society work together?" *Corporate Governance* 14 (3).

Smith, David Woodruff. 2013. "Phenomenology." In *Stanford encyclopedia of philosophy*, edited by Edward N. Zalta. http://plato.stanford.edu/archives/win2013/entries/phenomenology/ Access date: Jan 11, 2016.

Smucker, Jonathan M. 2014. "Can prefigurative politics replace political strategy?" *Berkeley Journal of Sociology* 58:2.

Snyder, Zack. 2013. *Man of steel.* United States: Warner Bros.

Social Enterprise Alliance. 2016. "About." Social Enterprise Alliance. https://socialenterprise.us.

Sociocracy for All. n.d. "History." Institute for Peaceable Communities, Inc., accessed August 5, 2016. www.sociocracyforall.org/why-sociocracy/history/.

Sofoulis, Zoë. 1988. "Through the lumen: Frankenstein and the optics of re-origination." PhD, History of Consciousness, University of California, Santa Cruz.

Sørensen, Eva. 2002. "Democratic theory and network governance." *Administrative Theory & Praxis* 24:693–720.

Sørensen, Eva, and Jacob Torfing. 2003. "Network politics, political capital, and democracy." *International Journal of Public Administration* 26 (6):609–634.

Sørensen, Eva, and Jacob Torfing. 2005a. "The democratic anchorage of governance networks." *Scandinavian Political Studies* 28 (3):195–218.

Sørensen, Eva, and Jacob Torfing. 2005b. "Network governance and post-liberal democracy." *Administrative Theory & Praxis* 27 (2):197–237.

Sørensen, Eva, and Jacob Torfing. 2007. *Theories of democratic network governance*. New York: Palgrave Macmillan.

Sørensen, Eva, and Jacob Torfing. 2009. "Making governance networks effective and democratic through metagovernance." *Public Administration* 87 (2):234–258.

Sørensen, Eva, and Jacob Torfing. 2011. "Enhancing collaborative innovation in the public sector." *Administration & Society* 43 (8):842–868.

Sosa, Braulio Machín, Adilén María Roque Jaime, Dana Rocíío Ávila Lozano, and Peter Michael Rosset. 2013. *Agroecological revolution: The farmer-to-farmer movement of the ANAP in Cuba*. 1st English ed. Habana, Cuba: Asociación Nacional de Agricultores Pequeños.

Spiegel, Herbert, and David Spiegel. 2004. *Trance & treatment: Clinical uses of hypnosis*. 2nd ed. Arlington, VA: American Psychiatric Publishing.

Spinoza, Baruch. 2002. *Spinoza: Complete works*. Indianapolis: Hackett Publishing.

Stackhouse, Max L. 1987. *Public theology and political economy: Christian stewardship in modern society*. Grand Rapids, MI: William B. Eerdmans Publishing.

Standing Rock Tribe. 2017. "History." Stand with Standing Rock, accessed July 25, 2017. http://standwithstandingrock.net/history/.

Stanisevski, Dragan. 2011. "The inheritance of a promise of democracy-to-come: Of resistance and tolerance." *Critical Policy Studies* 5 (3):299–309.

Starcross, Leigh. 2004. "Nietzsche was an anarchist: Reconstructing Emma Goldman's Nietzsche lectures." In *I am not a man, I am dynamite! Friedrich Nietzsche and the Anarchist tradition*, edited by John Moore, 29–39. Brooklyn, NY: Autonomedia.

Starhawk. 1999. *The spiral dance: A rebirth of the ancient religion of the Goddess*. 20th Anniversary ed. San Francisco: HarperOne. Original edition, 1979.

Stédile, Joao Pedro, and Horácio Martines de Carvalho. 2011. "People need food sovereignty." In *Food movements unite! Strategies to transform our food systems*, edited by Samir Amin. Oakland, CA: Food First Books.

Stengers, Isabelle. 2011. *Thinking with Whitehead: A free and wild creation of concepts*. Translated by Michael Chase. Cambridge, MA: Harvard University Press.

Stewart-Harawira, Makere. 2005a. "Cultural studies, indigenous knowledge and pedagogies of hope." *Policy Futures in Education* 3 (2):153–163.

Stewart-Harawira, Makere. 2005b. *The new imperial order: Indigenous responses to globalization*. London: Zed Books.

Stiglitz, Joseph. 2001. *Globalization and its discontents*. New York: W. W. Norton.

Stivers, Camilla. 1990. "Active citizenship and public administration." In *Refounding public administration*, edited by Gary L. Wamsley, Robert N. Bacher, Charles T. Goodsell, Philip S. Kronenberg, John A. Rohr, Camilla Stivers, Orion F. White and James F. Wolf, 246–273. Thousand Oaks, CA: Sage Publications.

Stivers, Camilla. 1994. "The listening bureaucrat: Responsiveness in public administration." *Public Administration Review* 54 (4):364–369.

Stivers, Camilla. 2000a. *Bureau men, settlement women: Constructing public administration in the progressive era*. Lawrence, KS: University Press of Kansas.

Stivers, Camilla. 2000b. *Gender images in public administration: Legitimacy and the administrative state*. 2nd ed. Thousand Oaks, CA: Sage Publications.

Stivers, Camilla. 2008. *Governance in dark times: Practical philosophy for public service*. Washington, DC: Georgetown University Press.

Stoker, Gerry. 2006. "Public value management: A new narrative for networked governance?" *The American Review of Public Administration* 36 (1):41–57.

Stone, Jerome A. 2015. "Natura: Discerning the immanent sacred." 10th International Whitehead Conference, Claremont, CA, June 5–8.

Storing, Herbert J. 1981. *What the anti-federalists were FOR: The political thought of the opponents of the constitution.* Chicago: University of Chicago Press.

Stout, Margaret. 2006. "A Samurai's lineage: Theoretical traditions in public administration." *Administrative Theory & Praxis* 28 (4):618–630.

Stout, Margaret. 2007a. "In remembrance of Fred Thayer." *Administrative Theory & Praxis* 29 (3):465–469.

Stout, Margaret. 2009a. "Enhancing professional socialization through the metaphor of tradition." *Journal of Public Affairs Education* 15 (3):289–316.

Stout, Margaret. 2009b. "You say you want a revolution?" *International Journal of Organization Theory and Behavior* 12 (2):291–309.

Stout, Margaret. 2010a. "Back to the future: Toward a political economy of love and abundance." *Administration & Society* 42 (1):3–37.

Stout, Margaret. 2010b. "Climbing the ladder of participation: Establishing local policies for participatory practice." *Public Administration and Management* 15 (1):46–97.

Stout, Margaret. 2012. "Toward a relational language of process." *Administrative Theory & Praxis* 34 (3):407–432.

Stout, Margaret. 2013. *Logics of legitimacy: Three traditions of public administration praxis.* Boca Raton, FL: CRC Press.

Stout, Margaret, and Jeannine M. Love. 2013. "Ethical choice making." *Public Administration Quarterly* 37 (2):278–294.

Stout, Margaret, and Jeannine M. Love. 2014a. "Fraternity, solidarity, and unity: Concepts grounded in competing ontologies." *Administrative Theory & Praxis* 36 (3):421–429.

Stout, Margaret, and Jeannine M. Love. 2014b. "The unfortunate misinterpretation of Miss Follett." *Public Voices* 13 (2):11–32.

Stout, Margaret, and Jeannine M. Love. 2015a. *Integrative process: Follettian thinking from ontology to administration.* Anoka, MN: Process Century Press.

Stout, Margaret, and Jeannine M. Love. 2015b. "Relational process ontology: A grounding for global governance." *Administration & Society* 47 (4):447–481.

Stout, Margaret, and Jeannine M. Love. 2016. *A radically democratic response to global governance: Dystopian utopias.* New York: Routledge.

Stout, Margaret, and Jeannine M. Love. 2017. "Integrative governance: A method for fruitful public encounters." *American Review of Public Administration* 47 (1).

Stout, Margaret, and Jeannine M. Love. 2018. "Competing ontologies and epistemologies: Which inform your qualitative research?" *Qualitative Research in Management and Organization, Albuquerque, New Mexico*, March 27–29.

Stout, Margaret, Koen P. R. Bartels, and Jeannine M. Love. 2014. "Collaborative governance: Why dispositions, styles of relating, and modes of association matter." Trans-Atlantic Dialogue, Lugano, Switzerland, June.

Stout, Margaret, Koen P. R. Bartels, and Jeannine M. Love. 2018. "Clarifying collaborative dynamics in governance networks." In *From austerity to abundance? Creative approaches to coordinating the common good*, edited by Margaret Stout. Bingly, UK: Emerald Publishing.

Stout, Margaret, and Carrie Staton. 2011. "The ontology of process philosophy in Follett's administrative theory." *Administrative Theory & Praxis* 33 (2):268–292.

Stout, Martha. 2007b. *The paranoia switch: How terror rewires our brains and reshapes our behavior – and how we can reclaim our courage.* Vol. 1. New York: Farrar, Straus and Giroux.

Strogatz, Steven H. 2003. *Sync: The emerging science of spontaneous order.* Vol. 1. New York: Hyperion.

Structure & Process. 2016. "Who is using Holacracy?" Structure & Process, accessed August 5, 2016. http://structureprocess.com/holacracy-cases/.

Success Works. 2002. *Working together – integrated governance*. Sydney: Institute of Public Administration Australia.

Suchocki, Marjorie. 1985. "Weaving the world." *Process Studies* 14 (2):76–86.

Susskind, Lawrence, Sarah McKearnan, and Jennifer Thomas-Larme, eds. 1999. *The consensus building handbook*. Thousand Oaks, CA: Sage Publications.

Sutich. 1969. "Editor's note." *Journal of Transpersonal Psychology* 1 (1):iv.

Suzuki, David, and Peter Knudtson. 1992. *Wisdom of the elders: Sacred native stories of nature*. New York: Bantam Books.

Swann, Robert. 1972. *The community land trust: A guide to a new model for land tenure in America*. Cambridge, MA: Center for Community Economic Development.

Swyngedouw, Eric. 2005. "Governance innovation and the citizen: The Janus face of governance-beyond-the-state." *Urban Studies* 42 (11):1991–2006.

Taylor, Charles. 1989. *Sources of the self: The making of the modern identity*. Cambridge, MA: Harvard University Press.

Teisman, Geert R., and Erik-Hans Klijn. 2002. "Partnership arrangements: Governmental rhetoric or governance scheme?" *Public Administration Review* 62 (2):197–205.

Tejerina, Benjamín, and Ignacia Perugorría. 2013. "Politics of the encounter: Cognition, emotions, and networks in the Spanish 15M." *Current Sociology* 61 (4):424–442.

Tejerina, Benjamín, Ignacia Perugorría, Tova Benski, and Lauren Langman. 2013. "From indignation to occupation: A new wave of global mobilization." *Current Sociology* 61 (4):377–392.

Thayer, Frederick C. 1981. *An end to hierarchy and competition: Administration in the post-affluent world*. 2nd ed. New York: New Viewpoints. Original edition, 1973.

Thayer-Bacon, Barbara. 2010. "A pragmatist and feminist relational (e)pistemology." *European Journal of Pragmatism and American Philosophy* 2 (1).

Thera, Nyanaponika. 2005. *The heart of Buddhist meditation: A handbook of mental training based on the Buddha's way of mindfulness*. Kandy, Sri Lanka: Buddhist Publication Society. Original edition, 1962.

Thistlethwaite, Susan Brooks. 2005. "The mourning of John Paul II." *Chicago Tribune*, April 3, 2.

Thomson, Ann Marie, and James L. Perry. 2006. "Collaboration processes: Inside the black box." *Public Administration Review* 66:20–32.

Thomson, Ann Marie, James L. Perry, and Theodore K. Miller. 2009. "Conceptualizing and measuring collaboration." *Journal of Public Administration Research and Theory* 19 (1):23–56.

Thorne, Kym, and Alexander Kouzmin. 2006. "Learning to play the 'pea and thimble' charade – the invisible and very visible hands in the neo-liberal project: Towards a manifesto for reflexive consciousness in public administration." *Administrative Theory & Praxis* 28 (2):262–274.

Tillich, Paul. 1973. *Systematic theology*. Chicago: University of Chicago Press.

Tilman, David, Kenneth G. Cassman, Pamela A. Matson, Rosamond Naylor, and Stephen Polasky. 2002. "Agricultural sustainability and intensive production practices." *Nature* 418 (August 8):671–677.

Timney, Mary. 2001. "Eco-nomics: Toward a theory of value for public administration." *Administrative Theory & Praxis* 23 (1):25–38.

Tocqueville, Alexis de. 2000. *Democracy in America*. Chicago: University of Chicago Press.

Toffler, Alvin. 1984. *The third wave*. Reissue ed. New York: Bantam Books. Original edition, 1980.

Tollefsen, Christopher. 2002. "Cooperative, coordinative, and coercive epistemologies." In *Realism & antirealism*, edited by William P. Alston, 150–166. Ithaca: Cornell University Press.

Tønder, Lars. 2005. "Inessential commonality: Immanence, transcendence, abundance." In *Radical democracy: Politics between abundance and lack*, edited by Lars Tønder and Lasse Thomassen, 203–218. New York: Manchester University Press.

Tønder, Lars, and Lasse Thomassen. 2005a. "Introduction." In *Radical democracy: Politics between abundance and lack*, edited by Lars Tønder and Lasse Thomassen, 1–13. New York: Manchester University Press.

Tønder, Lars, and Lasse Thomassen, eds. 2005b. *Radical democracy: Politics between abundance and lack*. New York: Manchester University Press.

Traditional. n.d. Wiccan Rede.

TRANSIT, Transformative Social Innovation Theory. 2014a. "About the project." Transformative Social Innovation Theory, accessed July 23, 2017. www.transitsocialinnovation.eu/about-transit.

TRANSIT, Transformative Social Innovation Theory. 2014b. "Discover our cases." Transformative Social Innovation Theory, accessed July 23, 2017. www.transitsocialinnovation.eu/about-transit.

Transition United States. 2013. "The 7 guiding principles of transition." Transition United States, accessed July 25, 2017. http://transitionus.org/initiatives/7-principles.

Tripathy, Jyotirmaya. 2006. "Towards an essential native American identity: A theoretical overview." *The Canadian Journal of Native Studies 2():*. XXVI (2):313–329.

Tugal, Cihan. 2014. "End of the leaderless revolution." *Berkeley Journal of Sociology* 58:3.

Uhl-Bien, Mary. 2006. "Relational leadership theory: Exploring the social processes of leadership and organizing." *The Leadership Quarterly Yearly Review of Leadership* 17 (6):654–676.

Uhl-Bien, Mary, and Sonia Ospina, eds. 2012. *Advancing relational leadership research: A dialogue among perspectives*. Charlotte, NC: Information Age Publishing.

UIA, Union of International Associations, ed. 2012/13. *Yearbook of international organizations*. 49th ed. Leiden: Brill.

UN, United Nations. n.d.-a. "About the UN: Overview." United Nations, accessed July 20, 2017. www.un.org/en/sections/about-un/overview/index.html.

UN, United Nations. n.d.-b. "Preamble." United Nations, accessed July 20, 2017. www.un.org/en/sections/un-charter/preamble/index.html.

UNCHE, United Nations Conference on the Human Environment. 1972. "Declaration of the United Nations Conference on the Human Environment." Stockholm, Sweden.

UNDP, United Nations Development Programme. 1999. *Human development report 1999*. Oxford: Oxford University Press.

UNFCCC, United Nations Framework Convention on Climate Change. 1995. Report of the Conference of the parties on its first session, United Nations, Berlin, March 28–April 7.

UNFCCC, United Nations Framework Convention on Climate Change. 1997. Report of the Conference of the parties on its third session, United Nations, Kyoto, December 1–11.

UNFCCC, United Nations Framework Convention on Climate Change. 2014. "Background on the UNFCCC: The international response to climate change." United Nations Framework Convention on Climate Change, accessed July 20, 2017. http://unfccc.int/essential_background/items/6031.php.

UNFCCC, United Nations Framework Convention on Climate Change. 2017. "The Paris agreement." United Nations Framework Convention on Climate Change, accessed July 20, 2017. http://unfccc.int/paris_agreement/items/9485.php.

UNRISD, United Nations Research Institute for Social Development. 2012. "Potential and limits of social and solidarity economy." In *Project brief 2*. Geneva: United Nations.

USFWC, United States Federation of Worker Cooperatives. 2016. "Home page." United States Federation of Worker Cooperatives, https://usworker.coop/home-2/ accessed May 18, 2016.

Vahabzadeh, Peyman. 2002. *Articulated experiences: Toward a radical phenomenology of contemporary social movements*. Albany, NY: State University of New York Press.

Van Buuren, Arwin, and Sibout Nooteboom. 2010. "The success of SEA in the Dutch planning practice: How formal assessments can contribute to collaborative governance." *Environmental Impact Assessment Review* 30:127–135.

Van Buuren, M. W., and Jurian Edelenbos. 2004. "Conflicting knowledge: Why is knowledge production such a problem." *Science and Public Policy* 31 (4):289–299.

van Gelder, Sarah, David Korten, and Steve Piersanti. 2011. "Ways the occupy movement changes everything." In *This changes everything*, edited by Sarah van Gelder, 13. San Francisco: Berrett-Koehler Publishers.

van der Steen, Martijn, Jorren Scherpenisse, Maarten Hajer, Olav-Jan van Gerwen, and Sonja Kruitwagen. 2015. *Learning by doing: Government participation in an energetic society*. The Hague: PBL Netherlands Environmental Assessment Agency.

van Stokkom, Bas. 2005. "Deliberative group dynamics: Power, status and affect in interactive policy making." *Policy & Politics* 33 (3):387–409.

Vangen, Siv, and Chris Huxham. 2012. "The tangled web: Unraveling the principle of common goals in collaborations." *Journal of Public Administration Research and Theory* 22 (4):731–760.

VeneKlasen, Lisa, and Valerie Miller. 2007. *A new weave of power, people & politics: The action guide for advocacy and citizen participation*. Rugby, UK: Practical Action Publishing.

Ventriss, Curtis. 1985. "Emerging perspectives on citizen participation." *Public Administration Review* 45 (3):433–440.

Verhoeven, Imrat, and Evelien Tonkens. 2018. "Joining the citizens: Forging new collaborations between government and citizens in deprived neighborhoods." In *From austerity to abundance? Creative approaches to coordinating the common good*, edited by Margaret Stout. Bingly, UK: Emerald Publishing.

Verney, M. N. 2004. "On authenticity." In *American Indian thought*, edited by Anne Waters, 133–139. Malden, MA: Blackwell Publishing.

Victor, Peter A., and Tim Jackson. 2015. "The trouble with growth." In *State of the world 2015: Confronting hidden threats to sustainability*, edited by Lisa Mastny, 37–49. Washington, DC: Island Press.

Vigoda, Eran. 2002. "From responsiveness to collaboration: Governance, citizens, and the next generation of public administration." *Public Administration Review* 62 (5):527–540.

von Bertalanffy, Ludwig. 1975. *Perspectives on general system theory: Scientific-philosophical studies*. New York: George Braziller Press.

Vote Leave. n.d. "Why vote leave." Vote Leave, accessed July 20, 2017. www.voteleavetakecontrol.org/why_vote_leave.html.

Vreeland, James Raymond. 2007. *International monetary fund: Politics of conditional lending, global institutions*. New York: Routledge.

Wachhaus, Aaron. 2014. "Governance beyond government." *Administration & Society* 46 (5):573–593.

Waldo, Dwight. 1980. *The enterprise of public administration: A summary*. Novato, CA: Chandler & Sharp Publishers.

Waldo, Dwight. 1984. *The administrative state: A study of the political theory of American public administration*. 2nd ed. New York: Holmes & Meier Publishers. Original edition, 1948.

Walker, Margaret. 1998. *Moral understandings: A feminist study in ethics*. New York: Routledge.

Wallerstein, Immanuel Maurice. 1998. *Utopistics, or historical choices of the twenty-first century*. New York: The New Press.

Walsh, Roger, and Frances Vaughan. 1993. "On transpersonal definitions." *Journal of Transpersonal Psychology* 25 (2):199–207.

Walters, Lawrence C., James Aydelotte, and Jessica Miller. 2000. "Putting more public in policy analysis." *Public Administration Review* 60 (4):349–359.

Walzer, Michael. 1984. "Liberalism and the art of separation." *Political Theory* 12 (3):315–330.

Wang, Zhihe. 2012. *Process and pluralism: Chinese thought on the harmony of diversity*. Edited by Nicholas Rescher, Johanna Seibt and Michel Weber. Vol. 23, *Process thought*. Frankfurt: Ontos Verlag.

Warren, Mark. 1992. "Democratic theory and self transformation." *American Political Science Review* 86 (1):8–23.

Warren, Mark R. 2001. *Dry bones rattling: Community building to revitalize American democracy*. Princeton, NJ: Princeton University Press.

Waterhouse, Jennifer, and Robyn L. Keast. 2012. "Strategizing public sector human resource management: The implications of working in networks." *International Journal of Public Administration* 35 (8):562–576.

Waters, Anne, ed. 2004a. *American Indian thought*. Malden, MA: Blackwell Publishing.

Waters, Anne. 2004b. "Language matters: Nondiscrete nonbinary dualism." In *American Indian thought*, edited by Anne Waters, 97–115. Malden, MA: Blackwell Publishing.

Waters, Anne. 2004c. "Ontology of identity and interstitial being." In *American Indian thought*, edited by Anne Waters, 153–170. Malden, MA: Blackwell Publishing.

Weber, Max. 1949. *The methodology of the social sciences*. New York: The Free Press.

Weber, Max. 1994a. "The concept of social action." In *Sociological writings: Max Weber*, edited by Wolf Heydebrand, 1–3. New York: Continuum Publishing Company.

Weber, Max. 1994b. "The concept of social relationship." In *Sociological writings: Max Weber*, edited by Wolf Heydebrand, 6–9. New York: Continuum Publishing Company.

Weber, Max. 1994c. "The types of social action." In *Sociological writings: Max Weber*, edited by Wolf Heydebrand, 3–6. New York: Continuum Publishing Company.

WEF, World Economic Forum. 2010. *Everybody's business: Strengthening international cooperation in a more interdependent world – report of the global redesign initiative*. Geneva: World Economic Forum.

Weick, Karl E. 1979. *The social psychology of organizing*. Vol. 2, *Topics in social psychology*. Reading, MA: Addison-Wesley Pub. Co.

Weick, Karl E. 2001. *Making sense of the organization*. Oxford, UK; Malden, MA: Blackwell Publishers.

Weiming, Tu. 1996. "Beyond the enlightenment mentality: A Confucian perspective on ethics, migration, and global stewardship." *International Migration Review* 30 (1):58–75.

Weisbord, Marvin Ross, and Sandra Janoff. 2000. *Future search: An action guide to finding common ground in organizations and communities*. San Francisco: Berrett-Koehler Publishers.

Wendle, John. 2016, March. "Syria's climate refugees." *Scientific American* 314 (3):50–55.

Wheatley, Margaret J. 2006. *Leadership and the new science: Discovering order in a chaotic world*. 3rd ed. San Francisco: Berrett-Kohler Publishers Inc. Original edition, 1992.

Whitaker, G. 1980. "Coproduction: Citizen participation in service delivery." *Public Administration Review* 40 (3):240–246.

White, Jay D., and Guy B. Adams, eds. 1994. *Research in public administration: Reflections on theory and practice*. Thousand Oaks, CA: Sage Publications.

White, Orion F. 1990. "Reframing the authority/participation debate." In *Refounding public administration*, edited by Gary L. Wamsley, Robert N. Bacher, Charles T. Goodsell, Philip S. Kronenberg, John A. Rohr, Camilla Stivers, Orion F. White and James F. Wolf, 182–245. Thousand Oaks, CA: Sage Publications.

White, Stephen K. 2000. *Sustaining affirmation: The strengths of weak ontology in political theory*. Princeton, NJ: Princeton University Press.

Whitehead, Alfred North. 1967. *Adventures of ideas*. New York: The Free Press.

Whitehead, Alfred North. 1979. *Process and reality: An essay in cosmology*. Edited by David Ray Griffin and Donald W. Sherburne. Vol. Corrected. New York: Simon and Shuster. Original edition, 1929.

Widder, Nathan. 2005. "Two routes from Hegel." In *Radical democracy: Politics between abundance and lack*, edited by Lars Tønder and Lasse Thomassen, 32–49. New York: Manchester University Press.

Wieman, Henry Nelson. 1946. *The source of human good*. Chicago: University of Chicago Press.

Wilber, Ken. 2011. *A theory of everything: An integral vision for business, politics, science, and spirituality*. Boston: Shambhala Press.

Wilde, Parke. 2013. *Food policy in the United States: An introduction*. New York: Routledge.

Williams, Paul. 2002. "The competent boundary spanner." *Public Administration* 80 (1):103–124.

Williams, Rhys H. 1999. "Visions of the good society and the religious roots of American political culture." *Sociology of Religion* 60 (1):1–34.

Williamson, Abby, and Archon Fung. 2004. "Public deliberation: Where are we and where can we go?" *National Civic Review* 93 (4):3–15.

Willoughby, Westel W. 1930. *The ethical basis of political authority*. New York: The MacMillan Company.

Wilson, Shawn. 2009. *Research is ceremony: Indigenous research methods*. Winnipeg, Manitoba, Canada: Fernwood Publishing Co., Ltd.

Wiredu, Kwasi. 1996. *Cultural universals and particulars: An African perspective*. Bloomington, IN: Indiana University Press.

Wolleben, Peter. 2015. *The hidden life of trees: What they feel, how they communicate*. Vancouver: Greystone Books.

Wood, Donna, and Barbara Gray. 1991. "Towards a comprehensive theory of collaboration." *Journal of Applied Behavioral Science* 27:139–162.

Woodlock, Peter D., and Richard A. Young. 2001. "The trade-off of reliability for relevance within a stewardship setting." *Managerial and Decision Economics* 22:315–326.

Woods, Ngaire. 2006. *The globalizers: The IMF, the world bank, and their borrowers*. Ithaca, NY: Cornell University Press.

WTO, World Trade Organization. 2017. "Accession in perspective." World Trade Organization, accessed July 19, 2017. www.wto.org/english/thewto_e/acc_e/cbt_course_e/c1s1p1_e.htm.

Yankelovich, Daniel. 1991. *Coming to public judgment: Making democracy work in a complex world*. Syracuse, NY: Syracuse University Press.

Yankelovich, Daniel. 1999. *The magic of dialogue: Transforming conflict into cooperation*. New York: Simon & Schuster.

Yogananda, Paramahansa. 1993. *Autobiography of a yogi*. 12th ed. Los Angeles: Self-Realization Fellowship. Original edition, 1946.

York, Michael. 2000. "Defining paganism." *The Pomegranate* 11 (11):4–9.

York, Michael. 2003. *Pagan theology: Paganism as a world religion*. New York: New York University Press.

Young, Iris. 1997. *Intersecting voices: Dilemmas of gender, political philosophy, and policy*. Princeton, NJ: Princeton University Press.

Young, Iris. 2000. "Hybrid democracy: Iroquois federalism and postcolonial project." In *Political theory and the rights of indigenous people*, edited by D. Ivison, P. Patton and W. Sanders. Cambridge: Cambridge University Press.

Zanetti, Lisa A. 2004. "Repositioning the ethical imperative: Critical theory, *recht*, and tempered radicals in public service." *American Review of Public Administration* 34 (2):134–150.

Zeiler, Thomas W. 1999. *Free trade world trade: The advent of the GATT*. Chapel Hill: University of North Carolina Press.

Zelko, Frank. 2013. *Make it a green peace! The rise of countercultural environmentalism*. Oxford: Oxford University Press.

Žižek, Slavoj. 2002. "A plea for Leninist intolerance." *Critical Inquiry* 28 (2):542–566.

Zukav, Gary. 1980. *The dancing Wu Li masters: An overview of the new physics*. New York: Bantam Books.

Zwerdling, Daniel. 1980. *Workplace democracy*. New York: Harper & Row.

Glossary

A

Atomistic Governance: In this ideal-type, existence is understood in physical terms that can be perceived through the senses. In this understanding, temporal beings and objects evolve from non-temporal finite sources. Individuality is characterized by stable identities that are pre-social and independent of the group. It employs empiricist epistemology and consequential ethics. This worldview fits naturalist belief systems. From this perspective, political representation is possible because identity is fixed. Thus, it fits the political theory of modern liberalism. Stressing competition and individual preferences, this perspective leads to the ideal of free market exchange within the social contract. The administrative theory that best fits this pluralist approach to both governance and economics is New Public Service. This approach seeks to balance the authority of administrative experts with citizen participation to augment traditional representative government.

B

C

***co-creating*:** A process through which all that exists collaborates in the relational, dynamic process of becoming, thereby synthesizing *eternal* and *changing* understandings of the source of existence. This generates a synergistic, qualitative value to all.

Co-Creationism: A hypothetical system of belief grounded in assumptions of ***co-creating*** and ***sacred immanence***. It reflects a faith in and affirmation of all beings and places as equally sacred co-creators, all drawing from an embodied void of creative potentiality in their Relational Becoming. Sacred acts are designed to increase understanding of these aspects of existence and to celebrate their implications for life. The synergistic value generated through these relational processes adds qualitatively to all of creation and helps motivate social norms.

***commoning*:** A set of economic and social practices in which all forms of economic activity are relationally determined by situated economic actors, thereby synthesizing *internal* and *external regulation*. Markets are reconnected to people and place, re-embedding the economy within society and making it answerable to the people.

***cooperation*:** In the context of economics, cooperation is the self-organizing and self-regulating coordination of production and exchange among radically democratic participants. This synthesizes *moderate* and *strong* regulation.

Coopetition: An economic paradigm in which economic actors compete against shared challenges in the pursuit of flourishing for all. Both ownership and production are rooted in ***commoning*** relationships that operate in ***cooperation***, which centers direct participation in the management of enterprises with an emphasis on local self-sufficiency when possible. Characteristics include: common ownership and stewardship of natural resources, the merging of capital and labor through cooperative enterprise, the linkage of producers and consumers through cooperative association, the collaboration of lenders and borrowers in community finance, and participative coordination of resource use, exchange, and distribution.

***creative emergence*:** An ontological assumption that all things emerge from a non-temporal, nonmaterial state through a process of becoming that is punctuated by moments of stability. This ontological condition synthesizes *static* and *dynamic states of existence.*

D

dialectical synthesis : The intellectual process through which contrasts between pairs of concepts (dialectic) are resolved by creating a wholly new third position (synthesis) that meets the driving concerns of the original concepts.

E

***embodied knowing*:** A process that synthesizes *internal* and *external justification* of truth claims through a combination of experiential perceptions (e.g., panexperientialism, tacit knowing, intuition, holistic perception, creative imagination) and intellectual conceptualizations given by one's epistemic community.

***embodiment*:** An ontological assumption that synthesizes *immanent* and *transcendent sources of existence* in which material and nonmaterial form an integral whole. Creative potentiality is manifest within all that is.

***emergent multidimensionality*:** An understanding of self that synthesizes *unitary* and *decentered identity.* The mind-body dualism is dissolved and the self is composed of constantly changing and interlocking material and nonmaterial elements that interact with the environment.

***emergent principles*:** Ethical principles that are co-created through the method of integration. This process synthesize *internal* and *external motivations* for ethical action.

Ensembling individuality: A psychosocial theory that combines ***relationality*** and ***emergent multidimensionality***. This is an understanding of individuality that is emergent and multidimensional and dynamic within a relational context that includes other human beings and all of creation.

F

Facilitative Coordination: An administrative approach that follows the principles of collaborative governance within nonhierarchical, ***responsive networks***. It achieves ***integrative collaboration*** through situational authority, evoking and facilitative leadership, and participatory processes. Situational authority is emergent and driven by the evolving needs of the situation to focus efforts on the group purpose, while drawing most effectively from the capacity of each member of the group.

Fragmented Governance: In this ideal-type there is no essential foundation from which any aspect of reality can be understood or described. Singular Individuality is characterized by disconnection from both a substantive core self and human groups. Identity is continually formed through individual choice in response to experience. This decentered atomism leads to both empirical and ethical relativism. Political representation is not possible because identity is ever-changing and there is no legitimate basis for authority over any individual. Therefore, individualist anarchism emerges as the only viable political form. Individuals must be free to pursue their own self-sufficiency or engage in trade with others without government interference. The administrative theory most aligned with this type is New Public Management given its promotion of privatization of previously public functions and deregulation of all types of private action.

G

H

Hierarchical Governance: In this ideal-type all of creation is assumed to be an imperfect copy of a transcendent source that is whole and complete. Human beings exhibit an individuality characterized by stable identities that are socially embedded within the group. People seek to become more perfect copies of the source of existence through logic and attention to moral rules; thus, this perspective fits with monotheistic religions that believe in an external divine source of existence. This lends itself to rationalist epistemology and an ethic of deontological obligation. These assumptions require political representation – someone or something with superior reason must speak for the source of being and determine Right. These assumptions fit logically with traditional forms of political monism (royalty or the Church), as well as classical conservative liberalism (republicanism). In economics these assumptions lead to a paternalistic welfare state hierarchically administered by government functionaries. Orthodox Public Administration is an approach that minimizes the authority of administrators to ensure political authority is maintained by elected by elected representatives.

Holographic Governance: In this ideal-type all of creation is encompassed within and perfectly reflects the transcendent source of existence. As a part of the whole, Particular individuality is characterized by a decentered identity that is socially embedded. The assumption that the divine is both internal and external to self leads to epistemological idealism. Action is guided by an ethical moral imperative; both Truth and Right can be found through careful introspection. These assumptions can be seen in pantheistic religions in which all beings are considered parts of the divine being. Representation is possible because individuals are interchangeable expressions of the whole. This worldview lends itself to the ideal of socialism and its collectively planned economy. Because these empowered citizen planners seek to ensure both socially and economically just outcomes, it is best aligned with New Public Administration. This approach empowers administrators to protect the interests of citizens, particularly those most vulnerable to market forces.

I

Integral Knowing: An epistemological approach that combines ***embodied knowing*** and ***situated knowing***. These forms of knowing are both perceptual and conceptual, explicit and implicit. Each member of an epistemic community accesses their own ***embodied knowing*** and then engages in a process of forming intersubjective agreement with others to mutually justify truth claims, thereby co-creating ***situated knowing***. Truths generated in this process remain open to ongoing questioning, evaluation, and change.

integration, method of: A group process developed by Mary Follett that includes dialogue and deliberation designed to work through differences in perspectives and values in order to produce shared understanding and agreement. The integrative method consists of four general phases that tend to be iterative in nature: (1) dialogic sharing, (2) disintegration of positions, (3) comparative revaluation, and (4) deliberative synthesis.

integrative collaboration*:** An approach to administration that transforms *administrative discretion* through ***power-with. All group members are understood as collaborators, enhancing both autonomy and mutuality among all group members. This form of active participation emphasizes self-organizing coordination of labor and reciprocal cooperation to achieve common goals across organizational boundaries.

Integrative Governance: In this ideal-type all of existence is understood as an ongoing process of becoming among interdependent beings, things, and places – each of which is a unique expression of existence. From this perspective we are a dynamic, mutually influencing multitudinous wholes composed of unique but related individual parts. This worldview provides a logically coherent basis for practices that include all concerned individuals, allowing for equal mutual influence and change in an ongoing political, economic, and social process. The aim of governance is progress of both the individual and society, as understood in both substantive and process terms. The greater the capacity for integrative action, the better the outcomes for all, enabling a greater emphasis of qualitative social and environmental bottom lines while considering quantitative economic outcomes. This approach to governance draws together philosophical assumptions of Relational Becoming, Ensembling individuality, Integral Knowing, and Co-Creationism, as the foundations for practical expression in the ethic of Stewardship, a politics of Radical Democracy, Coopetition in economics, and administration as Facilitative Coordination.

integrative pathways: The dialogical routes through which conflicting assumptions (dialectically opposed conceptual pairs) can enter into the process of integration in order to achieve dynamic synthesis.

J

K

L

M

N

O

P

***power-with*:** An understanding of power as having expansive potential rather than static limits – when more people are involved, more power is developed. From this perspective, power is emergent and synergistic rather than zero-sum. Politically, this understanding of power synthesizes *moderate* and *strong* positions on *authority*, re-envisioning sovereignty as cooperative.

Q

R

Radical Democracy: A political theory that fosters ***power-with*** within ***self-organizing confederalism.*** This approach retains sovereignty within each individual and utilizes participatory practices in the process of governance. It centers the freedom to engage in direct participation where practicable and delegate-style deliberative practices that enable un-centered, deeply nesting, and networking confederation from the most local to global levels. The function of governance is a shared responsibility in which leadership emerges and evolves based on the situation, including all affected groups in a collaborative process.

***relational assemblage*:** An ontological assumption that synthesizes *singular* and *pluralistic expressions* of existence, in which the One is co-created by the Many in an emergent process. This ontological perspective draws on the metaphor of the rhizome.

Relational Becoming: An ontological perspective, also called relational process ontology, which is comprised of ***embodiment***, ***relational assemblage***, and ***creative emergence.*** Becoming is understood as a seamless emergent process of creative, relational assemblage from embodied potentiality to actuality.

***relationality*:** A social condition that synthesizes *embeddedness* and *independence.* Individuals exist within interconnected webs in which all entities (humans, nonhumans, flora, physical objects, and places) co-determine identity.

***responsive networks*:** An organizational *structure* that synthesizes *hierarchical* and *matrix* forms. This organizing style enables a type of collaboration that achieves both the stability associated with hierarchy and the flexibility associated with competition. Every group (family, organization, community) exists within networks that are interconnected through overlapping memberships. These networks are emergent and responsive to the ongoing situation.

***reverent interconnectivity*:** An ethical stance that synthesizes *Right* and *Good.* It engenders a subject-subject relationship, generating both mutual care and relational mindfulness in reciprocal relationship.

S

***sacred immanence* :** A relational concept that considers synthesizes assumptions of a *theistic creator* and *materialist creation.* All things, beings, and places to be equally sacred and divine as co-creators that draw from an embodied source of potentiality.

***self-organizing confederalism* :** A political *structure* that synthesizes *centralization* and *decentralization* through un-centering. This multiscalar structure loosely binds autonomous local communities together into a system of government, building from the micro (neighborhood) to the macro (global). Following the principle of subsidiarity, decisions are made by political units at the scale and scope appropriate to the issue at hand, while considering the effects on other levels of analysis.

situated knowing*:** An epistemological process that resolves the dialectic between *foundational* and *coherentist structuration* of knowledge by synthesizing subjectivity and objectivity through intersubjective agreement. This form of knowing draws together the intrapersonal and interpersonal knowledge generated in ***embodied knowing and integrates them through an intentional, interactive process.

Stewardship: An ethic that combines the sense of ***reverent interconnectivity*** and a commitment to ***emergent principles***. The inherent value of relatedness and reverence for interconnectedness demands mutual care, responsibility, and answerability for our actions. It is a motivation, an attitude, and an act of both deciding and doing. It is understood as an internal, intrinsic motivation that stems from both philosophical commitments and experience. Stewards are neither self-interested nor self-sacrificing, but are rather mutually caring and respectful of the sanctity of all human beings and all of creation.

T

U

W

X

Y

Z

Index

Page numbers in *italic* indicate a figure and page numbers in **bold** indicate a table on the corresponding page.

For Product Safety Concerns and Information please contact our EU representative GPSR@taylorandfrancis.com Taylor & Francis Verlag GmbH, Kaufingerstraße 24, 80331 München, Germany

Batch number: 10726294

Printed by Printforce, the Netherlands